The **Industrial Relations Research Centre (IRRC)** is based at the University of New South Wales and was established in 1980 with the assistance of a federal government general development grant to the University. The Centre's function is to focus and stimulate industrial relations research, and to facilitate publication of research results. The policy of IRRC is to promote the use of research results in industrial relations practice, and to sponsor projects in applied research, the results of which will help inform public debate and policy making. This book is published in its Australian Studies in Industrial Relations series. Others in the series include: *Industrial Action* (Frenkel); *Wage Indexation* (Plowman); *Arbitrator at Work* (Dabscheck); *Unions against Capitalism?* (Frenkel and Coolican); *Control, Consensus or Chaos?* (Niland and Turner); *Wage Fixation in Australia* (Niland); *Alternatives to Arbitration* (Blandy and Niland); *New Technology* (Bamber and Lansbury); *Democracy in Australian Unions* (Davis); *Agenda for Charge* (Niland and Clarke) and *Australia's Economy under Labor* (Mahony).

Other works by this book's editors are listed on page ii. This edition was facilitated by the following two Australian Research Council Key Centres.

The **Key Centre in Strategic Management (KCSM)** was established as a national key centre at the Queensland University of Technology in 1989 with the assistance of grants from the Australian Research Council, the federal government's Department of Employment, Education and Training and the state government of Queensland. The Centre is closely linked with the University's Faculty of Business, which has a long and distinguished record of research, teaching and consulting across the range of business studies, including industrial relations. The Centre's mission is to further develop its role as a centre of excellence in teaching and research, especially in the field of strategic management and management education with a particular emphasis on employment relations. The Centre is directed by Professor Bamber.

The **Australian Centre in Industrial Relations Research and Teaching (ACIRRT)** was established as a national key centre at the University of Sydney in 1989 with the assistance of a grant from the Australian Research Council and the federal government's Department of Employment, Education and Training. The Centre is closely linked with the University's Department of Industrial Relations which has a long and distinguished record of research, teaching and consulting in this field. The Centre is pursuing a wide range of projects, particularly in the area of workplace industrial relations. Professor Lansbury was the Foundation Director of the Centre.

A selection of other works by this book's editors

Professionals and Management (Lansbury) University of Queensland Press

Militant Managers? (Bamber) Gower

'Technological Change and Industrial Relations', Special Issue, *Bulletin of Comparative Labour Relations* (Bamber and Lansbury) Kluwer

Senshin Shokoku nó Roshikankei, (Kuwahara, Bamber and Lansbury) Nihon Rodo Kenkŷu Kikôa, rev. Japanese edn of *International and Comparative Industrial Relations*

New Technology and Industrial Relations in Scandinavia (Graversen and Lansbury) Gower

New Technology: International Perspectives on Human Resources and Industrial Relations (Lansbury and Bamber) Unwin Hyman (Routledge)/Allen & Unwin

Current Issues in Labour Relations (Gladstone, Lansbury, Stieber, Treu and Weiss) de Gruyter

Managing Mangers (Snape, Redman and Bamber) Blackwell

Workplace Industrial Relations (Lansbury and MacDonald) Oxford University Press

Industrial Relations Teaching and Research: International Trends (Lansbury) Australian Centre in Industrial Relations Research and Teaching

Strategic Management of Organisational and Industrial Change (Patrickson and Bamber) Longman Cheshire

International and comparative industrial relations

A study of industrialised market economies

Second edition

Edited by
Greg J. Bamber and Russell D. Lansbury

To Betty, Val, Gwen, Owen, Nina, Alex and Kate,
and in loving memory of Freda and Doug
(Royalties from this book will contribute to research on cancer)

First edition published in 1987
by Allen & Unwin Pty Ltd

Second edition published 1993
by Routledge
11 New Fetter Lane, London EC4P 4EE

Simultaneously published in the USA and Canada
by Routledge
29 West 35th Street, New York, NY 10001

© 1993 Selection and editorial material Greg J. Bamber and Russell
D. Lansbury
© 1993 Individual chapters to their authors

Typeset in 10/11 point Times by DOCUPRO, Sydney, Australia
Printed and bound in Singapore

British Library Cataloguing in Publication Data

A catalogue record for this book is available from the British Library

Library of Congress Cataloging in Publication Data
has been applied for.

ISBN 0-415-10360-6

Foreword

The second English-language edition of *International and Comparative Industrial Relations* is a welcome contribution to the literature in this growing field of study and teaching. The book embodies the best principles of international scholarship. By assembling a premier group of experts from different countries to address a similar set of issues, Greg Bamber and Russell Lansbury have produced a book that provides rich and detailed country specific knowledge and information from which readers can make informed comparisons.

The field of international industrial relations is coming alive again after a period when most researchers focused on developments within their national systems. There seems to be a growing consensus that we now have more to learn from each other than we do from further self examination. This is understandable given the growing importance of world markets and regional trading blocs, the remarkable political transformations in Eastern Europe and the former Soviet Union, the advancing Asian economies, and the speed with which organisational and technological innovations cross national boundaries.

All these developments increase the range of options from which managers, union leaders, and government policy-makers can choose in shaping their own employment practices. Our challenge as teachers, researchers, students and practitioners is to determine which industrial relations institutions and practices can be effectively transferred across international borders and can be adapted satisfactorily to different local settings. Yet, as the material in this book attests, there are significant limitations to this transfer process, given the desire by most parties to maintain well established traditions and the fear of changing existing power relationships. Debates over these issues are likely to be at the forefront of industrial relations in many countries, firms, unions, and policy-making bodies for the rest of this century.

Professors Bamber and Lansbury provide a useful guide to how we might go about this cross-national learning. They point out that a variety of different analytical frameworks exist to support international comparisons. I believe these frameworks will become the focal points of important debates in our field in the years ahead. This book should serve as a valuable empirical point of reference in those debates.

I am delighted that the authors used the meetings and members of the International Industrial Relations Association to good avail in producing this book. My hope is that the Association will serve as host to similar international and comparative projects in the future.

Thomas A. Kochan
President 1992–95, International Industrial Relations Association; Leaders of Manufacturing Professor and George M. Bunker Professor of Management Sloan School of Management, Massachusetts Institute of Technology, USA. Author and co-author of many articles and books including: *Introduction to Collective Bargaining and Industrial Relations* and *The Transformation of American Industrial Relations*.

Contents

Figures

Tables

Abbreviations

ACAS	Advisory, Conciliation and Arbitration Service (UK)
ACCI	Australian Chamber of Commerce and Industry
ACSPA	Australian Council of Salaried and Professional Associations
ACTU	Australian Council of Trade Unions
ACTWU	Amalgamated Clothing and Textile Workers Union (USA)
ADGB	*Allgemeiner Deutscher Gewerkschaftsbund* (General Federation of German Trade Unions)
AEU	Amalgamated Engineering Union (UK)—merged in 1992 to form Amalgamated Engineering and Electrical Union
AFAP	Australian Federation of Air Pilots
AFL	American Federation of Labor
AFL–CIO	American Federation of Labor–Congress of Industrial Organizations
AIRC	Australian Industrial Relations Commission
ALP	Australian Labor Party
AMS	*Arbetsmarknadsstyrelsen* (Labour Market Board) (Sweden)
ASAP	*Associazione Sindacale Aziende Petrolchimiche* (Italian Employers' Association of Petrochemical Firms)
ASEAN	Association of South East Asian Nations
Assicredito	*Associazione Italiana Credito* (Italian Association of Employers in Credit)
BCA	Business Council of Australia
BDA	*Bundesvereinigung der Deutschen Arbeitgeberverbände* (Confederation of German Employers' Associations)

BIAC	Business and Industry Advisory Committee to the OECD
BLS	Bureau of Labor Statistics of the US Department of Labor
BNA	Bureau of National Affairs Inc (USA)
CAGEO	Council of Australian Government Employee Organisations
CAI	Confederation of Australian Industry (merged in 1992 to form ACCI)
CBI	Confederation of British Industry
CDU	Christian Democratic Union (Germany)
CEEP	*Centre Européen des Entreprises Publiques* (European Centre for Public Enterprises)
CF	*Ciuilingerjörsförbundet* (Swedish Association of Graduate Engineers)
CFDT	*Confédération française démocratique du travail* (French Democratic Confederation of Labour)
CFE–CGC	*Confédération française de l'encadrement*–CGC (French Confederation of Executive Staffs, the successor to the CGC)
CFL	Canadian Federation of Labour
CFTC	*Confédération française des travailleurs chrétiens* (French Confederation of Christian Workers)
CGC	*Confédération générale des cadres* (French General Confederation of Executive Staffs)
CGD	*Christlicher Gewerkschaftsbund Deutschlands* (Confederation of Christian Trade Unions of Germany)
CGIL	*Confederazione Italiana Generale del Lavoro* (Italian General Confederation of Labour)
CGT	*Confédération générale du travail* (French General Confederation of Labour)
CIA	Central Intelligence Agency (USA)
CIC	*Confédération internationale des cadres* (International Confederation of Executive Staffs)
CIDA	*Confederazione Italiana Dirigenti di Azienda* (Italian Confederation of Enterprise Managers)
CIG	*Cassa Integrazione Guadagni* (Italian Wages Integration Funds)
CIO	Congress of Industrial Organizations (USA)
CISAL	*Confederazione Italiana Sindacati Lavoratori Autonomi* (Italian Confederation of Unions of Autonomous Workers)
CISAS	*Confederazione Italiana Sindacati Addetti ai*

	Servizi (Italian Confederation of Unions in the Service Sector)
CISL	*Confederazione Italiana Sindacati Lavoratori* (Italian Confederation of Workers Unions)
CISNAL	*Confederazione Italiana Sindacati Nazionali Lavoratori* (Italian Confederation of National Unions of Workers)
CLC	Canadian Labour Congress
CNPF	*Conseil national du patronat français* (National Council of French Employers)
CNTU	Confederation of National Trade Unions (Canada)
Confagricoltura	*Confederazione Generale dell'Agricoltura* (Italian General Confederation of [Employers in] Agriculture)
Confapi	*Confederazione Italiana della Piccola e Media Industria* (Italian Confederation of Small and Medium Enterprises)
Confcommercio	*Confederazione Generale del Commercio* (Italian General Confederation of [Employers in] Commerce)
Confindustria	*Confederazione Generale dell'Industria Italiana* (General Confederation of Italian Industry)
CONFSAL	*Confederazione Sindacati Autonomi Lavoratori* (Italian Confederation of Unions of Autonomous Workers)
COPE	Committee on Political Education (USA)
CSU	Christian Social Union (Germany)
CWA	Communication Workers of America
DAG	*Deutsche Angestelltengewerkschaft* (German Salaried Employees' Union)
DBB	*Deutscher Beamtenbund* (Confederation of German Civil Service Officials)
DC	*Democrazia Cristiana* (Christian Democratic Party)
DGB	*Deutscher Gewerkschaftsbund* (German Trade Union Federation)
Domei	Japanese Confederation of Labour
DSP	Democratic Socialist Party (Japan)
EC	European Community
EETPU	Electrical, Electronic, Telecommunication and Plumbing Union (UK, merged in 1992 with Amalgamated Engineering Union)
ENI	*Ente Nazionale Idrocarburi* (Italian National Institute for Hydrocarbons)
ERM	Exchange rate mechanism (of EC)
ETUC	European Trade Union Confederation

FDGB	*Freier Deutscher Gewerkschaftsbund* (Free German Trade Union Federation) in the former German Democratic Republic
FDP	Free Democratic Party (Germany)
Federazione CGIL– CISL– UIL	Italian Inter-union Federation
FEN	*Fédération de l'éducation nationale* (French National Federation of Education)
FIET	*Fédération internationale des employés techniciens et cadres* (International Federation of Commercial, Clerical, Professional and Technical Employees)
FO	*Force ouvrière* (Workers' Force); also known as CGT–FO (France)
GATT	General Agreement on Tariffs and Trade
GCHQ	Government Communications Headquarters (UK)
GDP	Gross domestic product
GHQ	General Headquarters of the Allied Powers (Japan)
GNP	Gross national product
HR	Human resources
HRM	Human resource management
IBT	International Brotherhood of Teamsters (USA)
ICC	International Chamber of Commerce
ICFTU	International Confederation of Free Trade Unions
IG Metall	Union of Metal Industry Workers (Germany)
IG Chemie- Papier- Keramik	Union of Chemical, Paper and Ceramics Industry Workers (Germany)
ILO	International Labour Organisation
IMEs	Industrialised market economies
IMF	International Metalworkers' Federation
IMF–JC	Japan Council of Metalworkers' Unions
IOE	International Organisation of Employers
IRI	*Istituto per la Ricostruzione Industriale* (Italian Institute for Industrial Reconstruction)
ITSs	International Trade (union) Secretariats
IWW	Industrial Workers of the World (USA and Canada)
JCP	Japan Communist Party
JSP	Japan Socialist Party
LDEs	Less developed economies
LDP	Liberal Democratic Party (Japan)
LO	*Landsorganisationen i Sverige* (Swedish Trade Union Confederation)
MBL	Act on Co-determination at Work (Sweden)

MTIA	Metal Trades Industry Association (Australia)
NDP	New Democratic Party (Canada)
NIEs	Newly industrialising economies
Nikkeiren	Japan Federation of Employers' Associations
NLRA	National Labor Relations Act (USA)
NUM	National Union of Mineworkers (UK)
NUMMI	New United Motor Manufacturing–Toyota-General Motors joint venture (USA)
OECD	Organisation for Economic Co-operation and Development
OPEC	Organisation of Petroleum Exporting Countries
OSHA	Occupational Safety and Health Act, 1970 (USA)
PCI	*Partito Comunista Italiano* (Italian Communist Party)
PDS	*Partito Democratico della Sinistra* (Italian Democratic Party of the Left)
PGEU	Plumbers and Gasfitters Employees Union (Australia)
PLI	*Partito Liberale Italiano* (Italian Liberal Party)
PPPs	Purchasing power parities
PRI	*Partito Repubblicano Italiano* (Italian Republican Party)
PSDI	*Partito Socialista Democratico Italiano* (Italian Social Democratic Party)
PSI	*Partito Socialista Italiano* (Italian Socialist Party)
PTK	*Privattjänstemannakartellen* (Federation of Salaried Employees in Industry and Services) (Sweden)
QWL	Quality of Working Life
Rengo	Japan Trade Union Confederation (JTUC)
Rodosho	Ministry of Labour (Japan)
RSA	*Rappresentanza Sindacale Aziendale* (Italian Firm Union Representative)
RSU	*Rappresentanza Sindacale Unitaria* (Italian Unitary Union Representative at Firm Level)
SACO	*Sveriges Akademikers Centralorganisationen* also known as SACO/SR (Swedish Confederation of Professional Associations)
SAF	*Svenska Arbetsgivareföreningen* (Swedish Employers' Confederation)
SALF	*Sveriges Arbetsledareförbund* (Swedish Association of Supervisors)
SAP	*Socialdemokratiska Arbetar Partiet* (Social Democratic Labour Party) (Sweden)
SAV	*Statens Arbetsgivarverk* (National Agency for Government Employers) (Sweden)

Scala Mobile Wage indexation (Italy)
SED *Socialistische Einheitspartei Deutschlands* (Former East German Communist Party)
Shunto Spring labour offensive (Japan)
SIF *Svenska Industritjänstemannaförbundet* (Swedish Union of Clerical and Technical Employees in Industry)
SKTF *Svenska Kommunaltjänstemannaförbundet* (Swedish Union of Local Government Officers)
SLD Social and Liberal Democrats (UK)
SMEs Small and medium-sized enterprises
SMIC *Salaire Minimum Interprofessionnel de Croissance* (French national minimum wage)
SNCF *Société Nationale des Chemins de Fer* (French Railways)
SNECMA *Société Nationale d'Etude et de Construction de Moteurs d'Aviation* (French Aerospace)
Sohyo General Council of Trade Unions in Japan
Somucho Management and Coordination Agency (Japan)
SPD *Sozialdemokratishe Partei Deutschlands* (Social Democratic Party of Germany)
TCO *Tjänstemännens Centralorganisation* (Central Organisation of Salaried Employees) (Sweden)
TCO–OF *TCOs förhandlingsråd för offentliganställda* (Confederation of Professional Employees, Public Sector Negotiation Council) (Sweden)
TDL *Tarifgemeinschaft der Deutschen Laender* (German State Government Employers' Association)
TGWU Transport and General Workers' Union (UK)
THC Trades Hall Council (Australia)
TLC Trades and Labor Council (Australia)
TQM Total quality management
TUAC Trade Union Advisory Committee to the OECD
TUC Trades Union Congress (UK)
UAW United Automobile Workers (USA)
UCC *Union confédérale des ingénieurs et cadres* (Confederated Union of Engineers and Executive Staffs of CFDT) (France)
UCI *Union des cadres et ingénieurs* (Union of Executive Staffs and Engineers of FO) (France)
UGICA *Union générale des ingénieurs et cadres* (CFTC) (France)
UGICT *Union générale des ingénieurs, cadres et techniciens* (General Union of Engineers, Executive Staffs and Technicians of CGT) (France)

UIL   *Unione Italiana del Lavoro* (Italian Union of
              Labour)
ULA   *Union der Leitenden Angestellten* (German Union
              of Senior Managers)
UMW   United Mine Workers of America
UNICE   *Union des Industries de la Communauté
              Européenne* (Union of Industrial and Employers'
              Confederations of Europe)
USWA   United Steelworkers of America
VKA   *Vereinigung der Kommunalen Arbeitgeberverbände*
              (German Federation of Local Government
              Employers' Associations)
WARN   Worker Adjustment and Retraining Notification Act
              (USA)
WCL   World Confederation of Labour
WFTU   World Federation of Trade Unions
WIRS   Workplace Industrial Relations Survey (UK)
Zaibatsu   Group of holding companies based on a group's
              commercial bank (Japan)
Zenkoun   All Japan Council of Traffic and Transport
              Workers' Unions
Zenminrokyo Japanese Private Sector Union Council

Preface

This book summarises the traditions and issues in employment and industrial relations in nine significant industrialised market economies (IMEs)—the UK, the USA, Canada, Australia, Italy, France, Germany, Sweden and Japan. We discovered the need for this book while researching, consulting and trying to encourage people to understand international and comparative industrial relations and human resources (HR) in Australia, Britain, the USA and elsewhere.

In this fully revised edition of the book, the introductory and concluding chapters explore trends across IMEs in general. The book begins by showing why international and comparative industrial relations is an important area of study. It goes on to consider some of the relevant methodological problems and to evaluate some of the most influential theories in this field. (Some may prefer to defer reading these two general chapters until after they have read the more specific country chapters.)

A chapter is devoted to each of the countries, which all belong to the 'rich countries' club': the Organisation for Economic Co-operation and Development (OECD). The first four of these countries have comparable adversarial traditions: the UK, the USA, Canada and Australia. The next four are from the European continent: two are Latin countries, with strong postwar traditions of Communist and Catholic unionism: Italy and France. The other two from North-Western Europe have developed distinctive approaches to industrial democracy and skill formation: Germany and Sweden. The narrative starts with the country where industrialisation began (the UK) and finishes with one which reaped an advantage of being 'a late developer' (Japan). To aid comparisons, countries that display some similarities are considered in adjacent chapters. For example, the neighbouring chapters on Canada and Australia, France and Italy, Germany and Sweden can fruitfully be read alongside each other.

Each country is analysed according to a similar format, with an examination of the context—economic, historical, political, legal and social—and the characteristics of the major interest groups—employers, unions and governments. Then follow concise analyses of the main processes of industrial relations, such as legislation, plant or enterprise bargaining, centralised bargaining, arbitration and joint consultation. Important and topical issues are discussed, such as novel forms of Human Resources Management (HRM), labour law reform, technological change, employee participation, labour market flexibility and incomes policy. Periodically, these issues are controversial in most economies and valuable lessons can be learnt—and anticipated—from the experience of others. For each country there is a list of references and a historical chronology of major relevant developments, which is a helpful way of putting current events into perspective. The chapters also comment on prominent disputes and controversies (for example, the 1984–85 and 1992 British miners' protests about job losses in chapter 2 and the 1992 German public-sector pay dispute in chapter 8). Chapter 9 describes the altercations about the wage earner funds in Sweden, while chapter 10 illustrates how Japanese enterprises may differ fundamentally from those of most other countries. The Appendix includes a useful collection of comparative international economic and labour market data on these nine countries.

The first edition and the subsequent Japanese edition of this book were repeatedly reprinted and have been widely read all over the globe. According to an international survey of comparative courses, this book is one of the two most widely prescribed texts in its field around the world (Adams 1991:49). This success is a tribute to the perseverance and skill of all those who have helped. We much appreciate the constructive comments that readers have passed on. We are already planning to improve the next edition, so would be glad to receive any suggestions or corrections please to any of our inevitable errors (in spite of all the people who have cooperated), at the addresses below.

Despite the difficulties of working across different languages, cultures and disciplines, the contributors have patiently met our requests for updating, re-drafting and sometimes our reinterpretation of their original material. We are grateful that the contributors to this new edition include all except one of the original team that compiled the 1987 edition. We thank three new contributors: Annette Jobert, who co-authored the revised chapter on France; Oliver Clarke, who adds a concluding synthesis and helped in many other ways; and Gillian Whitehouse who, while co-authoring the revised Appendix, also adds more insights, for example, on women's issues. We appreciate assistance with the Appendix from the Australian Bureau of Statistics; Department of Employment, UK; International

Labour Organisation (ILO); OECD and the US Bureau of Labor Statistics (BLS). Unless otherwise specified, currencies cited throughout the book are in US$ at current exchange rates, as in Appendix Table A.7.

We are indebted to all those who have facilitated this project, including Tom Kochan, who wrote the Foreword to the new edition. Many people have commented on parts of the draft manuscript of this edition and/or helped in other ways, including: Roy Adams; David Akers; Val Bamber; Marco Biagi; Doug Blackmur; Breen Creighton; Geoff Dow; Margaret Gardner; John Goodman; Winton Higgins; Sid Kessler; Don Lambert; Sol Levine; Mick Marchington; Ian McLoughlin; John Mathews; Neil Millward; Jan Nixon (with assistance from Emma and Rachael); Joyce Rawlins; Irene Sanderson; Peter Scherer; Mark Shadur; George Strauss; Paul Sutcliffe and Di Yerbury.

The Industrial Relations Research Centre, University of New South Wales originally commissioned this book in their series with Allen and Unwin. We thank the chief executives of the university and the publisher for their longstanding personal interest and encouragement: John Niland and Patrick Gallagher.

We much appreciate the support of our colleagues (not least the library staff) in Australia at the Queensland University of Technology, the University of Queensland and the University of Sydney. Institutions in several other countries have also augmented our efforts over several years, including, in Japan, Dokkyo University and the Japan Institute of Labour; in Sweden, the Arbetslivcentrum; in the UK, the University of Durham; in the USA, Harvard University and the Massachusetts Institute of Technology.

Our debts extend to other friends too numerous to mention, including all those who were associated with the first edition. But our greatest debt is to our families, to whom this book is dedicated.

Greg Bamber   and   Russell Lansbury
Key Centre in Strategic   Department of Industrial
  Management   Relations
Queensland University of   University of Sydney
  Technology   City Road, Sydney
George Street, Brisbane   NSW 2006, Australia
QLD 4000, Australia   Fax 612 6924729
Fax 617 8641766   (or 5523105)
(or 8641811)

                        March 1993

Note: We acknowledge that parts of this Preface draw on Roger Blanpain's Foreword to this book's first edition.

Contributors

Greg J. Bamber is Professor and Director, Australian Research Council Key Centre in Strategic Management, Queensland University of Technology, Brisbane. Formerly he was Director of Research, Durham University Business School, England; he has a BSc (Hons) from the University of Manchester Institute of Science and Technology and a PhD from Heriot-Watt University, Edinburgh. He is currently investigating the use of 'Japanese' and other high-performance management strategies in 'western' enterprises and is completing a book, *The Strategic Management of Organisational and Industrial Change* (with Margaret Patrickson). His other publications include *Militant Managers?* and *New Technology: International Perspectives on Human Resources and Industrial Relations* (co-editor). His interests include employee involvement, management education, the management of professional and managerial employees and job flexibility. He researches and consults with international organisations, governments, employers and unions.

Oliver Clarke is currently Visiting Professor at Michigan State University's School of Labor and Industrial Relations. He has also had visiting assignments at the universities of: British Columbia, Wisconsin-Madison, Western Australia, New South Wales and Leuven, and at Curtin University of Technology, Perth, also the American Graduate School of International Management, Glendale, Arizona. After working in industry, where he trained in engineering, he became Secretary of a major British employers' association. Then, after a period as Research Fellow at the London School of Economics and as a management consultant, he served for eighteen years in the Organisation for Economic Co-operation and Development in Paris, where he coordinated its work on industrial relations.

Edward M. Davis is Director of the Labour–Management Studies Foundation and Professor, Graduate School of Management,

Macquarie University, Sydney. He holds a Master of Arts from Cambridge University, England; a Master of Economics from Monash University, Melbourne and a PhD from La Trobe University, Melbourne. His recent research and publications have been mainly on organisational and technological change, employee participation and union government. He is the author of *Democracy in Australian Unions* and co-editor of *Democracy and Control in the Work Place*. With Valerie Pratt, he co-edited *Making the Link: Affirmative Action and Industrial Relations* (three annual volumes).

Friedrich Fuerstenberg was born in Berlin. After receiving a doctorate in Economics at Tubingen University (1953), he did research at the New York State School of Industrial and Labor Relations, Cornell University (1953–54) and the London School of Economics and Political Science (1956–57). After working as Superintendent of the Central Training Department at Daimler–Benz AG in Stuttgart and as Managing Director of the Research Institute for Cooperatives in Erlangen, he was appointed as a full Professor at the Technical University in Clausthal in 1963. From 1966 until 1981 he was a Professor at Linz University, Austria and Head of the Sociological Division of the Austrian Institute for Labour Market Research. From 1981 until 1986 he was a Professor at Bochum University, Germany. Since 1986 he has been Professor of Sociology, Bonn University. He was President of the International Industrial Relations Association, 1983–86. In 1991 he was awarded an honorary doctorate by Soka University, Tokyo and published 'Structure and Strategy in Industrial Relations' as a special issue of the *Bulletin of Comparative Labour Relations*, no 21.

Janine Goetschy is a senior researcher at the *Centre National de la Recherche Scientifique* (CNRS), Paris. Her publications are in the fields of comparative industrial relations and industrial sociology with special reference to industrial democracy and neo-corporatist aspects. She also lectures in a number of French Universities. In recent years she has been conducting research in Brussels on the 'social' dimensions of the EC and is currently engaged in a project on industrial relations developments in the Nordic countries.

Olle Hammarström received an MBA from Gothenburg School of Economics and Business Administration in 1967, and worked as a consultant in personnel administration before joining the Sociology Department of Gothenburg University. He worked as a researcher and change-agent during the first generation of industrial democracy experiments in Sweden 1969–74, and later joined the Ministry of Labour as a policy adviser in the field of industrial democracy and work environment, and as a liaison officer with labour market organisations. He joined the *Arbetslivcentrum* (Swedish Work Life Centre) as a Research Director in 1978. Since 1981 he has been a senior official of the Swedish Union of Clerical and Technical Employees in Industry (SIF). He has published several books and articles on industrial democracy and industrial relations. In 1976–77, he worked at the Australian Department of Employment and Industrial Relations and the Australian Department of Productivity. He was a Visiting Research Fellow with the Department of Industrial Relations at the University of Sydney 1990–91, funded by the Swedish Work Environment Fund to undertake a comparative study of labour market policies in each country (with Rut Hammarström).

Annette Jobert is a senior researcher at the *Centre National de la Recherche Scientifique* (CNRS), Paris, where she specialises in the sociology of work and industrial relations. Her current projects include studies of the development of collective bargaining, ways of classifying jobs and qualifications, and the development of consultation in European multinational enterprises. Her publications include: *Les Classifications dans l'Entreprise: Production des Hiérarchies Professionnelles et Salariales* (jointly with F. Eyraud, P. Rozenblatt and M. Tallard) Paris: La Documentation Française; and 'La négociation collective dans les entreprises multinationales en Europe' in G. Devin ed. *Syndicalisme: Dimension Internationale* Paris: Editions Européennes Erasme.

Yasuo Kuwahara is a Professor of Economics at Dokkyo University and Senior Research Associate at the Japan Institute of Labour (both in Tokyo). He is a graduate of Keio University (Tokyo) and the New York State School of Industrial and Labor Relations, Cornell University, USA. Previously, he worked at Nippon Light Metal Co. Ltd, and at the Organisation for Economic Co-operation and Development as a consultant and adviser. He has taught at Yokohama National University, St Paul University, and Hosei University as a Visiting Lecturer, and has published over fifty papers and books on technological change, foreign direct investment, equal employment opportunities and industrial relations.

Russell D. Lansbury is Professor and Head of the Department of Industrial Relations at the University of Sydney, Australia. He holds degrees in Psychology and Political Science from the University of Melbourne and a PhD from the London School of Economics and Political Science. Professor Lansbury has worked in personnel and industrial relations for British Airways in London, and has held visiting positions at various universities in Europe and North America. In 1984 he was a Senior Fulbright Scholar at both MIT and Harvard University, USA. He was the Foundation Director of

the Australian Centre for Industrial Relations Research and Teaching
(ACIRRT) at the University of Sydney. He has acted as a consultant
to governments in Australia and the International Labour Organisation on industrial relations issues. He is author and editor of numerous academic articles and books on topics such as industrial
democracy, technological change and the role of management in
industrial relations.

Claudio Pellegrini graduated in labour history at the University of
Rome in 1972. Subsequently he worked for an Italian union (CGIL)
as an editor, labour educator, and collective bargaining representative at the national level. Between 1978 and 1984 he studied for
and obtained a PhD in Industrial Relations from the University of
Wisconsin at Madison, USA. He currently teaches in the Faculty of
Sociology, University of Rome, Italy. He has published several
articles on industrial relations in the construction industry, on collective bargaining and on managements' and unions' rights.

Ed Snape teaches human resource management (HRM) and industrial relations in the Department of Human Resource Management
at the University of Strathclyde, Glasgow, Scotland. He has degrees
in economics and industrial relations from the University of Durham
and the University of Wales. Previously he worked at the University
of Teesside, Middlesbrough and at Durham University Business
School (both in the north of England). He has recently completed
a book, *Managing Managers* (with Tom Redman and Greg Bamber).
His current research interests are in HRM and quality management.

Mark Thompson received his PhD from the New York State School
of Industrial and Labor Relations, Cornell University, USA. He
taught at McMaster University and then, since 1971, in the Faculty
of Commerce, University of British Columbia. In addition, he spent
two years as a member of the Research and Planning Department,
International Labour Office, Geneva, Switzerland. He has been a
visiting scholar at the University of Texas, El Colegio de Mexico,
Cornell University and the University of Warwick, England. He was
appointed William M. Hamilton Professor of Industrial Relations in
1985. He is a member.of the National Academy of Arbitrators and
has served as President of the Canadian Industrial Relations Association and on the executive of the Industrial Relations Research
Association (USA). His research interests include public sector
industrial relations, labour relations in Mexico and the role of
management in Canadian industrial relations. He has published
articles in *Relations Industrielles, British Journal of Industrial Relations, Industrial Relations,* and *Industrial and Labor Relations
Review.*

Hoyt N. Wheeler became a full Professor in 1981 at the College of Business Administration, University of South Carolina, where he helped to establish a new graduate program in personnel and industrial relations, and a local chapter of the Industrial Relations Research Association of which he was the founding President. After obtaining a BA in Political Science at Marshall University and a law degree from the University of Virginia, he practised labour law as a partner in a law firm from 1961 to 1970. He received his PhD in 1974 from the University of Wisconsin. He taught at the University of Wyoming from 1973 to 1976; during this time he became an active labour arbitrator. From 1976 to 1981, he taught at the University of Minnesota. He is the co-coordinator of the International Relations Association Study Group 'The Rights of Employees and Industrial Justice'. His publications include *Industrial Conflict: An Integrative Theory,* and *Workplace Justice: Employment Obligations in International Perspective,* co-edited with Jacques Rojot (both published by the University of South Carolina Press).

Gillian Whitehouse teaches in the Department of Government at the University of Queensland, Brisbane, Australia, where she was also an undergraduate and post-graduate student. She is currently involved in research focusing on cross-national studies of work and industrial relations, gender studies, and relations between government and business. In 1991 she undertook a study visit to Canada. Her recent publications include articles in the areas of equal pay and the impact of legislation on workplace gender inequality.

1

Studying international and comparative industrial relations
Greg J. Bamber and Russell D. Lansbury

Most studies of industrial relations focus on the *institutions* that are involved with collective bargaining, arbitration and other forms of job regulation. Some broader approaches see industrial relations as dealing with all aspects of the employment relationship, including personnel/human resource management (HRM). The contributors to this book have begun to move towards such broader approaches.[1]

Although the study of industrial relations focuses on the means by which employment relationships are regulated, it must also take account of the wider economic and social influences on the relative power of capital and labour, and the interactions between employers, workers, their collective organisations and the state. A full understanding of industrial relations requires an interdisciplinary approach which uses analytical tools drawn from several academic fields including: history, sociology, psychology, politics, law, economics, accounting and other elements of management studies. Industrial relations, then, has a dual character: 'it is both an interdisciplinary field and a separate discipline in its own right' (Adams 1988).

Adopting an internationally comparative approach to industrial relations requires not only insights from several disciplines, but also knowledge of different national contexts. Some scholars distinguish between *comparative* industrial relations and *international* studies in this field. For them, comparative industrial relations may involve describing and systematically analysing two or more countries. By contrast, international industrial relations involves exploring institutions and phenomena which cross national boundaries, such as the labour market roles and behaviour of inter-governmental organisations, transnational enterprises and unions (cf. Bean 1985:3). This is a useful distinction, but, again, we veer towards a broader perspective, whereby *international* industrial relations includes a range of studies that traverse boundaries between countries.[2]

This book emphasises an *internationally comparative* approach by analysing nine different countries—all are industrialised market economies (IMEs). In other words, it combines comparative and international approaches to the subject. In this introductory chapter we begin by examining the important reasons for studying comparative and international industrial relations; we then go on to discuss the difficulties and problems in this field, highlight some of the major issues and review several theories which can help to explain different national patterns of industrial relations. There are aspects of an institutional approach to international industrial relations issues in each of the country chapters. However, such issues are discussed more explicitly in the introductory and, in particular, in the concluding chapter.

Why study internationally comparative industrial relations?

There are many ways in which comparative studies can contribute to knowledge about industrial relations. One of the main reasons for studying the experiences of other societies is to gain a better insight into our own country's institutions and practices. 'If one's environment never changes', argues Kahn-Freund, 'one tends to assume that an institution, a doctrine, a practice, a tradition, is inevitable and universal, while in fact it may be the outcome of specific social, historical or geographical conditions of the country' (1979:3). The reasons for studying internationally comparative industrial relations include the need to understand the relative significance of various factors such as technology, economic policies, laws and culture in determining the type of industrial relations system adopted by different countries.

Employment issues are important in all countries. The growth of international commercial and industrial links has made it imperative for governments, employers and unions to be aware of the patterns and idiosyncrasies of labour markets in other countries. For example, certain governments try to maintain up-to-date analyses of industrial relations in other countries. Countries send labour *attachés* to their most important foreign embassies. Also, to be sure of obtaining appropriate supplies, the Japanese steel companies aim to forecast their future needs for raw materials. Therefore, some of these enterprises have monitored industrial relations in the Australian mines and docks, and have exploited industrial disputes there to advantage; for example, when negotiating to buy coal and other raw materials (Hill et al. 1983). The realisation that employment standards are important in determining fair international trade between states has further heightened the need for the comparative study of labour relations and its role in export competitiveness (Servias 1989; Van Liemt 1989). In the Uruguay Round of the General Agreement on Tariffs and Trade (GATT) for instance, many IMEs pressed for the inclusion of a 'social clause' in bilateral and multi-lateral trade agreements.

The study of industrial relations practices in other countries can provide the basis for reforms in our own country and has important implications for public policy. Most countries are confronting social change, whereby there are proposals to adapt industrial relations institutions to new circumstances. An internationally comparative approach can facilitate industrial relations reform by indicating alternative institutions or procedures which other countries have used in an attempt to solve particular problems. However, programs of reform based on the experience derived from another context can also have unanticipated consequences. A former British Conservative government introduced an Industrial Relations Act in 1971 which was based partly on US experiences—such as enforceable contracts and unfair industrial practices—and also on Australian experiences, notably in relation to the crucial role it accorded to union registration. Among other objectives, the Act aimed to constrain unions and thereby reduce the number of disputes (see ch. 2). Nonetheless, this Act induced a great deal of industrial conflict. Following a change of government, this Act was repealed in 1974. It was seen as a failure by employers as well as unions, thereby demonstrating the difficulty of attempting to initiate fundamental change by grafting a series of industrial relations practices derived from one country onto another. Hence Kahn-Freund argues:

> We cannot take for granted that rules or institutions are transplantable . . . any attempt to use a pattern of law outside the environment of its origin continues to entail the risk of rejection . . . Labour law is part of a system, and the consequences of change in one aspect of the system depends upon the relationship between all elements of the system. Since the relationships may not be similar between the two societies, the effects of similar legislation may differ significantly as between the two differing settings (1974:27).

Another reason for studying internationally comparative industrial relations is to assist with the construction of theories. Such an approach can be a useful way of verifying hypotheses or of producing generalisations derived from research findings from different national contexts. Many researchers have criticised the relative lack of theory in the study of industrial relations in general (Barbash & Barbash 1989). This lack reflects the contributions to the field of policy-makers and practitioners, as well as academics; many of their studies are directed towards settling a particular dispute or issue and tend to be predominantly descriptive, without much of an analytical framework (see Giles 1989).

A further factor adds to the complexity of this field: analysts have to collect much information about more than one country before being able to make generalisations. There is also a tendency to focus on the formal institutional and legal structures as a basis for comparison, rather than on the more complex informal practices and processes. Strauss (1992) advances the interesting proposition that it is fruitless to seek to 'design a complete full-grown theory of comparative industrial relations' at this stage of the field's development. Rather, he suggests it is more appropriate to 'creep towards a field of comparative industrial relations' by developing generalisations and testable hypotheses which explain differences among countries, and which may subsequently provide the basis for developing useful theories. He draws attention to advantages to be gained from studying close pairs of countries with somewhat similar economies, cultures and historic traditions. This permits the researcher to hold many characteristics constant and examine those which vary between each country. 'By looking at differences we seek uniformities, universal rules which explain these differences' (Strauss 1992:1).

As an illustration of such a comparative approach, Lansbury et al. (1992) matched Swedish and Australian plants in the automotive components industry. They examined productivity levels in each of the plants and sought to determine which variables explained differences in performance. The superior levels of productivity achieved by the Swedish plant appeared to be related not only to levels of investment but also to industrial relations in the broadest sense, including: the degree of consultation between management and the workforce, type of work organisation and degree of teamwork. However, the study also demonstrated the difficulty of seeking to hold characteristics constant, even when the products being manufactured and the processes used are identical.

What and how should we compare?

One of the challenges of comparative studies is the choice of 'what' and 'how' to compare. As Schregle (1981:16) argues: 'international comparison in industrial relations requires the acceptance of a reference point, a scale of values . . . a third factor to which the industrial relations systems or phenomena of the countries being compared can be related'. He illustrates his argument by considering three examples: labour courts and labour disputes; collective agreements; and collective bargaining. In each case there are problems of distinguishing the formal institutions themselves from the functions which they perform. Thus, a comparative study of labour courts in Western Europe immediately encounters the difficulty that the functions of these bodies differ so markedly. In France, for example, the labour courts deal with individual as distinct from collective disputes, while the Swedish labour court is competent to deal with little more than disputes arising out of the interpretation of collective agreements. Employment discipline or industrial justice is an issue in all countries, so is an especially appropriate focus for comparative analysis (see ch. 3), even though there are many international differences in terminology. There are challenges in communicating even between English-speaking countries: for instance, there are differences in the style and legal status of a British *collective agreement*, an American *labour contract* and an Australian *industrial award*. Nevertheless, each of these instruments has a broadly similar role. Hence, it is important to compare the role of particular institutions, irrespective of the terminology used.

The lack of a common language and terminology may create confusion. As Blanpain (1993) points out: 'identical words in different languages may have different meanings, while corresponding terms may embrace wholly different realities'. He notes that the term 'arbitration' (or 'arbitrage' in French) which usually means a binding decision by an impartial third party, can also signify a recommendation by a government conciliator to the conflicting parties. There can also be difficulties in distinguishing between the law and the actual practice. For example, while Australia has formally practised 'compulsory arbitration' since the beginning of this century, there is relatively little 'compulsion' in practice and the arbitration tribunals rely mainly on advice and persuasion (see ch. 5).

The collection of comparative data also poses challenges for those studying this field; for example, the definition of industrial disputes differs between countries (see Appendix). In Australia and Britain, generally there is no explicit distinction between conflicts of *right* and of *interest*, though in one Australian state (New South Wales) and New Zealand a legal distinction between rights and interest was proposed in the early 1990s as part of wide-ranging reforms of labour law. These innovations received a mixed reception by the parties. However, in the USA, Sweden and many other countries, this distinction is important. Conflicts of right concern the interpretation of an *existing* contract or award, such as which pay grade applies to a particular individual or group of workers. However, conflicts of interest arise during collective bargaining about a new demand or claim, such as for a general pay increase or a reduction in working hours. In practice, conflicts of interest are usually collective disputes. In France, Italy and many other countries, conflicts of right are further divided into individual and collective disputes. The general intention is that different settlement procedures will apply to the different types of dispute. In some countries only conflicts of interest can lead to lawful strikes or other forms of sanction, but conflicts of right should be settled by a binding decision of a labour court or similar body.

An illustration of the way in which institutions are reshaped by different environments may be seen in the former British colonies. Although many of these countries inherited the English legal system and other institutions from Britain, most of them have subsequently modified or transformed this legacy. Many of the American (ch. 3), Canadian (ch. 4) and Australian (ch. 5) approaches to industrial relations are as different from each other as they are from Britain's (ch. 2). In Japan (ch. 10), following the Second World War, the occupying forces imposed American-style labour laws and managerial techniques. These were not completely rejected, but were subsequently reshaped by the Japanese to suit their particular circumstances (Shirai 1983; Gould 1984). In the latter years of the twentieth century, as they adopt more globally-oriented strategies, Japanese transnational enterprises are increasingly exporting their approaches to managing production, human resources (HR), work organisation and industrial relations. Although these approaches have been strongly criticised (e.g. Parker & Slaughter 1988), business leaders tend to see them as successful, so many non-Japanese enterprises are trying to emulate Japanese role models. This is illustrated vividly in a best-selling book on the automobile industry, a study of 'Japan's revolutionary leap from mass production to lean production—and what industry everywhere can learn from it' (Womack et al. 1990; also see Bamber, Shadur & Howell 1992).

Theoretical approaches

It is important to bear in mind that ideology is a significant issue— and sometimes a problem—in shaping the framework within which research questions are formulated (Korpi 1981:186–7). Industrial relations research in the English-speaking countries, for example, tends to focus on procedural and institutional approaches to problem-solving, predominantly within a pluralist framework (as discussed later). Some writers have also tried to formulate broader theories to explain similarities and differences between countries. From a radical Left perspective, industrial relations issues tend to be seen as only one component of a larger concern with economic and social change and relationships between classes. In some countries, such as Sweden and France, there is a combination of approaches so that Marxist-oriented research is tempered by a pragmatic orientation towards public policy (Doeringer et al. 1981). Another approach has been developed in the USA by political economists. In the next part of this chapter we examine these approaches and indicate their strengths and weaknesses.

The way in which different countries handle similar industrial relations issues can be illustrated by reference to technological change. We suggest that in societies which have a predominantly adversarial approach to industrial relations—such as Britain, Australia, USA and Canada—the parties find it more difficult to cope with technological change than those which have more of a social partnership approach to industrial relations—such as the Nordic countries and Germany. Based on observation of the way in which new technology has been introduced in these countries and the degree to which conflict is engendered between the parties during this process, hypotheses can be developed to begin to explain different approaches (Bamber & Lansbury 1989). Hence, countries that share an inheritance of occupationally-based unionism, relatively weak unions and employers' associations, an inconsistent government role in industrial relations (depending upon which political party holds office), and adversarial traditions of labour–management relations, tend to take a 'distributive bargaining' approach to technological change (cf Walton & McKersie 1965). By contrast, those countries with industry-wide unions, stronger employer associations and a more consensual tradition of industrial relations, tend to take a more 'integrative bargaining' approach to the issue. They also appear to be able to introduce technological change with less industrial conflict.

Gill and Krieger's (1992) study of technological change in a comparative perspective drew similar conclusions. They conducted a major survey of managers and employee representatives throughout the twelve members of the European Community (EC) to ascertain the degree of participation which was exercised during the introduction of new technologies. Far from being 'harmonised', Gill and Krieger found that practices differed significantly between countries and concluded that the degree of employee involvement in decision-making depended on several variables including: the bargaining power of organised labour; managements' attitudes; legal regulation; and the degree of centralisation of the industrial relations system. The EC countries which were found to be most favourable on the majority of these variables were: Germany, Denmark, the Netherlands and Belgium.

There are, of course, exceptions to these broad hypotheses.

Nonetheless, these examples illustrate how we can draw on international studies to generate testable hypotheses. We must still be wary, however, of the pitfalls that confront those who seek to develop grand theories to incorporate all societies in such an analysis.

In the next few pages, we focus on unions and collective bargaining and recap the debates about convergence and industrialisation. We summarise the notion of modified convergence, and consider radical critiques, contributions by political economists and the concepts of divergence and strategic choice. This leads us to discuss the application of theory to practice and the challenge of explanation. Initially, however, we turn to the idea of an industrial relations system.

Systems approach

Dunlop (1958) developed an approach based on a notion of an 'industrial relations system'. This includes three sets of 'actors' and their representative organisations ('the three parties'): employers, workers, and the state. (In some Western European countries, the parties are known as 'the social partners'.) These parties' relations are determined by three environmental contexts: the technology; market forces; and the relative power and status of the parties. Dunlop defined *the network of rules* which govern the workplace (e.g. the web of rules about pay and conditions) as the *output* of the industrial relations system. Dunlop's approach has been influential among a generation of scholars in the English-speaking countries and elsewhere; it was a notable attempt to identify a theoretical framework for industrial relations. Walker (1967) was influenced by Dunlop and went on to urge that we should transcend the dominant descriptive approaches to 'foreign industrial relations systems' and concentrate on identifying the role, importance and interaction of different factors which shape and influence industrial relations in different national contexts. Others enlarged on Dunlop's approach (e.g. Blain & Gennard 1970; Craig 1975).

Various critics accept that Dunlop's framework is useful as 'a model within which facts may be organised, but stress that it must not be understood as having a predictive value in itself' (Gill 1969). Criticisms of the systems approach include its neglect of the importance of such behavioural variables as motivations, perceptions and attitudes (Bain & Clegg 1974). Dunlop ignored the insights about the importance of informal work groups that were developed by his Harvard colleagues, the 'human relations school' (e.g. Mayo 1949). Moreover, Dunlop's approach tends to concentrate on the rule-making institutions and the settlement of conflict rather than examining the causes of conflict and the role played by *people* in making decisions about the employment relationship (Hyman 1975). In spite of the attempts to develop a systems approach, it is by no means a generally accepted theory.

Collective bargaining

Nevertheless, Dunlop's approach was a point of departure for several British writers, including Flanders (1970) and Clegg (1976), who concentrate on unions and on collective bargaining. Drawing on data from six of our nine countries, Clegg argues that variations in the dimensions of collective bargaining are the main influences on union behaviour. He defines union behaviour as: density of membership (for a definition, see Appendix), external structure, internal government, workplace organisation, strikes, attitudes to industrial democracy and political action.

For Clegg, collective bargaining covers both the negotiation and the administration of agreements. In spite of the assumed distinction between collective bargaining and arbitration, many arbitration awards in Australia are, in fact, the outcome of collective bargaining (see ch. 5). Thus a more important distinction is not between collective bargaining and arbitration, but between collective bargaining and either political action or unilateral regulation.

Clegg identifies six dimensions of collective bargaining as: extent, level, depth, union security, degree of control and scope. He contends that:

> The extent and depth of collective bargaining and the degree of union security offered by collective bargaining are the three dimensions which influence trade union density. The level of bargaining accounts for the extent of decentralisation in union government, including the power and independence of workplace organisations, and decentralisation in turn helps to explain the degree of factionalism within unions . . . (1976:118).

Clegg argues that the dimensions of collective bargaining are themselves mainly determined by the structures of management and of employers' organisations; 'but where the law has intervened in the early stages, it may have played an equally important part, or even a more important part, in shaping collective bargaining' (1976:118). He submits that the theory is confirmed by data from five countries. However, it is not so applicable in France, 'because collective bargaining is not the main method of trade union action there' (1976:119). Political action is more important for French unions, but Clegg fails to find a simple explanation for this.

Clegg's approach is narrower than Dunlop's, for Clegg seems to ignore the economic, social and technological environment while concentrating on collective bargaining and the 'web of rules'. Clegg holds that collective bargaining is the principal influence on union behaviour, yet unions are part of collective bargaining. Thus, in Clegg's theory it is unclear which aspect is cause and which is effect. While Clegg does not provide an adequate theory of union behaviour, his approach does provide a stimulus for those who wish to construct theories of comparative industrial relations. Ideally, however, such theories would also have to explain the behaviour of managers, employers' organisations and governments, rather than accepting it as given, as Clegg does.

Adams (1981) and Sisson (1987) seek to develop the collective bargaining approach in an international context, but they both focus on the role of employers. Adams points out that employers' attitudes and behaviour towards unions differ significantly between Europe and North America. In the former, typically, employers are organised into strong associations that engage in collective bargaining with unions (and sometimes with the state). By contrast, in North America, employers have generally not formed strong associations and even where they have, it is much less usual for them to engage in collective bargaining. Adams holds that these differences are attributable to the differing early political or economic strategies of the various labour movements and the resulting differing degrees of state intervention into industrial relations arrangements.

Sisson argues that there could be no adequate theory of collective bargaining which overlooked the interests of management. Furthermore, there has been widespread failure to appreciate how the role of employers in collective bargaining varies from country to country. Sisson compares the role of employers and their organisations in the development of collective bargaining in seven IMEs. He also concludes that differences between the countries were rooted in historical experience, particularly flowing from the impact of industrialisation. Hence, in Western Europe, including Britain, multi-employer bargaining emerged as the predominant pattern largely because employers in the metal working industries were confronted with the challenge of national unions organised along occupational or industrial lines. By contrast, single-employer bargaining emerged in the USA and Japan because the relatively large employers that had emerged at quite an early stage in both countries were able to exert pressure on unions to bargain at the enterprise or establishment level. When legislation was introduced requiring employers to recognise unions (in the 1930s and 1940s), they had already exerted a profound influence on the labour movement and were able to deny unions the platform from which to push for more effective national unionism—especially in Japan.

He argues that the key features of collective bargaining—whether single-employer or multi-employer—are not easily changed, except in crisis periods. He instances the lack of success of attempts to extend the scope of collective bargaining at the workplace level in several Western European countries, excluding Britain. Sisson also makes the important point that most attempts to change the collective bargaining system by legislation are unlikely to have the intended effect, unless they take into account the parties' wishes (as illustrated by the above-mentioned experience of the British 1971 Act). Thus there are significant forces in most countries which tend to prevent major deviations from their industrial relations traditions.

Hence Sisson does not find convergence between collective bargaining systems, even though employers may share the motive of seeking to maintain managerial control through collective bargaining.

Controversies about convergence

A focus for much of the theorising about comparative industrial relations (and especially about industrialisation) has been the debate about whether there has been convergence or divergence between the different patterns of institutional behaviour found in various countries, especially the IMEs. One of the most influential postwar comparative books argued that industrial societies would gradually become more alike. Although their book was first published in 1960 and has often been misinterpreted, the arguments of Kerr et al. (1973) remain influential, especially in English-speaking countries. Their core proposition was that there is a global tendency for technological and market forces associated with industrialisation to push national industrial relations systems towards uniformity or 'convergence'. They argued that there is a *logic of industrialism*, even though the process has various patterns in different countries. Among the 'universals' of the logic are the development of a concentrated, disciplined workforce with new and changing skills, and a larger role for governments in providing the infrastructure required for industrialisation. An essential part of the logic of industrialism is the growth or imposition of a pluralistic consensus which provides an integrated body of ideas and beliefs. Each industrialising society develops an industrial relations system, which becomes increasingly tripartite as industrialisation proceeds.

Figure 1.1 illustrates schematically the logic of industrialism, showing how the various social changes are related to the prime cause: technology. Convergence between advanced industrial socie-

Figure 1.1   The logic of industrialism

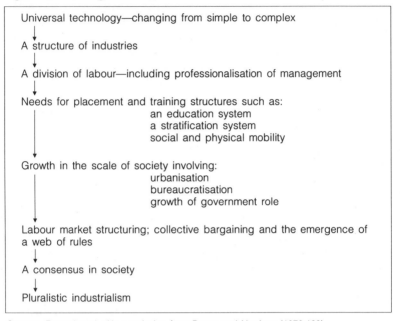

Source: Reproduced with permission from Brown and Harrison (1978:129).

ties occurs most readily at the technological level, at plant and industry levels, or at urban levels, and then ultimately at national levels. However, Kerr et al. did concede that total convergence was unlikely because of the persistence of political, social, cultural and ideological differences. Kerr later (1983) modified his views and argued that convergence is a *tendency* that is not likely to precipitate identical systems among industrialised countries. He also noted that while IMEs at the macro-level might appear to be similar, differences at the micro-level could be quite profound. Further, industrialisation on a world scale is never likely to be total because the barriers to it in many less-developed economies (LDEs) are insurmountable. Nevertheless, he still held the central assumptions of the original study—namely, that the basic tensions inherent in the process of industrialisation had been overcome by modern industrial societies and that there would be a growing consensus around liberal–democratic institutions and the pluralist mixed economy. Relations between 'managers and the managed' would be increasingly embedded in a web of rules agreed to by both parties, so that industrial conflict would 'wither away' (Ross & Hartman 1960).

Modified convergence

Many writers have criticised the 'liberal–pluralist' approach of Kerr et al. For example, Chamberlain (1961) saw their book as:

> . . . long on categories and classifications and impressionistic observations, but . . . short on analysis. It is perhaps best described as a latter-day descendant of the 19th century German school of economic history, whose hallmark was a literary exposition of the transition from one idealised state of economic development to another.

Other critics have focused on the 'deterministic view of the future' represented by industrialisation as an 'invincible process' (Cochrane 1976). According to Bendix (1970:273), 'seldom has social change been interpreted in so *magisterial* a fashion, while all contingencies of action are treated as mere historical variations which cannot alter the logic of industrialism'. Arguably, Kerr et al. were too concerned with maintaining the *status quo*, controlling conflict, defending the existing institutions and imposing an ethno-centric, American, perspective on the rest of the world.

Doeringer (1981) is less critical, but argues that convergence should be seen in a different form compared with that envisaged by Kerr et al. Doeringer argues that countries develop alternative solutions to common industrial relations problems; thus all industrialised countries show a tendency to institutionalise their arrangements for rule-making about employment, even though their particular approaches vary. Differences between countries, therefore, are not simply random but are rooted in their individual responses to the underlying compulsions of industrialisation. He analyses convergence using a three-part framework: first, as the result of responses to problems common to all industrial relations systems; second, as the process by which gaps in areas in the institutional industrial relations arrangements are filled; and third, as the reali-sation that, over time, all industrial relations systems selectively respond to multiple and often incompatible goals. Hence, what may appear as differences between systems may be due simply to dif-ferences in the goals which are being pursued at a particular point in time.

Piore (1981) also doubts that the convergence thesis is a general theory of comparative industrial relations. Thus, he observes that certain aspects of industrial societies tend to converge while others diverge, depending upon time and circumstances. An alternative approach suggested by Piore is to focus on the role of regulatory institutions in the industrial relations of different societies. He argues that capitalist economies pass through a distinct series of regulatory systems in the course of their historical development. As technology and industry change, they outgrow the regulatory structures initially adopted and the system has increasing difficulty maintaining itself in balance. The result is an economic and social crisis which can be resolved only by the development of a new set of institutions.

Late development

In comparison with the work of Kerr et al. and that inspired by it, Dore (1973) has a more modest approach. He too aims to account for international differences, but he focuses on Japan and Britain. He places less emphasis on technology than Kerr et al., and highlights the importance of other factors: the emergence of giant corporations and the spread of democratic ideals of egalitarianism.

In examining Japanese industrial relations, Dore identifies a 'late-comer' effect. Since Japan began to industrialise relatively late (a century after Britain), it was able to learn from the experience of the countries which had already been through that process. He argues that late-developers had been able to adopt organisational forms and institutions which were more suited to industrialisation than are those of countries which industrialised relatively early. Dore concludes that employment arrangements were becoming more alike, but Japan, rather than any Western country, was the model to which other countries were converging. There have been general criticisms of Dore's thesis and specific criticisms of some of his detailed interpretation; however, his approach has considerable potential in this field. 'By concentrating on only two country cases and dealing with these cases in a consistently and systematically comparative fashion, Dore succeeded in minimising the danger of lapsing into either vacuous description or superficial comparison' (Shalev 1980:40).

Towards divergence?

Poole (1986) and Streeck (1988) refuel the earlier convergence debates. They outline several factors which operate in most IMEs to induce structural change, but hold that these are leading to diverse outcomes or 'divergent evolutionary trajectories'. Streeck likens this situation to the growing variety in the use of technology and the structure of work organisation whose present trend has been described as an 'explosion'—with different strands of development moving away from each other in different directions—as opposed to 'implosive' convergence towards one central 'best practice'.

The changes in the structure of employment are causing unions to experience a loss of power. These changes include: shifts in employment from the industrial to the service sector; the growth of a 'secondary sector' of small subcontracting firms and of a marginal workforce in unstable employment ('dualisation'); increases in part-time work and white-collar jobs; the growing use of HRM techniques, including worker-involvement schemes; and the increasing participation of women. Although these changes are widespread, they are likely to have very different consequences for employers, governments and unions, depending on their organisational base. Thus, where union density is low, it is likely to decline further; whereas where density is high, it is likely to remain stable or even grow.

Union strategies for coping with structural changes are also likely to differ in accordance with their current situation. Heterogeneity is increasing not only between, but also within, national industrial relations systems. A growing 'individualisation' within the workforce is eroding the membership base of unions and resulting in three different responses. There is, first, de-unionisation—with unions organising only a few of the many groups with divergent interests which form the labour force; second, the decomposition of the labour movement resulting from inter-organisational fragmentation; third, the preservation of formal organisational unity at the national or sectoral level, but at the price of heightened internal policy conflict. Streeck warns that the ability of the unions to manage internal heterogeneity (and thereby preserve a strategic continuity) will be put to severe test in the coming years in all developed industrialised countries. To maintain even a modicum of centralised decision-making, unions will require major organisational and institutional change. Australian unions, for instance, appear to be implementing significant innovations (see ch. 5).

Flexibility

Changes in markets and production methods are resulting in strong pressures for the decentralisation of industrial relations and for custom-made rules for particular plants or enterprises, even within the most centralised systems of industrial relations. In recent years, 'flexibility' has been seen as an important issue (Bamber, Boreham & Harley 1992), though its meaning and application have varied widely. Streeck argues that industrial relations systems are polarising around three types of flexibility as a response to the changing economic environment. First, there is the 'neo-liberal model' of flexibility through recourse to the external labour market (or a 'return to the market'), especially where there are weak unions and few legal provisions for employment protection. This response is most likely in relatively low wage, mass production sectors or economies (e.g. Britain; see ch. 2). Second, there is the 'dualistic model' which combines internal flexibility and external employment rigidity for the core workforce, on the one hand, with external flexibility in the employment of a sizeable marginal workforce, on the other (e.g. Japan; see ch. 10). Third, there is a 'quasi-corporatist model' which involves high internal flexibility as a compensation for continuing external rigidities (or 'flexibility within centralism'). This occurs mainly where there is a strong labour movement that is able to intervene in political decision-making. Internal flexibility, in this case, is accomplished and mediated through institutions which provide for union–management cooperation (e.g. systems of co-determination as in Germany and Sweden; see chs 8 & 9). The economic viability of this form of flexibility depends on whether markets can be found which place a premium on high skills and worker commitment, and that have the potential to underwrite the costs of joint regulation.

A logical conclusion from such analyses is that industrial relations should no longer be treated as distinct from the rest of the economy (as it was by writers such as Flanders, who focused on collective bargaining). Rather, the terms of employment relationships are becoming increasingly sensitive to changes in economic conditions. The influence which unions are able to wield depends upon their strategic choices and institutional opportunities. Hence, the introduction of flexibility can be achieved against union opposition through the restoration of managerial prerogatives (the 'neo-liberal model') or without union participation but through enlightened HRM policies (the 'dualistic model'). Alternatively, unions may participate in decisions and operations of integrated flexible production systems (the 'quasi-corporatist' model).

Alternative approaches

Most of the writers in the orthodox industrial relations tradition could be described as liberal pluralists in terms of their ideological perspectives. The most far-reaching critiques of the orthodox pluralist approaches to the study of industrial relations are by radical scholars (e.g. Mills 1959; Mandel 1969). Such critics argue that the orthodox approaches are parochial and generally ignore the world outside a narrow definition of industrial relations. They hold that, at most, the wider society is included in the pluralists' models only through narrowly circumscribed channels of 'adjustment' and 'feedback' (Hyman 1980). Most Marxists, for example, generally see industrial relations merely as derivative of the patterns of economic ownership, political domination and of relations of production. Therefore, much of their analysis has been concerned with examining such broader issues as capital accumulation and class struggle. However, from their writing—which focuses mainly on other issues—we generally have to infer the radical interpretations of industrial relations.

Goldthorpe (1984), for instance, argues that in confronting macro-economic problems, societies have diverged from the pluralistic mould which hitherto held sway; hence the convergence thesis should no longer be seen as appropriate. On the one hand, there are countries like Norway, Austria, Germany and Sweden (see chs 8 & 9) where inequalities between capital and labour have been mitigated by corporatist state policies; these seek to 'harmonise' the interests of employers, unions and the state. By contrast, in countries like Britain and the USA (see chs 2 & 3), traditional labour market institutions (e.g. collective bargaining) have been undermined by market forces that have operated to overcome perceived rigidities. This has resulted in a tendency towards dualism in which the workforce is separated into core and peripheral employees. The former may remain unionised and within the collective bargaining framework, albeit in a more decentralised mode, while the latter are employed under more individualistic work arrangements characterised by contractual forms of control (see chs 2 & 11).

Goldthorpe is pessimistic about the long-term likelihood that such corporatist and dualist structures could continue to coexist within the same society. Rather, the logical and political implications of each approach were so dramatically opposed to the other that this would lead to increasing tension between them, resulting in the ultimate dominance by one of another. In other words, any compromise would be unstable and ineffective in resolving macro-economic problems. Thus, either the corporatist system would triumph or the more market-based, dualistic industrial relations system would become the norm. However, different societies find their own solutions depending upon social, economic and political pressures.

Political economy

Certain political economists have drawn upon social, political and economic theory in an attempt to compare some aspects of industrial relations. They have argued that the pluralists have either ignored or denied the interaction between politics (or power relations) and industrial relations, while Marxists have not provided a satisfactory framework for analysing the labour markets and associated political processes.

In an analysis of union strategy and political economy in five Western European countries (Lange et al. 1982; Gourevitch et al. 1984), this Harvard group supports a 'divergence thesis', arguing that in those sectors where it has representation, the unions responded to the economic crisis since the early 1970s in quite different ways (also see Goldthorpe 1984). Four broad approaches are identified in the responses of Western European unions. First, a *maximalist* response has been associated with some of the French unions, especially those on the Left, as demonstrated by their refusal to play any role in the 'management of the crisis' at the firm, sectoral or national levels. This is seen as an illustration of the subordination of union policy to the strategic and tactical interests of the French Communist Party, with the CGT playing the role of a 'transmission belt' for the Party (see ch. 7). Second, an *interventionist* approach has been followed by some of the Italian unions which have sought to intervene at the firm, sectoral and national levels in order to develop incremental policies to relieve the economic crisis (see ch. 6). Third, a *defensive-particularistic* strategy has occurred where groups of workers have sought to protect themselves in the face of income and job insecurity, using rank-and-file power bases to veto changes with which they disagree. This has been characteristic of some British unions (see ch. 2). Fourth, a *corporatist* strategy has been associated with unions which collaborated with the state and employers in areas such as incomes policies and broader economic and social programs. This approach has been epitomised by unions in Sweden and, to some extent, in Germany, especially during periods of Social Democratic government (see chs 8 & 9). These categories are not intended to precisely fit different national union movements, but are merely intended as ideal–typical illustrations of how unions differ both within and between the countries of Western Europe.

Lange et al. also outline four different characteristics which have distinguished these union movements: market strength, political influence, inter-union relationships and expectations. While these writers are able to demonstrate the existence of important differences between the union movements of Western Europe, they rather neglect such areas of common interest as confronting multinationals and defending members' job security. They also focus on a rather limited period, namely 1945–80 in general, and the 1970s in particular. Events since the publication of the first volume of their work (e.g. the accommodation between some of the French unions and the Mitterrand socialist government), illustrate the current difficulty of predicting even a few years ahead. A more important limitation of such approaches, however, is the focus on the macro-level and the neglect of rank-and-file perspectives. For this reason, they emphasise the role of the state and the role of union confederations, which although important, are only two elements in the wider spectrum of industrial relations.

Towards divergence in unionism?

Based on data from the USA and other IMEs, Freeman argues that 'far from converging to some modal type, trade unionism . . . traditionally the principal worker institution under capitalism developed remarkably differently among Western countries in the 1970s and 1980s' (Freeman 1989). While union density rose or at least was maintained at high levels in much of continental Europe and Canada, it declined significantly in the USA and, to a lesser extent, in Japan, the UK and Australia (see Appendix). This divergence in density occurred despite such common factors as increasing trade, technological transfer and capital flows between countries, which might have been expected to exert pressures for similarities.

The USA has adopted a different route from most other IMEs with regard to unionisation and industrial relations in recent years (see ch. 3); no other country has gone as far towards 'the union-free nirvana of the rabid opponents of trade unionism' (Blanchflower & Freeman 1989). Yet the USA also exhibits a mixture of two opposing trends: a near collapse of unionism in the private sector, but a relatively stable level of unionisation in the public sector. One of the main causes of decline in private-sector unionism in the USA is that unions there have significantly greater effects on wages than do unions in other countries—which gives US management an exceptional profit incentive to oppose them. Unless the decline can be arrested, Blanchflower and Freeman forecast that unions in the USA will be 'relegated to a few aged industrial sectors and to public and some non-profit sectors, producing what can be called ghetto unionism'. In order to recover their position in the 1990s, unions, they argue, will have to emphasise their 'collective voice' role, drawing on international experience and experimenting with new initiatives. The election of President Clinton in 1992 aroused renewed union hopes of a revival in their fortunes.

We should not be surprised to see conflicting perspectives emerge in parallel debates and controversies which are taking place in Europe and the USA. As Streeck argues in relation to European developments, unionists are faced with a choice of strategy between 'optimistic conservatism' and a 'productionist strategy' (Streeck 1987). The former strategy assumes that the economic and industrial environment has not undergone a permanent change and that economic cycles will allow unions to resume their traditional roles and functions involving a predominant concern for wage bargaining and securing non-wage benefits for their members. Alternatively, unions can adopt a 'productionist strategy' in which they assist employers to develop a cooperative and committed workforce who will comply with the new production systems, thereby avoiding the marginalisation of the unions and an associated decline of union membership levels.

The diversity of responses by unions, employers and governments to changing conditions in Western Europe is emphasised by Clarke (1990), who notes that when 'surveying the European scene today it is difficult to see much of a convergence of industrial relations systems'. Nevertheless, there is a conspicuous difference between, on the one hand, Norway, Sweden, Finland and Austria, and, on the other hand, most other countries. The first group still largely enjoys relatively low unemployment; its unions have not had to face substantial membership loss and they continue to have a strong influence on (mainly) social democratic governments.

Strategic choice: Another point of departure?

Collective bargaining specialists, Kochan et al. (1984), offer another contribution. Although it focuses on the changing patterns of American industrial relations, Kochan et al. take an inter-disciplinary approach and their work has a comparative application. They seek to add a dynamic component, which they call 'strategic choice', to Dunlop's analysis. They propose a framework that differentiates between three levels of decision-making (macro, industrial relations system and the workplace) and three parties (employers, unions and governments) and which identifies the relatively independent effects of the levels on employment relations.

The concept of strategic choice is not new and has previously been used in economics and organisational behaviour, but there are considerable differences in the way this concept is considered by Kochan et al. They use a matrix to encompass the three levels of strategic decision-making. As shown in Figure 1.2, the columns of the matrix represent the three key parties who make strategic decisions. The rows represent three levels at which these decisions can be made. The effects of particular decisions, however, may appear at levels other than those where the decisions are made.

Examples of strategic decisions made at different levels are illustrated in Figure 1.2. Strategic choices in the bottom row are those associated with individual workers or work groups and their relations with the immediate work environment. In the middle row are decisions associated with the practice of collective bargaining and implications of personnel policy. Strategic choice in the top row

Figure 1.2 Industrial relations strategy matrix

Decision level	Nature of Decisions		
	Employers	Unions	Government
I Macro or global level for the key institutions	The strategic role of human resources; policies on unions; investments; plant location; new technology; and outsourcing	Political roles (e.g. relations with political parties and other interest groups); union organising (e.g. neutrality and corporate campaigns); public policy objectives (e.g. labour law reform); and economic policies (e.g. full employment)	Macro-economic and social policies; industrial policy (protection vs free trade)
II Employment relationship and industrial relations system	Personnel policies and negotiations and strategies	Collective bargaining policies and negotiations strategies (employment vs income)	Labour and employment standards law; direct involvement via incomes policies or dispute settlement
III Work place individuals and groups	Contractual or bureaucratic; and individual employee/workgroup participation	Policies on employee participation; introduction of new technology; work organisation design	Regulation of worker rights and/or employee participation

Source: Reproduced with permission from Kochan, McKersie and Cappelli (1984:23).

is concerned with macro or organisation-wide matters. As discussed in chapter 3, due to their job-control traditions US unions have not generally emphasised decisions at this highest level, although this may change. By contrast, Western European unions have been more involved in the decisions at the highest level, within the tradition of tripartite discussions between governments, unions and employers. The emphasis given by the different parties to decisions at various levels tends to change according to circumstances. The greater attention given by American employers to macro-level strategy in recent years has initiated a transformation in industrial relations in the USA (see ch. 3).

However, a strategic approach does not dispense with the need for institutional analysis (Thurley & Wood 1983:2). Other writers criticise the use of strategic choice as a concept. Although Hyman (1987) is explicitly concerned with how Marxist analysis can relate to strategic matters, he raises some significant questions. For example: 'If capitalist production is subject to the determinism of economic forces or laws external to the individual enterprise, what latitude is there for strategic choice?' In other words, are choices in industrial relations made by individual managers (or unions, for that matter) constrained by their external environment over which they have little control? If so, how credible is it to describe the parties as acting 'strategically' in industrial relations? A thorough treatment of strategic choice must emphasise the inevitable contradictions of capitalism, so Hyman redefines management strategy as 'the programmatic choice among alternatives none of which can prove satisfactory'. He reminds us that we are glossing over the complex realities of organisational power if we assume that management as a whole has a unified 'strategic choice'.

After such criticisms and in order to foster a substantial international project on comparative employment relations, Kochan et al. (1992) have refined the strategic choice framework. In this new approach, Kochan et al. advance four propositions. First, that it is increasingly appropriate to adopt a broad approach to employment relations, drawing from HRM as well as from older and narrower approaches to industrial relations, as the literature on strategic HRM emphasises that employers may aim to coordinate their industrial relations and HR strategies with their broader corporate policies (cf. Purcell 1989). Second, the individual components of an employment relations system cannot be understood in isolation, for they interact with each other. Third, distinct competitive strategies tend to be associated with different types of employment practices; for example, cost-cutting mass production strategies are coupled with low pay, low skills and adversarialism, but high-quality and innovatory strategies are coupled with higher pay, better training and more cooperative industrial relations. Shifts in business strategies may be reflected in changes in industrial relations outcomes at all three levels. Fourth, corporate governance arrangements and public policies are vital determinants of employment relations practices. This approach pays more attention to the role of the state, which is less crucial in the USA than in most other countries and therefore tends to be neglected by many US writers.

This new framework is conceptualised in Figure 1.3. It exemplifies, on the left side, explanatory forces, and on the right, outcomes in terms of economic and social performance. In the centre, it illustrates as variables, four key employment relations practices: first, issues of staffing, employment security and job mobility; second, pay arrangements; third, skill formation, education, training and social welfare benefits; and fourth, work organisation and employee participation.

Kochan et al.'s framework for comparative analysis provides a

Figure 1.3   Framework for analysing comparative industrial relations and human resources issues[a]

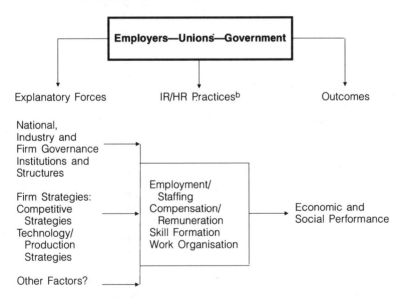

Notes: [a] We appreciate the input of H. Druke and R. Lansbury to this framework.
    [b] Within any single country industrial relations/human resources (IR/HR) practices vary across industries, firms and over time, and all the variables in the model may be shaped by different combinations of employer, union and government influence.

Source: Adapted with permission from an original in Kochan, Locke and Piore (1992).

novel approach to analysing differences in employment relations practices at the levels of national and corporate policy-making, collective bargaining and workplace interaction. This framework should not be viewed as a substitute for studying the political economy of employment relations and the broader historical, social and legal contexts, but it helps to conceptualise such studies and thus assists understanding the dynamics of comparative industrial relations.

The importance of strategies developed by employers, unions or governments varies between countries and may be influenced by the prevailing values, ideologies, economic conditions and power relationships. Furthermore, the strategies which dominate industrial relations in a particular enterprise, industry or country may vary over time.

Applying theory to practice

Recent developments in industrial relations have provided challenges for industrial relations theorists and practitioners (e.g. Giles & Murray 1988). It is not surprising that in a period of apparently declining union power when there is a transformation of collective bargaining, traditional approaches to the analysis of labour and management issues are being challenged. However, as we try to develop fuller and more satisfactory explanations, it becomes more important to draw on insights from several disciplines rather than relying only on one.

Even though the role of the state may appear to be declining, following the deregulation of the economy in many Eastern European countries and IMEs, the insights from political economy will still be useful. As there is an increased role for markets in determining industrial relations outcomes, a micro-economics paradigm will also be relevant, especially as micro-economic labour market reform is high on the agenda of many governments, employers and unions around the world. Moreover, a significant number of economic policy-makers are realising the desirability of attempting to incorporate into their analyses institutional concerns and insights from industrial relations (cf. Oswald 1985;1987).

New approaches are needed in order to interpret increasingly complex and seemingly contradictory developments. There is increasing globalisation of capital and hence greater competition. Changes in the nature of production, such as the advent of flexible specialisation (Piore & Sabel 1984) means that the search for improved labour and capital flexibility is international in its extent and influence. Yet given the different institutional bases of national

industrial relations systems, the manner in which changes are introduced, mediated and handled, can lead to different outcomes. Thus,
in a sense, convergence at the global level in terms of economic
forces and production technologies, may result in divergence at the
national and intra-national level as these forces are mediated by
different institutions with their own traditions and cultures (cf. Poole
1992). This provides further support for the arguments advanced
above for paying close attention to the linkages between historical,
political and economic factors and industrial relations outcomes,
rather than making broad generalisations concerning tendencies
towards convergence or divergence between systems.

Conclusion: The challenge of explanation

The differences between industrial relations in economies which are
at different stages of industrialisation (let alone those at similar
stages) are so vast as to defy a single theoretical explanation. Yet
the quest continues for conceptual approaches which will help to
explain why particular systems develop. Various writers in the
pluralist tradition provide some categories which are useful ways
for organising our work as summarised above, but they tend to have
a restricted focus and some make naive assumptions about the
maintenance of consensus. Certain radical writers usefully focus on
critical issues and on rank-and-file workers themselves, but some
tend to dwell unrealistically on a presumed inevitability of increasing class conflict. They also tend to deny any autonomy to industrial
relations processes, while the pluralists tend to exaggerate such
autonomy. The reality is that class and industrial relations issues are
both important, as shown by some sociologists and political economists.

Each approach is partial. Political economists show how there
has been a growing divergence, even between Western European
nations. They provide convincing explanations of national union
strategies in the polity, but neglect the increasing initiating role
played by employers. On the other hand, the importance of managerial strategies is highlighted by such writers as Kochan et al.

When analysing the patterns of labour–management relations in
their own countries, the contributors to the present book have been
most influenced by pluralist approaches. But readers should draw
selectively from other approaches in an attempt to make sense of
the various aspects of the complex realities of the real world. The
development of comparative industrial relations as a viable and
robust field is still in its infant stage and as yet we do not have a
comprehensive analytical approach to the subject. We agree with

Strauss who concludes that 'eventually perhaps the work of model builders and systems theorists may fruitfully interact and the field of comparative industrial relations may flourish at the intersection of these seemingly disparate approaches. But much creeping will be required before we can run' (1992:6). This is an exciting challenge for students of comparative industrial relations and we hope that this book may help with the necessary mapping of the terrain and pathfinding.

2 Industrial relations in Britain
Greg J. Bamber and Edward J. Snape

There has been much change in employment and industrial relations in recent years, as shown in this and the following chapters. In the USA, management has arguably been the prime mover in exercising 'strategic choice' in the transformation of US industrial relations, with unions generally in a reactive mode (ch. 3). An increasing proportion of enterprises have sought to maintain a non-unionised workforce and to implement more sophisticated and strategic human resources management (HRM) techniques. By contrast, in Australia, following the election of the Labor government in 1983, many observers held that the leadership of the Australian Council of Trade Unions (ACTU) was the prime mover. In the post-1983 period, the ACTU set the agenda of reform, not only in the industrial relations arena but also in a broader field, encompassing equal employment opportunities, superannuation, education and training, and health and safety (ch. 5).

In Britain since 1979, the Conservative government has set the tone in industrial relations with its step-by-step reform of employment law and its attempts to foster an 'enterprise culture'. Some commentators argue that there has been a fundamental *change* towards a 'new industrial relations' (e.g. Bassett 1986), but several scholars counter that the general pattern is of *continuity,* especially if we take a historical perspective and avoid focusing only on a few much-publicised cases (e.g. MacInnes 1987; Sisson 1992).

Accordingly, this chapter discusses continuities and changes in industrial relations. It describes the long-established traditions of collective organisation and voluntarism, and it shows how the roles of unions, employers, the state and the legal regulation of the employment relationship have developed. Initially, however, we summarise the economic and political context.

The United Kingdom (UK)[1] has a total population of 57 million people and a 79 per cent labour force participation rate. Apart from

Sweden, this rate is higher than any of the other nine countries covered in this book. (Such statistical data cited in each chapter are elaborated and discussed in more detail in the Appendix.) The UK has relatively fewer people employed in agriculture (2.1 per cent of civilian employees) than any other Organisation for Economic Co-operation and Development (OECD) country (on the OECD, see the Appendix, note 2). About 29 per cent of its civilian employees work in industry; the remaining 69 per cent work in services (according to OECD definitions). There has been a greater decline in its 'industry' category since 1970 than in any other OECD country. In spite of the relative growth of services, there was a steep rise in unemployment, from 1.2 per cent of the working population in 1965 to nearly 12 per cent by 1986, by which time the UK had a higher unemployment rate than any of the other countries discussed in this book. The rate fell in the late 1980s, but rose again in the early 1990s. In terms of gross domestic product (GDP) per capita—an approximate indicator of labour output—the UK (along with Australia) appears to be at the lowest level of the nine countries.[2] Although the rate of inflation declined during the 1980s, the UK still experienced a higher inflation rate in the 1985–90 period than most of the comparable countries.

British politics have been dominated by two political parties since 1945 (see Chronology). The Conservative Party's support is strongest in the more prosperous south of England, and more generally amongst the business and farming communities, which provide much of its income. The Labour Party's support is strongest in Wales, Scotland and the north of England, particularly in industrial working-class communities. The Labour Party is mainly funded by the unions. There are several other political parties, including nationalist parties in Scotland and Wales, and a centre party, the Social and Liberal Democrats (SLD).

The fragmentation of the parliamentary opposition has helped the Conservatives to retain political power since Margaret Thatcher became Prime Minister in 1979. In the 1992 general election, the share of the popular vote was 43 per cent Conservative, 35 per cent Labour, 18.3 per cent SLD, and 2.4 per cent Nationalists. However, Parliament is elected on the basis of 'first past the post' in each constituency and since the Conservative and Labour parties' votes are concentrated in particular strongholds, the other parties find it difficult to win many parliamentary seats.

In spite of the Conservatives' domination of much of Britain, in the north of England they managed to win only a third of the vote, and only a quarter in Scotland. The stark contrast between the Conservative south and Labour-held Scotland was a major factor

behind the high level of support for greater political devolution—
and even independence—for Scotland.

In the 1989 European Parliamentary Elections, the Green Party
made its first significant impression in Britain with nearly 15 per
cent of the vote, but under the 'first past the post' system it won
no seats. Although the Green Party has not emerged as a significant
political force, environmental issues are now on the political agenda
as the major parties have begun to adjust their policies accordingly.
Britain used to have a small Communist Party which was influential
in some unions, but the Party was disbanded as the Soviet Union
disintegrated. Compared with Italy and France, relatively few people
in the British labour movement have embraced revolutionary political ideologies.

The industrial relations parties

Even before industrialisation began in the late eighteenth century,
the early capitalists were changing the basis of society. Workers
were seen as 'hands', as expendable resources for whom the
employer had no responsibility beyond the legal obligations of
contract (Fox 1985). Workers responded to this view and by the
early nineteenth century had begun to organise collectively to defend
themselves in unions. Unlike the position in Sweden, Japan and
some other countries which industrialised relatively late, in Britain
the notion of a 'vertically-bonded works community' hardly developed; industrial relations were generally adversarial rather than
paternalistic.

Unions

Many British unions can trace their roots back to the mid-nineteenth
century or earlier. The earliest unions were formed by skilled
craftsmen. Widespread unionisation of so-called semi-skilled and
unskilled manual workers began in the late nineteenth century,
whilst relatively few white-collar workers joined a union until after
the Second World War. British unions can be classified as craft,
general, industrial or white-collar, depending on their origins and
predominant membership—though this categorisation has become
blurred as unions have gained members in more than one category.
It may be more useful to see unions as either 'closed' or 'open',
according to whether or not they restrict recruitment to particular
categories of workers (Turner 1962). Although there were 1384 UK
unions recorded in 1920, by the end of 1990 there were only 323
(Certification Office 1991). However, membership was concentrated

into a small number of larger unions, with the largest 23 unions accounting for over 81 per cent of the total membership.[3]

There is a complex structure of multi-unionism in many industries. According to the 1990 Workplace Industrial Relations Survey (WIRS) of a large sample of workplaces with at least 25 employees, there is an average of 2.5 unions among the 53 per cent of WIRS workplaces that recognise unions (Millward et al. 1992). Multi-unionism is a legacy of the long and continuous history of most unions. Many have grown in an *ad hoc* manner, recruiting wherever the opportunities arose. Union mergers have further complicated the structure, often bringing together disparate occupational and industrial groups (as illustrated in Table 2.1).

Many have argued that it might simplify collective-bargaining structures if British unions were organised by industry, with one union representing the workers in each main industry. This structure was recommended by a British union delegation which advised on the reconstruction of the West German unions in the late 1940s (see ch. 8). Whilst there are some quasi-industrial unions in Britain, for example in steel, railways and coal mining, there are also specialist unions in these industries for skilled, white-collar, supervisory and managerial workers. Further, as these industries decline, there is pressure on such unions to merge with those that cover other industries, hence the development of industrial unionism is unlikely.

The complexity of union structure is especially evident in private-sector manufacturing industry; workers may belong to different unions depending on their job, skill level and whether they were traditionally seen as manual or non-manual employees. Membership patterns vary between establishments, employers and localities; therefore an employer may deal with several unions within one establishment, even on behalf of a group of workers with similar jobs. There have been inter-union disputes in some industries, but the possible problems associated with multi-unionism have increasingly been offset by the practice of having multi-union negotiating committees, both at workplace and industry levels.

Unlike most other Western European countries, Britain has only one main union confederation: the Trades Union Congress (TUC). By 1991, 74 unions (including most of the large ones), representing 84 per cent of British union members, were affiliated to the TUC. It has a longer continuous history than most central confederations in other countries; established in 1868 to lobby government, this has remained a primary role. However, in the period after the Second World War in particular, it has nominated union representatives to various quasi-governmental agencies and tripartite bodies, though this role has been reduced since 1979. In contrast with its counterparts in many other countries, the TUC has no direct role in

Table 2.1 The fifteen largest British unions

Unions	Membership (000s) 1980	Membership (000s) 1990	% Change 1980–90	Summary Description
Transport & General Workers' Union	1 887	1 224	–35	General/open; has white-collar section
GMB (General, Municipal & Boilermakers' Union)[a]	1 180	865	–27	General/open; has white-collar section
National & Local Government Officers' Association	782	744	–5	Public services; white collar
Amalgamated Engineering Union[b]	1 251	702	–44	Ex-craft; now fairly open. White-collar section split from union in 1985
Manufacturing, Science and Finance[a]	683	653	–4	White-collar, technicians & supervisors in private and public sectors
National Union of Public Employees	699	579	–17	Public service; mainly manual
Electrical, Electronic, Telecommunication & Plumbing Union[b]	439	367	–16	Ex-craft; now fairly open; has white-collar section
Union of Shop, Distributive & Allied Workers	450	362	–20	Fairly general, but based in retailing
Royal College of Nursing	181	289	+60	'Professional union'. Apart from EETPU, only top 15 union not in TUC
National Union of Teachers	273	218	–20	Largest schoolteachers' union
Union of Construction, Allied Trades & Technicians	312	207	–34	Building industry union; some craftsmen elsewhere
Confederation of Health Service Employees	216	203	–6	Health service staff
Union of Communication Workers	203	203	–0	Post Office & British Telecom workers
Banking, Insurance & Finance Union	141	171	+21	Financial services union, competes with non-TUC staff associations
Society of Graphical & Allied Trades[a]	254	169	–33	Ex-craft union printing/paper industries
Total membership of all other unions	3 685	2 854	–23	
Total membership of all unions	12 636	9 810	–22	

Note: a The 1980 membership figures for these unions have been adjusted to take account of amalgamations.
b These two unions merged in 1992 to form the Amalgamated Engineering and Electrical Union.

Source: Calculated from Annual Reports of the Certification Office.

collective bargaining and it cannot itself implement industrial action. British unions have generally been too jealous of their own autonomy to allow the TUC a more powerful role. It has played an important role in regulating inter-union relations, conciliating in major industrial disputes and training union representatives. However, during the early 1990s, even this limited role came under attack from some of the large affiliates, who claimed that the TUC duplicated many of the services already provided by individual unions. The need to cut costs when there is falling aggregate membership, discussed later in this chapter, means that calls for a rationalisation of the TUC are likely to continue.

Besides establishing the TUC to lobby government, the unions were instrumental in the establishment of the Labour Party in 1906. This was seen as a necessary complement to the industrial activities of the unions, particularly after a series of adverse legal judgements meant that new legislation was required to re-establish union rights.

Individual unions may affiliate to the Labour Party, contributing to its funds through a 'political levy' on members, from which individuals may 'opt out' if they wish. Unions also sponsor individual candidates, usually Labour, in parliamentary and local government elections. In 1988, 36 unions were affiliated to the Labour Party, providing nearly 80 per cent of the party's income. Links between the Labour Party and the unions continue to be close, not least because many union activists are also Labour Party members. Since the mid-1980s, however, the Labour Party leadership has attempted to distance the party from the unions in order to try to establish its independence in the eyes of the electorate.

The level and density of union membership has varied since the Second World War. Bain and Price (1983) identify three broad phases. First, between 1948 and 1968 membership grew, but at a lower rate than the growth in potential membership, hence density fell slightly. This was due to structural shifts within the economy as low union density industries, such as services, increased their share of employment and the proportion of women and white-collar employees grew.

Second, the level and density of membership grew rapidly in the 1970s as workers were attracted to unions by the 'threat' effect of rising prices and the 'credit' effect of rapid pay increases in a period of high inflation. Also, the period 1974–79 was notable for a legal and political climate generally favourable to union growth, under the Wilson–Callaghan Labour governments, so that employed membership density was as high as 51 per cent in 1980. At that time Britain appeared to be in the middle of the range of OECD countries' union density rates (see Appendix).

The beginning of the third phase coincided with the return of a

Conservative government in 1979, the acceleration of the structural decline in manufacturing employment, and the onset of the early 1980s' economic recession. The rise in unemployment reduced union membership, partly because most of the unemployed allowed their membership to lapse. Union membership continued to decline, however, even when employment grew in the late 1980s, largely because many new jobs were part-time and were concentrated in private-sector services where unions found it difficult to recruit. Union density declined during the 1980s in most OECD countries, so that although by 1988 UK membership density was only 41.5 per cent, it was still about halfway up the range for OECD countries, and higher than in the other countries discussed in this book except Sweden and Australia.

In view of changing technologies and forms of work organisation, the traditional categories of 'manual' and 'non-manual' workers are increasingly difficult to separate—but many employers, unions and other authorities still try to maintain a distinction. Manual workers are much more likely to be unionised (43 per cent) than non-manual staff (35 per cent).[4] Nevertheless, non-manual workers constitute an increasing proportion of total union membership. Much of this growth has taken place in separate white-collar unions, and some unions also organise managerial and professional employees, especially in the public sector (Bamber 1986). The increasing importance of non-manual unions has helped to change the style of union leadership and has implications for the future political allegiance of unions, since their members and officials may lack the Labour traditions of manual-worker trade unionists.

Union density is higher among men (44 per cent) than women (about 33 per cent) and among full-time workers (43 per cent) than part-timers (22 per cent). There are significant differences in density between industries. Thus the private services have lower union density—for example, it is only 15 per cent in retailing and 11 per cent in hotel and catering, compared with a density of 41 per cent in manufacturing. According to WIRS, the number of workplaces that recognised union(s) for collective bargaining declined from 66 per cent in 1984 to 53 per cent in 1990 (Millward et al. 1992).

The 'closed shop' has been an important factor. In a closed shop, workers must join a union either before (pre-entry) or soon after (post-entry) starting a job. Most manual unions have preferred closed shops wherever possible and many employers also welcomed such an arrangement to ensure that stewards[5] speak for the whole workforce, and also as a means of stabilising industrial relations, for example by controlling union structure in the workplace (McCarthy 1964). The extent of the closed shop increased significantly during the 1970s. By 1978, around 23 per cent of all employees were covered, the majority by post-entry closed shops (Dunn & Gennard 1984). However, the closed shop declined from covering nearly 5 million employees in 1980 to only half a million employees by 1990 (Millward et al. 1992; cf. Stevens et al. 1989). This decline reflected structural change in industry and employment as well as the gradual removal of legal protection; by 1988 it was deemed to be unfair for an employer to enforce a post-entry closed shop by dismissing an employee for non-membership. By 1991, the enforcement of pre-entry closed shops was also unlawful.

Employers

The plurality and fragmentation of the employers' associations is at least as complex as that of the unions, but there has been less research on employers' associations. Employers began to form their own collective organisations during the nineteenth century, largely as a reaction to the growth of unionism. One of the largest employers' associations, the Engineering Employers' Federation, was established in 1896 and in the following year it led a national 'lock-out' of workers in opposition to union calls for an eight-hour day.

Employers' associations are not merely reactive; they have taken important initiatives in the development of collective bargaining procedures, especially in the early twentieth century (Gospel & Littler 1983). Increasingly, employers' associations also provide a range of services relating to trading activities, though in many sectors such services are provided by separate trade associations (Armstrong 1984).

Traditionally, many employers' associations engaged in collective bargaining on a multi-employer, industry-level basis. In recent years there has been a trend towards single-employer bargaining in such sectors as chemicals, engineering, banking and publishing. Some larger firms have left their associations, largely because they wanted more control over their own industrial relations and because multi-employer bargaining had apparently failed to neutralise union activity at the workplace (Sisson 1987). Between 1980 and 1990, private-sector firms' membership of employers' associations fell from 29 to 13 per cent (Millward et al. 1992). Although employers' associations have become less important, in some sectors they still operate procedures for resolving industrial disputes and their other members still seem to value at least some of their services, for example, training, consultancy and advice; however, more firms are turning directly to lawyers and government agencies for the latter.

The Confederation of British Industry (CBI) is approximately the employers' equivalent of the TUC. Formed in 1965 following a merger between three separate employers' confederations, the CBI has more resources than the TUC. It has individual firms and employers' associations in membership and more than half of Britain's workers are employed by CBI members. The CBI has become an important lobbyist on behalf of employers but, like the TUC, its powers are limited and it does not participate in collective bargaining.

The decline of multi-employer bargaining arrangements has involved individual companies taking a more direct role in industrial relations. By the 1960s, many first-line supervisors were involved in negotiations with stewards, usually on an informal basis. More recently, formal collective bargaining has increasingly taken place at company, division or workplace level; employers have often seen the level at which bargaining takes place as a key issue. Most large companies have structured themselves into a multi-divisional form, with some devolution of budget and personnel responsibilities, but head offices still retain a powerful role. HRM became a more important and specialised function than formerly, especially in the larger firms, and there was a growth in the relative number, pay and status of such specialists after the 1960s. Since 1979, however, there has been much debate on whether or not the HRM function has been losing influence as line managers began to take more responsibility for their own HRM and industrial relations (Legge 1988).[6]

Collective bargaining

In some industries, such as engineering, multi-employer bargaining developed in the late nineteenth century. In others, 'joint industrial councils' were set up after the First World War to conduct industry-level bargaining between employers' associations and unions. By the early 1920s, multi-employer bargaining was established in Britain, covering most of the major industries. Such industry-level machinery was encouraged by the government as a way of constructing orderly procedures between the parties. Bargaining regulated pay and conditions as well as establishing negotiating and disputes procedures. Agreements were usually in writing, while negotiations and dispute settlement followed formally agreed procedures. This industry-level process rarely included a role for stewards, as bargaining was usually conducted by full-time union officers and was not carried out at the workplace. In most unions, stewards were not mentioned in the union rules as much more than the collectors of union subscriptions.

After the Second World War, stewards increasingly became

involved in bargaining with management within the workplace, particularly where there were piecework pay systems. This was partly because the tight labour markets of the immediate postwar years enhanced workers' bargaining power. Stewards derived much of their power from their ability to pressurise local managers into making concessions, sometimes under the threat of industrial action (as portrayed by Peter Sellers in the classic film *I'm All Right Jack*).

In the mid-1960s, there was an upward trend in the number of unofficial[7] strikes in manufacturing. Many commentators were denigrating Britain as a strike-prone country, with chaotic industrial relations, which prompted employer interests to call for action. (In fact, in so far as it is possible to compile an international 'league table' of dispute-proneness, Britain was near the middle of it in the mid-1960s, as it was subsequently; see Appendix.) Unions were also increasingly concerned about the courts encroaching on their ability to engage in lawful industrial action (Davies & Freedland 1984:738ff.). Therefore, in 1965 the government set up a Royal Commission, chaired by Lord Donovan, to study industrial relations, 'with particular reference to the Law' (Donovan 1968:1). The Donovan Report concluded that Britain had two systems of industrial relations: on one hand, there was industry-level bargaining, but on the other, this was extensively supplemented by workplace bargaining. The latter involved local managers and stewards bargaining over pay and conditions, individual grievances and job control issues. Employers' associations, senior management and full-time union officials tended not to be involved in workplace bargaining, which led to verbal agreements and implicit understandings rather than to formal written agreements and procedures.

In certain sectors, industry agreements set a 'floor' to pay levels, but substantial additions were negotiated at workplace level. Workplace bargaining was also concerned with detailed issues such as piece rates and working practices, which industry-level negotiations could not regulate effectively. According to Donovan, the extent of informal, fragmented and autonomous workplace bargaining was a cause for concern. These three aspects increased the likelihood of local unofficial industrial action and made managing more difficult. Donovan's prescription was a formalisation of workplace bargaining, which should thereby avoid the potential disorder of informality. Donovan put the onus on managers to reform their own bargaining practices and recommended the establishment of a government agency to promote reform: hence the Commission on Industrial Relations was born (Palmer 1983:189ff.).

Most collective bargaining in Britain is voluntary; private-sector employers are under no legal obligation to bargain. The content of collective agreements is for the parties themselves to determine.

Traditionally most agreements concentrated on *procedures* for negotiating and settling differences rather than the *substantive* terms and
conditions of employment. In contrast with many other countries,
collective agreements are not legally enforceable; they are backed
only by the relative power of the bargaining parties and their wish
to maintain mutual goodwill. Especially compared to North American 'contracts' but also to Australian 'awards' (see chs 3–5), most
British agreements are concise, extending to only a few pages, and
they do not usually specify a fixed-term duration. A few longer-term
agreements have been negotiated; however, most general pay rates
are reconsidered annually, and most procedural agreements specify
the period of notice which either party agrees to give before terminating the agreement.

In the WIRS samples, the coverage of collective bargaining
declined from 71 per cent in 1984 to 54 per cent in 1990 (Millward
et al. 1992). Although it has declined, collective bargaining is still
an important method of pay determination. Taking smaller workplaces into account, the basic pay of about 40 per cent of all employees
is determined by collective bargaining (*The Times*, 25 September
1992). Those working in private-sector services are the least likely
to be covered by collective bargaining (33 per cent), whilst coverage
is much greater in manufacturing (51 per cent) and the public sector
(78 per cent) (Millward et al. 1992). In view of such differences
between bargaining arrangements in these three broad sectors, we
discuss each in turn.

Manufacturing

Donovan's analysis focused on manual workers in manufacturing,
particularly engineering, thus tending to understate the diversity of
bargaining arrangements. Nevertheless, the Donovan reforms have
to some extent been realised, with workplace bargaining becoming
more orderly. The role of stewards became more formally
recognised in the 1970s, and more convenors[8] and stewards' committees were established. Except at small establishments, the parties
generally formalised their grievance-handling and negotiation procedures; nevertheless, these are still less formal than North American collective bargaining or Australian arbitration.

Since the 1970s, single-employer bargaining has developed at
the expense of multi-employer arrangements in some industries. In
such cases the significance of industry-wide pay bargaining has so
declined that Donovan's analysis is no longer relevant. However,
multi-employer bargaining at industry-level continues to be significant in some industries; even where its relevance in determining
pay levels has declined, it often continues to be important for

determining issues such as hours of work, holidays, overtime and shift premiums.

Public sector

Union density is higher in the public sector, partly because the state has in most cases obliged the employers to bargain with unions. Bargaining has usually been centralised and workplace representatives did not generally become important until the 1970s, following widespread militancy in the public sector. This was largely because traditional pay relativities with the private sector were being disturbed by government incomes policies. Even so, the development of workplace bargaining in the public sector has been uneven and bargaining is still more centralised than in most private manufacturing industries. Nonetheless, the public sector has been changing as the government has privatised significant elements of it and has directed that the remaining elements either prepare for privatisation or adopt more 'commercial' management styles.

In 1991, John Major, the new Conservative Prime Minister, launched his 'Citizen's Charter' proposals. Designed to improve the quality of service provided by public-sector organisations, customers were to be provided with published service standards, supported by complaints procedures and in some cases by compensation schemes. The aim was to introduce a form of market discipline into the public sector; it was envisaged that this would have a major impact on HRM, working practices and industrial relations. For example, the introduction of performance-related pay for employees was to be encouraged as part of the Citizen's Charter reforms.

Service sector

Employment in the private-sector service industries has grown since the 1970s, as manufacturing has declined and parts of the public sector have been privatised. There are proportionately more part-time and temporary workers (who are overwhelmingly women), sub-contracting, franchising and non-unionised firms in this sector than in the other two. Private services have the lowest union densities and the least-developed bargaining arrangements. Where it exists, bargaining is more centralised than in manufacturing, with single-employer bargaining at the level of the firm (rather than the establishment) being the norm—for instance in large enterprises in the finance and retailing sectors.

Management styles can be characterised along a spectrum from *collectivism* to *individualism* (cf. Purcell 1987; Marchington & Harrison 1991). We could generalise that in most parts of the public sector collectivism has reigned, while individualism has prevailed in most private-sector service enterprises, except perhaps in the very large ones such as the major banks and retail chains which are more bureaucratic.

Bargaining scope

Particularly in manufacturing and the public-sector, the *scope* of bargaining typically involves a wide range of issues, including remuneration, hours of work, holidays, overtime and shift-working arrangements, pensions and other working conditions. In addition, unions may bargain over issues such as staffing arrangements, recruitment, redundancy and working practices.

Occasionally unions have attempted to extend the scope of bargaining to include the wider issues of corporate policy, such as investment, marketing and product strategies. For example, in the mid-1970s a multi-plant 'combine group' of stewards from Lucas Aerospace devised an alternative corporate plan (Wainwright & Elliott 1982). However, employers have usually seen such issues as management prerogatives and have rarely been willing to negotiate on them.

During the early 1980s, several unions sought to extend the scope of collective bargaining to regulate technical change. They attempted to negotiate 'technology agreements' which would oblige employers to involve unions in decision-making. Employers would be required to disclose information about their plans; they would usually have to avoid redundancies and new health hazards, whilst providing retraining where appropriate. Unions also demanded a reduction in lifetime hours of work, joint regulation of any personal data that might be collected, and training for their own 'technology stewards' who would negotiate and monitor these innovations. British unions were influenced by similar policies adopted by Scandinavian unions (see ch. 9). Some British unions did negotiate technology agreements, but few employers were willing to concede to the spirit of such demands. Most technical change was introduced unilaterally by employers; they might consult with *employees,* but they were reluctant to consult and negotiate with *unions* on such issues (Bamber & Lansbury 1989). Notwithstanding a great deal of media attention to a few disputes about technological change (as illustrated later), employees and their unions usually do support technological change rather than resisting it (Daniel 1987). Although there had been much controversy in the early 1980s about the advent of microelectronics, by the early 1990s microelectronic devices were generally taken for granted and attracted less attention.

The role of the state

Throughout much of the nineteenth century the law was hostile to unionism and many unionists are still wary of legal intervention. The law has tended to provide only a minimum framework within which voluntary collective bargaining has taken place between employers and unions. Unlike most other countries, in Britain there is no law setting out a specific right to strike; instead, unions have had certain statutory immunities protecting them from liability when invoking sanctions.

For most of the twentieth century, governments have encouraged the parties to develop voluntary collective bargaining arrangements. Governments have legislated to provide individual rights for employees. These include the right to have statements of terms of employment, redundancy payments, remedies for unfair dismissal, healthy and safe workplaces, maternity arrangements, and protection from victimisation for union activity. Most of these rights were established by Labour governments after 1964; Conservative legislation has diluted certain details, but at least until the 1980s there was a broad consensus about the desirability of most of the provisions.

The issue of equal opportunities in the labour market has attracted increasing attention in Britain, though perhaps less so than in Sweden, North America and Australia. Under various British laws enacted since 1970, discrimination in employment on the grounds of race or gender is illegal. In the 1970s, the government established the tripartite Commission for Racial Equality and Equal Opportunities Commission to provide information and to help monitor and enforce these laws. Nonetheless, it has proved difficult to enforce this legislation. As with unfair dismissal cases, enforcement largely depends on individuals complaining to an industrial tribunal.

Low pay

The state has had a limited role in regulating pay and conditions in certain industries. It began setting up trade boards or wages councils in 1909, whereby representatives of employers and unions, along with independent members, could determine legally enforceable minimum terms and conditions for their industry to be monitored by a wages inspectorate. This was in industries such as agriculture, clothing manufacture, retailing, hairdressing, hotels and catering, where there was little effective collective bargaining. Wages councils have probably never covered more than 15 per cent of workers.

The purpose of wages councils was to 'plug the gaps' in the coverage of voluntary bargaining arrangements rather than to establish a comprehensive statutory system or a general minimum wage, as there is in many other countries. Several wages councils have been merged and others have been abolished, occasionally on the initiative of the unions, who have in some cases argued that the presence of a wages council may discourage the development of voluntary arrangements. Some large firms opposed abolition, arguing that the absence of statutory minima allows smaller firms in particular to undercut prices by driving pay down.

The post-1979 Conservative government saw wages councils as restricting 'flexibility' in the labour market and 'pricing people out of jobs' by keeping pay levels 'artificially' high. In 1986, the government removed young people from wages council protection and limited the councils to the setting of a single minimum hourly rate and an overtime rate. In addition, the government denounced the International Labour Organisation (ILO) minimum wage-fixing convention (see ch. 11), releasing itself from any obligation to maintain such procedures. In 1992, the government announced its intention finally to abolish the remaining 26 wages councils.

Economic policy and incomes policies

Since the 1940s, British governments have repeatedly used incomes policies in an attempt to control inflation and offset balance of payments difficulties. Some governments opted for a statutory policy, often with a quasi-independent body to vet proposed pay increases with penalties for those breaking the norm, whilst other governments preferred to follow a voluntary approach, seeking to win the support and compliance of unions and employers by persuasion. The 1974–79 Labour government, for example, introduced a 'social contract', offering pro-union legislation and Keynesian economic policies in exchange for voluntary pay restraint, in an accord with the TUC. This was effective for at least two years in so far as there was a substantial reduction in the rate of pay and price inflation, and in stoppages. But the social contract had collapsed by 1978–79 with the onslaught of industrial action in a 'winter of discontent'. Incomes policies were not successful in constraining pay increases over the longer term. Typically, periods of restraint were followed by periods of 'catching up' as unions, especially those in the public sector, sought additional pay increases to compensate.

The post-1979 Conservative governments took a different approach by rejecting formal incomes policies, preferring instead to adopt monetary and fiscal restraint as a way of dealing with inflation in the private sector, with direct controls and 'cash limits' in the public sector. This strategy amounted to a rejection of a Keynesian consensus; the defeat of inflation became the key medium term priority, and the commitment to full employment was abandoned. Whilst by the mid-1980s the government was having some success in controlling inflation, such gains disappeared in the economic boom of the late 1980s. By then, the main concern was that pay had continued to rise more quickly than prices, contributing to a loss in competitiveness which was offset only by a fall in the exchange rate. In 1990 when the UK joined the European exchange rate mechanism (ERM), whereby Sterling was linked to the value of other European currencies, some argued that the time was right to reintroduce incomes policies, or at least some form of pay restraint, to try to curb pay and price rises and maintain UK competitiveness. However, the Conservatives, even after the replacement of Mrs Thatcher as Prime Minister in 1990, remained set against incomes policies, and their re-election in 1992 suggests that such 'corporatist' approaches will not reappear in the foreseeable future. (Later in 1992, the UK withdrew from the ERM as the Sterling exchange rate continued to decline.)

Conciliation and arbitration

The British state has long intervened in industrial relations by acting as a third party in employer–employee relations; conciliation and arbitration services were formerly provided by a government department. By the 1970s the government was so committed to pay restraint that many felt that these services should be more independent of its influence. Hence, the 1974 Labour government abolished the Commission on Industrial Relations and established the Advisory, Conciliation and Arbitration Service (ACAS). ACAS is governed by a tripartite council consisting of employer and union nominees and government-nominated academics. Thus, the government sought to distance itself from the settlement of particular industrial disputes. The services of ACAS are a supplement to, not a substitute for, collective bargaining. ACAS services are free and include the provision of advice to employers, individuals and unions on all aspects of industrial relations and employment policies. ACAS officials carry out conciliation, but they appoint academics and other independent experts as mediators and arbitrators. Unlike the position in many other countries, arbitration is neither compulsory (as in Australia) nor legally binding (as in North America and Australia). Although ACAS had been established by a Labour government, it continued under the Conservatives, though they did curtail the use of arbitration in the public sector and cut ACAS's role in conducting inquiries.

Legal reforms

The state has made other attempts to reform industrial relations. By the 1960s there was increasing concern at Britain's relatively poor economic performance, with slow growth, high inflation and recurrent balance of payments difficulties. Some commentators argued that Britain's industrial relations system was largely to blame, with restrictive working practices and unofficial strikes making industry uncompetitive. Accordingly, industrial relations reform has been high on the political agenda.

Although the Donovan Commission had argued for *voluntary* reform to formalise workplace bargaining, since the 1960s successive governments have also resorted to various forms of legislation. The Conservatives' 1971 Industrial Relations Act sought to legislate for fundamental and rapid reform. Following the US example, this Act aimed to make collective agreements into legally enforceable contracts. The unions boycotted much of the Act and most large employers did not use it, thereby rendering it largely ineffective. Most of the Act was repealed by Labour in 1974 (see ch. 1).

After 1979, Conservative governments adopted a more gradualist approach than the 1971 Act. They enacted significant new laws at two-yearly intervals throughout the 1980s (Mackie 1989). The legislation limited the ability of unions to organise industrial action; it narrowed union immunities from action by employers through the courts, especially in the case of secondary industrial action. Workers were allowed to picket only at their own place of work, thus further restricting their ability to secure support from other workers. Since 1984, to be lawful, industrial action has to be preceded by a secret ballot of the workers concerned. A union cannot lawfully discipline a member who refuses to support industrial action, even where the majority have voted in favour.

The legislation has also made it more difficult for unions to consolidate and extend union membership by removing the statutory union recognition procedures of the 1974–79 Labour government, and by preventing unions from ensuring that only unionised sub-contractors are used by their employer. Furthermore, the Conservative government rescinded the Fair Wages Resolution, which had originated in 1891. Its most recent version had obliged government sub-contractors to recognise the freedom of its workers to join a union, and to offer terms of employment not less favourable than those established for similar activities.

In addition, the 1980s' laws required secret membership ballots to elect union executive committees and national leaders directly, and to approve the continuation of a 'political fund'. The explicit aim was to ensure that unions were responsive to the wishes of their members on the assumption that ballots would moderate the influence of militant activists. One implicit aim was to reduce the number of union political funds and thereby to erode financial support for the Labour Party. Paradoxically this law prompted unions to improve their communications with their members. Several public-sector unions established political funds for the first time, concerned that campaigns aimed at resisting government policies on the public services would be seen as 'political'.

Conservative governments and the unions

The Conservatives argued, then, that the unions had become too powerful and that major legal changes were necessary to disempower them. Unions were seen as a barrier to the development of a more flexible, entrepreneurial economy—a view reflected in the government's employment policies.

As a major employer, government employment policies are important, both directly and also through their influence as an example to other employers. Traditionally, the government aimed to be a 'good' employer, offering secure employment and reasonable terms and conditions and encouraging union membership. However, the Thatcher government appeared to reject much of this legacy. Parts of the public sector were privatised by selling whole corporations or divisions, and elsewhere by introducing 'flexibility' through subcontracting such services as transport, cleaning and catering which could be portrayed as peripheral.[9] The effect was to reduce the number of public-sector employees and also to undermine union organisation, job security, pay and other conditions of employment.

In 1984, the government withdrew union membership and employment protection rights for staff at the Government Communications Headquarters (GCHQ), claiming that this was necessary for 'national security'. Existing GCHQ staff were offered £1000 in return for the loss of their rights. Only a few actually refused the offer and the unions claimed that staff morale was badly affected by the controversy. The unions reacted angrily, claiming that the government had breached the ILO convention on freedom of association and protection of the right to organise. One union also complained to the European Commission on Human Rights. The union challenge in the courts was, however, unsuccessful. The whole issue contributed to a further deterioration of relations between the government and the unions, which sank to low levels in the most significant industrial dispute in Britain since the general strike of 1926, the 1984–85 miners' dispute.

The miners' dispute

Coal mining was nationalised by a Labour government in 1947. Since then the industry's workforce declined as capacity was reduced and productivity increased. The National Union of Mineworkers (NUM)[10] had generally accommodated this decline, partly because the management had developed a close working relationship with the union, and also perhaps because of the general availability of alternative employment until the early 1970s. There was, however, a growing frustration amongst miners about the decline; against this background the NUM elected a radical Left-wing leader, Arthur Scargill, in 1981.

By the early 1980s, the management was becoming more aggressive and commercial in its approach and many pit closures seemed likely. This set the scene for confrontation in 1984, following the announcement of two closures. Under the NUM's own rules, a full national strike would have required a national ballot of the members. It did not hold such a ballot, however, in spite of the calls from some members and many outsiders. The union's strategy was to allow the more militant local area unions to declare their own strikes and then for others to follow their example, forcing them to do so by picketing if necessary. The leaders reasoned that a majority of members might not vote for a national strike, because it would appear that only a minority were threatened by the closures. Moreover, the employer, government and media propaganda could sway members to vote against a strike. Some miners tried to force other areas out and to close power stations, steelworks and other coal-using plants by mass picketing. This attracted much public attention, especially when there were violent confrontations between pickets and police. Some pit villages were divided between strikers and non-strikers, with cases of violence and intimidation.

Several sets of negotiations broke down acrimoniously. The NUM refused to accept the closure of 'uneconomic pits', whilst British Coal insisted on its 'right to manage' and to implement closures. Thanks to imported coal and oil, and to the high level of coal stocks, no power cuts were necessary. The miners were supported by donations of food and money from community groups and other British and overseas unions. Nevertheless, the strike was increasingly seen as a failure; more and more of the NUM's funds were being seized by the courts, and few other unions had given practical support. A drift back to work developed and the strikes were called off a year after they had begun.

In the wake of the dispute, some sections of the NUM broke away to set up a rival Union of Democratic Mineworkers (UDM); subsequently, pit closures continued. British Coal introduced a new disciplinary code and proposals for six-day shift working at several new pits. The NUM opposed such developments and industrial conflict continued to bedevil the industry on a sporadic local basis. At national level, however, the union was too weak to take industrial action. Subsequently, productivity increased substantially; miners were keen to earn bonus payments to make up for lost earnings and more and more 'marginal' collieries were closed.

In the years following the dispute, employment fell continuously and output per person-shift almost doubled between 1985 and 1992. Remuneration included more overtime pay and locally-determined incentive bonuses, while the split between the NUM and the UDM continued to weaken the unions. By the early 1990s, British Coal was profitable and being prepared for privatisation. It faced a crisis, however, because the privatised electricity generating companies, the largest customers, were buying much less coal and more cheaply than when electricity was generated in the public sector. Commercial realities meant that management sought ever higher productivity. In 1992, British Coal and the government announced the closure of most of the remaining pits. Following extensive public protests, which included Conservative Members of Parliament and the clergy as well as miners, the government deferred some of the proposed closures; but again, the mining industry was the focus of major political and industrial controversy.

The experiences of the mining industry illustrate several features of British industrial relations in the 1980s and 1990s: a tougher management style; the weakness of the labour movement; and a public mood unsympathetic to militant union action. As in many other industries, competitive pressures were setting the scene for change in industrial relations.

The Wapping printing dispute

Another landmark dispute took place in 1986 at Rupert Murdoch's News International. In a carefully planned manoeuvre, this company transferred production of its newspapers to Wapping (East London) without the agreement of the unions, with the aim of adopting new technology and working practices. At the new plant, which was surrounded by barbed wire, there were violent clashes between police and pickets. There was also considerable conflict between the printing unions and the Electrical, Electronic, Telecommunication and Plumbing Union (EETPU) which had colluded with Murdoch, assisting him with the recruitment of employees for the new plant. But in spite of subsequent attempts by the EETPU to organise the plant, management refused union recognition. Arguably the Wapping episode helped to pave the way for other newspaper publishers to introduce changes in working practices with little or no union opposition.

The coal mining and national newspaper industries had long been seen as union strongholds. If the powerful miners and printers could be defeated, what chance was there for weaker unions? The union defeats in these key industries, along with similar examples of a renewed managerial assertiveness in steel and car manufacturing earlier in the decade, fuelled the view that a new 'macho-management' style was being adopted. This was apparently reflected in the generally lower level of strike action after 1980. With the exception of 1984, the year of the miners' dispute, the annual number of days lost due to industrial action was never above 6.5 million in the 1980s, compared to an annual average of around 13 million in the 1970s. Pay issues continued to be the main apparent 'cause' of strikes.

Of course, factors other than employer policies could explain this decline, including higher unemployment, lower inflation and a favourable growth in real incomes for many of those in employment. But the government's uncompromising stance on certain public sector disputes was significant, as was its legislation, although perhaps less directly. Towards the end of the 1980s, as employment growth resumed and unemployment fell, the level of stoppages did increase for a while, though it did not return to the levels of the previous decade, thus lending some support to the view that the 1980s witnessed the advent of a 'new industrial relations'.

Current and future issues

HRM policies

Despite much discussion of a more strategic approach to the management of employment and industrial relations, most employers still seem to be engaging in opportunism and 'muddling through' rather than adopting a strategic approach (Sisson 1992:30). Whilst there was much talk—for instance, about the importance of training and equal opportunities—there was rather less systematic management action and unions did not appear to be actively pursuing these issues (Millward et al. 1992). Some employers withdrew union recognition, but relatively few tried to copy the 'union busting' initiatives of certain American employers (Claydon 1989; Snape & Bamber 1989). Nonetheless, employers at new establishments generally prefer either a single union or no union.

Several unions have made concessions at new sites to gain bargaining rights and members. These new agreements often give sole bargaining rights to the union concerned, sometimes in exchange for an undertaking not to invoke sanctions but rather to submit any disputes to final-offer (pendulum) arbitration on disputes of interest—hence the term 'no-strike deals' (Bassett 1986). Multinational enterprises (especially Japanese ones) pioneered such agreements, for instance between Toshiba and the EETPU (Trevor 1988), and between Nissan (and subsequently Toyota) and the Amalgamated Engineering Union (AEU) (Wickens 1987). Such deals are usually accompanied by HRM strategies that embrace a range of techniques from sophisticated selection and training, performance-related pay and performance appraisal (Storey 1989; Towers 1992). The use of such techniques has become more prevalent since the 1970s.

The EETPU in particular sought such agreements, often in direct competition with other unions. Critics condemn them as 'sweetheart deals', since management may choose the union without reference to the workforce, even though another union may already have members in the establishment. In spite of much discussion about these agreements, particularly those on new 'greenfield' sites, by 1990 they covered no more than 2 per cent of establishments that have arbitration arrangements (Millward et al. 1992). Nevertheless, they may have a longer-term significance because of their influence on existing management–employee relations. Even on older 'brownfield' sites where much union organisation has survived relatively intact, many employers have sought to introduce changes. In some cases they have sought to negotiate concessions from the unions, particularly on the introduction of more flexible working practices. Employers have also sought more flexibility through greater use of temporaries and part-time employees (IMS 1986). Particularly in those industries subject to privatisation and/or increasing competition, such changes have often been introduced with little if any union resistance. These developments contributed to the improved productivity performance of UK manufacturing industry during the late 1980s (Metcalf 1989).

Whilst they have attracted less publicity than the 'greenfield' no-strike deals, management initiatives on total quality management (TQM) and a range of HRM innovations are accelerating. The adoption of HRM techniques may represent a more fundamental challenge to unionisation than did the relatively isolated examples of macho-management referred to earlier. Some HRM approaches threaten to marginalise unions by directly communicating with employees, developing the role of the first-line supervisor, and generally seeking a higher degree of employee commitment while offering other benefits to the workforce (Storey 1992). Examples of sophisticated (and paternalistic) HRM are particularly apparent in enterprises that have generally avoided unionisation (e.g. IBM, Mars and Marks & Spencer). However, such approaches to HRM are not the only explanation of why employees in non-union settings do not join unions (McLoughlin & Gourlay 1992). HRM, then, represents a more subtle strategy than macho-management, and is less easily written off as merely an attempt by management to exploit a possibly temporary power advantage over the unions.

Single-union strategies

It was the EETPU's enthusiastic pursuit of two single-union deals which led to its expulsion from the TUC. The EETPU had signed a single-union deal with Orion Electric even though Britain's largest union, the Transport and General Workers' Union (TGWU), had already recruited some workers but had been denied recognition by the company. The EETPU signed a similar agreement with Christian Salvesen to cover two new transport depots without consulting three other unions that were already recognised at Christian Salvesen's other depots. Following complaints by the other unions through the TUC's disputes procedure, the EETPU was instructed by the TUC to cancel both agreements and to make a joint approach to the employers with the other unions concerned. The EETPU refused to accept the TUC's instructions and so was suspended and eventually expelled at the 1988 Congress.

Underlying this controversy was a longer-running rivalry between the EETPU and some other unions. The EETPU had come close to expulsion in 1985 when it and the AEU accepted government funding for ballot expenses in contravention of a TUC policy. Also, the EETPU's above-mentioned role at Wapping had made it unpopular in the TUC. Some analysts had identified the EETPU, and possibly other unions such as the AEU, with the notion of American-style 'business unionism': a pragmatic form of unionism emphasising the provision of benefits and services to a relatively highly skilled membership and with a cooperative (though not a weak) approach to employers. The pursuit of single-union deals fits with such a vision of unionism.

In contrast, the large general unions, often Left-led and with a higher proportion of less-skilled members, have tended to emphasise the need to organise the emerging 'peripheral' labour force, comprised largely of women, temporary and part-time workers. These, it is claimed, are the 'new servant class', who are particularly in need of union protection. Such unions put forward a campaigning, more overtly political, approach, often emphasising the need to win and defend statutory employment rights.

Following its expulsion, the EETPU attempted to foster closer links with several staff associations and non-TUC unions. Whilst there was some recruitment competition between the EETPU and the TUC unions, and the EETPU established links with groups from several TUC unions, at most workplaces inter-union relations generally remained cordial. Whilst some affiliates were still hostile to the EETPU being readmitted to the TUC, there was a reconciliation in 1992 following the merger between the EETPU and the AEU to form the Amalgamated Engineering and Electrical Union.

Employee involvement and European Community influences

Especially during the 1960s and 1970s most union strategies at workplace level depended on stewards. This was a period when stewards thrived, with many larger employers taking considerable trouble to negotiate and consult with them. On average, stewards represent 20 members. Between 1984 and 1990 this average remained constant; however, there was a decline, from 82 per cent to 71 per cent, in the number of workplaces with recognised unions which had a steward or equivalent lay union representative. This decline particularly affected smaller establishments (Millward et al. 1992).

Approximately 29 per cent of the WIRS sample have consultative committees. These provide a forum for labour–management discussions on issues such as health, safety and welfare facilities, which might be beyond the scope of collective bargaining. These committees differ from collective bargaining as issues are *discussed*, but not formally *negotiated*. Joint consultation does not necessarily displace collective bargaining; it sometimes develops furthest alongside high levels of union activity, particularly in the public sector. Since the 1970s, management has fostered more direct employee communications (Marchington & Parker 1990). Employers have introduced team briefing groups, quality circles, TQM, and more direct forms of employee involvement, communications and profit-sharing in an attempt to increase levels of commitment and productivity. Such schemes have often bypassed the unions, and might also be seen as an attempt to forestall any future calls for more rigorous forms of industrial democracy from governments or the EC (Bamber & Snape 1986).

There has been much debate about the so-called 'social dimension' of the EC internal market. This includes further moves to facilitate labour mobility within the member countries and harmonise employment rights, including maternity leave and atypical working hours. The Thatcher government and employers were hostile to these EC initiatives, particularly if they introduced greater labour market regulation and conferred new statutory rights, for example in the area of industrial democracy. Such moves were seen by the British government as running counter to its aim of increasing labour market flexibility. Significantly, Britain was the only EC member which did not endorse the EC Social Charter (see ch. 11).

Historically, British unions and their members have tended to be less than enthusiastic about formal channels of co-determination such as worker directors (cf. ch. 8), fearing that such schemes might provide a rival channel of representation to established collective bargaining procedures. Nevertheless, perhaps because of its negative experiences under the post-1979 Conservative government, and with little prospect of an upturn in union membership and influence, the TUC officially embraced the EC Social Charter. If implemented, the Charter could induce significant innovations in many workplaces, possibly including works councils.

Conclusions

In 1979, few would have predicted the extent of change that would be apparent by the 1990s. A Conservative government which rejected the postwar liberal-pluralist consensus had abandoned governmental responsibility for the level of employment and attempted to reassert the primacy of market forces. This is only part of the story. The neo-corporatist experiments of the 1970s were replaced in the 1980s by monetarist policies that included tight budgets, deregulation, privatisation and new employment legislation, which sought to create a more flexible labour market and an 'enterprise culture'. The recessions of the early 1980s and early 1990s, along with the intensification of competition in world markets, contributed towards the continued deindustrialisation of the former 'workshop of the world' and helped to change the context of employment.

As working practices were reformed, manufacturing productivity improved, particularly in unionised plants in the early part of the 1980s (Wadhwani 1990). The level of union membership and strikes declined sharply. Interestingly, however, there was a parallel decline in unionisation and strikes in Australia, even though for most of the 1980s it had an apparently 'pro-union' government.[11] This implies that those seeking to explain the changes in industrial relations in the UK should look not only at UK government policies, but also at trends in international markets and at structural change. It is also important to recognise the substantial continuities in British industrial relations as well as the changes. Claims about a 'new industrial relations' may yet prove premature, if, as many suggest, there has not been a fundamental change in union and employee attitudes. A future economic upturn may once again be accompanied by an increase in strikes and a growing reluctance to accept further reform to working practices if the balance of power shifts away from employers (cf. Metcalf 1989). Having reviewed some of the competing arguments about whether there has been a radical change or a general continuity in the patterns of industrial relations, we adopt a middle position. British industrial relations are undergoing a *transition*; they are not yet transformed, but besides the evident continuities much change is apparent.

In spite of the unions' setbacks and divisions, the labour movement still has some power and is formulating new strategies, although the leaders of the British unions seem to be less adept at the formulation and implementation of longer-term strategies than their counterparts in Scandinavia, Austria or even Australia. However, opinion polls show that the popularity of unions increased in the 1980s, even though their membership decreased; British unions are also too well established for membership densities to fall to, say, the American or French levels (see chs 3 & 7) in the foreseeable future.

Margaret Thatcher's successor, John Major, promised to change Britain into a classless society. Nonetheless, he inherited her program of economic and social policies, with further proposed changes to the law on employment and the unions after his winning the 1992 general election. Despite much Conservative rhetoric about deregulation, these changes may increase the legal regulation of industrial relations, unions and strikes. The further integration of the EC would be likely to continue this tendency.

EC influences may underlie key developments in British industrial relations in the 1990s. Britain's economic policies are likely to become more closely aligned with those of her EC partners, and the social dimension of European integration may increasingly influence employment policies (see ch. 11). A future Labour government would probably be more receptive to the EC's social dimension. Along with the TUC, the Labour Party has agreed that, if elected, it would retain much of the Conservative's employment legislation. But a Labour government would generally pursue policies more favourable to the unions. Whichever party is in government, the law will continue to play a key role and the trend away from the British tradition of 'voluntarism' will continue.

A chronology of British industrial relations

1349   Ordinance of Labourers sets up pay determination machinery (the first recognisable labour legislation).

1563	Prohibition of workers' 'conspiracy' and 'combination' to raise wages.
1780–1840	Period of primary industrialisation.
1799–1800	Combination Acts provide additional penalties against workers' 'combinations'.
1811–14	'Luddites' begin smashing machines.
1824–25	Repeal of Combination Acts.
1829	Grand General Union of Operative Spinners formed.
1834	'Tolpuddle martyrs' transported to Australia for taking a union oath.
1851	'New model unions' formed, mainly of skilled craftsmen.
1868	First meeting of TUC.
1871	Trade Union Act gives unions legal status.
1880–99	Growth of militancy and development of 'new unionism' amongst unskilled workers.
1891	Fair Wages Resolution of the House of Commons.
1899	TUC set up Labour Representation Committee, which became the Labour Party in 1906.
1901	House of Lords' Taff Vale Judgement holds that a union could be liable for employers' losses during a strike.
1906	Trades Disputes Act gives unions immunity from such liability, if acting 'in contemplation or furtherance of a trade dispute'.
1909	House of Lords' Osborne Judgement rules that unions could not finance political activities.
1913	Trade Union Act legalises unions' political expenditure if they set up a separate fund, with individuals able to 'contract out'.
1917–18	Whitley reports recommend joint industrial councils.
1926	General strike and nine-month miners' strike.
1927	Subsequent legislation restricts picketing and introduces criminal liabilities for political strikes.
1945	Election of Labour government.
1946–51	Repeal of 1927 Act; nationalisation of the Bank of England, fuel, power, inland transport, health, steel etc.
1951	Election of Conservative government.
1962	National Economic Development Council established.
1964	Election of Labour government. House of Lords' *Rookes v. Barnard* judgement holds that union officials threatening industrial action could be sued for 'intimidation'.
1965	Trades Disputes Act overturns the 1964 decision.
1968	Donovan report advocates voluntary reform of industrial relations.

1969	Labour government proposes legal reforms, but is successfully opposed by the unions.
1970	Equal Pay Act. Election of Conservative government.
1971	Industrial Relations Act legislates for reform; most unions refuse to comply. It also introduces the concept of 'unfair dismissal'.
1974	A miners' strike precipitates the fall of the Conservative government.
1974	Trade Union and Labour Relations Act replaces the 1971 Act, but retains the 'unfair dismissal' concept, sets up ACAS and signals a new Social Contract.
1974	Health and Safety at Work etc. Act.
1975	Employment Protection Act extends the rights of workers and unions; Equal Pay Act implemented.
1976	Race Relations Act.
1978–79	'Winter of discontent'.
1979	Election of Conservative government.
1980	Employment Act restricts unions' rights to enforce closed shops, picket and invoke secondary action; it weakens individuals' rights (e.g. in relation to unfair dismissal, maternity leave etc.).
1981	Breakaway from Labour to form Social Democratic Party.
1982	Employment Act restricts closed shops, strikes and union-only contracts.
1984	Trade Union Act requires regular secret ballots for the election of officials, before strikes, and to approve the continuance of political funds.
1984–85	Miners' strike.
1986	Wages Act restricts the scope of Wages Councils.
1986	News International moves to Wapping.
1988	TUC expels EETPU.
1988	Employment Act removes all legal support for post-entry closed shops.
1990	Employment Act ends pre-entry closed shops, further restricts unions and their scope for invoking industrial action. Margaret Thatcher replaced as Prime Minister by John Major.
1992	Re-election of Conservative government (the fourth consecutive defeat for the Labour Party).
1993	EC aims to be 'a single market'.

3 Industrial relations in the United States of America
Hoyt N. Wheeler

Both the relative power of the American economy and the global influence of its managerial and industrial relations models justify the effort necessary to understand it, despite the difficulties posed by its exceptionalism and complexity. The magnitude of the American economy is illustrated by its GDP of $5330 billion and population of over 252 million, both by far the largest of any country discussed in this book. The impact of American influence can be observed in the chapters reporting other national systems. This influence derives from the early development of professional management techniques in the USA; the USA's guidance and financing of the post-Second World War recovery; and the size and worldwide scope of American multinational corporations.

The historical, economic and political context

Prior to industrialisation, beginning in the 1790s, American skilled craftsmen formed unions. According to the widely accepted view, this was in response to downward pressures on pay that were produced by growing and increasingly competitive markets. According to this view, being pre-factory, unionisation was not, as might be expected in Marxist theory, stimulated by changes in the mode of production (Commons 1913). It is also generally believed that the skilled trades nature, practical goals, and economic strategy of these early, pre-factory unions had a permanent influence on American unions (Sturmthal 1973). It should be noted, however, that as is often the case in matters of American labour history, 'Versions of the past [serve] aims of the present' (Cooper and Terrill 1991:46). Marxist scholars, not surprisingly, (see, for example, Foner 1947) disagree with the above analysis, seeing the market as only 'hastening' the inevitable development of working-class organisations among the wage-earning class.

The industrialisation of the USA, which was later than that of Britain, began in the period 1810–40. From the mid-1820s to 1860, manufacturing developed in a broad range of industries, with textiles being among the most significant (Lebergott 1984:130, 136). Prior to the 1850s, however, production was mainly in small shops and in workers' homes. This extensive use of part-time home-working ameliorated the labour shortage that existed throughout this period (Taylor 1951:215). The establishment of the factory system in the 1850s and 1860s brought into the industrial system large numbers of native rural women and children, and eventually many immigrants from Ireland, Britain, Germany and other countries. These early factory workers did not unionise. This may have been partly because their pay was generally comparable to American farm earnings and higher than those of factory workers in Europe. In addition, vigorous repression of unionisation by employers, both directly and through government action, inhibited unionisation. It may also be that the high rate of worker mobility to other jobs, and considerable social mobility, hindered the development of the solidarity among workers that would have facilitated widespread organisation of unions (Lebergott 1984:373, 386–7; Wheeler 1985).

In spite of the difficulties, skilled craftsmen did form national unions in the 1860s. Also, the social reform-oriented Knights of Labor rose to prominence in the 1880s. By 1886, they organised 700 000 mainly unskilled workers. Unlike the craft unions, which focused on wages and working conditions of their members, the Knights aimed at reforming society as a whole, turning back the clock to an earlier and better time before the rise of capitalism. Their strategy was 'cooperation,' which meant forming worker cooperatives. The Knights had only a brief time in the sun. In the same year that they reached their peak of membership—1886—the craft unions organised on a national basis into the American Federation of Labor (AFL). These pragmatic 'business' unions drove the Knights from the field. By the turn of the century, the Knights had ceased to be an important force. This experience of idealistic unionism rising for a time—only to fall before pragmatic economic unionism—has occurred several times in the history of American labor (Taft 1964).

Around 1900, building on a large home market made accessible by an improved transportation system, large corporations achieved dominance in American industrial life. These complex, impersonal organisations required systematic strategies for managing their workers. Responding to this need, Frederick Taylor, the father of 'scientific management', and his industrial engineer disciples gained a powerful influence on the ideology and practice of management in the USA (Hession & Sardy 1969:546–7). These ideas became widely accepted in this country some time before they were accepted in Europe and other parts of the world. By declaring 'scientific' principles for the design of work and pay, the Taylorists undermined the rationale for determining these matters through power-based bargaining by unions. Added to this difficulty for the unions was the continuing vigorous opposition of the capitalists, who had both enormous power and high prestige. Nevertheless, the craft unions were able to survive and prosper in the first two decades of the century, partly because of the cooperative mechanisms put into place during the First World War, and their patriotic support of the war. During this same period the craft unions were challenged by the rise of the first powerful American union of the Left, the Industrial Workers of the World (IWW). The IWW, or 'Wobblies' (a title allegedly derived from their drinking habits), combined philosophies of anarchism and syndicalism with tactics that included songs and martyrs, to rise to prominence during the pre-war years. Like the reformist Knights, they had a brief moment of glory. However, during the First World War (which they opposed) and the post-war reaction to the Russian revolution, they were crushed by the forces of capitalism and patriotic fervour.

By the 1920s, a combination of the influence of Taylorism, employer use of company-dominated unions as a union-substitution device, tough employer action in collective bargaining, widespread use of anti-union propaganda by employer groups, and a hostile legal environment had reduced even the proud and once-powerful craft unions to a very weak position.

It was during the Great Depression of the 1930s that American unions rose from the ashes and, for the first time, penetrated mass-production industry, organising large numbers of factory workers. Working conditions and pay had deteriorated. There was a changed political environment with the election of President Franklin D. Roosevelt in 1932. A great wave of strikes, most of which were successful, broke out in 1934. The Wagner Act was passed in 1935, giving workers for the first time a federally guaranteed right to organise and strike. The unions, organised by industry rather than by craft (United Automobile Workers, United Mine Workers, United Steel Workers), adopted the strategy of mass organising campaigns. This strategy and the fact that the unions were united in a new labour movement—the Congress of Industrial Organizations (CIO)—led to unionisation of cars, steel, rubber, coal and other industries (Bernstein 1970; Wheeler 1985).

In the 1940s and 1950s the unions continued to grow and to develop the collective bargaining system. Since the 1950s, they have organised large numbers of government employees, but have declined in strength overall. In the early 1990s, American unions covered less than 16 per cent of the workforce. Until recently, they had been comparatively militant, although the number of working days lost due to industrial stoppages decreased in the 1980s (but at least part of the apparent reduction reflects the change in the basis of collecting stoppage data; see Table A.21).

Employment patterns in the USA are probably prototypical. The services sector employs 71 per cent of civilian employees (along with Canada this is a higher percentage than any other OECD country); 26 per cent are employed in industry, and only 2.8 per cent in agriculture (less than any of the other countries discussed in this book except Britain).

The level of unemployment in the USA has historically tended to be higher than that in Australia, Japan and most of Western Europe, but this relationship reversed relative to Europe in the 1980s. By the early 1990s, the USA had a lower unemployment rate (about 7 per cent) than most of the other 8 countries except Germany, Sweden and Japan. Between 1985 and 1991 the consumer price index increased by 28 per cent, which was less than in most of the other 8 countries covered here, apart from France, Germany and Japan (see Appendix).

Although the USA is heavily engaged in international trade, exports of goods constitute only 5.7 per cent of its GDP—smaller than any other OECD country. The relative unimportance of exports to the economy reflects the USA's large home market which creates a greater potential for self-sufficiency than exists in most other countries. However, for more than a decade large international trade deficits have been a major problem for the economy.

American politics is largely politics of the centre. The two major parties, Republicans and Democrats, that dominate national politics, have generally absorbed and moderated the ideas of more extreme groups. However, during the Great Depression of the 1930s, Franklin Roosevelt's Democrats moved some distance to the Left, and in the early 1980s, Ronald Reagan's Republicans moved to the Right. Even in these instances, substantial segments of the other major party moved in the direction set out by the party in power, thereby shifting the centre. Distinctions between them are further blurred by the fact that, unlike most political parties in other English-speaking countries, party discipline is weak.

Nevertheless, the two political parties *do* differ with respect to the area of the centre that they occupy. The Democrats, while not a labour party, are clearly more Leftward inclined than the Republicans. In general, they have more 'liberal' political goals, and are more supportive of government action to achieve social and economic justice. As a party, the Democrats enjoy the support of the unions.

Under Ronald Reagan and his successor George Bush the Republicans moved further to the Right, drawing upon traditional American notions of individualism and distrust of 'big government,' a 'backlash' reaction to demands of blacks for opportunity and equality, and what was for a time at least a rising tide of religious fundamentalism. They also used appeals to patriotism to salve the wounds to national pride inflicted by the loss of the Vietnam War, George Bush as a presidential candidate 'wrapping himself in the flag' during his successful 1988 presidential campaign. This has been combined with a new move toward market-oriented economic policies, increases in military expenditures (until very recently), and record high government-budget deficits, that have been associated with strong, but uneven, economic prosperity until the recession of the early 1990s. The effects on American politics of the massive changes in the former Soviet Union and Eastern Europe are likely to be important, but are difficult to predict accurately.

Since the 1950s policy issues relating to unions and collective bargaining have not often been high on the national agenda, but there has been a great deal of legislative activity in the broad area of employment relations. Legislative initiatives in the areas of minimum wages, termination of employment, race and sex discrimination in employment, pensions, health and safety, plant closing, drug testing, discrimination against disabled workers, and polygraphs (lie detector machines) all drew a great deal of attention and produced a plethora of new laws in the 1980s and early 1990s.

Nature of industrial relations

The industrial relations system in the USA consists of two rather distinct sectors: a unionised sector and a non-union sector. These two sectors interconnect in many ways and share common legal and social underpinnings, but do differ significantly.

The *unionised sector* has historically been characterised by openly adversarial relations between labour and management (Barbash 1981:1–7). The traditional American view sees unions and management as performing the functions of serving rather discrete, and fundamentally opposed, interests. The conflict between unions and management is circumscribed, however, by the limited goals of American unions. As the unions are still mainly concerned with the 'pure and simple' goals of the founders of the American labour movement, i.e. better wages, hours and conditions of work, and do not wish to be broadly involved in management, their challenge to management has been rather constrained. They have been willing to enter into what the old radical trade unionists called a 'treaty with the boss'—a collective bargaining agreement covering those matters that concern them, even giving up the right to strike for the duration of this 'treaty'. Conflict in the unionised sector is further bounded by the recognition by managers and unions that there are some broad areas of mutual interest.

The end result in the unionised sector is a rather stable situation where conflict is legitimate but bounded as to grounds, timing, and emotional intensity. The main threat to its stability is endemic managerial resistance to unions, which from time to time results in efforts to move establishments from the unionised sector to the non-union sector—either by dis-establishing a union in an existing location or moving the work to a southern or western location where unions are weak. In the late 1980s and early 1990s, managers and unionists who are proponents of labour–management cooperation (one of the issues discussed at length below) have challenged the basic adversarial nature of the American system. It remains to be seen whether this is a fundamental change or merely a tactical expansion of the area of accepted common interest.

The *non-union sector* is characterised by broad management discretion and control over the terms and conditions of employment. This is limited only by labour-market constraints, protective labour legislation, the desire of managers to avoid unionisation, and the strong influence of a 'positive' managerial philosophy that holds that firms 'ought to' offer favourable conditions of employment to employees. This sector includes private white-collar employment, electronics, small firms, most of the textile industry, most of the service sector, and manufacturing employees in a variety of industries. The main threat to the stability of this sector is the sporadic efforts of unions to organise it.

The environment of industrial relations

The *economic* environment has always had a powerful influence upon the American industrial relations system. The predominant employers are large private-sector enterprises. American unions were created to deal with, and have adapted to, operating in a capitalist economy dominated by such firms. Government's role in the economic system, although it has fluctuated over the years, has largely remained more limited than in other countries. Economic growth has helped to produce relatively favourable terms and conditions of employment for the majority of workers in the USA since the Second World War.

A reduction in demand for American goods was part of the general decrease in demand during the post-1974 recession, and was exacerbated by the competition from high quality goods produced in other countries. In the home market, competition from higher quality or lower cost foreign goods has particularly affected major industries such as cars, textiles and steel. In these and other industries, improvements in technology, encouraged by this competition, have caused workers to be replaced by machines. To further complicate matters, the type of labour demanded has been changed both by new technology and the shift of the American economy from manufacturing to services. All of this has weakened the bargaining power of labour. In periods of relative economic growth, collective bargaining demands and results are generally more favourable to labour. However, with a return to general prosperity in the late 1980s, unions remained weak and wage improvements were only moderate. The early 1990s' recession did not change this situation.

The *political* environment in the USA, with its representative democratic institutions, has historically provided a structure for the development of both free trade unions and free management. The political strength of capital and its representatives has always been sufficient to preserve broad areas of managerial discretion from government regulation. The balance of political forces has also permitted the development of reasonably strong trade unions and the imposition of some governmental constraints upon managerial freedom in the industrial relations arena. The government endorsed the formation of private-sector unions during the period 1935–47. The Federal government established bargaining with its own employees, and many state and local governments followed suit in the 1960s and 1970s. However, in some areas of the USA, particularly in the south, state and local governments do not permit collective bargaining by their employees.

During the 1980s and early 1990s the political environment accentuated the trend toward ever increasing management power in industrial relations. Conservative national administrations 'deregulated' the transport industry, increasing competition and placing downward pressure on wages. They have lessened the influence of government upon employers generally by moderating the enforcement of laws protecting workers from health and safety hazards and discrimination. Reagan appointees to the agency responsible for ensuring workers the right to organise (the National Labor Relations Board) instituted major policy changes unfavourable to unions. All of this has combined with the heightened conservatism of the Republican appointed Federal judiciary to create a very hostile legal environment for unions. There is a dramatic example of the effects of the political environment upon union power in the recent strike by 13 000 United Auto Workers against Caterpillar Corporation. After a five-month strike, Caterpillar announced that it would, as permitted by the law, permanently replace workers who refused to cross the picket line and return to work. Under pressure of this threat, the union ended the strike and ordered the strikers back to work. One of the union's main goals is to persuade Congress to change the law that permits this devastating employer tactic.

The major participants in industrial relations

In the USA, of all the participants in the industrial relations system, it is the employers who have generally been the most powerful of the actors.

Employers and their organisations

As Kochan has written, 'Management is the driving force in any advanced industrial relations system' (1980:179). In the USA and in other industrialised countries this derives, at least in part, from the crucial role of management in ensuring the efficiency and survival of work organisations. It may further stem from the high general social status of managers and their relatively high position in the organisational hierarchy.

In 1992 the non-union sector of the American workforce included more than 80 per cent of the workers. Throughout most of this sector, redundant workers can be laid off in whatever order the employer desires, and terminated for any or no reason. Furthermore, the conditions under which employment takes place are essentially employer-determined, limited only by labour-market forces and the protective labour legislation (discussed below).

In some non-unionised firms, the conditions of employment are relatively favourable. 'Personnel welfarism' has been a strong movement in the USA since the early years of the twentieth century. Modern personnel practice is oriented toward HRM—the notion that the labour factor of production is valuable, worth investing in, and worth preserving (Heneman et al. 1980:6). In this 'enlightened' view, it is in the interests of the corporation as a whole to attract, retain and improve workers. It is a unitary perspective that sees no necessary conflict between the interests of managers and other workers (Feuille & Wheeler 1981:255–7).

Employers' organisations are relatively unimportant in the USA (Adams 1980:4). In contrast to many other countries, there have never been national employers' confederations engaging in a full range of industrial relations activities. In the non-union sector, however, there have long been employers' organisations with a mission to avoid the unionisation of their members' employees. The

National Association of Manufacturers was formed for this purpose in the nineteenth century. At both the regional and national levels, the Chamber of Commerce includes union avoidance in its activities. These employer groups and others engage in anti-union litigation, lobbying, and publicity campaigns. They, along with management consultants, engage in the lucrative business of educating employers in techniques of union avoidance.

There has been a considerable increase in employer anti-union activities since the mid-1970s. These actions have ranged from locating plants in non-union areas in the south and west (the so-called 'Sun-Belt'), to openly violating the labour laws, to providing higher pay than the union range. The reasons for this increase are not entirely clear. It may be, at least in part, the result of a movement arising from the lower levels of management in protest against the strictures which unions impose on the performance of work (Piore 1982:8). This is especially ironic as many union rules were developed in the context of management application of the Taylorist notions of scientific management described earlier (Taylor 1964). Another cause of increased employer resistance may be managers seizing the opportunity to defeat their historic adversary when it is weak. The acceptance of unions by American managers has always been somewhat grudging, and based more upon necessity than choice.

The unions

The fundamental characteristics of the American labour movement are as follows:

1 goals which are largely those of 'bread and butter' unionism;
2 a strategy that is mainly economic;
3 collective bargaining as a central well-developed activity;
4 relatively low total union density;
5 strength vis-à-vis the employer on the shop floor;
6 an organisational structure in which the national union holds the reins of power within the union;
7 financial strength;
8 leadership drawn largely from the rank-and-file.

Selig Perlman long ago argued that the American labour movement exhibited a 'Tom, Dick and Harry' idealism—an idealism derived from the ordinary worker (1970:274–5). Perlman believed that unions, because they reflected the aspirations of their members, adopted those goals which seemed most important to the workers. These goals, said Perlman, had nothing to do with the imagined utopia of the Marxist 'intellectuals', but rather with the 'pure and simple' goals espoused by such labour leaders as Samuel Gompers, the 'father' of the American labour movement. Perlman's argument still affords a basic understanding of the American labour movement. Although American unions have also pursued wider goals, and are now newly interested in cooperation with management to increase worker feelings of self-worth, what has endured has been their emphasis upon practical improvements in wages, hours and conditions of work. Of course, unions in other countries have also sought 'bread and butter', but American unions have focused more closely upon this outcome than have most others.

The ideology of American unions is still much as it was expressed in 1911 by Samuel Gompers:

> The ground-work principle of America's labour movement has been to recognize that first things must come first. The primary essential in our mission has been the protection of the wage workers, now; to increase his wages; to cut hours off the long workday, which was killing him; to improve the safety and the sanitary conditions of the workshop; to free him from the tyrannies, petty or otherwise, which served to make his existence a slavery (Gompers 1919:20).

American unions have relied upon collective bargaining, accompanied by the strike threat, as their main weapon. This strategy has influenced the other characteristics of the American labour movement. It has provided the basis for an effective role on the shop floor, as the day-to-day work of administering the agreement requires this. It has required unions to be solvent financially in order to have a credible strike threat. It has resulted in an organisational structure in which the power within the union is placed where it can best be used for collective bargaining—the national union (Barbash 1967:69). Centralisation of power over strike funds in the national union has been a crucial source of union ability to develop common rules and to strike effectively. It has facilitated, and perhaps even required, an independence from political parties that might be tempted to subordinate the economic to the political. It is one reason why there is a relatively low total union density, as collective bargaining organisations have a concern about density only as it pertains to their individual economic territories. It has also contributed to one of the concomitants of low density—weak political power.

Although American unions have emphasised collective bargaining, they have also engaged in politics. Their political action has for the most part taken the form of rewarding friends and punishing enemies among politicians and lobbying for legislation. They have avoided being involved in the formation of a labour party. The

American Federation of Labor–Congress of Industrial Organizations (AFL–CIO) Committee on Political Education (COPE) and similar union political agencies are major financial contributors to political campaigns. The goals of such political activity have often been closely related to unions' economic goals, being aimed at making collective bargaining more effective. However, the American labour movement has also been a major proponent of progressive political causes such as laws on civil rights, minimum wages, plant closing notice, and other subjects of benefit to citizens generally.

Why is the USA unique among the countries discussed in this book in having no labour party? First, it would be difficult to operate as an independent national political force when representing only a small proportion of the workforce. Second, American workers have traditionally been highly independent politically, often voting in ways other than those desired by their union leaders. Third, the limited American experience with separate labour parties has not been favourable. Formed in 1828, the Working Men's Party was arguably the first labour party in the world. Its collapse, and the severe problems that it engendered, caused unions to steer clear of a repeat of that experience. Some later attempts were made, but were not much more successful. These were probably hindered by the historic difficulty of forming any third party in the USA. Fourth, the idea of a labour party is one which has often been urged by Left-wing unionists who were the losers in struggles for control of unions in the 1930s and 1940s, and were purged during the 'Red-scare' years of the 1950s. The failure to form a labour party may be accounted for in part by the narrow economic orientation of American unions, making the unions themselves and their federations seem logically to be the exclusive organisations for labour. Although others are puzzled by the American failure to have a labour party, American trade unionists are unable to see why they should do such a peculiar thing.

Yet, in the 1980s, the AFL–CIO did move towards greater identification with a party (the Democratic Party) than has been the case in the past. This move was accompanied by many statements by labour leaders which provide evidence of a new awareness of the importance of politics. It is possible that having 8 years of Ronald Reagan as President helped to stimulate this awareness, which was heightened by their experience under George Bush.

The structure of the American labour movement is rather loose compared to that of other Western union movements. The AFL–CIO is a federation of national unions that includes approximately 85 to 90 per cent of American union members. It has been strengthened in the 1980s by the reaffiliation of such major unions as the International Brotherhood of Teamsters (IBT), United Auto Workers

(UAW), United Mine Workers (UMW) and several others. This has given the American labour movement the greatest degree of cohesiveness that it has seen in 30 years. The AFL–CIO serves as the chief political and public relations voice for the American labour movement, resolves jurisdictional disputes among its members, enforces codes of ethical practices and policies against racial and sex discrimination, and is American labour's main link to the international labour movement.

The national unions have been described as occupying the 'kingpin' position in the American labour movement (Barbash 1967:69). They maintain ultimate power over the important function of collective bargaining, in a large part through their control of strike funds. The national unions can establish and dis-establish local unions and can withdraw from the AFL–CIO if they wish. The national presidents of unions are generally considered to be the most powerful figures in the American labour movement.

The local unions perform the day-to-day work of the labour movement. They usually conduct the bargaining over the terms of new agreements and conduct strikes. They administer the agreement, performing the important function of enforcing the complex set of rights that the American collective bargaining agreement creates. Social activities among union members take place at the local level, where there exists what there is of a union culture in the USA (Barbash 1967:26–41).

In 1991, unions had as members some 16.6 million employees, which constituted about 16 per cent of employed wage and salary workers. This compares to having 17 million people as members and 16.8 per cent of wage and salary earners in 1988. Their collective bargaining agreements covered 18.8 million workers. Although slipping slightly in terms of workforce percentage, they did manage to gain some 90 000 members between 1987 and 1988 (Bauman 1989). In contrast, they had lost 891 000 members between 1979 and 1980. Since 1988, membership has held relatively steady.

Over the last decade and a half, government and service employee unions such as the American Federation of Teachers; the Communication Workers of America; the American Federation of State, County and Municipal Employees; Letter Carriers; and the Firefighters, have experienced substantial growth. One of the old construction unions, the International Union of Operating Engineers, has also grown impressively. It is mainly in the manufacturing sector that union membership has been lost, as unions such as the United Rubber Workers; the Oil, Chemical and Atomic Workers; the United Automobile Workers; and the Amalgamated Clothing and Textile Workers have experienced heavy membership declines (Bureau of the Census 1989).

The composition of the American labour movement has gradually come to include more white-collar and female workers. In 1973, 24 per cent of organised workers were white-collar workers. By 1988 this figure was about 40 per cent. In 1973, 23 per cent of organised workers were female—in 1988, 36 per cent. As one would expect from the national shift of employment to non-manufacturing, the majority of union members now work in non-manufacturing occupations.

The American labour movement is generally considered an exceptional case because of its apolitical 'business unionism' ideology, focusing rather narrowly on benefits to existing membership. The most convincing explanations for this are historical (Kassalow 1974). First, there is no feudal tradition in the USA, which has made the distinctions among classes less obvious than in much of Europe and, unlike Australia, the USA lacks any other special historical circumstances giving rise to strong class feelings. Second, American capitalism developed in a form that allowed fairly widespread prosperity. Third, the great diversity of the population has always hampered the organisation of a broad-based working-class movement. Fourth, the early establishment of voting rights and free universal public education eliminated those potential working-class issues in the nineteenth century. Fifth, social mobility from the working class to the entrepreneurial category blurred class lines, creating a basis for the widely-held belief in the 'log cabin to White House' myth. In consequence, the American labour movement has seldom defined itself in class terms. Additionally, the historic experience of American unionists was that class-conscious unions, i.e. those that assumed the 'burden of socialism', tended to be repressed by the strong forces of American capitalism. A related but somewhat different explanation (Sturmthal 1973) is that American labour formed an economic strike-based strategy in its early years because this was appropriate to the conditions of labour shortage under which it began, and it has continued to pursue this course, even when it might be inappropriate.

Government

Government has three main roles in industrial relations: the direct regulation of terms and conditions of employment; regulation of the manner in which organised labour and management relate to each other; and as an employer.

Historically, the direct regulation of terms and conditions of employment was limited to the areas of employment discrimination, worker safety, unemployment compensation, minimum wages and maximum hours, and retirement (Ledvinka 1982). In 1964, the government acted to prohibit discrimination in employment on the grounds of race, colour, sex, religion, national origin or age. It has also proscribed discrimination against disabled persons and Vietnam War veterans. Most recently, since 1992, it acted to broadly prohibit discrimination against disabled workers.

The government has addressed problems of worker safety, mainly through the Federal Occupational Safety and Health Act 1970 (OSHA), state health and safety laws, and state workers' compensation laws. OSHA mandates a safe workplace, both by imposing a general duty of safety upon employers and by providing a detailed set of regulations for each industry. Employers violating safety and health standards are subject to fines and remedial orders. Workers' compensation laws provide for medical care and income protection for workers injured on the job. Also, they encourage safety indirectly by increasing the costs of insurance for employers experiencing a large number of on-the-job injuries.

Unemployment compensation is provided for on a state-by-state basis, but with some Federal control and funding. It involves payments to people who become involuntarily unemployed and are seeking work. The duration of payments is less than in most of the other countries covered in this book. It is usually limited to a period of 26 weeks, although with Federal support this may be extended to 39 weeks in a particular state when unemployment is high (Commerce Clearing House 1987:4409). Federal and state wage and hour laws provide for a minimum level of pay and a premium pay rate for overtime work. In 1992 the minimum pay level was $4.25 per hour, but there is a lower 'training' wage for young workers. As to overtime, employers are required to pay one and a half the employee's regular rate of pay for hours worked in excess of 40 in a particular work week. In addition, the national government uses its power as a purchaser of goods and services to require those doing business with it to pay the prevailing rates of pay in their region, and one and a half times the regular rate of pay for all hours worked in excess of eight in a work day.

Retirement benefits are regulated in two main ways. First, through the Social Security system employers and employees are required to pay a proportion of wages (7.65 per cent each in 1992) into a government fund. It is out of this fund that pensions are paid by the government to eligible retired employees (Social Security Act). The second way in which government controls pensions is by regulation of the private pension funds that are set up voluntarily by employers. The Employee Retirement Income Security Act of 1974 requires retirement plans to be financially secure, and insures these plans. It also mandates that employees become permanently vested in their retirement rights after a certain period.

There are a number of long-standing issues in the area of government regulation of conditions of employment. A major public policy debate has long taken place over the minimum wage laws. As in Britain, many economists believe that such laws tend to create unemployment, particularly among the young. This belief has led to proposals for a sub-minimum wage for this group of workers, for whom unemployment has been particularly high. Opponents of this idea see it as creating unemployment for adults and greater employer exploitation of low-wage workers. The debate leading up to the 1989 changes in the law was curiously muted; the only disagreement between a mainly Democratic Congress and a Republican President was over the *amount* of increase and the adoption of a youth training wage.

In the field of sex discrimination laws, the concept of 'comparable worth' was much debated in the 1980s (see Appendix). This is the notion that different jobs should carry equal rates of pay if they are worth the same to the employer. That is, the job of secretary, which is mostly held by women, should pay as well as that of a truck driver, which is mostly held by men, if its worth is comparable. The chief argument against this theory is its difficulty of application. In 1991, sexual harassment gained visibility as an issue because of charges of this conduct raised against a nominee for the Supreme Court, Clarence Thomas, who had headed the government agency charged with enforcing anti-discrimination laws. Also in 1991, Congress enacted amendments in the employment discrimination laws. They reversed restrictions which had made it more difficult for employees to assert claims under the law. These restrictions had been read into them originally by a conservative Supreme Court. Over the years occupational safety and health laws and pension regulations have been challenged by employers and conservative politicians because of their cost to employers and their alleged ineffectiveness.

Government regulation of the labour–management relationship consists largely of a set of ground rules through which these actors establish, and work out the terms of, their relationship. Through the National Labor Relations Act (NLRA) of 1935, as amended in 1947 and 1959, government provides a structure of rules that establishes certain employee rights with respect to collective action. The right to organise and bargain, as well as the right to refrain from organising and bargaining, is set out in the law. These rights are made effective through the establishment of an election process for workers to choose whether they want union representation, and the prohibition of certain 'unfair labour practices' on the part of employers and unions.

Since the late 1970s, there has been a continuing debate over the adequacy of laws protecting workers' rights to form and join unions. Management spokespeople have argued that unions are too powerful and should not be encouraged by more benevolent organising rules. The unions have maintained to the contrary, citing numerous violations of employee rights by many employers. The unions argue for reforms to facilitate the enforcement of laws prohibiting discrimination against workers for union activity, and to expedite the process of choosing union representation. Union leaders have gone to the extreme of suggesting repeal of the NLRA as useless. The reality is that employers can violate the labour laws with impunity, knowing the enforcement mechanisms are too weak to do them much damage. The unions tried to correct these problems in their support of the proposed Labor Law Reform Act of 1977. The failure of this legislative initiative in 1978 was a crushing blow to the political credibility of organised labour. This was one of the main spurs to increased union political activity in the 1984 Presidential election and since. The main effort by labour to change these laws at present is the proposed Workplace Fairness Act which would prohibit employers from permanently replacing striking workers (as discussed above in relation to the Caterpillar strike).

Since 1959, the government has regulated the internal affairs of unions. Federal law creates a 'Bill of Rights' for union members, requiring that unions accord them rights of free speech and political action. It also punishes union officials who mishandle union funds and outlaws certain anti-democratic practices by unions. In 1991, an election held under government supervision resulted in a slate of 'reform' candidates taking power in the historically corrupt Teamsters union (IBT).

An explosion of Federal employment legislation took place in 1988. In that year the Employee Polygraph Protection Act placed limitations on the use of lie detectors by employers. These machines, notorious for their unreliability and degrading uses, were being widely used by employers for both pre-employment testing and investigations of employee wrongdoing. This increased protection of employees was balanced, however, by the Drug-Free Workplace Act of 1988. This applies to employers that do business with the Federal government and strongly encourages drug testing and punishment of employees for both on- and off-duty drug use. Employer actions in this area have received further encouragement from regulations of the US Department of Transportation and Department of Defense requiring broad drug testing of employees in those industries. Drug testing of Federal and railroad employees, at least under some circumstances, was approved by the US Supreme Court in two 1989 decisions (*National Treasury Employees Union v. Von Raab*; *Skinner v. Railway Labor Executives Ass'n*). The issue of employee drug testing is a battleground on which the traditional protections of individual human dignity are under siege by public panic over a crisis in drug use.

An additional piece of legislation adopted in 1988 is the Worker Adjustment and Retraining Notification Act (WARN), or 'plant closing' law. This Federal statute requires employers, with some exceptions, to give 60 days advance notice of a plant closing or a mass layoff.

This trend in government action has continued into the 1990s. The changes in the employment discrimination laws mentioned above make it easier for workers to prevail in their claims. The adoption of these changes was an important attempt by Congress to reverse the weakening of these laws by conservative judges. Perhaps of more practical importance is the Americans With Disabilities Act which, since 1992, has imposed on most employers the obligation to make reasonable accommodation to the needs of disabled employees. This may even include protection for employees with infectious diseases such as AIDS.

Government is an employer of considerable consequence. In 1988 it employed 17.2 million workers. Government employment, including both national and state levels, increased by 32 per cent between 1970 and 1988 (Bureau of the Census 1989; Bauman 1989). In 1988 37 per cent of government workers were unionised, the same proportion as in 1983 (Bauman 1989).

The rapid increase in public-sector unionisation in the 1960s and 1970s was probably the most important development in the American labour movement since the 1930s. Teachers initiated this, as they successfully protested about declines in their salaries and benefits relative to those of other workers. Unionisation spread rapidly through most areas of government employment. As a result of this wave of unionising, there has been an important change in the composition of the American labour movement, with public-employee unions now representing slightly over one-third of union members. It remains to be seen to what degree this will affect the basic goals and activities of the movement.

The main processes of industrial relations

In the non-union sector, employers have devised a set of HRM practices to systematically determine pay and conditions of work. With respect to compensation, a combination of job evaluation and individual performance evaluation systems is common. The range of possible wage rates to be paid to workers in a job of, say, clerk are determined by an assessment of the worth of the job to the firm, i.e. job evaluation. A particular employee is assigned a wage rate within this range depending upon seniority, performance, or other factors. In addition to pay, fringe benefits such as health insurance, pensions, vacations and holidays are determined by company policy. All of this is done with an eye to the external labour market, with total compensation having to be adequate to attract and keep needed workers.

With respect to conditions of work, non-union employers establish job design and conditions in two principal ways. First, there is what has been called the 'conventional management theory' approach, in which jobs are standardised and specialised, in the spirit of Frederick Taylor (1964). Jobs are designed in such a way as to maximise efficiency. Second, the 'behavioural science' approach, originally founded in human relations theory, looks to the internal motivation of workers to provide efficient and high quality production. It attempts to design jobs in such a way that workers can fulfil their goals and the employer's at the same time. The enrichment of jobs, or at least their enlargement to provide more variety, is a major thrust of this notion. Quality circles and other schemes for worker participation in the design of jobs are consistent with this approach.

Collective bargaining, which chiefly determines the outcomes in the unionised sector, has reached an advanced stage of development in the USA. Since the 1940s, collective bargaining has produced a high standard of living for most unionised workers, protection for the worker interest in fair treatment and a complex and detailed set of rules governing the employment relationship, while generally preserving the managerial ability to ensure efficiency.

The collective bargaining structure is highly fragmented, and this fragmentation is increasing. Single company or single plant agreements are the norm in manufacturing. Most collective bargaining takes place at such levels. Even where national agreements exist, as in the car industry, substantial scope is left for local variation. Yet, in this large and diverse country, there is diversity as to this also, and much bargaining still occurs at higher levels (Mills 1978:120–4).

Third party intervention is widespread. In the private sector, government mediators are active in the negotiation of new agreements, and their work is generally admired. In negotiations involving government employees, many state laws provide for binding arbitration of unresolved disputes over the terms of a new agreement. This is especially common where the government employees involved, such as fire fighters or police officers, are considered to be 'essential'. Interest arbitration of the terms of a new agreement is very rare in the private sector. However, in both the private and public sectors, rights arbitration of disputes over the application and interpretation of an existing agreement is nearly always provided for in collective bargaining agreements. Decisions of arbitrators have historically been treated by the courts as final, binding and unappealable; although their finality has been weakened somewhat since the 1970s (Feuille & Wheeler 1981:270, 281).

Although there is considerable variety in collective bargaining agreements (contracts), they share certain nearly universal aspects. Most are very detailed, although the craft-union contracts are less so. Agreements generally cover wages, hours of work, holidays, pensions, health insurance, life insurance, union recognition, management rights, and the handling and arbitration of grievances. Most agreements have a limited duration, usually of one, two or three years.

A broadly representative sample of 400 major contracts maintained by the Bureau of National Affairs, Inc. (BNA), provides a picture of the scope of American collective bargaining that has changed since the early 1980s (BNA 1992). Discharge and discipline provisions, as well as arbitration clauses, are found in 97 per cent of this sample. Holidays, which are provided for in 99 per cent, amount to nine or more days per year in 48 per cent (1983—83 per cent) of the contracts. Vacation provisions are found in 91 per cent of the contracts, with 62 per cent of contracts providing for a maximum of five weeks vacation per year. All of the contracts in the sample contain wage provisions, and 25 per cent (1983—48 per cent) of them contain some form of automatic adjustment in wages to reflect inflation. Safety and health provisions appear in 86 per cent of the contracts. Provisions covering hours and overtime are found in 99 per cent of the contracts, with the eight-hour day being provided for in a very large proportion of these. Life insurance is provided for in 99 per cent of the contracts, hospital insurance in 83 per cent (down from virtually all as late as 1989), and dental insurance in 83 per cent (1983—65 per cent). By contrast, provisions for health and dental insurance are rare in British collective agreements. Pensions are mentioned in virtually all American contracts, but the details of pension plans are often set out in separate agreements. Seniority rights are established in 90 per cent of the contracts. These rights, which are crucial in American practice, may cover benefits, such as vacations, or the right to retain an existing job or be promoted to another one. Union promises not to strike are found in 96 per cent of the contracts.

At least for unionised workers, the relative lack of government welfare programs in the USA is somewhat compensated for by the extensive protections included in these agreements. However, the very substantial declines in holidays, and automatic wage adjustments, although balanced by gains in other areas, reflect the decreased strength of American unions in what has traditionally been their bailiwick. Furthermore, although union wages and benefits continue to be substantially higher than those of non-union workers, their *increases* have been slightly smaller than those of non-union workers in several recent years.

During the 1980s substantial pressures were brought to bear upon unions to reduce wages. In the early 1980s the chief response to this was union agreements to general wage cuts in what was known as 'concession bargaining' (Mitchell 1983:83). Although the unions often obtained a *quid pro quo* for these concessions, such as membership on a corporate board of directors, it was an extraordinary event for established unions to agree to a reversal of the historic upward trend of wages in collective bargaining. This wave of concession bargaining was followed by a series of 'two tier' wage agreements in which certain workers, usually new employees, received a lower rate of pay for doing the same work as other employees, violating the traditional union rule of equal pay for equal work. The two tier system provides a means for employers to reduce labour costs without offending (and perhaps losing) their experienced workers, while at the same time permitting the experienced majority of workers at the firm to protect their wages at the expense of the minority of newer workers. However, as was obvious from the outset, there is tremendous potential for dissatisfaction of newer workers, conflict among groups of workers, and difficulty in attracting new hires. Not unexpectedly, after peaking in popularity in 1985, when they were adopted in 11 per cent of contracts, they lost popularity. In 1992 they were included in only 5 per cent of agreements (BNA 1992). These in turn have been replaced by lump sum payments in lieu of wage increases, which have the effect of putting money in employees' hands immediately but not being a part of the basic wage for purposes of future increases. Perhaps more importantly, unlike wage increases, lump sum payments do not 'roll-up' into other parts of the wage package such as vacations, overtime pay, shift differentials and holidays (Kempski 1989).

Collective bargaining dealt with a variety of challenging issues in the late 1980s and early 1990s. The rapid rise of health care costs, most of which had been borne by employers, has prompted them to shift some of this burden to employees, and unions and employers to work together to contain these costs. Profit-sharing plans have been proposed and accepted at such firms as Weyerhauser, Chrysler and Uniroyal-Goodrich. Child care has become a major item on the union bargaining agenda for the 1990s, although employer interest in providing these benefits appears to be limited. Corporate mergers and acquisitions have given rise to union insistence on 'successorship clauses' in contracts with such diverse employers as Bloomingdale's Department Stores, and Firestone. In such a clause the company agrees to require a buyer of the business to retain the union relationship. Technological changes have sparked agreements on early retirement, preferential hiring, pay continuance guarantees and retraining (Kempski 1989).

Although the American collective bargaining system is currently being widely criticised for its adversarial nature and obsolescence, a review of its accomplishments in the 1980s and early 1990s provides clear testimony to its strength and flexibility. It may bear some share of blame for the problems of American competitiveness, at least for its invention of automatic wage adjustment based upon increases in the consumer price index (COLA clauses), which raised wages unexpectedly during the high inflation of the 1970s. However, in reviewing the adjustments that it has made to the enormous economic disturbances of the past two decades, one is struck with its ability in times of change to meet the efficiency requirements of management while providing workers with as much protection as possible.

Issues of current importance

Of the many issues concerning American industrial relations, let us discuss three, in particular: industrial justice, labour–management cooperation and union decline.

Industrial justice

Industrial justice has become one of the most widely discussed issues, chiefly because of increasing public dissatisfaction with the common law doctrine of employment-at-will. Under this legal doctrine an employee can be dismissed at any time, for any (or no) reason. Historically, the only exceptions to this rule have been statutory prohibitions against dismissals that discourage union membership or discriminate on other forbidden grounds, and contractual obligations that the employer voluntarily assumes.

In the unionised sector, employers agree to refrain from dismissing or disciplining employees except for 'just cause'. To enforce this, American collective bargaining agreements provide for a multi-step grievance procedure, with the ultimate step being arbitration by an outside neutral, employed jointly by the union and management. The concept of 'just cause' is one that has been reasonably well defined in the decisions of arbitrators. A distinction is made between 'major' offences, such as theft and insubordination, and 'minor' offences. For a major offence a worker can be discharged immediately upon first offence. For a minor offence, 'progressive' discipline must be used. Progressive discipline means the imposition of progressively more severe discipline, ordinarily beginning with an oral warning, and moving to a written warning, suspension, and eventually discharge for repeated offences. An employer is also required to impose discipline evenly across employees (Elkouri & Elkouri 1973).

The contrast between the protections available to unionised workers and minority employees on the one hand, and other workers on the other hand, has led to proposals for a general system of legislative protection of all workers (Stieber 1980). One state, Montana, has adopted such legislation. Also, numerous court decisions have weakened the employment-at-will doctrine. Courts have held that employees cannot be terminated for refusing to violate a law or for 'whistle blowing' when an employer violates a law or endangers public safety. They have found employers liable for money damages for terminating employees in violation of the implied obligation of good faith and fair dealing, and for acting contrary to provisions in employee handbooks. Terminating an employee in an abusive manner can also give rise to a claim of unjust termination.

Labour–management cooperation

Labour–management cooperation's prominence as an issue is perhaps the most unusual feature of the current discussions about industrial relations in the USA. This is somewhat odd in a system that is still characterised by adversarial relations between management and unions. But the pressures of international competition and the Japanese example, among other things, have caused a re-examination of the foundation principle of the necessity of labour–management conflict. Recognition that there are broad areas of common interest amenable to a problem-solving approach, known as win/win or integrative bargaining, is not new. However, the emphasis upon this has reached new highs in recent years. This trend has been encouraged by scholarly writing, such as Kochan, Katz and McKersie's influential *The Transformation of American Industrial Relations* (1986), the establishment and activities of a Bureau of Labor–Management Relations and Cooperative Programs in the US Department of Labor, the 1978 Labor–Management Cooperation Act adopted by the Federal Congress, and the 1988 report of the President's Advisory Committee on Mediation and Conciliation.

Cooperation takes many forms. Scanlon and Rucker plans, which share productivity gains with workers, have been around for many years, as have joint health and safety committees. More recent innovations are quality circles, quality of working life (QWL) programs, and even scattered instances of union representation on corporate boards of directors. Some of these have been initiated by strategic management decisions aimed at improving productivity or quality. In some instances, innovations such as membership on corporate boards have come in exchange for union wage concessions. A number of union leaders, such as Douglas Fraser, former president of the United Auto Workers, and Morton Bahr, president of the Communication Workers of America (CWA), have become vigorous advocates of increased direct worker participation in the decisions that affect their working lives. The shop floor version of this amounts to adding *direct* industrial democracy to the more traditional *representative* industrial democracy.

There are numerous well-publicised instances of successful ventures in labour–management cooperation. These include the experience at New United Motor Manufacturing Inc. (NUMMI); a joint venture between General Motors and Toyota; General Motors' Saturn contract with the UAW; non-adversarial negotiations between Xerox and the Amalgamated Textile Workers Union (ATWU); and the relationship worked out between National Steel Co. and the United Steelworkers of America (USWA). The claimed benefits are improved satisfaction of workers, higher productivity and better quality. There have, however, been numerous, less well-publicised examples of failures of attempts at cooperative programs. There has also developed in some unions something of a rank-and-file anti-cooperative movement. The 'New Directions' movement in the UAW is the prime example of this. Another problem is the credibility of managements in proposing cooperation while working avidly to destroy or avoid unions, thereby removing the grounds for the trust that is necessary for cooperative programs. In spite of the difficulties, however, there does seem to be a generally shared opinion among managers and many union leaders that cooperation is a necessary condition for economic survival in a competitive world.

Union decline

The decline of the union movement is an issue receiving increasing attention in the USA. Union density has slipped substantially since 1980 (see Appendix). A number of reasons are probably associated with its decline, including:

1 the shift in the economy from manufacturing to services;
2 the challenges of technological change and foreign competition;

3   employer anti-union activities, both positive and negative;
4   changing employee preferences and values away from 'bread
    and butter' (Allen & Keaveny 1988:697–700).

Furthermore, the recession of the early 1980s hit hardest at unionised basic industries, causing massive losses of union members.
These industries recovered somewhat in the late 1980s but did not
return to former levels of employment, and are unlikely ever to do
so. It may also be that equally important causes of union decline
are the failure of unions to exert sufficient efforts to organise new
members and a rising tide of employer opposition.

The opposition of employers to unions has been especially
intense since the mid-1970s. Attempts to dis-establish existing
unions reached new highs in the 1980s, as did convictions of
employers for fighting against unions in violation of labour laws.
In 1992, the unremitting opposition to unions of most employers
has become a fact of industrial life. Given the well-known inability
of the labour laws to protect workers from employer retribution, it
is hardly surprising that unions have experienced difficulty in
organising new members.

It perhaps bears repeating that employer power is very great in
the USA in both the political and economic spheres. To the extent
that changes in the law are needed for unions to regain and preserve
power, change is blocked by the superior political power of employers. This, in turn, makes it more difficult to operate in the sphere
of economic action, as the example of the Caterpillar strike shows.
Friends of labour in the USA have been known to look across the
Northern border and cry 'Oh, Canada' in wistful admiration of the
Canadian legal system which is more friendly to unions (Geoghegan
1991). Added to this is a high unemployment rate in the early 1990s,
which also makes economic action difficult. It is also easy to
understand why American unions are having trouble regaining the
ground they lost when employment has declined in sectors which
traditionally have been organised.

The crucial question is whether the American labour movement
can survive the current difficulties and re-emerge as a powerful,
lively movement. The alternative is for it to slip into a moribund
condition, as it did in the 1920s—a period not unlike the 1980s and
early 1990s in political and social climate. Another possibility is a
dramatic slide to the Left, changing from an economic orientation
to a more political one. However, neither of these outcomes seems
likely. Although the unions appear to have a new awareness of the
importance of politics, it is still politics directed at achieving their
survival for collective bargaining. It seems most unlikely that American unions will become as political as those in Western Europe and

Australia. It is also unlikely that they will wither away under the various pressures described above. American unions still have millions of members. As those who have worked with labour's 'grassroots' can testify, its ranks are filled with energetic, dedicated and intelligent unionists who appear to be capable of weathering the storm.

In the hazardous business of forecasting the future of the American labour movement there are both positive and negative auguries that could be used as guides. On the positive side, the unions have achieved an improved rate of victories in representation elections, including major wins involving air traffic controllers (whose earlier union was crushed by Ronald Reagan), over 2000 employees at Arcata Graphics (where a group of unions was defeated in a highly publicised strike in the 1960s), and a surprisingly little-noted success in anti-union South Carolina in a Mack Truck plant. Organising effectiveness is increasing as a number of unions, some of them working in conjunction with the Industrial Union Department of the AFL–CIO's Organising Department, improving the coordination of their efforts. The renewed militancy of miners and their use of non-violent techniques drawn from the civil rights movement in the Pittston strike, and the success of international cooperation among unions in the BASF lockout are hopeful signs. Labour's willingness to innovate is shown by the adoption of new forms of membership that go back to their historic roots as benevolent associations, and their renewed receptiveness to labour–management cooperation and employee ownership. Recent increases in absolute numbers of union members, noted above, are also encouraging.

On the negative side, the continuing competitiveness of the international economy gives support to those in management who oppose unions as fetters to efficiency and profitability. Furthermore, until there is once again a shortage of labour, which is the condition under which a strike-based strategy is most effective, the ability of unions to achieve large gains in collective bargaining is probably going to remain limited. Demographic forecasts do furnish some hope in this regard. Loss of major strikes, such as at Eastern Airlines and Caterpillar, and endemic problems with democracy and honesty, continue to hurt the unions' public image. Perhaps most importantly, the continuing aversion of the legal system to unions remains a severe problem.

Conclusion

The pressures of international competition have, for the American industrial relations system as for others, opened a Pandora's box of troubles. Kochan et al. argued that these pressures and others had already, in the early 1980s, fundamentally changed the nature of the American system. Yet, in the 1990s, the extent and depth of these changes still are not clear.

Certainly, the move from oligopolistic markets to competitive ones has created the need for many industries in the USA to create new ways to organise work and cut costs. It may be that the necessary level of quality of some goods, such as automobiles and electronic equipment, cannot be attained without developing cooperative mechanisms that are inconsistent with the adversarial American model. However, it is unclear whether more cooperative work methods can endure under American capitalism, where the 'fast buck' is held in reverence, the pressures of predatory take-over artists keep management constantly squeezing for more profits, managers hold opposition to employee collective action to be a holy cause, and hierarchical habits are deeply ingrained. The trust that is the foundation stone of labour–management cooperation is difficult to build in such an environment. Management choosing to share power with union and non-union workers in the highest councils of corporate decision making is also something about which this writer is highly sceptical. It seems that the best chance for cooperation lies on the shop floor where the workers have expertise, power, and the desire to exercise both of these.

Meanwhile, the traditional collective bargaining structure in the USA has fared rather well. It has devised means to cut labour costs. Unions have generally not opposed the adoption of new technology, and have bargained innovations in cooperation, profit sharing, health care costs, and holidays. Child care may be the next frontier. Similarly, in the unionised sector, the grievance and arbitration procedures continue to guarantee worker protection from, as put earlier, the 'tyrannies, petty or otherwise, which served to make [the worker's] existence a slavery'.

In the non-union sector, many employers are adopting progressive and positive employment policies, making workers' jobs both better and better paid. The network of laws has increased, providing new protections for workers, although the enforcement of both old and new laws may not be sufficiently energetic. Also, rights of human dignity of employees are being challenged by new employer anti-drug policies.

An enduring concern is the continued strength of the American labour movement which, like those in many other countries, has declined in recent years. However, as noted earlier in this chapter, in labour's Pandora's box of troubles there is, as there was in Pandora's, one important remaining item—hope. There is also a fundamental logic to collective action by workers that is not repealed by international competition. Indeed, the historical roots of American unions lie in a time when markets-expanded in this young country, forcing workers to gather together in a protective response. In sum, the parties in the American industrial relations system continue to muddle through. As the only certainty appears to be change, a history of muddling through reasonably well is rather reassuring.

A chronology of US labour–management relations

1794	Federal Society of Cordwainers founded in Philadelphia—first permanent US union.
1828	Working Men's Party founded.
1834	National Trades Union founded—first national labour organisation.
1866	National Labor Union formed—first national 'reformist' union.
1869	Knights of Labor founded. A 'reformist' organisation dedicated to changing society, which nevertheless was involved in strikes for higher wages and improved conditions.
1886	Formation of the American Federation of Labor (AFL), a loose confederation of unions with largely 'bread-and-butter' goals. Peak of membership of the Knights of Labor (700 000 members), which then began to decline.
1905	Formation of the Industrial Workers of the World, the 'Wobblies', an anarcho-syndicalist union.
1914–22	Repression of radical unions because of their opposition to war, and during 'Red-scare' after Russian Revolution.
1915	Establishment of the first company-dominated union, Ludlow, Colorado.
1920s	Decline and retrenchment of the American labour movement.
1932	Election of Franklin D. Roosevelt as President of USA—a 'New Deal' for unions.
1934	National Labor Relations (Wagner) Act, gave employees a federally protected right to organise and bargain collectively. Also, formation of Congress of Industrial Organizations (CIO), a federation of industrial unions.
1934–39	Rapid growth of unions covering major mass production industries.
1941–45	Growth of unions and development of the collective bargaining system during the war.

1946	Massive post-war strike wave in major industries.
1947	Enactment of Taft–Hartley Act prohibited unions from certain organising and bargaining practices.
1955	Merger of AFL and CIO to form the AFL–CIO.
1959	Landrum–Griffin Act, regulating the internal operations of unions.
1960	New York City teachers' strike—the beginning of mass organisation of public employees.
1962	Adoption of Executive Order 10988 by President John F. Kennedy, providing for limited collective bargaining by Federal government employees. Also the beginning of the movement of the National Education Association toward collective bargaining by teachers.
1960–80	Growth of unionism of public employees. Decline of union density in manufacturing.
1977–78	Defeat of Labor Law Reform Bill in Congress, as employer movement in opposition to unions gained strength.
1980	Election of President Ronald Reagan—new Federal policies generally adverse to organised labour.
1981	Economic recession.
1988–89	Federal legislation on drugs, lie detectors, plant closing, minimum wages. Court decisions on drug testing and termination of employment.
1991	Federal legislation prohibiting discrimination against disabled workers. Federal legislation strengthening employment discrimination laws.
1991–	Serious economic recession.
1992	Election of President Bill Clinton—the first Democrat president for 12 years—with policies more in tune with organised labour.
1993	Passage of Family Leave Act, providing for employee unpaid leave.

4   Industrial relations in Canada
Mark Thompson

Students of comparative industrial relations have usually ignored
Canada, treating it as part of a North American continental system
or a minor variant of US industrial relations. While the two nations
have similar legal regulation of industrial relations, unions with
formal organisational links, and plant-level collective bargaining,
Canadian industrial relations now constitute a distinctive system. It
is extremely decentralised, with high levels of conflict, a thriving
labour movement, and frequent legislation to deal with labour
problems. Periodically, industrial relations are perceived as serious
national or regional issues. Although there is no national consensus
on reform, governments do amend statutes from time to time in an
effort to reduce conflict.

The economic, social and political context

The economic, social and political contexts of Canadian industrial
relations are different from most other developed nations. Canada
enjoys a standard of living equal to, or higher than, the more
prosperous nations in Western Europe (see Appendix). But, like
Australia, Canada depends heavily on the production and export of
raw materials and semi-processed products—mineral ores, food
grains, and forest products. Although Canada enjoys a comparative
advantage in the production of most of these commodities, their
markets are unstable and these industries generate limited direct
employment. A large manufacturing sector does exist in the central
provinces, but efforts to stimulate its expansion beyond 20 per cent
of the gross national product have failed. Canada lacks a large
domestic market, and its manufacturers usually must compete with
much larger US firms in third countries. Early in the 1980s, traditional Canadian manufacturing industries, such as clothing, automobiles, and electrical products suffered severely from offshore

competition, but most of the sector recovered by the end of the decade. Another sharp decline occurred in the early 1990s, and recovery was slow and weak. Lacking a large domestic market, Canada usually exports about 28 per cent of its gross national product and imports almost as much. These transactions are dominated by the USA, which is Canada's largest trading partner. Apart from proximity and a complementarity of the two economies, Canadian–American trade relations are encouraged by extensive US ownership in many primary and secondary industries and a free trade agreement covering most economic sectors.

Canada has a mixed economy, with active roles for both public and private sectors, often in the same industries. Older public-sector enterprises typically were created for pragmatic reasons—provision of a necessary service, development of natural resources or the preservation of jobs. Thus, many public utilities, transportation and communications companies are government owned. In the 1970s, government ownership served nationalistic goals—the reduction of foreign ownership or stimulation of technological development. Public-sector companies and their industrial relations generally are run with relatively little political interference. A number of government enterprises and operations were privatised in the 1980s and 1990s, without materially altering the basic role of government.

Canada's most pressing economic problems in the 1980s were unemployment and inflationary pressures, difficulties it shared with most other developed nations. After a period of inflation in the mid-1970s, unemployment, always substantial by international standards, rose sharply and remained high, as Table 4.1 demonstrates. Fears of renewed inflation caused the central bank to restrain demand by raising interest rates.

Two sets of government policies were adopted to deal with inflation. Between October 1975 and September 1978, the Federal government imposed an anti-inflation program, which included comprehensive wage and price controls, limits on growth in government spending and restrictive monetary and fiscal policies. Nine of the nation's ten provinces enacted legislation to put their own public sector employees, normally within provincial jurisdiction, under the Federal program. Although opinions differ about the impact of the program, the rate of inflation declined during its life, and the rate of wage increases fell even more sharply. However, both labour and management resented the restrictions in the program, so it was not extended. In the early 1980s, the national bank adopted a modified monetarist economic policy, which kept interest rates high, restrained the growth in the supply of money and accepted the basic thrust of US economic policy by maintaining a relatively stable relationship between the two nations' currencies. When the recession

Table 4.1   Earnings, prices and unemployment

Year	Rate of change of average earnings (%)	Annual rate of change, consumer price index (%)	Annual rate of unemployment (%)
1974–78	11.5	9.2	7.1
1979–83	10.6	9.7	9.0
1984	3.0	4.4	11.2
1985	3.0	4.0	10.5
1986	2.8	4.1	9.5
1987	2.7	4.4	8.8
1988	4.8	4.1	7.8
1989	5.0	5.0	7.5
1990	5.3	4.8	10.3
1991	5.5	5.6	10.4

Source: Statistics Canada *Canadian Economic Observer,* various issues; *Historical Statistical Supplement,* 1989/90.

of the period grew more serious, Federal and provincial governments re-imposed wage controls for the public sector only in an effort to reduce government spending and divert expenditure to the private sector. These policies provoked scattered labour disputes and held public-sector compensation down, but did little to reduce deficits or stimulate the private sector.

Politically, Canada has a modified two-party system. The Liberal Party has dominated Federal politics for the past 50 years, occasionally forming a minority government or yielding power to the Conservatives, who won large majorities in 1984 and 1988. The Liberals are a pragmatic, reformist party, with a traditional base of support in Quebec. The Conservatives are a right-of-centre party, normally drawing votes from the eastern and western regions, though they ran strongly in Quebec in 1984 and 1988. While it has a market orientation, the Conservative government did not embrace the social and economic policies of the Thatcher or Reagan administrations.

The New Democratic Party (NDP), with a social-democratic philosophy and strong union support, has a small number of parliamentary seats and 15 to 20 per cent of the popular vote. Other parties appear from time to time. In the early 1990s, a pro-independence party from Quebec and a conservative party from the western provinces both had Members of Parliament. None of the Federal parties is strong in all the provinces, and provincial parties have normally governed in Quebec and British Columbia. A large provincial pro-independence party exists in Quebec, though both

French- and English-speaking citizens voted to remain in Canada in a 1980 referendum.

Official efforts to deal with economic problems have been hindered by the nation's political structure. Like Australia, Canada is a confederation with a parliamentary government. The ten provinces hold substantial powers, including the primary authority to regulate industrial relations, leaving only a few industries, principally transport and communications, to Federal authority. The political structure reflects strongly-held regional sentiments, accentuated by distance and language. The second most populous province, Quebec, is predominantly French-speaking and has continuing separatist tendencies. The provinces, often led by Quebec, not only have resisted any efforts to expand Federal powers, but periodically demand greater powers for the provinces.

In an effort to establish certain guarantees for Quebec, the Liberal government produced the nation's first written constitution in 1982. It included a Charter of Rights which contained a number of protections for individuals and groups from government action. Among these are freedom of association and speech and the right to live and work anywhere in the nation, all of which have potential impact on industrial relations law and practice.

As a 'new' country, Canada has received immigrants throughout its history. The largest source of immigrants has been Britain, followed by other European countries after 1945 and citizens of developing Commonwealth nations in the 1960s and 1970s. Most of the immigrants came to improve their economic status, including a tradition of working-class politics. Simultaneously, the relatively conservative political tradition of the USA has been a powerful model to Canadians. These influences, combined with a parliamentary political system and its acceptance of third parties, have combined to produce a value system which includes both the individualism of an expanding capitalist economy and the collectivism of mature industrial nations in Western Europe. Thus, conservative governments occasionally have nationalised private companies and NDP regimes have encouraged small businesses. Even political parties which govern for long periods of time nationally, such as the Liberals, may alternate between conservative and liberal economic policies.

The industrial relations parties

The unions

The Canadian labour movement has displayed steady, though unspectacular, growth since the 1930s, despite a long-standing tradition of disunity. Membership reached 4.1 million in 1991, which constituted 36.5 per cent of non-agricultural employees, an increase from 1.4 million and 32.2 per cent in 1960. This membership was divided among three national centres and a large number of unaffiliated unions.

The greatest penetration of unionism is in primary industries, construction, transport, manufacturing and the public sector. In the late nineteenth and early twentieth centuries, Canadian unions were established first in construction and transportation, mostly on a craft basis. During the 1930s and 1940s, industrial unionism spread to manufacturing and primary industries, without including white-collar workers in the private sector. Since the late 1960s, the major source of growth in the labour movement has been the public sector. First public servants, then health and education workers, joined unions. Professionals, notably teachers and nurses, had long been members of their own associations, and these transformed themselves into unions as their members' interest in collective bargaining grew. By 1980, virtually all eligible workers in the public sector had joined unions. In the public sector junior managers are permitted to unionise, while supervisors in the private sector are effectively denied the right to collective representation. Table 4.2 shows the relative rate of unionisation by industry.

Approximately 280 unions operate in Canada, ranging in size from under 20 to over 300 000 members. Two-thirds are affiliated with one of the central confederations discussed below, with the remainder, mainly in the public sector, independent of any national body. The ten largest unions contain 42.1 per cent of all members. A variety of union philosophies are represented. Most of the old

Table 4.2 Union members as a percentage of paid workers[a]

Industry group	Per cent unionised
Public administration	79.1
Fishing and trapping	45.9
Transportation, communication and other utilities	53.4
Construction	53.5
Forestry	45.2
Manufacturing	36.3
Service industries	34.6
Mines, quarries and oil wells	30.8
Trade	11.5
Finance and agriculture	less than 5.0

Note: a 1989 data.

Source: Ministry of Supply and Services *Annual Report of the Minister of Supply and Services Under the Corporations and Labour Unions Reporting Act, Part II* Ottawa: Ministry of Supply and Services, 1991.

craft groups still espouse apolitical business unionism; a larger number of unions see themselves fulfilling a broader role and actively support the NDP and various social causes. A few groups, principally in Quebec, are highly politicised and criticise the prevailing economic system from a Marxist perspective. But rhetoric aside, the major function of all unions is collective bargaining.

The role of US-based 'international' unions is a unique feature of the Canadian labour movement that historically affected its behaviour in many ways. Most of the oldest labour organisations in Canada began as part of American unions—hence the term 'international'. The cultural and economic ties between the two countries encouraged the union connections, while the greater size and earlier development of US labour bodies attracted Canadian workers to them. For many years, the overwhelming majority of Canadian union members belonged to such international unions, which often exerted close control over their Canadian locals. But the spread of unionism in the public sector during the 1960s and 1970s brought national unions to the fore, as internationals were not active among public employees. As a result the proportion of international union membership declined from over 70 per cent in 1966 to under 45 per cent in 1982.

Persistent complaints about the quality of service in Canada, American labour's support for economic protectionism and increased Canadian nationalism created pressures for change within the labour movement. During the 1970s, a few unions in Canada seceded from internationals, and the largest international in Canada—the UAW—separated in 1985. But a more common (and successful) change was agreement to grant special autonomous status to Canadians in international unions. In the past, internationals encouraged a conservative form of business unionism in Canada, discouraged political involvement and exerted powerful influence over the policies of national centres. While a role in these areas continues, the impact of policies originating in the USA is low and seems destined to decline further.

The most important central confederation in Canada is the Canadian Labour Congress (CLC), with about 100 affiliated unions who represent over 50 per cent of all union members. CLC members are in all regions and most industries except construction. It is the principal political lobbyist for Canadian labour, but is weaker than many national centrals in other countries. It has no role in bargaining; nor does it have any substantial powers over its affiliates, unlike central confederations in Germany and Scandinavia. The CLC's political role is further limited by the constitutionally weak position of the Federal government, its usual contact point in many areas the labour movement regards as important, such as labour legislation, regulation of industry or human rights. In national politics, it officially supports the NDP. The CLC has chartered federations in each province to which locals of affiliated unions belong. Some of these bodies wield considerable influence in their provinces.

The Confederation of National Trade Unions (CNTU) represents about 5 per cent of all union members, virtually all in Quebec. It began early in the twentieth century under the sponsorship of the Catholic Church as a conservative French-language alternative to the English-dominated secular unions operating elsewhere in Canada. As Quebec industrialised during and after the Second World War, members of the Catholic unions grew impatient with their lack of militancy and unwillingness to confront a conservative provincial government. In 1949, following an illegal strike against a powerful employer supported by the provincial government, the Catholic unions abandoned their former conservatism and moved into the vanguard of rapid social change in Quebec. In 1960, the federation adopted its present name and severed its ties with the Catholic Church. Since then, ideological competition has prevailed in the Quebec labour movement, and the CNTU has become the most radical and politicised labour organisation in North America. It has supported Quebec independence actively and has adopted Left-wing political positions. Unlike the CLC, it has a centralised structure which gives officers considerable authority over member unions. Because of its history, current political posture and the large provincial public sector in Quebec, the CNTU membership is concentrated among public employees.

In 1982, a third labour central was formed. A group of construction unions had left the CLC a year earlier because they resented pressure from the CLC to grant greater autonomy to their Canadian sections. They also maintained the craft tradition of business unionism (see ch. 3) and opposed the social and political activism of the CLC leadership. The CLC voting structure favoured public sector unions and reduced the power of construction unions. Ten of the dissident unions, representing over 5 per cent of all union members, formed the Canadian Federation of Labour (CFL). The new group is apolitical, though it quickly established ties with the Federal government. Both the CLC and the CFL have avoided any open hostilities since the latter appeared, but the issues separating them remain, so the potential for conflict is great.

Management

The high degree of foreign ownership in the Canadian economy affects general management strategy, but seldom industrial relations. Over 20 per cent of the assets of all industrial firms are foreign-owned, chiefly by US corporations. Foreign ownership clearly affects significant managerial policy decisions, such as product lines or major investments. But the impact of non-Canadians on industrial relations decisions appears to be slight. Foreign owners prefer to remain in the mainstream of industrial relations for their industries rather than imposing corporate policies in Canada.

Most Canadian managers have only a limited commitment to collective bargaining. Firms with well-established unions accept the presence of labour organisations. Efforts to dislodge existing unions are rare, and in industries with a long history of unionism—for example transportation, mining or heavy manufacturing—unionism is accepted as a normal part of the business environment. Even in these industries, however, employers are reluctant to recognise unions voluntarily at new plants. A common policy is to transport many of the basic elements of collective agreements into these new locations. If unions do seek recognition through legal procedures, management resistance is weak.

Non-union firms on the other hand, strive to keep unionism out, some by matching the wages and working conditions in the unionised sector, others by combinations of paternalism and coercion. A small number of firms in sectors where unions are weak have active union-substitution policies, which replicate many of the forms of a unionised work environment with grievance procedures, quality circles or mechanisms for consultation.

Unionised firms in Canada normally have a full-time industrial relations staff, though seldom a large one. Collective bargaining rounds usually occur at intervals of between one and three years, so it is not feasible for most firms to maintain large staffs for that purpose, and many such staff also have non-industrial relations duties. Small firms rely heavily on lawyers to perform industrial relations staff functions. Most industrial relations decisions, such as decisions to take strikes or the level of first wage offers, are highly centralised, i.e. taken at the corporate level.

Traditionally, Canadian employers have preferred appeals to government or short-term strategies for dealing with labour problems. There is some evidence that this pattern changed in the 1980s. Large employers responded to economic pressures by stressing improved communications with their employees and unions in efforts to generate greater employee commitment to raising productivity and quality. Labour–management cooperation increased in importance. Many of these initiatives are not reflected in collective agreements or other documents, keeping them relatively informal. While the lasting impact of these initiatives remains uncertain they do represent a break with past practice.

The organisation of employers varies among regions. No national organisation participates directly in labour relations, although a number do present management viewpoints to government or the public. Since most labour relations law falls under provincial jurisdiction, few industries have national bargaining structures. In two provinces, Quebec and British Columbia, local economic conditions and public policy have encouraged bargaining by employer associations, normally specialised bodies for that purpose. Elsewhere single plant bargaining with single unions predominates, except in a few industries with many small firms, such as construction, longshoring or trucking, where multi-employer bargaining is the norm.

Government

The government in Canada has a dual role in industrial relations—it regulates the actors' conduct and employs large numbers of people both directly and indirectly.

Government regulation of industrial relations is very specific, although it rests on an assumption of voluntarism. Each province, plus the Federal government, has at least one Act covering labour relations and employment standards in the industries under its jurisdiction. Most governments also have separate labour relations statutes for the public sector. Employment standards legislation generally set minima for such areas as wages, vacations or holidays. In a few areas, such as maternity leave, the law has led most employers. Although the details vary considerably, labour relations legislation combines many features of the US National Labor Relations Act (Wagner Act) and an older Canadian pattern of reliance on conciliation of labour disputes. Each statute establishes and protects the right of most employees to form unions, and sets out a procedure by which a union may demonstrate majority support from a group of employees in order to obtain the right of exclusive representation for them. The employer is required to bargain with a certified union. A quasi-judicial labour relations board administers this process and enforces the statute, although the legislation often specifies the procedural requirements in detail.

Labour relations legislation imposes few requirements on the substance of a collective agreement, though the exceptions are significant and expanding. For many years, Canadian laws have effectively prohibited strikes during the term of a collective agreement, while also requiring that each agreement contain a grievance procedure and a mechanism for the final resolution of mid-contract disputes. More recently, statutes have added requirements that the parties bargain over technological change and that management grant union security clauses. The Federal labour code and a few provinces also provide rights of consultation for non-union workers. Separate legislation exists federally and, in eight out of the ten provinces, for employees in the public sector. These statutes normally apply to government employees and occasionally to quasi-government workers such as teachers or hospital workers. They are patterned after private-sector labour relations Acts except for two broad areas. The scope of bargaining is restricted by previous civil service personnel practices and broader public policy considerations. Technological change is also often outside bargaining. In a majority of provinces, there are restrictions on the right to strike of at least some public employees. Police and firefighters are the most common categories affected by such limits, but there is no other common pattern of restrictions. Employee groups without the right to strike have access to a system of compulsory arbitration. While a statute requires arbitration, the parties normally can determine the procedures to be followed and choose the arbitrator.

Although public sector collective bargaining has been an established feature of Canadian industrial relations since the 1960s, the conduct and results of bargaining was restricted in 1982 and 1983. Governments in several jurisdictions sought to combat the prolonged recession by reducing the size of their expenditures. A politically acceptable means was to cut the number and compensation of public employees (at least in real terms). Many governments chose to make these cuts by legislation, rather than through bargaining, leaving public-sector unions with very little to negotiate. By 1987, however, all jurisdictions had removed formal restrictions on collective bargaining, though spending limitations remained. Early in 1991, the Federal government and five provinces introduced new restrictions on public-sector compensation increases, again in response to declining revenues caused by a serious recession. These serious economic conditions and the decline in labour militancy and negotiated wage increases, limited the practical impact of these policies.

The processes of industrial relations

The major formal process of Canadian industrial relations is collective bargaining, with union power based on the ability to strike. Joint consultation is sporadic and generally confined to issues such as safety; although, in some areas, these are quality-of-working-life activities which consist of consultation in the work area on production methods. Other formal systems of worker participation in management are rare. Arbitration of interest disputes is largely confined to the public sector.

Collective bargaining

Collective bargaining in Canada occurs on a decentralised basis. The most common negotiating unit is a single establishment–single union, followed by multi-establishment–single union. Taken together these categories account for almost 90 per cent of all units and over 80 per cent of all employees. Company-wide bargaining is common only in the Federal jurisdiction, where it occurs in railways, air lines and telecommunications. The importance of provincial legislation and practice impedes the formation of wider bargaining units. However, geographic concentration or the policies of the parties in industries such as automobiles have resulted in *de facto* company-wide, multi-provincial bargaining units. In response to increased union militancy, employer associations expanded in the 1970s, especially in the construction industry, and contracted again in the 1980s as union pressures subsided.

Despite the decentralised structure of negotiations, bargaining often follows patterns. Although there are no national patterns in bargaining, one or two key industries in each region usually influence provincial negotiations. In larger provinces, such as Ontario and Quebec, heavy industry patterns from steel or autos tend to predominate.

The results of bargaining are detailed, complex, collective bargaining agreements. Few of the terms are the result of the law, and negotiated provisions typically include: pay, union security, hours of work, vacations and holidays, layoff provisions and miscellaneous fringe benefits. Grievance procedures are a legal requirement and invariably conclude with binding arbitration. In addition, there are often supplementary agreements covering work rules for specific situations or work areas. Seniority provisions are prominent features in almost all collective agreements, covering layoffs, promotions or transfers, with varying weights given to length of service or ability.

In the workplace, agreements regulate behaviour rather closely. Negotiated work rules are numerous and many parties are litigious, so rights arbitrations are frequent and legalistic. In turn, this emphasis on precise written contracts often permeates labour–management relationships.

Another outcome of collective bargaining is labour stoppages, the most controversial feature of Canadian industrial relations. In four key industries Canada generally loses more working days due to industrial disputes than any other country discussed in this book (see Appendix). There have been frequent allegations, never really proven, that the nation's economic growth has been seriously hindered by labour unrest. These concerns are especially notable because Canadian society generally has low levels of social conflict.

Historically, strike levels have moved in cycles. There was a wave of unrest early in the twentieth century, another around the First World War, a third beginning in the late 1930s and a fourth in the 1970s (see Table 4.3). By international standards, the two salient characteristics of Canadian strikes are their length and the concentration of time lost in a few disputes. Involvement is medium to low (7 to 12 per cent of union members annually), and the size of strikes is not especially large (350–450 workers per strike, on average). The largest five or six strikes typically account for 35 per cent of all time lost. In recent years, the average duration of strikes has been 10–20 days. These characteristics have not been explained fully, but may be due to the existence of major companies, such as General Motors or International Nickel, and large international unions taking strikes at individual production units incapable of inflicting major economic loss on the parent organisations.

Mediation has long been a common feature of Canadian collective bargaining. Two models currently exist. A tripartite board may be appointed and given authority to report publicly on a dispute; alternatively, single mediators function without the power to issue a report. In most jurisdictions participation. in mediation is a precondition for a legal strike. Although elements of compulsion have diminished, over half of all collective agreements are achieved with some type of third-party intervention.

Outside of the public sector, compulsory arbitration of interest disputes is rare. However, special legislation to end particular dis-

Table 4.3   Strikes and lock-outs

Year	Number	Workers involved	Days lost (1000)	Average length	% of working time
1966–70	572	291 109	5709	19.6	0.35
1971–75	856	473 795	7309	15.4	0.38
1976–80	1105	618 743	7824	12.6	0.35
1981	1048	338 548	8878	26.2	0.37
1982	677	444 302	5795	13.0	0.25
1983	645	329 309	4444	13.5	0.19
1984	576	184 929	3890	21.0	0.18
1985	829	162 231	3125	19.2	0.13
1986	657	483 615	7109	14.7	0.28
1987	655	273 058	3669	13.4	0.15
1988	549	206 787	4905	23.7	0.18
1989	630	444 551	3724	8.4	0.13
1990	579	270 512	5682	18.8	0.18
1991	460	249 001	2580	10.4	0.09

Source: Labour Canada *Bureau of Labour Information* unpublished data.

putes is not uncommon in public sector or essential service disputes. Back-to-work laws are extremely unpopular with the labour movement and have contributed to the politicisation of labour relations in some areas. In the public sector, interest arbitration is common. Arbitrators are usually chosen on an *ad hoc* basis from among judges, lawyers or academics. The process is legalistic without the use of sophisticated economic data. When collective bargaining first appeared in the public sector, there were concerns that compulsory arbitration would cause bargaining to atrophy. Experience of the 1970s demonstrated that collective bargaining and compulsory arbitration can coexist successfully, though the availability of arbitration does reduce the incidence of negotiated settlements.

Issues of current and future importance

For most observers, the most important issue in Canadian industrial relations has been time lost due to strikes. In 1982, the incidence of strikes fell sharply as the economy suffered a severe recession and unemployment rose, though the number of strikers declined much less. Time lost and the number of strikes remained low throughout the 1980s and early 1990s. Despite public concern about strikes, there have been few efforts to deal with their underlying causes or even to understand them better. Certainly, the fragmented structure of bargaining is one factor that contributes to the pattern of strikes. Yet the causes of fragmentation lie in the nation's governmental structure and politics. Provincial governments resist virtually any effort to limit their powers and the paramount importance of Quebec separatism on the national political agenda has restrained any impulses of the Federal government to extend its authority over economic issues. Employers traditionally prefer to seek political solutions rather than work actively to improve industrial relations.

During the 1970s changes in the world economy affected Canada's regions quite differently. Energy-consuming and manufacturing areas in Ontario, Quebec and the eastern provinces suffered, while the western half of the country generally benefited as energy-producing and resource-rich areas. The recession of the early 1980s tended to reverse this pattern, and Ontario led the nation in its economic recovery. These changes affected industrial relations, but Canada lacked any national institutions for dealing with them. Labour, management and government were all divided by regional, economic, political and language lines. As the economy recovered, these divisions seemed to increase.

Governments have attempted to deal with labour unrest in a

variety of ways. One model is the encouragement of consultation. During the 1970s there were a number of initiatives directed at establishing tripartite systems of consultation as practised in Western Europe. None of these initiatives had any lasting impact.

The Federal government later required employers planning to terminate 50 or more employees to establish a joint planning committee, half of whom were to be elected by the employees, in an attempt to eliminate the need for redundancies or to minimise the impact of redundancies on individuals. Impasses within the committee are resolved by arbitration. In several provinces employers are required to form joint committees to administer safety and health programs. Since experience with these institutions is still limited, it is difficult to predict their impact or extension. They represent a sharp departure from the North American traditions of government limiting its role in the workplace to the promulgation of minimum standards and the maintenance of a sharp distinction between the unionised and non-union sectors in matters of collective representation. The labour movement remains suspicious of legislation that might undermine its monopoly of representation, and few of these committees have functioned well. The Federal labour ministry sponsored several 'sectoral committees' in the 1980s. These joint labour–management bodies were established in industries such as automobile manufacture, basic steel production and forest products to advise the government on active staffing policies, development (or maintenance) of foreign markets or planning for redundancies. These committees are too new and small to have had a significant impact on other industrial relations processes.

A second model for dealing with labour unrest has been to impose legislative controls on the exercise of union power. One province enacted a new labour relations act along such lines and two others considered similar policies. As in post-1979 Britain, government in these jurisdictions is more anxious to legislate against labour than most employers, so the long-run prospects for this model are not good.

Constitutional protections

Another issue arises from the Charter of Rights proclaimed as part of the new Canadian Constitution in 1982. Previously, an 1867 Act of the British Parliament had established the structure of Canadian government, and Canada relied on the British tradition of an unwritten constitution and the supremacy of Parliament to protect individual and collective rights. Several provisions of the new Charter with potential implications for industrial relations were included without much debate. Thus, their impact will not become clear until complaints are reviewed by the courts. These rights include: freedom of association, freedom of speech, the right to pursue a livelihood in any province, and protection against discrimination on the basis of age, sex and race. It is almost inevitable that the courts will apply some of the Charter's protections to industrial relations.

Several issues appear likely to arise. Restrictions on the scope of bargaining and the right to strike that governments impose on their own employees may be challenged as a violation of the freedom of association. Employer communications during a union organising campaign may fall under the protection of freedom of speech, thereby strengthening management's hand in anti-union campaigns. The earliest judicial decisions under the Charter did not upset existing industrial relations practices, however.

Whatever the outcome of these or other issues arising from the Charter, an almost inevitable result will be increased litigation and the remaking of certain long-standing policies entrenched in labour law and the parties' practices.

Political role of the labour movement

Although many Canadian unions and union leaders are active in partisan politics, the labour movement has been unable to define a political role for itself. Officially, the CLC supports the NDP, but two problems beset the parties in this alliance. Federally, the NDP has not been successful in raising its share of the popular vote (and legislative seats) beyond about 20 per cent. The CLC is thus left to deal with governments whose election it has opposed. The tensions created by this situation have hampered efforts to establish mechanisms for consultation on economic policies.

Secondly, the labour movement has been unable to deliver large blocs of votes to the NDP, though financial contributions and the diversion of staff to the party are invaluable. As a consequence, when the NDP has governed provincially, it has not been a 'labour' party in the British or Australian modes.

The practical result of these problems is that the CLC has vacillated between wholehearted commitment to the NDP and a more independent posture as a workers' lobbyist to governments of any party. To further complicate the situation, most public-sector unions avoid political endorsements and the CFL is strongly apolitical. Provincially, the picture is brighter for the NDP. In 1992, the party controlled three provincial governments. In each of these jurisdictions there were legislative changes beneficial to organised labour. Historically, innovations have spread to non-NDP provinces. Labour is being consulted in the formulation of a variety of social and economic policies.

The founders of the NDP had the British Labour Party as a model, but were unsuccessful in achieving their goal federally. The American tradition of labour acting as an independent political force has adherents in Canada, despite limited relevance in a parliamentary political system. Despite its recent success provincially, the NDP has never demonstrated a capacity to govern for more than five years. It thus appears that the labour movement will continue to search for an effective political role.

Conclusion

Industrial relations seldom have been a major issue in Canadian life, but the system is caught up in the central concerns of the nation— the division of powers between provinces and the national government, the relative importance of the public and private sectors, relations with the USA and other trading partners and economic performance. The outcomes of each of these issues will be in doubt for the remainder of the century. While industrial relations will contribute to the resolution of these issues, the future direction of the system is likely to be determined by broader trends in Canadian life. But decisions on economic policy, changes in industrial structure and a new constitution will ensure that flux and unrest in the Canadian industrial relations system remain high in the future.

A chronology of Canadian labour–management relations

1825	Strike by carpenters in Lachine, Quebec for higher wages.
1825–60	Numerous isolated local unions developed.
1867	Confederation—Canada became an independent nation.
1872	Unions exempted from criminal and civil liabilities imposed by British law.
1873	Local trade assemblies formed Canadian Labour Union, first national labour central.
1886	Trades and Labour Congress (TLC) formed by 'international' craft unions.
1902	'Berlin Declaration', TLC shunned unions not affiliated to international unions.
1906	Canadian chapter of Industrial Workers of the World founded.
1907	Canadian Industrial Dispute Investigation Act—first national labour legislation, emphasised conciliation.

1919	Winnipeg General Strike—most complete general strike in North American history.
1921	Canadian and Catholic Confederation of Labour formed, Quebec federation of Catholic unions.
1925	British courts ruled that the Canadian Constitution put most labour legislation within provincial jurisdiction.
1927	All-Canadian Congress of Labour founded.
1935	Following the National Labor Relations (Wagner) Act in the USA, there were demands for similar Canadian legislation.
1937	Auto workers strike at General Motors, Oshawa, Ontario, established industrial unionism in Canada.
1939	TLC expelled Canadian affiliates of US Congress of Industrial Organizations (CIO).
1940	CIO affiliates joined All-Canadian Congress of Labour to form the Canadian Congress of Labour (CCL).
1943	Order-in-Council P.C. 1003 guaranteed unions' right to organise (combining principles of US Wagner Act with compulsory conciliation).
1949	Miners in Asbestos, Quebec, struck in defence of law, initiating 'quiet revolution' in Quebec.
1956	Merger of TLC and CCL to form the Canadian Labour Congress (CLC).
1960	Canadian and Catholic Confederation of Labour severed ties with the Catholic church to become the Confederation of National Trade Unions.
1967	Federal government gave its employees bargaining rights; other jurisdictions followed suit.
1975	Federal government imposed first peacetime wage and price controls.
1982	Construction unions withdrew from CLC to form Canadian Federation of Labour.
1987	Charter of Rights and Freedoms (enacted in 1982) took effect.
1991	Legislated pay freeze imposed on Federal government employees.
1992	Major revisions to labour legislation in Ontario and British Columbia, making use of replacement workers illegal.

5   Industrial relations in Australia
Edward M. Davis and Russell D. Lansbury

Like Canada, Australia was colonised by the British, has a wealth of mineral and energy resources and is sparsely populated. Australia has a population of 17 million people and a GDP of $298 billion. Australia has developed a services sector which is almost as predominant as in the USA and Canada. Thus, out of its total civilian employment of 8.4 million people, 69 per cent are employed in services, 25 per cent in industry and less than 6 per cent in agriculture (see Appendix). However, Australia's economy remains highly dependent on raw materials and rural products which comprised 46 per cent of exports in 1988 (Gregory 1991).

Strong economic growth in the middle of the 1980s and a reduction in real wages enabled the labour market to expand and reduced the rate of unemployment. However, deteriorating economic conditions resulted in an unemployment rate above 10 per cent in 1992. Having fallen to 2.6 per cent in 1984, the Consumer Price Index also rose to 8.0 per cent by 1989–90. With a tightening of government economic policy and a sharp downturn in 1990–91, the Consumer Price Index fell to 5.3 per cent in 1990–91 and is expected to be less than 2 per cent by 1992–93. Both the rate of wage increases and days lost through industrial disputes also declined over the last decade, although in the case of disputes, there were some sporadic outbursts of discontent.

Unlike the other three English-speaking countries discussed in this book, Australia has had a Labor government in office since 1983. It is the longest-serving Australian Labor government at the national level. The Federal parliament remains the formal and symbolic focus for Australian political democracy, but the Australian executive and legislature are also particularly important, as are the six state governments.

The legal, political and economic environment

Australia was founded in 1901. When the former colonial governments agreed to establish the Commonwealth of Australia, they insisted that the new Federal government should have only a limited jurisdiction over industrial relations. Thus, under the Constitution of the Commonwealth of Australia (1901), Federal government was empowered to make industrial laws only with respect to 'conciliation and arbitration for the prevention and settlement of disputes extending beyond the limits of any one State' (Section 51, para. 35).

Employers were initially hostile to the Commonwealth Court of Conciliation and Arbitration (the forerunner to the Australian Industrial Relations Commission), established under the Conciliation and Arbitration Act (1904), since it forced them to recognise unions registered under the Act and empowered these unions to make claims on behalf of all employees within an industry. Having earlier rejected the notion of compulsory arbitration, the unions changed their stance after some disastrous defeats during the strikes of the 1890s. Under the 1904 Act they could force employers to court even if they were unwilling to negotiate, and once the court made an award (that is, ruled on pay or other terms of employment), its provisions were legally enforceable. Despite their initial opposition to the system, employers soon found that they could use arbitration procedures to their advantage and generally supported the system (see Macintyre & Mitchell 1989). The establishment of systems of conciliation and arbitration at the Federal and state levels marked an important departure from the British-style industrial relations which had characterised Australia before the 1890s. That British traditions played a large part in Australian industrial relations was unsurprising. British law and notions of unionism were major imports in the nineteenth century, when the foundations of Australia's contemporary industrial relations system were established.

The system of arbitration includes both Federal and state industrial tribunals. Until 1956, the Commonwealth Court of Conciliation and Arbitration carried out both arbitral and judicial functions. Since then, the industrial division of the Federal Court has administered the judicial provisions of the Act while the Australian Industrial Relations Commission (AIRC), as it is now known (hereafter referred to as the Commission), has carried out non-judicial functions. Federal awards which cover approximately a third of the workforce tend to set the pattern for all other tribunals, so that a high degree of uniformity has emerged despite the multiplicity of tribunals. Although the Commission is empowered to intervene only in disputes extending to more than one state, most important cases fulfil this requirement or can be made to do so. Either party to a dispute may refer a case to the Commission, or it may intervene of its own accord 'in the public interest'. Thus, the powers of the Commission have become more extensive than originally intended. Some states have expressed concern at the drift of control to the Federal level; others have been in favour.

In 1988 the Labor government replaced the Conciliation and Arbitration Act 1904 with the Industrial Relations Act 1988. The new Act was similar in approach in many ways to its predecessor. Under it, all Federal unions are required to register with the arbitration authorities (represented by the Industrial Registrar) in order to gain access to the tribunal and to enjoy full corporate status under the law. Registration requirements operate for large employers and employers' associations, but registration is more significant for unions since it establishes the conditions for union security. The Act prescribes that a union will not be registered if there is already one in existence to which employees can 'conveniently belong'. While this has helped to reduce inter-union disputes, it has also inhibited the development of new unions and helped preserve some whose principal industry has declined. The 1988 Act stipulated that unions seeking registration must have a minimum of 1000 members and be industry-based. The intent was to deter the further proliferation of small, craft-based unions. Existing unions with under 1000 members must make a case before the Registrar in a bid to maintain their registration.

The Federal government moved to amend the Act in 1990, increasing the minimum size of Federal unions to 10 000 members. There was substantial opposition to this bold proposal. Indeed the then Confederation of Australian Industry lodged a complaint with the International Labour Organisation claiming that the proposal breached the principle of freedom of association, and in any case could not be justified on economic or other grounds. The amendments took effect from 1991 and existing smaller unions will have to meet this requirement in March 1993. However, it will still be possible for smaller unions to establish that special circumstances justify their continued registration.

Since Federation, conservative political parties have generally dominated Federal government. During their intermittent periods in office at the Federal level, Labor governments made some significant changes in the economic management of the nation and were more sympathetic to union interests than their conservative counterparts. However, once in government, most political parties have tended to favour protectionist policies. This has resulted in the creation of a manufacturing sector which has produced goods for a small domestic market behind high tariff barriers. These barriers, however, have not prevented the decline of manufacturing employment which has resulted from a combination of structural and technological changes in the Australian economy. The tariff policy was originally designed to insulate the Australian economy from cheap imported goods and provide employment for an expanding labour force. It also enabled wages to be determined by tribunals more on social and equity grounds than in accordance with productivity and market forces. Many protected industries, anticipating the chill winds of unrestricted competition, tenaciously lobbied governments to retain significant tariff levels. The move of the Whitlam Labor government (1972–75) to reduce tariffs by 25 per cent 'at a single stroke', was strongly criticised both by Australian unions and employers as having led to increased levels of unemployment, especially in industries vulnerable to overseas competition.

The Federal Labor government, since 1983, has sought to 'phase in' tariff reductions and stimulate competition. The lengths to which government policy should go to encourage competition has remained a matter of debate. In addition, while some have advocated the rapid dismantling of protective barriers, others have argued for a more selective and cautious approach.

Industrial relations in Australia are influenced by the nature of its mixed economy. There is a heavy concentration of power in a relatively small number of large enterprises. As in comparable countries there is a very uneven distribution of employees across organisations. The comprehensive Australian Workplace Industrial Relations Survey found that the largest 1 per cent of workplaces, each employing 500 or more employees, accounted for 24 per cent of all employees. At the other end of the scale workplaces with between 5 and 19 employees, representing 75 per cent of all workplaces, accounted for 23 per cent of all employees (Callus et al. 1991:19). Looking at the workforce from a different angle, governments at the Federal, state and local levels employ approximately one-quarter of the total labour force and have an important impact on industrial relations practices.

The major parties

Employers' associations

The early growth of trade unions in Australia encouraged the development of employers' associations and led them to place greater emphasis on industrial relations functions than their counterparts in some other countries. Numerous employers' associations have a direct role or interest in industrial relations (Plowman 1989). However, there is great variation in the size and complexity of employers' associations from small, single-industry bodies to large organisations which attempt to cover all employers within a particular state. In 1977, the Confederation of Australian Industry (CAI) was established as a single national employers' body, almost 50 years after the formation of the Australian Council of Trade Unions (ACTU). In 1983, a group of large employers set up the Business Council of Australia (BCA) partly as a result of their dissatisfaction with the ability of the CAI to service the needs of its large and diverse membership. Membership of the BCA comprises the chief executive officers of each member company, which has given it a high profile and significant authority when it makes pronouncements on matters such as industrial relations.

Since the mid-1980s there have been several important departures from the CAI. These included large affiliates such as the Metal Trades Industry Association (MTIA) (1987) and the Australian Chamber of Manufacturers (ACM) (1989). One repercussion has been employers airing their different viewpoints at events such as National Wage Case hearings. In 1992 the CAI attempted to present a more united front and to attract back former affiliates by merging with the Australian Chamber of Commerce to form a new organisation, the Australian Chamber of Commerce and Industry (ACCI). The unions have generally appeared more united in recent years under the umbrella of the ACTU.

Trade unions

The establishment of the arbitration system in the early years of this century encouraged the rapid growth of unions and employers' associations. By 1921, approximately 50 per cent of the Australian labour force was unionised. Union density has fluctuated; during the depression of the early 1930s it dropped to little over 40 per cent. The 1940s witnessed a steady increase in density and a peak of 65 per cent was achieved in 1953. Surveys of the labour force conducted by the Australian Bureau of Statistics suggest that union density has suffered a steep decline since the mid-1970s. In 1976, 51 per cent of all employees were in unions (56 per cent males; 43 per cent females). By 1990 this had dropped to 41 per cent (45 per cent males; 35 per cent females) (Australian Bureau of Statistics 1990).

Factors contributing to the fall in union density have included the relative decline in employment in manufacturing, a bastion for unions, and strong growth in the more poorly-unionised services sector (approximately 68 per cent of the workforce). Significant growth in part-time and casual employment, also poorly unionised, has been an additional factor. The sharp fall in coverage has sparked a vigorous debate on reform within the movement (see below). The typical Australian union is small by international standards but varies considerably in size from fewer than 50 members to 200 000. Around 34 of Australia's unions enrol 30 000 or more members and this represents approximately 73 per cent of total union membership. As in Britain, unionism originally developed on a craft basis but with the growth of manufacturing, general and industrial unions became more common. The basic unit of organisation for the Australian union is the branch, which may cover an entire state or a large district within a state. Plant-level or workplace organisation tends to be informal, but shop-floor committees and shop steward organisations have developed more rapidly in recent years, in both blue- and white-collar sectors (see Peetz 1990).

Nevertheless, unionism in Australia tends to be comparatively weak at the workplace level, reflecting the reliance of many unions on the arbitration system rather than enterprise-level bargaining to achieve their objectives (see Lansbury & Macdonald 1992). The Australian Workplace Industrial Relations Survey revealed that union members were present in only 43 per cent of workplaces with five or more employees (Callus et al. 1991:48–53). However, this proportion rose to 80 per cent among workplaces with 20 or more employees. Yet, as Callus et al. argue, neither the presence of a union nor the proportion of the workforce which is organised give a very clear account of the role or impact of unions in the workplace. While two-thirds of unionised workplaces had one or more delegates, in one-third of workplaces there was no workplace union representative at all. Callus et al. drew a distinction between 'active' and 'inactive' workplace trade unionism. Confirming the weakness of unions in the workplace, only 26 per cent of workplaces in the survey had 'active' unions, where delegates spent more than one hour per week on activities other than recruiting members and where evidence of activity existed in the form of a union committee or regular membership meetings.

The main confederation for both manual and non-manual unions is the ACTU. It was formed in 1927 and currently embraces approximately 125 unions and covers around 95 per cent of all trade unionists. The ACTU expanded considerably following its merger with two other confederations which formerly represented white-collar unions. The Australian Council of Salaried and Professional Associations (ACSPA) joined the ACTU in 1979 and the Council of Australian Government Employee Organisations (CAGEO) followed in 1981. The ACTU's considerable influence over its affiliates was reflected at ACTU Congresses and Conferences throughout the 1980s and early 1990s which saw Executive recommendations, almost without fail, endorsed by affiliates (Davis 1992). Officers of the ACTU also play key roles in the presentation of the unions' case before the Australian Industrial Relations Commission and in the conduct of important industrial disputes.

As in the UK and USA, then, there is now only one main central union confederation. This is in contrast to many western European countries which have several confederations. Nevertheless, in each of the states, trades and labour councils also play a significant role in industrial relations. Although the state trades and labour councils are formally branches of the ACTU, they generally have a much longer history than the ACTU and display some independence in the way they conduct their affairs.

By the early 1990s Australian unions were in the midst of an extraordinary period of change. Encouraged by ACTU policy and spurred on by Federal legislation, unions sought to implement far-reaching reform. The goal has been the restructuring of unions into some 20 industry or occupational unions. The ACTU President reported in 1991 that 'dozens of amalgamations' were underway. The target for unions is the establishment of larger, better-resourced unions, better able to serve their members and assist them in workplace bargaining.

Government

As the role of Federal government in Australian industrial relations is restricted by the Constitution, it has commonly used fiscal, monetary and other tools to influence industrial relations. It has also sought to take advantage of the High Court's interpretation of the Constitution in order to extend its influence in the industrial arena. The Court's interpretations of the Federal government's powers in industrial relations, however, have varied over the years. This has given rise to inconsistencies and uncertainties and has often served to restrict the powers of the Industrial Relations Commission. The existence of a bicameral legislature, in which the Senate has the power to review, amend or reject Bills proposed by the House of Representatives, checks the powers of the Federal government when it lacks a majority in the Senate. This has frequently been the case.

The lack of legislative power, particularly over prices and incomes, has frustrated Federal governments of all political persuasions. During the period of the Fraser Liberal–National Party government (1975–83) there were occasional strong exchanges between the Federal government and the Commission. For instance, in 1977 the Fraser government argued strenuously that its economic policy would be prejudiced unless the Commission's decisions on wage adjustments were framed in accordance with government wishes. The Commission responded that it was 'not an arm of the Government's economic policy [but] an independent body . . . required under the Act to act according to equity, good conscience and the substantial merits of the case' (Isaac 1977:22).

The 1972–75 Whitlam Labor government sought to establish pace-setting conditions for its employees and encouraged the extension of union coverage. The election of the Conservative government led by Malcolm Fraser in 1975 brought considerable change. The conditions of public servants began to fall behind those prevailing in the private sector, and legislation was introduced which strengthened the ability of the government as an employer to lay-off or dismiss workers at will. A further measure was the cancellation of the system whereby members' dues in the two largest public sector unions had been deducted from wages. The post-1983 Labor government repealed those laws regarded as least palatable by the unions and restored the automatic payroll deduction of union dues. Public-sector employees failed, however, to regain their place as pace-setters. Indeed, experience during the 1980s suggested a growing disparity in remuneration for public- and private-sector employees.

A feature of industrial relations over the last decade has been the strength of ties between senior ministers in the Federal Labor government and senior union officials. Contributing factors are that Bob Hawke, Labor Prime Minister from 1983–91, was a former President of the ACTU and two of the three Ministers for Industrial Relations during this period were former ACTU officials. Paul Keating, who launched a successful challenge for the leadership of the Labor Party and became Prime Minister in December 1991, is also well known for his ties to the ACTU. The ACTU's influence in government decision making is therefore set to remain strong. Labor's loss of office and the election of a Liberal–National Parties Coalition would see a sharp reduction in union influence at this level.

Industrial relations processes

Although Federal awards have precedence, the state systems of industrial relations are still very important. Problems arising from overlapping jurisdiction of the state and Federal tribunals have long been a source of concern to reformers, but changes have been difficult to achieve. Since the late 1980s, however, agreements have been reached between the state and Federal governments on the dual appointment of Heads and other members of the state industrial tribunals to the Federal Commission. This is an important step to the possible future development of an integrated national industrial relations system. The Australian system of arbitration is compulsory in two senses. First, once engaged, it requires the parties in dispute to submit to a mandatory procedure for presenting their arguments. Second, tribunal awards are binding on the parties in dispute. Awards specify minimum standards of pay and conditions which an employer must meet or else face legal penalties. It is necessary to distinguish between the formal provisions of the arbitration system and the way it works in practice. In reality, there is a considerable amount of direct negotiation between the parties. Agreements directly negotiated between employers and unions may co-exist with or take the place of arbitrated awards. Once these agreements have been ratified by the Commission, they are known as 'consent awards' and may deal comprehensively with the terms and conditions of work in particular workplaces or supplement existing agreements.

Following a survey of 60 major unions, Niland (1976) reported that three-quarters of the respondents claimed to be using direct negotiation or bargaining procedures in dispute resolution. Some 30 per cent were negotiating solely within the conciliation and arbitration framework, 20 per cent were operating completely outside the system, while 50 per cent were using a mixed approach. These findings provided support for an earlier study by Yerbury and Isaac (1971) which reported a substantial increase in the relative importance of directly negotiated agreements at both the Federal and state levels. Yerbury and Isaac noted the emergence of a 'peculiar hybrid of quasi-collective bargaining' which, they argued, could well become the dominant feature of industrial relations in Australia. During the late 1980s there were moves towards greater industry and enterprise bargaining within limits set by the Commission. Decisions made at the centre were designed to encourage a more decentralised focus or 'managed decentralism' (McDonald & Rimmer 1989). The term points to the continuing hybrid nature of the Australian industrial relations system.

The settlement of disputes

One of the principal motivations behind the introduction of compulsory arbitration was to render strikes unnecessary. The 'rule of law' provided under arbitration was supposed to displace the 'barbarous expedient of strike action'. For many years the Conciliation and Arbitration Act contained a provision making strike activity illegal and subject to penalties. Although this provision was removed in 1930, Australian workers have never been granted the right to strike and remain liable to dismissal and action for damages incurred by employers. It is interesting to note that some of the proponents for reforming the Australian industrial relations system in the direction of US style collective bargaining have baulked at the 'right to strike' being granted to Australian workers.

Another sanction, used sparingly by tribunals, has been to deregister a union which has acted in defiance of a tribunal order. Since deregistration has tended to be difficult and complex, tribunals have generally hoped that its threat would be sufficient. Threats, though, made little impact on the Builders Labourers' Federation, deregistered in 1986; its members were quickly absorbed by other unions leaving only the shell of a once powerful union.

One of the main effects of arbitration has been to shorten the duration of strikes but to increase their frequency. Although international comparisons of strike statistics are notoriously difficult (see ch. 11 and Appendix), the Australian experience is illuminating. During the 1960s and 1970s it was among those countries with a relatively high number of strike days per 1000 people employed. For instance, in a study by Creigh and Makeham (1982) of 20 OECD countries, Australia came sixth with an annual average of 675 working days lost per 1000 employees between 1970 and 1979. The five countries with a higher strike propensity were Italy, Iceland, Canada, the Irish Republic and Spain. Close behind Australia were the UK and the USA. A relatively adversarial style of industrial relations prevailed in Australia, in comparison with countries such as Japan, Germany and Sweden, which recorded many fewer strike days each year per 1000 employees.

Since 1983, the Federal Labor government has presided over a more peaceful industrial relations climate. In the period 1982–87, compared with 1978–82, Australia's record of industrial disputes improved considerably. During the 1980s, average working days lost through disputes per 1000 employees were halved. Since the end of 1982, no calendar year has seen working days lost exceed 300 per 1000 employees per year and in the main, annual averages have ranged between 200 and 250 (Australian Bureau of Statistics 1990). Beggs and Chapman (1987) have argued that while changing macroeconomic conditions played a part in this absolute and relative decline in the impact of industrial stoppages, so too did the ALP–ACTU Accord (see later in this chapter).

The Australian Workplace Industrial Relations Survey further undermined the popular impression that Australian workplaces are stricken with conflict. It revealed that nearly three-quarters of workplaces with more than four employees had never experienced any type of industrial action (Callus et al. 1991). When launching the publication of the survey, the then Minister for Industrial Relations, Senator Peter Cook, commented:

> In the year preceding the survey (1988–89), only 12 per cent of workplaces had been involved in some form of industrial action. In most cases, these were stop-work meetings, involving information sessions and the like as well as stoppages per se. Moreover, whether one relies on the account of managers or union representatives, management–employee relations are generally perceived as reasonably harmonious. (Cook 1991:4)

The BCA has been less sanguine. In a survey of BCA member companies (which represent larger firms), the National Institute of Labour Studies reported that, during the twelve month period prior to its survey in 1988, two-thirds of establishments were affected by stoppages of less than a day's duration, with 50 per cent affected by stoppages of a day or more. It should be noted, however, that BCA member companies generally have larger than average workplaces.

There are other expressions of industrial conflict besides industrial stoppages. These include: accidents, absenteeism, labour turnover, working to rule, bans and limitations (see Hyman 1989). There is much less comparative data available on such forms of conflict. Yet there is some evidence to suggest an increase in the use of bans during the past decade. A ban is defined as 'an organised refusal by employees to undertake certain work, to use certain equipment or to work with certain people' (Sheehan & Worland 1986:21). One of the reasons put forward for this is that 'bans minimise loss of pay and make it more difficult for employers to apply legal sanctions against unions' (Frenkel 1990:14).

The term 'silent strike' has been used to describe such phenomena as labour turnover, absenteeism and even industrial sabotage. The Australian Workplace Industrial Relations Survey reported that voluntary labour turnover (thereby excluding dismissals, retirement and retrenchments) was 19 per cent and that an average of 4.5 per cent of employees was absent each day. This compares with a rate of absence due to strikes of about 0.23 per cent. The Australian Automotive Industry Council has estimated that turnover and absenteeism adds about A\$850 to the ex-factory cost of an automobile manufactured in Australia (Automotive Industry Council 1990:1). These statistics help to place strikes and their costs in perspective.

The determination of wages

The arbitration system has led to a relatively centralised wages system. This has been achieved by increasing the influence of the

Federal Commission over key wage issues despite constitutional limitations. Its predecessor, the Commonwealth Court of Conciliation and Arbitration, initially became involved in fixing a minimum wage in 1907 when it described the 'basic wage' as intended to meet 'the normal needs of an average employee, regarded as a human being living in a civilised community'. The basic wage was set at a level sufficient to cover the minimum needs of a single income family unit of five and became the accepted wage for unskilled work. The custom of wage differentials (margins) for skills, developed in the 1920s, based largely on historical differentials in the metal and engineering trades.

The Court thus began to regulate wages and differentials through its decisions on the 'basic wage' and 'margins' at National Wage Case hearings. These are a much publicised ritual and occur at regular intervals, with usually one National Wage Decision per year. The employers, unions (through the ACTU) and governments (at Federal and state levels) each make submissions to the Commission, which later hands down a decision. This determines changes to wages and conditions which apply to nearly all employees throughout Australia. In 1967, the Commission ended the system of basic wage and margins in favour of a 'total' award. It also introduced the concept of a national minimum wage, representing the lowest wage permissible for a standard work week by any employee.

During the early 1970s, the Commission sought to adjust the relative structure of award wages in different industries and to limit over-award increases. But by 1973–74, the contribution of increases determined at National Wage Cases to total wage increases had declined to approximately 20 per cent as unions bargained directly with employers for large over-award payments (Howard 1977). Collective bargaining had therefore become the dominant force in wage increases, its leading settlements being generally extended to the whole economy (Isaac 1977:14). Faced with both rapidly rising inflation and unemployment, the Labor government moved to restore the authority of the Commission (Lansbury 1978). In 1974, both the Federal government and the ACTU asked the Commission to introduce automatic cost-of-living adjustments to wages, to offset the effect of increased prices (i.e. full wage indexation). Non-Labor state governments and private employers opposed this approach.

In 1975, the Commission issued guidelines on the principles and procedures of the new wage-fixing system. Under these guidelines, no wage increase could be granted without the permission of the Commission (Yerbury 1980a). In December 1975, however, the newly-elected Conservative government, led by Malcolm Fraser, opposed full wage indexation mainly on the grounds of the depressed state of the economy. It also argued that the unions had failed to comply with the Commission's indexation guidelines. Between 1975 and 1981, partial rather than full indexation was the norm. In other words, the wage increases determined by the Commission were regularly below the increases in the Consumer Price Index. The system of wage indexation was abandoned by the Commission in 1981 (Dabscheck 1989). A round of direct negotiations followed, similar in style to the collective bargaining round of 1974. Some very large pay increases were won and these began to flow-on to other sectors. At the same time, there was a sharp fall in demand for goods and services and unemployment rose. The Fraser government then initiated a 'wage pause' within the Federal public service and successfully sought its general implementation by the Commission.

The Accord

The election of the Hawke Labor government in 1983 returned the Commission to a powerful role in wage determination. The Accord agreed between the Labor Party and the ACTU included a return to centralised wage determination with wage adjustments for price movements and, at longer intervals, for movements in national productivity (Lansbury 1985). In late 1983 the Commission agreed to reintroduce wage indexation. Among the principles announced by the Commission, however, was the requirement that each union pledge to make no 'extra claims' in return for receiving wage indexation.

To the surprise of many commentators, most unions accepted this condition and there has since been little movement in wages beyond the nationally determined pay rates. Those unions seeking to press for wage increases outside the Accord have found themselves isolated and their campaigns have usually proved unsuccessful. Prominent examples have included the Plumbers and Gasfitters Employees Union (PGEU) in 1986–87 and the spectacular case of the Australian Federation of Air Pilots (AFAP) in 1989. The PGEU found itself confronted with legal armory used by employers to force the lifting of specified bans on building sites. This resulted in substantial damages being incurred by the union and its return to the centralised wages fold. The AFAP fared even worse. Opposed by government and airline employers, it failed to make any gains for its members and found its base decimated. These exceptional episodes point to the more general observation of national wage guidelines by unions. The guidelines are discussed in more detail later in this chapter.

Although opinion has been divided over the effectiveness of the

Accord, two researchers have argued that it was responsible for generating an extra 313 000 jobs between 1983–89 (Chapman & Gruen 1990). This represented a 4 per cent rise in employment and a 2 per cent reduction in unemployment. On this reasoning, the Accord produced about one-fifth of the 1.6 million new jobs during this period. A major factor was significant restraint in real wages; indeed, the authors estimate that real wages fell by 10 per cent between 1983–89.

As might be imagined, this sparked debate within the union movement with some arguing that unions should have done more to reverse the fall in real wages. ACTU officials contended, however, that the impact of the fall in real wages was more than offset by increased employment (thereby increasing household incomes), tax reform, improved superannuation and a raft of more generous social welfare provisions. These, it were claimed, had led to higher standards of living. The ACTU also pointed to the greater influence exercised by union representatives over economic, industry and social policies. The Accord, for instance, set out 'agreed policy details' on the treatment of prices and non-wage incomes, on taxation, and on supportive policies covering industrial relations legislation, social security, occupational health and safety, education, health and Australian government employment. Although the Accord has undergone a number of significant 'adjustments', known colloquially as Mark I to Mark VII, it has consistently provided the framework for the development of union and government policies on economic, industry and social matters. The various phases of the Accord (from Mark I to Mark VII) are summarised in Figure 5.1.

The original Accord (which later became known as Mark I) envisaged Federal government support for full wage indexation. As can be seen in Table 5.1, the National Wage Case Decisions in 1983, 1984 and 1985 provided for full wage indexation, although they simultaneously delivered reductions in real wages through a mixture of delays in the adjustment of money wages and other factors. The severe economic crisis of 1985–86 however, seen in the rapid and largely unanticipated fall in the exchange value of the Australian dollar, the accompanying stimulus to inflation, soaring levels of foreign debt and increasing levels of interest rates, led the government to abandon its commitment to full wage indexation. Wage fixing became a more complicated business thereafter.

Landmark Commission decisions

The 1987, 1988 and 1989 National Wage Case Decisions broke the nexus between price and wage movements. Wage increases, for the

Figure 5.1 The Accord—Mark I to Mark VII—selected features

Mark I	1983–85	Commitment by Federal government and the ACTU to the maintenance of real wages, controls on prices and non-wage incomes and supportive government policies.
Mark II	1985–86	ACTU reduced NWC claim from 4.3% to 2.3% in return for compensating tax cuts; 3% phased increases in occupational superannuation.
Mark III	1987–88	Two-tier wage system, which initiated moves towards productivity bargaining.
Mark IV	1988–89	Package of wage increases and tax cuts linked to restructuring and greater efficiency at industry and enterprise levels.
Mark V	1989–90	Package of wage increases, tax cuts and social wage improvements linked to structural efficiency and award restructuring.
Mark VI	1990–92	Package of wage increases, tax cuts, increased superannuation, improved social welfare benefits and access to enterprise bargaining linked to greater structural efficiency and continued award restructuring.
Mark VII	1993–96	Package of agreed reforms, with enterprise bargaining the primary path to wage increases: but award-based increases possible as an alternative; proclaimed central goal: to cut unemployment.

greater part, were linked to measures that increased, or were seen as likely to increase, productivity and performance. The 1987 National Wage Case Decision became known as the two-tier decision because it introduced a split system of wage adjustments. (This is quite different from the US notion of two-tier collective bargaining.) A first tier provided for an initial A$10 to be paid to all workers. This was followed by a further A$6 'across the board' some eleven months later. A second tier permitted further wage increases of up to 4 per cent. This depended on unions and employers agreeing to improve efficiency in their industry or workplaces. The Commission requested that the parties consider reforms to restrictive work and management practices, multi-skilling and broadbanding of work classifications, reduction of demarcation barriers and changes to award classifications.

The 1988 National Wage Case Decision took a similar path. It allowed increases of 3 per cent (and A$10 six months later) on the condition that discussions occur between employers and unions on 'structural efficiency'. Unions and employers were required to agree to review their awards, looking at issues such as skill-related career paths, award relativities, flexibility, minimum rates, and 'any cases where award provisions discriminate against sections of the

Table 5.1 Wage and price movements

Quarters	Change in CPI (%)	National wage increases	Date paid
1983 March/June	4.3	4.3%	Sept 1983
Sept/Dec	4.0	4.1%	April 1984
1984 March/June	– 0.2	—	—
Sept/Dec	2.7	2.6%	April 1985
1985 March/June	3.8	3.8%	Nov 1985
Sept/Dec	4.3	2.3%	July 1986
1986 March/June	4.0	—	—
Sept/Dec	5.5	—	—
1987 March/June	3.5	A$10.00	March 1987
Sept/Dec	3.4	A$ 6.00[a]	Feb 1988
		+4.0%	Varied
1988 March/June	3.5	—	—
Sept/Dec	4.0	3.0% + A$10.00	from Sept 1988[b]
1989 March/June	4.0	—	—
Sept/Dec	4.2	3.0% + 3.0%	from Aug 1989[c]
1990 March/June	3.3	—	—
Sept/Dec	3.4	—	—
1991 March/June	– 0.1	2.5%	from April 1991
Sept/	0.6	—	—

Notes: a Taking the A$10.00 and A$6.00 together, this represented a 3.6% increase for full-time adult males.

b The date for the initial 3% payment depended on the finalisation of agreement between employers and unions, on structural efficiency. The A$10.00 was to be paid as a second instalment at least six months later.

c The Commission determined that again there should be a six month interval between instalments.

Sources: Australian Bureau of Statistics, *Consumer Price Index*, Cat. No. 6401.0 and National Wage Case Decisions 1983–91.

workforce'. This resulted in a mixture of industry-by-industry and employer-by-employer negotiations. The decision reflected the central role of the Commission while it also supported moves towards the establishment of enterprise agreements between employers and unions.

The 1989 National Wage Case Decision followed on. The Commission granted a wage increase in two instalments as the lever to maintain pressure for reform. The first increase of A$10.00 to A$15.00 (or 3 per cent) was to be paid following scrutiny of proposals for award restructuring by the Commission while the second would depend on the progress made. The post-1987 decisions had therefore provided the opportunity for unions and employers to address issues which had long bedevilled economic performance, but had been widely regarded as immutable.

At the 1990 National Wage Case, Federal and state governments, the ACTU and employer groups requested the Commission to encourage greater reliance on enterprise bargaining. In addition, the ACTU and the Federal government asked the Commission to ratify the agreement struck by them in February 1990 (known as Accord Mark VI). This sought centrally-determined increases to wages and superannuation and the opportunity for further wage increases negotiated at industry or enterprise levels. The Commission, however, in its April 1991 National Wage Case Decision, rebuffed the government and ACTU, in particular declaring that employers and unions had not achieved the maturity required for greater reliance on enterprise bargaining.

The ACTU condemned the Commission's Decision and encouraged its affiliates to win pay increases by negotiating directly with employers. There followed a period of extraordinary acrimony with bitter attacks made on the Commission by leading union officials and senior government ministers. Bargaining, however, against the backdrop of economic recession proved difficult and only a minority of workers gained the benefits sought by unions. Later in 1991 the Commission began a new National Wage Case which heard submissions on the future of wage fixation. Governments, unions and employers again argued for greater reliance on enterprise bargaining. In its second 1991 Decision the Commission refashioned the principles governing wage fixation giving greater encouragement to enterprise bargaining. Nonetheless, unions and employers remained obliged to pursue 'structural efficiency' and their agreements were to be subject to scrutiny by the Commission. The Commission therefore continues to play an important part in wage-fixing; although this may change in the event of the election of a conservative Federal government. The conservative coalition has committed itself to reducing the role of the Commission in its drive for a deregulated enterprise focus for employee relations.

Current and future issues

Industrial democracy

In the early 1970s, under the influence of two reforming Labor governments (led by Prime Minister Whitlam at the Federal level and Premier Don Dunstan in South Australia), industrial democracy attracted considerable attention. There was much discussion of the need to extend decision-making rights to workers, establish joint councils and committees in the workplace, and place worker representatives on management boards. In addition it was argued by proponents of industrial democracy that jobs should be redesigned to facilitate the more direct control of workers over their worklife (see Lansbury 1980).

Many employers indicated their support for reform, cherishing the hope that change would reduce problems such as absenteeism and poor quality work and encourage improved productivity. For their part unions wished to see the rights of their members extended and gave their blessing, through the ACTU, to both representative and participative schemes which led to an increase in workers' decision-making power. They made it clear that they strongly opposed plans which failed to provide for the sharing of gains flowing from the implementation of industrial democracy.

Under the 1975–83 Conservative Federal government and mounting levels of unemployment, the pressure for industrial democracy ebbed away. Unions became increasingly concerned with the defence of members' jobs and wages, and employers found themselves under less pressure to display a commitment to industrial democracy (see Davis & Lansbury 1986).

The change of Federal government in 1983 led to renewed interest. The Accord emphasised the need for government, employer and union involvement in macro-economic and social-policy decision-making. To this end the government established tripartite committees and councils at national and industry levels. Some, such as the Economic Planning Advisory Council, proved influential in the determination of government policy. The Accord also argued specifically for workers' involvement in decision-making on technological change. More generally, it stressed that 'consultation is a key factor in bringing about change in industry . . . (at) industry, company and workplace level' (ALP–ACTU 1983:9).

The 1980s saw several important developments. Both Federal and state governments took steps to legislate for improved occupational health and safety. Crucial roles were identified for joint union–management workplace committees with rights to relevant information, powers to inspect the workplace, and the right to be consulted on all changes which affect health and safety. Many union–employer agreements have gone further, granting employee representatives access to the facilities required to perform their duties and in some cases rights to stop the production process when deemed necessary. The extent of effective employee participation in occupational health and safety matters is usually related to the vigour of the unions covering members in the workplace and the attitude of management. The outcome across workplaces is inevitably mixed.

Adhering to its commitment in the Accord, the Hawke government supported the ACTU in a lengthy case before the Commission on employee rights to information and to consultation over technological change. Under the terms of the Commission's Termination, Change and Redundancy Decision of 1984, employers were required to consult their employees and unions before introducing major changes to production methods or to organisational structure. In addition, where redundancies were contemplated, the length of notice was increased. Account was taken of length of service so that, for instance, four weeks' notice were granted to any employee with five years service or more. Unions welcomed this decision. Many employers were less enthusiastic, seeing the decision as increasing costs and impinging on managerial prerogative.

In 1986 the Federal government published a policy discussion paper on Industrial Democracy and Employee Participation. The paper stated that, 'employee participation is now a major Government priority and the government sees it as essential to a successful response to the significant challenges of the present time' (Department of Employment and Industrial Relations 1986). It pointed to alternative paths the government might take in its pursuit of more employee participation. Three in particular were noted: the enactment of legislation; stimulating progress through financial incentives and assistance; and encouragement through government provision of resources, education and training, and information.

The National Wage Case Decisions of the late 1980s reflected the declared enthusiasm of government, unions and employers for more consultation and employee participation. They also provided the most effective stimulus to greater employee participation in the workplace. The 1987 Decision advocated pursuit of improved efficiency and stressed that the approach adopted by unions and employers should rely on 'cooperation and consultation' (National Wage Case Decision 1987). The 1988 Decision argued that further restructuring should be done 'primarily by consultation and at minimal cost' (National Wage Case Decision 1988). And in its 1989 Decision the Commission was explicit in its support for 'appropriate consultative procedures to deal with the day-to-day matters of concern to employers and workers' (National Wage Case Decision 1989).

Equal opportunity in employment

During the 1980s, issues related to women in the workplace attracted increasing attention. In large measure this was linked to the remarkable growth in female participation in the workforce. In 1961, women comprised approximately 25 per cent of the workforce; by 1981 this had increased to 37 per cent and by 1990 it reached 41.5 per cent (Eccles 1982; *Women and Work* 1990). Features of this expansion were the increasing propensity of married women to enter the workforce and the rapid growth of part-time work. Indeed the proportion of the labour force working part-time doubled between 1970 and 1990, moving from 10 per cent to 20 per cent. Part-time work has remained a female preserve; only one-fifth of this group are male.

The growth of women in the workforce has not, however, been accompanied by their greater dispersal across industries and occupations. Women workers have continued to be concentrated in a small number of industries and occupations. Women are over-represented in industries such as wholesale and retail trade; finance, property and business services; community services and recreation and personnel. Similarly, in occupational terms, over 50 per cent of female employees are concentrated in two groups; clerical, and sales and personal services. Features of these industries and occupations are relatively low rates of pay and poor conditions. The result has been that women's earnings on average have remained below male earnings. At the end of 1989 women's full-time, ordinary time earnings were 83 per cent of the comparable male rate.

These conditions have focused attention on measures to improve women's pay and conditions. The decisions of the Commission in 1969 and 1972 on Equal Pay have been criticised for their failure to achieve equal pay in practice. The 1980s saw pressure from the ACTU and various women's groups designed to encourage the Commission to reassess the value of work in female-dominated occupations. One response of the Commission has been to point to the opportunities to revise pay rates following the National Wage Decisions of the late 1980s. The results so far are patchy. It would appear that some predominantly female groups have significantly improved their relative position—others have not.

The Federal Affirmative Action (Equal Employment Opportunity for Women) Act 1986 covers all private sector employers with 100 or more employees. These employers are obliged to take eight specific steps designed to remove discrimination towards women and promote equality in employment. Two of the steps entail respectively consultation with unions and with employees on the desired approach. The evidence so far, however, indicates indifferent compliance (Davis & Pratt 1990).

Child care, maternity and paternity leave, equal employment opportunity and affirmative action, and efforts to tackle sexual harassment attracted increasing attention during the 1980s. By the end of the decade there were signs that such matters were treated as industrial in nature rather than exclusively women's issues. Further, the belief that employers will be assailed by shortages of labour in the 1990s has induced many to improve child care and related conditions in order to attract and retain women workers.

Industrial relations reform

Since the mid-1980s, proposals to change Australia's industrial relations arrangements can be divided into three competing groups. The first has advocated the maintenance of the centralised system. The second has proposed radical decentralisation. The third has argued for greater decentralisation within a centralised framework, or 'managed decentralism'.

The Hancock Committee of Review was appointed by the Hawke Labor government soon after it assumed office. Its task was to assess the changes required to develop a more effective system of industrial relations. After a two-year inquiry it delivered its report (1985) which argued strongly for the retention and consolidation of the existing system albeit with certain important modifications. It proposed a restructuring of the Federal tribunal into two bodies: an Australian Industrial Relations Commission with powers similar to the existing Commission and a new Labour Court to replace the industrial division of the Federal Court. It also proposed widening the new Commission's powers to deal with all disputes which arose between employers and employees.

At the heart of the report was the conviction that the relatively centralised system facilitated the enforcement of incomes policies. This was seen to be an important factor in the wider struggle to reduce unemployment and inflation. The Committee was unconvinced that dismantlement of the existing structure and, for instance, greater reliance on bargaining would be of benefit; indeed this was described as 'a leap in the dark'.

The ACTU's *Australia Reconstructed* followed two years later. It was cast in the midst of a sharp fall in the foreign exchange value of the Australian dollar and increasing inflation. The report itself was the product of a 'Mission' of senior union officials to Austria, Britain, Norway, Sweden and West Germany. Mission members returned arguing that the successful pursuit of macro-economic goals required an integrated mix of fiscal, monetary and incomes policies combined with social welfare and labour market policies. Echoing the Hancock Report, *Australia Reconstructed* supported the retention of centralised wage fixing but it also saw that wages' policy should be interlinked to approaches on taxation and social welfare and should be affected by considerations for productivity, international competitiveness and investment. In particular, wage determination should foster training and skill enhancement as a means to achieving greater efficiency and wealth creation.

The BCA's report, entitled *Enterprise-Based Bargaining: A Better Way of Working*, threw down a challenge to supporters of the centralised system. The BCA argued that the key to improved competitiveness was a shift to enterprise-based negotiations. Moreover it argued that the traditional focus on industrial relations should be abandoned and replaced by an employee relations 'mindset'. The latter would stress the mutuality of employee–management interests and the virtues of individualism and flexibility. The BCA stirred a hornet's nest. Commentators argued that the report assumed away the existence of industrial conflict and reflected a return to 'unitarism': 'management knows best' (Dabscheck 1990).

The BCA had commissioned an extensive survey of the plants of its member companies and it had also compared and contrasted the performance of selected Australian and overseas plants. The findings emanating from the research were used to back the BCA's proposals. But both the research methodology and interpretation of the results were questioned. As put by two researchers, 'the case study methodology appears unscientific and the results sparse and unconvincing' (Frenkel & Peetz 1990).

At the state level, the government of New South Wales published a Green Paper entitled *Transforming Industrial Relations in New South Wales* (Niland 1989) which argued in similar vein to the BCA for a shift towards more enterprise bargaining. A point highlighted was the need to 'lower the centre of gravity' in industrial relations decision making so that more responsibility rested on the shoulders of workplace supervisors and union delegates. Although some of the Green Paper's recommendations were accepted by all the major parties affected, of the remainder some upset employers, some disturbed unions and yet others provoked the New South Wales Industrial Commission. Employers, for instance, were vigorously opposed to the suggestion that workers should have the legal right to engage in industrial disputes over their 'interests'. Such disputes would typically occur at the expiry of the previous agreement (disputes during the life of an agreement would remain illegal). Unions mounted an energetic campaign against recommendations to increase the size of penal sanctions and to encourage the formation of enterprise unions. Furthermore, the President of the New South Wales Commission was eloquently critical of proposals to restructure the operation of the state's tribunal (Fisher 1990). The New South Wales government subsequently implemented many of the Green Paper's recommendations in a controversial Industrial Relations Act (see Lansbury 1991).

A prominent employers' organisation, the Metal Trades Industry Association, proposed that the Commission should retain a pivotal role. National Wage Cases should continue to examine economic and industrial matters and, on the basis of conclusions drawn, set the framework for wage bargaining at the industry or enterprise level. This approach has sought to combine the advantages of a centralised approach while providing broader scope for direct bargaining between the parties. 'Managed decentralism' (McDonald & Rimmer 1989; Evans 1989) also appears to have attracted support from the ACTU and the Labor government. It was the path taken by the Industrial Relations Commission in its October 1991 National Wage Case Decision.

During 1992, amendments were made to the Federal Industrial Relations Act. The Labor government limited the authority of the Commission to vet enterprise agreements, thereby making it easier for employers and unions to bargain over wages and conditions at the workplace. The role of National Wage Cases, so prominent in the 1980s, will be significantly reduced. Even in this more decentralised environment, however, the government still remains committed to an incomes policy. The ACTU agreed in Accord negotiations with the Keating government that any wage increases which they seek will be consistent with maintaining an inflation rate comparable with Australia's major trading partners. Should wages pressure lift inflation above this level, the government can be expected to reduce employers' contributions to employees' superannuation, and government funding of the social wage may also be reduced. Thus, there is likely to be greater emphasis on enterprise bargaining and a diminished role for the Commission in the foreseeable future. It remains to be seen, however, whether this will result in a fundamental and long-lasting change to the industrial relations system.

Conclusion

The 1980s and early 1990s proved to be a period of significant changes in Australian industrial relations which included the nature and strategies of the major parties and the structure of rules and regulations governing industrial relations. There was considerable economic turbulence with mixed progress made in the quest to reduce high levels of inflation and unemployment. The Australian Labor Party had governed at the Federal level for only three years between 1949 and 1983. Following its victory in 1983 it retained government at least until the mid-1990s. In 1993 it was re-elected for an unprecedented fifth consecutive term.

The parties in industrial relations underwent significant change during the 1980s. The major employer peak council, the former CAI, was beset by the departure of many of its leading affiliates. The impression of employer diversity was further strengthened by the emergence of a newly formed and high-profile employer pressure group, the BCA. By contrast, for unions, the 1980s witnessed unparalleled moves towards strategic coordination under the umbrella of the ACTU. The various state and Federal industrial tribunals also experienced great change. Reviews of the Federal and most state systems of industrial relations resulted in alterations to the structure of the tribunals. Moreover, the focus of the tribunals shifted following the 1987 National Wage Case Decision. The Federal Commission's traditional approach to wage determination was jettisoned in favour of moves to link wage increases to measures designed to improve efficiency.

As Australia moves through the 1990s, employers, unions and governments will have both common and divergent concerns about future directions. Employers will be concerned with their economic performance in the face of increasingly competitive markets, especially as tariff barriers are lowered further. Many employers will continue to give high priority to HRM strategies and to a greater enterprise focus in their industrial relations. They will, however, be closely monitoring the outcome of enterprise agreements to see whether the promise of increased productivity is realised.

Unions will also be concerned with industry and enterprise performance since poor performance and low competitiveness have constrained economic growth and exacerbated unemployment. Unions will be looking closely at enterprise bargaining, charting the repercussions for members' wages, conditions and rights at work. Of particular concern will be the position of low-paid workers. In addition, the ACTU and affiliated unions will be busy with the reshaping of the union movement. Major restructuring is seen as necessary in the quest to deliver improved services to members and so impress upon employees the relevance of unionism. Unions fear that failure to prove their relevance will result in diminished membership and reduced influence. They find neither outcome attractive.

Federal and state governments of all political persuasions will remain preoccupied with both the broader economic problems facing Australia and the related need for micro-economic reform. At the Federal level, the Labor government will continue to support an integral role for unions in national, industry and enterprise decision making as well as a role for the Commission. By contrast, in the mid-1990s most states have conservative governments which seek to limit union power and influence and pursue a diminished role for arbitration tribunals. It seems certain that industrial relations will retain its place at the heart of political and economic debate in Australia.

Australian industrial relations chronology

1788	European settlers arrived in New South Wales, with separate British colonies established subsequently.
1856	Unions won recognition of the eight-hour day. The Melbourne Trades Hall Council (THC) was formed.
1871	Sydney unions created a Trades and Labor Council (TLC); Brisbane and Adelaide unions followed.
1879	First Inter-Colonial Trade Union Conference.
1890–94	The Great Strikes. Following defeat by combined employer and colonial government power, unions founded Labor parties in each colony.
1901	Commonwealth of Australia founded.
1904	Commonwealth Conciliation and Arbitration Court established under the Commonwealth Conciliation and Arbitration Act, with powers of legal enforcement.
1907	The *Harvester* Case established the principle of the basic wage above which the Court could award a margin for skill.
1916	Widespread union opposition to the Labor government's conscription policy.
1917	The All-Australian Trade Union Congress adopted a socialist objective.
1927	Founding of the Australian Council of Trade Unions (ACTU).
1929	The Conservative government defeated in a Federal election called over proposed weakening of the Conciliation and Arbitration Court.
1949	A major coal strike, begun around economic demands, saw the Federal Labor government take strong action to defeat the Miners' Union.
1950	Penal provisions, known as bans clauses, written into awards, enabled employers to seek an injunction from the court restraining unions taking industrial action.
1955	The Australian Labor Party split, with a breakaway group becoming the Democratic Labor Party.
1956	Following the Boilermakers' Case, the Arbitration Court was disbanded. The Conciliation and Arbitration Commission was set up with arbitral functions, and the Industrial Court with judicial responsibility.
1967	Metal Trades Work Value Case—the determination of a basic wage and margins was discontinued and a 'total wage' was introduced in lieu.
1969	The jailing of a union official for failure to pay fines

	for contempt of court led to extensive strike action throughout Australia.
1972	A Federal Labor government was elected after 23 years of Liberal Coalition government.
1975	Wage indexation introduced; Labor government dismissed.
1977	The CAI established as a national employers' confederation.
1979	The Australian Council of Salaried and Professional Associations affiliated with the ACTU.
1981	The Council of Australian Government Employee Organisations merged with the ACTU; wage indexation abandoned.
1983	Hawke Labor government elected. ALP–ACTU Prices and Incomes Accord became the lynch-pin of government policy. Return to centralised wage fixation and full wage indexation. Formation of Business Council of Australia.
1985	Report of Committee of Review of Australian Industrial Relations Law and Systems.
1987	Landmark National Wage Case Decision.
1988	Elaboration of structural efficiency principle. New Federal Industrial Relations Act.
1989	Award restructuring. Domestic airline pilots' dispute.
1990	Accord Mark VI agreed between the ACTU and Federal government.
1991	Acrimony over the April National Wage Case Decision. October National Wage Case Decision condones shift to more enterprise bargaining.
1992	Paul Keating replaces Bob Hawke as Prime Minister. Further movement towards decentralisation of bargaining, including amendments to the Industrial Relations Act, 1988.
1993	Keating Labor government re-elected for an unprecedented fifth consecutive term of Labor government.

6 Industrial relations in Italy
Claudio Pellegrini

This chapter starts by putting Italian industrial relations into an economic, historical and political context. It describes the various union confederations, employers' organisations and the role of the state. It then continues by considering the different levels and content of collective bargaining and concludes by commenting on recent issues.

Italy has a total population of 58 million people with a civilian employment participation rate of only 60 per cent. This is a lower participation rate than in any of the other countries discussed in this book. One reason for this is that the official participation rate for women is only 44 per cent, which is less than in the other countries (see Table A.2; the OECD average for women is 55 per cent).

In terms of employment, Italy's agricultural sector (9.0 per cent) is larger than those of the other countries, even though it has declined from 34 per cent in 1959. Italy has the second largest industrial sector (32 per cent); only Germany's is larger. As another Italian characteristic, there is a relatively large clandestine or 'informal' economy, which is unrecorded and untaxed. Some estimate that it amounts to 20–30 per cent of GDP. This characteristic disguises the real rates of GDP, employment participation and unemployment.

Italy's official GDP is $1089 billion; it has a GDP per capita of $19 000. In the period 1973–79, the GDP yearly percentage increase was 3.7, while the average yearly percentage change in the EC was 2.5. In the period 1979–89, Italy also maintained above average growth; the GDP percentage increase was 2.5 per cent versus an EC average of 2.2 (OECD 1991).

Like most other industrial countries, according to the official statistics Italy has experienced a substantial rise in its unemployment rate, which doubled between 1970 and 1993 from 5.3 per cent to over 11 per cent (see Table A. 5), but in the south the figure is much higher: in 1991, around 19.9 per cent compared to 6.5 per cent in the north and centre of the country. More than half of the unemployed are young people looking for their first job (Accornero 1989). There is a major cleavage between the north and south of Italy. The labour force participation rate is much lower in the south, while pay levels are higher in the north. Although the south constituted 41 per cent of the land and 36.3 per cent of the population, in 1987 it contributed only 21.7 per cent of total industrial employment. Such regional differences have a major influence on collective bargaining.

Another aspect of the economic context is the role played by exports, which represent about 20 per cent of the GDP. However, Italy depends entirely on imported oil. Since 1973, the increased oil price and labour costs have made it more difficult for firms to maintain their foreign markets, which played a crucial role in the economic growth during the sixties. Moreover, Italy's average rate of price inflation between 1979 and 1984 was 16 per cent, higher than in any of the other countries discussed (Salvati 1985). In the period 1985–91 the increase was 44 per cent, higher than any other country apart from the UK and Australia. Productivity, as measured by output per unit of labour for marketed goods and services, increased on average 3.9 per cent per year in the period 1981–89, but, if the years of recession 1982–83 are not considered, the average increase is 4.5 per cent.[1] In the same period (1981–89) the total cost of labour in real terms increased 1.8 per cent per year. Gross earnings increased 1.4 per cent per year but net earnings increased only 0.3 per cent per year, due to fiscal drag (see Table

Table 6.1 Economic indicators

	% change in productivity (output/unit of labour) for marketed goods and services	1981 Total labour costs Lire 000/ employee	1981 Gross earnings Lire 000/ employee	1981 Net earnings Lire 000/ employee	Wage Integration Fund (millions of hours)
1981	3.6	14 642	10 835	8936	577
1982	1.0	14 612	10 730	8592	619
1983	2.7	14 749	10 741	8380	746
1984	8.7	14 913	10 926	8554	813
1985	2.7	15 111	11 031	8586	717
1986	2.8	15 316	11 065	8460	647
1987	5.1	15 878	11 549	8862	533
1988	6.3	16 537	12 029	9101	418
1989	2.6	16 939	12 137	9180	342

Source: Bank of Italy: Annual Reports.

6.1). Net earnings in 1989 were only 54.2 per cent of total cost of labour while in 1981 they were 61 per cent. The average take-home pay in Italy was 80 per cent of gross earnings, the average level for the nine countries examined. The high level of public deficit is an increasing source of concern. It was 11.1 per cent of GDP in 1989 and 10.8 per cent in 1990, mostly caused by interest payments (89.7 per cent in 1990); the total stock of public debt exceeded the GDP for the first time in 1990 (Economist Intelligence Unit 1991). The deficit is partly due to the increased cost of welfare payments, the national health service, and the increasing cost of public employment (earnings increased more in the public sector than in the private sector). The quality of the services provided by the public sector is, however, very low. The quality of marketed public services such as post, telecommunications, railways, air transport and electrical energy has steadily deteriorated causing great concern among business leaders, who need good services in order to compete internationally.

Another important development in the Italian economic structure is the increasing role that has been played by small firms. Between 1971 and 1981 the percentage of employment in the manufacturing sector working in units between 10 and 49 employees went from 20 to 26 per cent while larger units decreased their proportional percentage. The decentralisation in the economic structure was caused by several elements. The employers tried to avoid the rigidities of larger manufacturing units where unions were stronger. However, the growth of small production units gave rise in several areas to integrated manufacturing systems known as industrial districts (Pyke et al. 1990). These districts specialise in certain products that are manufactured by a large number of small firms carrying out various stages of production. This allows the district to obtain significant economies of scale without the rigidities of large corporations.[2] Industrial districts are well adapted to the flexible production processes needed for changing market requirements. Several other elements made the system successful, such as an artisan tradition, strong family ties and local government assistance.[3] The strong performance of this new type of manufacturing process made an important contribution to overall economic growth.

The political context

After the fall of Fascism and the end of the Second World War, the major political parties that emerged were: the Christian Democratic Party (*Democrazia Cristiana*, DC), a Catholic-oriented interclass moderate party; the Communist Party (*Partito Comunista Italiano*,

PCI) which from its revolutionary origins became a reform-oriented party and has played the role of the major political opposition; the Socialist Party (*Partito Socialista Italiano*, PSI), a social democratic party; other small centre-oriented political parties such as the Liberal Party (*Partito Liberale Italiano*, PLI), the Republican Party (*Partito Repubblicano Italiano*, PRI) and the Social Democratic Party (*Partito Socialista Democratico Italiano*, PSDI); a Right-wing party, Italian Social Movement (*Movimento Sociale Italiano*, MSI), which is the heir of the Fascist tradition. More recently Left oppositional parties have developed, such as the Radical Party, the Green Movement and local leagues.[4]

Between 1945 and 1947 all the anti-Fascist parties, including the PCI, formed a Coalition government of national unity. In the 1948 Cold War climate, following the electoral success of the DC, the PSI and the PCI were excluded from government. The DC party, with about 35 per cent of the vote, has always been in power since then. Between 1948 and 1964 the governments were based on a coalition between DC and other small centre parties; after 1964 the PSI also entered the coalition (Ginsborg 1990).

What are the consequences for industrial relations of this political setting? While in countries such as Britain, Germany, Sweden or France the functioning of the democratic system is based on the competition between conservative and labour parties, which have been alternatively in power, in Italy the main political opposition, the PCI, has never been in power since the post-war Government of National Unity that ended in 1948. The lack of change between the two major parties resulted from the Communist Party (in its roots if not in its policies) being seen as too far to the Left to gain more support or to form a coalition with other parties. In other words, the PCI was not considered a legitimate competitor for the national government. Some observers have called this situation 'blocked democracy' and believe it has negative consequences for the functioning of the political system. The party always in power perceived little risk of being challenged and became less accountable and less efficient in administration.

In the realm of industrial relations, unlike other European countries, a union–government relationship based on accords or social contracts (as in Australia, Sweden or Britain) is more difficult to achieve and to enforce in Italy. First, because a government based on the major pro-labour party has never been in power; second, because the presence of competing unions with different political orientations makes it difficult to reach a long-lasting union commitment; and finally, because the weakness of Italian government coalitions prevents the enforcement of the agreements and the delivery of government promises that were part of the accord (Regini 1987; Golden 1988).

It should be also added that between 1976 and 1979 the PCI supported the government in Parliament but did not participate in the Cabinet. This was the only feasible solution, because after the electoral success of the PCI in 1976, the PSI refused participation in governments that did not have support from the PCI. The period of so-called National Solidarity (in those years political terrorism was rampant in Italy) lasted until January 1979. Afterwards the PCI, which was losing support, went back to Opposition. The government since then has been formed by a coalition between DC, PSI, and all the other centre parties. The President of the Cabinet, for the period June 1981–April 1987, was no longer a DC member but a member of PRI, Giovanni Spadolini, until November 1982 and of PSI, Bettino Craxi. In 1987 the presidency of the Cabinet reverted to the DC (Giovanni Goria, Ciriaco De Mita, and Giulio Andreotti). However, in 1992, the presidency was returned to the PSI (Amato). Because the government is based on a Coalition, conflicts among parties, or divisions within the major party, often end in a political crisis and the formation of a new government or early elections. The instability of governments often disguises the stability of the Coalition that is in power. It is true, however, that weak Coalitions make it difficult to carry out government policies, especially when unpopular decisions have to be made (for instance for the reduction of governmental spending or to prevent tax evasion). The parties are trying to initiate a change in the political system that could produce stronger government; for instance a change in the electoral procedure. Other possibilities are also under discussion but an agreement has not been reached.

After 1988 the PCI under Achille Occhetto accelerated its transformation into a social democratic party and in 1991 changed its name to the Democratic Party of the Left (PDS). This produced a split and one group formed a new political organisation (*Rifondazione Comunista*, Communist Refoundation).

The industrial relations parties

In the analysis of industrial relations it is important to take into consideration some historical background. First, we should consider the late capitalist development of Italy; for instance, in 1901, only 238 out of every 1000 employees were in the industrial sector compared with 632 in Britain (Barbadoro 1973:21). Second, the weak democratic tradition; men over 30 gained the right to vote in 1912 and women voted for the first time in 1946 in the first free general election after Fascism (voters had to choose between the monarchy and a republic and had to elect the Constituent Assembly to draft the new Constitution). Both elements help to explain the strength of the revolutionary and Socialist tradition within Italian labour. Third, the large role played by the organisations of agricultural workers explains the importance in the union structure of the local geographical organisations called Chambers of Labour (*Camere del Lavoro*). Fourth, in order to explain the absence of unions based on craft, we should also mention that unionism in Italy took shape at the turn of the century (much later than in Britain) and that Socialists played a determinant role. At that time the Second International considered industrial unionism the most appropriate form of organisation because it was the most conducive to worker unity, and because it was more suited to the organisation of the large manufacturing plants, which were emerging at that time as the key factor in the industrial sector.

The Fascist period between 1922 and 1944 caused an end to the existence of all the established unions. The corporatist experience left its marks in the following period, particularly in terms of centralisation of the decision-making process and use of governmental intervention in industrial relations and it also reinforced the industrial basis of unionism. For all these reasons, after 1944 all the confederations had no doubt about organising along industrial lines.

Another element to be considered is the presence of the Catholic tradition before and after Fascism. Compared with other countries according to Jemolo (1963:6):

> the Italian Catholics were the last to join in organising the
> worker forces, in studying social problems . . . There was too
> long a tradition of agreements between the wealthy classes and
> the Church.

The situation changed at the turn of the century. The *Encyclica Rerum Novarum* in 1891 encouraged the formation of Catholic organisations in the industrial sector and competition with the Socialist-oriented Chamber of Labour favoured the emergence of Catholic trade unionism. In 1918 the *Confederazione Italiana dei Lavoratori* was formed. In the same period, Catholics became active in the political arena for the first time since 1870 when the papal states had been annexed by the emerging Italian reign.

The unions

The three major union confederations are the *Confederazione Generale Italiana del Lavoro* (CGIL), with about 5 million members; the *Confederazione Italiana Sindacati Lavoratori* (CISL), with 3.5 million; and the *Unione Italiana Lavoratori* (UIL), with 1.5 million. Also included in the membership are retired employees who belong to a separate structure. Without the retirees, the membership in 1990 for CGIL, CISL and UIL was 2.7, 2.0 and 1.1 million respectively. Union membership increased dramatically after 1969. In that year the three confederations had 2.6 million, 1.6 million and 0.7 million members respectively; altogether the rate of unionisation increased from 29 per cent in 1969 to nearly 50 per cent in 1980 with a decline afterwards to 40 per cent in 1988 (Santi 1988; but see also Table A.20). The largest organisation, CGIL, is Socialist- and Communist-oriented; the CISL has a large, but not exclusively, Catholic component; the UIL has ties with Socialist and small centre parties.

The relationship between unions and political parties has a long, complex history and only the most important phases and their consequences are highlighted in this chapter.[5] In 1944, the representatives of the major political parties that were opposed to the Fascist regime (Communist, Catholic and Socialist) signed an agreement which later led to the formation of CGIL. The three political components that formed the confederation remained together until 1948 when there was a rupture in the Coalition government which had included Socialists and Communists. As a consequence there was a split in the CGIL. The Catholic component left the CGIL in 1948 and formed the CISL. In 1950 the Republicans and Social Democrats also left the CGIL and formed the UIL. Socialists remained in the CGIL but gained strength, particularly in the UIL (Beccalli 1972). During the 1950s, the links between political parties and unions were more direct and the latter had little room for autonomous decisions. During the 1960s, however, inter-union cooperation began to emerge, together with a new political climate (a centre-left coalition) and the development of national and plant bargaining, particularly after 1969. Accordingly, the unions became more independent politically. In 1973, when the three union confederations formed the *Federazione CGIL–CISL–UIL*, it was also decided that their leaders could not hold office in political parties or be members of Parliament (Weitz 1975).

Obviously the political climate has an influence on union attitudes and decisions. It is important, however, to understand that there is a plurality of party allegiances, so compromise is usually necessary between and within each organisation if the unions want to act together. Besides the three major confederations in Italy there are also other unions. In 1950 the *Confederazione Italiana Sindacati Nazionali Lavoratori* (CISNAL) was founded by the heirs of the Fascist tradition. This confederation, however, plays no significant role in Italian industrial relations. In Italy there are also independent union organisations (so-called '*sindacati autonomi*') which are particularly strong in the public sector, education, hospitals and transportation. The main peak councils are: *Confederazione Italiana Sindacati Autonomi Lavoratori* (CISAL), present particularly in the municipalities and railways; *Confederazione Sindacati Autonomi Lavoratori* (CONFSAL), particularly strong in education and public employees; *Confederazione Italiana Sindacati Autonomi Servizi* (CISAS) in the services. In the late 1980s many other strong independent unions were formed in the educational system, in transportation and health services (Bordogna 1989). These unions were able to mobilise a large percentage of employees and gained a place in the collective bargaining process with the government.[6]

Managers (*dirigenti*) also have their own organisations. The main peak council is *Confederazione Italiana Dirigenti d'Azienda* (CIDA), with about 100 000 members. Forty per cent of them are in the industrial sector where the unionisation rate was 40 per cent in 1988 (Pellegrini 1989).

In analysing the union structure inside and outside the workplace it is important to keep in mind that there are differences between the legal framework, collective bargaining provisions and the *de facto* situation. From 1948 until 1970 the unions were not present as such in the workplace. By agreement with *Confindustria* there were internal commissions (*commissioni interne*) which were elected by all the employees, mainly to administer the national agreements. The main competing unions presented candidates for the Commission, but the latter was not formally a union structure as in the case of the French *comité d'entreprise* or the German *Betriebsrat* (see chs 7 and 8).

During the 1960s, when the economic situation was improving, the unions were enjoying more power and they tried to establish union representatives (*Rappresentanza Sindacali Aziendali* RSA), a position similar to the *vertrauensmann* in Germany. In 1970 the Workers' Statute was enacted. Consequently workers had the right to establish RSA in the workplace, and to have them recognised as such by the unions most representative in the country or that had signed national–local collective agreements applied in the workplace. The leaders of each RSA have the right to a certain amount of working time for union activity, based upon the size of the firm, and are protected from dismissal.

During the early 1970s, there was also a large increase in the number of industrial disputes (see Appendix). During these conflicts new forms of worker representation were emerging based on shop stewards (*delegati*) for each work unit. Together the shop stewards formed the factory council (*consiglio di fabbrica*). Both union and non-union members were eligible to vote and to be elected (Sciarra 1977). When the three main confederations formed the unitary structure in 1972 they decided to recognise the factory council as the union structure in the workplace, and the *delegati* enjoyed the legal protection given to RSA by the Workers' Statute in 1970. Thus, at their workplace, employees had only one form of representation which was also the basis of union organisation and played a major role in collective bargaining at plant level (Regalia et al. 1978).

One problem after the establishment of the *Federazione CGIL–CISL–UIL* was to ensure representation of all the major confederations within the factory councils. This was facilitated by the growth of all unions after 1970 and by the reduction of the friction between them. It is still possible, however, for a union that does not have members elected in the council to have their representatives as RSA (this is rarely the case). In 1981 there were 32 021 factory councils with 206 336 shop stewards representing more than 5 million workers (ETUI 1985).

Outside the workplace, together with the *Federazione CGIL–CISL–UIL*, united federations were also formed between the structure of CGIL, CISL and UIL at the (vertical) industrial level and at (horizontal) geographical level in the cities and regions. When the unitary federations were formed, the goal was to proceed gradually towards a merger. In the transitional period the statute of the unitary federations simply gave an equal number of seats to each confederation regardless of its actual membership, thus none of them risked being engulfed. The merger, however, did not occur. On the contrary, differences between the unions began to emerge in the late 1970s, due to unfavourable economic conditions and greater political competition which forced unpopular decisions. Decision-making within the unitary structure became cumbersome, since majority rule could not be used and compromises acceptable to all three constituents had to be found. In 1984, following the change of the national indexation system, the unitary structure collapsed. Since then each confederation has regained autonomy of action. This does not prevent unity on specific issues. At the plant level, however, the situation was more difficult because the workers' councils were based on the proposal of a unitary structure and a future merger among the unions. It took a long time to try to establish new rules related to the electoral procedures and the structure of worker representation. These are controversial, and in the absence of specific enterprise-level agreements, elections of employee representatives are not held regularly.

Employers' organisations

The most important employers' organisation for private employers is the *Confindustria*, which represents associations of the largest firms, in particular in the manufacturing and construction sectors. Firms may join both the regional multi-sector association and the national sector one: the two together form the *Confindustria*. In 1990 the *Confindustria* had 106 local associations and about 100 000 local units representing 3 750 000 employees. The local units were distributed geographically in the following way: 57 per cent in the north, 20 per cent in the centre and 23 per cent in the south; the employees had the following distribution: 74 per cent in the north, 15 per cent in the centre and 11 per cent in the south. Some firms do not belong to a local association but only belong to a national sectoral association, of which there are nearly 100.

Confindustria has two main objectives: one concerns industrial relations and the other concerns the broader economic, technical and political needs of their members. During the 1970s, *Confindustria* merged the various metalworking associations into a new organisation, the Italian Metalworking Industry Federation (*Federmeccanica*), which is exclusively concerned with industrial relations. There was a similar merger in the chemicals sector. Public sector manufacturing enterprises have their own associations only for the purpose of collective bargaining. The most important is *Intersind*, which, since 1958, has represented the Institute for Industrial Reconstruction (IRI), a group consisting of 260 firms and 330 000 employees in 1987. The other public sector employer association is the Employers' Association for the Petrochemical Firms (ASAP) with 100 firms and 125 000 employees of the National Institute for Hydrocarbons (ENI), mainly in the chemical and energy sectors.

Private employers also have collective organisations in the commercial sector (*Confcommercio*) and in agriculture (*Confagricoltura*), the latter with 648 000 local units. In the banking and credit sector there is *Assicredito* with 400 members and 300 000 employees. Small firms are represented by *Confapi*, which, in 1987, had 30 000 members and employed 850 000 people; it has 18 national agreements signed with different unions. Craft shops and small businessmen (*artigiani*) also have their own organisations and several collective agreements with unions on a sectoral basis; the same is true also for the cooperatives.

Within the *Confindustria* there has been a tense relationship between large industrial groups and other firms (Lanzalaco 1990). This has hindered the maintenance of a unified strategy towards the unions and governments. In the past, there have also been differences in the employer policies between capital- and labour-intensive industries, with the latter being more concerned with labour costs.

The *Confindustria* plays an important role in coordinating national bargaining in the major industrial sectors, and has a direct role in bargaining with the union confederations on agreements that apply to the entire country; this role has become particularly important because, since 1975, bargaining levels at the national level have played a central role (see later). In the past, the public sector employers have been innovative and have often been the first to make agreements during bargaining rounds. More recently, retrenchments in the public sector have imposed severe constraints on their innovative role. However, in the IRI group there was an important agreement, in 1984, which established joint committees for consultation on a large variety of issues related to strategic decisions and industrial relations policies. Although in the political arena the *Confindustria* traditionally had strong ties with the Christian Democratic Party (Martinelli & Treu 1984:287), relations have been subject to strain due to a shifting balance of power within the *Confindustria* and within the Christian Democratic Party.

The role of the state

As in Britain before the 1960s, there was relatively little legal intervention in Italian industrial relations in terms of regulation of the parties. The new constitution established in 1948 had some provisions regarding the recognition of unions and the right to strike, but, nevertheless, legislation on this issue was not enacted. Traditionally, many matters related to social security and labour market institutions have been regulated by law. The importance of collective bargaining in determining conditions of employment has always been recognised by the government and, in 1959, all the existing agreements were transformed into law (so called *erga omnes* provisions). They constitute a minimum (often ameliorated by further legislation and bargaining) that applies to all (Giugni 1972).

Legislation, however, has played an increasingly important role since the late 1960s, but labour law does not regulate the bargaining process, the size of the bargaining unit, nor the right to strike (in 1988 a law was passed that limits the right to strike in essential public services). Besides the earlier mentioned Workers' Charter, other important laws regulate social security and minimum pay during lay-offs (Treu 1981). In many cases, these laws were the result of direct bargaining between unions and government and were subsequently approved by Parliament and codified by law. In others, they were based on national agreements between employers and unions. Bargained legislation was particularly important during the

1970s when unions initiated many changes in the social, as well as the political, arena. This is partly related to the above-mentioned immobility of the political structure; the unions became vocal on emerging national issues. Thus the unions compensated for the shortcomings of the political system (Giugni 1973:37–46). The unions did succeed in winning reforms of the social security arrangements. However, they also sought reforms related to housing, health services, transport and fiscal policies. In these latter areas they were less successful.

The government also intervenes as a mediator during collective bargaining, particularly on national or industry level agreements (Veneziani 1972). This mediation role increased during the late 1970s, and many settlements were possible only because the employers' costs were subsidised by the state. The government can also have a major impact when bargaining with the unions in the public sector, which in Italy is relatively large; besides administration and education it includes many services (such as health services, transport, telephone) and a significant industrial sector. Altogether it is estimated that 28.1 per cent of all dependent employees are in the public sector (Ferraresi 1980:134). In many cases changes in agreements are first obtained and experimented in the public sector. In 1983 a new law was passed (93/1983) that tried to formalise the process of collective bargaining in the public sector. Three levels of collective bargaining were established: one for the entire sector for general issues; a second one for six major groups (education, health, state government, local government, public firms and governmental agencies); and a third one at the local level. The military, police, judges, diplomats and top managers were excluded from the bargaining process. Since 1983, two agreements at the higher level have been made and they have dealt with the issues of content of bargaining, union representation and strike regulation. The system is, however, still developing.

Government intervention is also crucial if and when major industrial corporations face economic difficulties and ask for the prolonged use of Wage Integration Funds (CIG), which guarantee up to 80 per cent of pay during lay-off (D'Harmant & Brunetta 1987). The CIG has two main forms: the ordinary one is financed by employers' contributions and used during temporary crises for three-month periods, renewable up to one year; the special one is used for more serious crises, is not time-limited, and is funded by the state. The CIG has become essential for facilitating technological and structural change. Since 1980, it has been used more and more frequently; in the second part of 1990 about 1 per cent of the labour force were covered by CIG. Another important form of relationship between unions and government is the increased union representation in social security organisations at national and local levels, and in many administrative structures and consulting bodies (Treu & Roccella 1979). The unions also participate in local commissions to help the unemployed (*Commissioni di Collocamento*). By legislation, the employer has to communicate job vacancies to the commissions, which provide candidates on the basis of family needs and of seniority on the unemployed list. Highly skilled workers and top level white-collar employees are excluded from these provisions. The employers have always opposed this limitation to their selection of the employees and, except in the larger firms, they have usually been able to avoid the provisions (Reyneri 1989). In 1991 the law reduced to a small percentage the number of vacancies to be filled on the basis of position in the unemployed list.

The process of industrial relations

In Italy there are three major bargaining levels: national, industry, and plant or firm. In some sectors, such as agriculture or construction, there is also collective bargaining at a regional level. The three major collective bargaining levels have played different roles over the years and in general they deal with different issues (Baglioni 1991). Italian contract deadlines are not as important in the bargaining process as in the USA. Agreements are often signed months after the expiration of the contract and are applied retrospectively when possible, or a lump sum of money is given to the employees to compensate for losses. During the bargaining process there are also strikes that usually last only a few hours or one day at the most. The number of working days lost through industrial disputes in Italy is high compared with most of the other countries covered in this book (see Appendix). Italy appears to be in an even worse position in relation to the number of workers involved in disputes (Franzosi 1989); however, since the mid-1980s there has been a significant decline.

Strikes are the most widely used form of union action (there is no tradition of product boycotts). Strikes often are held together with widely attended street demonstrations. As in France (see ch. 7) the Italian unions do not have strike funds. There are no peace clauses in agreements and consequently strikes can be held at any stage in solidarity with other workers or in opposition to government decisions and for issues not strictly related to wages and working conditions.

National bargaining

Agreements at the national level between major employers' associations such as *Confindustria* and the union confederations played an essential role during the 1950s, became less important between 1965 and 1975 when bargaining increased at the plant and industry levels, but became important again after 1975. The most crucial issue bargained at this level is the national indexation agreement (*scala mobile*). Other national agreements relate to hours, holidays, use of the CIG (later transformed into law) and payments in relation to seniority retirement or voluntary retirement. The bargaining process at this level is strongly centralised and highly politicised. Although unions consult members before and after the agreements, there is little rank and file participation. Nonetheless, bargaining is given wide media coverage as in Australia and Britain, unlike in the USA where the bargaining structure is too decentralised to be given national attention.

National bargaining became prominent again after 1975 for many reasons. First, in a period of economic recession there was little scope for bargaining at lower levels where employers' resistance was high; secondly, in centralised bargaining the unions could use their influence in the political arena; finally, the employers could benefit from a type of bargaining that inevitably involved governments eager to reach a settlement and, therefore, often willing to mediate and share the cost of settlements (Treu 1983).

A crucial issue that is bargained at national level is the *scala mobile* which guarantees automatic wage increases based upon the price index of a selection of basic goods. The functioning of the *scala mobile* is determined by agreement between unions and employers' organisations. Since the Second World War it has often been modified; in 1969, for instance, differential increases based on gender or geographical difference were eliminated. A major change was agreed in 1975, to gradually eliminate differences in the *scala mobile* based on occupation or skill level. Henceforth, after 1977, for every point of increase in the index, all employees were to receive the same increase. The 1975 agreement increased the percentage of wages covered by indexation, from 64 per cent in 1974 to 90 per cent in 1977 (Altieri et al. 1983). After 1977 the *scala mobile* had many, and often unforeseen consequences. The persistently high level of inflation and the high percentage of wages affected by indexation, flattened wage differentials and left little room for wage bargaining. Moreover, the apparently higher levels of pay pushed employees into higher tax brackets. This made it more difficult for unions to influence the real levels of pay. The unions that defended the indexation system were blamed for the high level of inflation. The government and many employees increasingly demanded that the unions should concede changes in the *scala mobile*.

In the early 1980s the issue was a major industrial relations controversy and bargaining at other levels did not progress because everything depended on the solution of this central problem (Flanagan et al. 1984). The parties compromised in 1983, with the intention of cutting inflation to 13 per cent in that year. To achieve this, unions and employees agreed to reduce indexed pay increases by 15 per cent and to limit the increases in all sector agreements to small, fixed amounts between 1983 and 1985. At the plant level there would be no increases for 20 months (Dal Co & Perulli 1986). The unions agreed to allow tougher management control of absenteeism and more flexible use of working time. The unions also agreed that increases should be differentiated by skill level and that plant bargaining should not deal with issues covered at other bargaining levels, as had been happening since 1969. This agreement also set up an arbitration system to foster the settlement of grievances and to avoid local disputes. For its part, the government agreed to reduce taxes, limit price increases in public utilities to 13 per cent, pay an increasing share of the employer contribution to the cost of social insurance and to increase welfare subsidies related to family size. The government also promised to improve the operation of the labour market agencies, the CIG, the national health system and pensions.

The agreement was seen by many as a further step towards the centralisation of bargaining and towards the establishment of stable trilateral bargaining between employers, unions and government. However, in 1984 when the three parties met again to evaluate the accord, there was disagreement within the *Federazione CGIL–CISL– UIL* about the decision to concede a further reduction of indexation in exchange for concessions on fiscal and other issues. CISL, UIL and the Socialist component of CGIL agreed that there were the conditions for a settlement while the Communists disagreed. According to them, during 1983 the workers had made the agreed-upon sacrifices while the government, on the other hand, had not honoured its promises, particularly with regard to prices and taxes. The result was a serious split between the unions and the end of the *Federazione CGIL–CISL–UIL*. The government decided to use a decree (based upon the accord with CISL and UIL) in order to put a ceiling on the amount of indexation that could be paid in 1984. The PCI asked for a national referendum on the issue which was held in 1985 and supported the government decision (54.3 versus 45.7).

In December 1985 a new indexation system was agreed in the public sector; in May 1986 this agreement was accepted also in the private sector. Under the agreement wages are adjusted every six months and, for a certain amount of the salary (580 000 lire), the new system provides full coverage while, for the remaining part, the coverage is limited to 25 per cent. The acceptance of the new system has been facilitated by lower inflationary levels since 1987 (Faustini 1987). In subsequent years national bargaining has continued. Unions and government reached agreement in 1988 on matters of fiscal policy that changed the tax brackets and introduced a mechanism for the correction of the fiscal drag. The agreement with the government also covered the issue of individual payments to the national health service (families below a certain income do not have to contribute). With the private employers, the main agreement has been on special contracts for training and work (in 1987) and on new rules for bargaining. Agreements on non-standard contract of employment ('solidarity contracts', part-time contracts) have played a significant role as a source of manpower flexibility in the second part of the 1980s. The overall importance of this level of negotiation, especially with employers, has declined in the second half of the 1980s in favour of enterprise bargaining. At this level, however, bargaining is still taking place and, in 1990, agreements were reached in the area of vocational training and labour market management.

In 1991, it was not possible to reach a new centralised agreement regarding the *scala mobile* and the labour cost structure (the existing agreement and the related legislation expired at the end of 1991). The government tried to mediate the controversy but did not succeed. The general election to be held in the spring of 1992 was imminent and the political parties preferred to avoid such a controversial issue.

Industry level bargaining

Agreements are signed for various segments of the economy by national unions. In the industrial sector there are four major contracts: metals, textiles, chemicals and construction. There are three agreements in agriculture and nine in the public sector. Even though there has been a reduction in the number of contracts, one union may be involved in negotiating many agreements. Altogether there are about 20 national unions in each confederation and in the manufacturing sector there are more than 30 agreements with private employers' associations; four with public employers, seven with associations of small firms and eight with the association of small businesses.

Industry agreements began to play a larger role in the mid-1950s, but in the 1970s they became very important. Major bargaining rounds have been held about every three years since 1969. As in

Australia, the metals agreement often sets a pattern which others follow.

From 1969 to 1976 such industry-level bargaining extended the settlements won in union strongholds to the entire country. This was particularly important given the differences between the north and the south. In many cases the agreements specified minimum conditions. These could be improved depending on the bargaining strength of the unions at plant level. Industry agreements have been used increasingly by the courts as a standard in disputes, even for employers that had not signed the contracts either directly or through their associations. Industry agreements usually exclude topics that have been regulated by national bargaining (or legislation). The latter has a larger scope and extends to issues such as retirement, insurance and unemployment compensation, unions and employee rights.

Industry agreements tend to focus on job classifications and descriptions, hours and overtime, incentive systems, holidays and vacations, discipline, union rights, and the disclosure of information to unions. In the metals agreements, for instance, the entire work-force is classified into eight classes. Classes 2–5 are shared both by white- and blue-collar workers; consequently the traditional rigid separation between these categories has been reduced. The unions have generally achieved their goal of narrowing the differentials in pay and fringe benefits between these categories. However, in relation to pay, it is now recognised that this has been carried too far. Inflation and *scala mobile* flat-rate increases reduced the average differential between white-collar workers and blue-collar workers to 30 per cent. In the 1983 bargaining round the parties agreed on expanding differentials again. Nonetheless, the skilled and professional employees were still dissatisfied. This has become a crucial issue for unions because it has prompted more employers to give increases to employees individually, thus undermining the union role in representing the workforce collectively. In the 1980s, there was a small reduction in the 40-hour standard week in some manufacturing sectors and there is usually a limit of 150 hours overtime per year. Each employee has four weeks of vacation.

In the area of union rights in the workplace, the most important provisions are those related to the direct check-off of dues and allowed time off for union activity. By law each employee can use up to eight hours each year for union meetings during working time, within the plant. The unions usually use part of the paid time in order to employ a shop steward for full-time union activity (these provisions are often improved by sector and plant agreements). Collective bargaining has also been used to influence employers' strategies in terms of investments, plant size, subcontracting and

technological change. Information disclosure provisions were negotiated in the late 1970s and were considered a first step towards
increased industrial democracy. As in Britain, the results have been
disappointing partly because of employer resistance and partly
because of lack of union expertise (Pellegrini 1983:204). In the early
1980s, this level of bargaining was frustrated because of the difficulties and delays in reaching agreements at the higher level (particularly on *scala mobile*). In the bargaining round of 1983, the key
issues were related to technological change, training, flexibility on
hours of work, and increases in the workers' classifications (Giugni
1984). In the bargaining round that started in the spring of 1987,
the most innovative issue was the definition and assignment of
employees in the new category of *cadres* (*quadri*) that was established by legislation in 1985. Previously there were only three
groups of employees: top managers (*dirigenti*), white-collar staff
(*impiegati*) and blue-collar workers (*operai*). The new category
includes the higher level of white-collar workers, technicians and
lower levels of management.

Another new area introduced in collective bargaining was that
of affirmative action in favour of people with disabilities and other
disadvantaged groups. The new agreements have extended information rights and the formation of bilateral commissions that have
increased joint administration. Wage increases were distributed in
different amounts among categories with the purpose of increasing
differentials. Another element was the introduction of rules for
greater flexibility in the deployment of employees. It was also
agreed that industry and plant bargaining should not overlap in their
content.

Plant and enterprise collective bargaining

Plant level collective bargaining has been important since 1969 as
more stewards have been recognised in the workplace. In the early
1970s unions first extended the scope of bargaining in plant agreements and later in sector or national agreements. After 1974, the
role of plant bargaining became more limited. A recent study shows
that the likelihood of a firm or plant having a plant agreement
increases with its size. In the area of Milan, 70 per cent of plants
with more than 150 employees have a plant contract (Cella & Treu
1989).

During plant bargaining stewards play a major role in formulating the claim, while the bargaining is usually conducted by full-time
union officials. Plant agreements usually last for a fixed term and
are renewed after national agreements, but negotiations can be
reopened at any stage for issues that become relevant. The content

of the agreements differs depending on the size of the plant, the type of product and the method of production. In general, at the plant level the main issues are supplementary pay increases, the distribution of working hours and overtime, assignment of jobs to the national classifications, increasing stewards' facilities, health hazards, canteen costs and food quality. Information rights have, to a certain extent, increased the unions' sympathies for the economic constraints faced by firms, but plant bargaining continues to be confrontational. Such bargaining is the main process used by employees to influence managerial decisions; it often involves workers invoking sanctions.

In recent years there have been more *ad hoc* joint committees formed by stewards and managers for handling issues on a more cooperative basis. In the economic recession the main controversies were related to lay-offs and other forms of employment reduction or mobility, and with the consequences of technological change (Garonna & Pisani 1986). A survey of 1168 local agreements (CESOS 1988) shows that in 34 per cent of cases a new agreement was reached in the second half of 1986 and 1987. The proportion was much higher in firms with more than 500 employees, and in firms where there were major structural changes. The issues most dealt with were employees' rights (60.7 per cent), selection of employees to be placed under the integration fund (61.7 per cent), hours (53.3 per cent), wages (50 per cent), work organisation (30 per cent), and job classification (25 per cent). A major development for large enterprises was the introduction into agreements of profit-sharing plans or wage increases linked to performance.

Conclusion

There are many reasons why it was not possible to repeat the 1983 type of agreement. In 1984 the government faced larger deficits and could no longer use economic incentives to facilitate a settlement. The political situation was also different because for the first time the Prime Minister was a Socialist. The greater involvement of the Socialist Party in government policies, its efforts to show that they were winning the battle against inflation and the increased strife with the PCI, had consequences in the industrial relations arena and all unions were affected. The divisions between the unions should not be seen, however, as a mere resurgence of the political parties' influence over them, because their differences were also rooted in their bargaining strategies and goals.

In the second half of the 1980s, national trilateral concertation and centralised agreements were not the most appropriate level of negotiations: because of fundamental changes that occurred in all firms, the increased levels of profitability made it more useful to bargain at the local level (Locke 1990). Centralised agreement with the government remained in the area of fiscal policies and labour market management.

After 1985, the tension among the unions decreased but there was no longer a formal unitary structure among the three major confederations. In every bargaining round there is argument about appropriate representation—who is representing whom. These problems of union representation require new legislation. The confederations have reached a preliminary accord on the rules for electing representatives at firm levels. The election process should lead to a future structure (RSU, Unitary Union Representatives) which balances the role of union members and non members. The agreement has yet to be implemented.

One of the areas for future change will be related to labour relations in units below 15 employees in the private sector (small businesses). This area was excluded from the Workers' Statute, but the majority of employees (about 8 million) work in such units. For this reason, in May 1990, new legislation (108/1990) was passed that entitles employees fired without just cause, to reinstatement in the job or compensatory payment (from 2.5 to 6 times the monthly wage). The law also provides for a conciliation–arbitration procedure. Small enterprises and industrial districts face new challenges in terms of technological change and increased international competition. An important role in shaping future directions will depend on government policies, union strategies (in many regions where small enterprises flourish unions have a considerable strength), and entrepreneurs' ability to respond to the new challenges.

An important future problem will be the improvement in quality of public-sector services. Employees in this area have gained more than average in terms of pay and working conditions, but the quality of service has not improved. The gap between public- and private-sector employees will cause increasing difficulties. Moreover, conflict and strikes tend to be more frequent in the public services. The entire area of public employment needs dramatic changes. A first step in the direction of conflict regulation in the public-sector services was the law 146/1990 which established a set of rules for preventing and limiting the damaging effects of strikes in essential services.

After the 1992 election the new government, with a very small majority, faced serious economic problems. In July 1992, in a new central agreement, it was decided to eliminate the indexation system In its place the government granted a small monthly salary increase (20 000 lire). Bargaining at the enterprise level on pay issues was suspended for 1992 and 1993. The government committed itself to anti-inflationary measures, with the aim of reducing inflation to 2 per cent by 1995. Later in 1992 the economic situation deteriorated again; the government devalued the lire and removed it from the European exchange rate mechanism. These events were likely to make it difficult to keep inflation low. Moreover, in order to reduce the deficit, the government approved a series of new taxes and budget cuts. In October 1992, the unions called a general strike asking for changes to aspects of government policy which were seen as unfair. In the union view, the economic burden was falling heavily on employees, while affecting the self-employed to a lesser degree because fiscal controls over them were ineffective. The outcome of this confrontation was uncertain. A solution to the economic crisis was elusive in view of the political instability and voter dissatisfaction with the traditional political parties.

Another emerging issue at the social level is the integration of an increasing number of immigrants from non-EC countries. This is a new development for Italy, which historically has been a country of emigration. There has been legislation to regularise the status of immigrants, but social tensions are beginning to develop. Hitherto immigrants have worked in the service sector or as independent dealers, but their presence in agriculture and construction will create new industrial relations challenges.

Finally, it should be mentioned that further steps towards European integration in 1993 (see ch. 11) are leading to increasing competition in sectors previously sheltered. In the banking sector, public construction, transport, and health services the effect will be strongly felt and major restructuring will take place.

A chronology of Italian industrial relations

1848	First printing workers' associations.
1872	National Printing Union formed.
1891	*Rerum Novarum* papal encyclical.
1893	The Italian Federation of Chambers of Labour (*Federazione Italiana delle Camere del Lavoro*) is formed by the union organisations of 12 northern cities.
1906	The General Confederation of Labour (*Confederazione Generale del Lavoro* CGL) is founded including the Chambers of Labour and national unions.
1907	The Catholics Economic and Social Union is founded (*Unione Economico-Sociale dei Cattolici d'Italia*).
1918	The above union becomes the Italian Confederation of Labour (*Confederazione Italiana dei Lavoratori* CIL).

1922	After the March on Rome, Mussolini becomes Prime Minister.
1922	CGIL holds its last Congress.
1926	Only Fascist unions allowed, which together with the Employers' Confederation formed the National Council of Corporations (*Consiglio Nazionale delle Corporazioni*) as part of the Corporate state.
1943	Fall of Fascism in the south. It remained in power in the north until 1945.
1944	Rome trade union Pact among Communists, Christian Democrats and Socialists provides for the creation of the CGIL.
1945–48	Coalition government of anti-Fascist political parties, including Socialists and Communists.
1948	The Christian Democrats (DC) win a parliamentary majority and exclude Left-wing parties from government. Catholics leave the CGIL and later form the CISL.
1949	Social Democrats and Republicans also leave the CGIL and later form UIL. Socialists continue in CGIL, which remains the largest peak council.
1962	After a period of economic expansion, union weakness and bitter competition, union unity develops in some manufacturing sectors.
1963	The Socialists join the Coalition government.
1969	Following intense industrial conflict, new unitary forms of workers representation develop and unions end formal political links.
1970	The so-called Workers' Charter favours and protects unions.
1973	Three major peak councils unite to form *Federazione CGIL–CISL–UIL*.
1974	The *Federazione* and the employers change the *scala mobile* indexation system. Lower paid workers are particularly favoured.
1977–79	The Communist Party supports the government, but with no direct participation in it.
1983	Tax structure and *scala mobile* changed after two years of controversy. Changes in other areas are also put into effect or promised with the leading role of government as mediator.
1983	A new law is passed that formalises collective bargaining in the public sector.
1984	Negotiations for another national agreement dealing with the indexation system break off. Only CISL and

UIL agree with the government offer. *The Federazione CGIL–CISL–UIL* ends. The government enforces the accord reached with CISL and UIL by decree.

1985   The referendum narrowly supports cuts in wage indexation (54.3 per cent versus 45.7 per cent). New bargaining rounds are held related to the indexation system and hours of work.

1985   New legislation introduces the new category of *cadres*. (Before there were only three groups of employees: top managers, white- and blue-collar workers.)

1986   A new indexation system agreed in the private sector; the coverage is reduced.

1983–85   The President of the Coalition government is a Socialist (Craxi).

1988–89   Autonomous unions challenge the leading role of the established confederation in the public sector.

1990   A new law is passed that gives some protection from unfair dismissal in small enterprises (less than 15 employees).

1991   New legislation regulates labour market, unemployment benefits and wage integration funds. Employers and unions begin a new round of central negotiations on *scala mobile*.

1992   A new central agreement between the social partners and government abolished the *scala mobile*. To reduce the public deficit, the government enacted tax increases and budget cuts.

7 Industrial relations in France[1]
Janine Goetschy and
Annette Jobert

France has a population of 56 million and a GDP of $1192 billion. Although France and Britain have a similar size of population and GDP, the growth rate in France for the 1989–90 period was 2.6 per cent, compared with only 1.6 per cent in Britain. France has 64 per cent of its civilian employees in the service sector, with 30 per cent in industry. It still has a relatively large agricultural sector, which employs about 6 per cent of civilian employees (compared with only about 2 per cent in Britain). Its main trading partners are Germany, Italy and its other EC neighbours. France can be characterised as apparently having a lower union density than any of the other countries featured in this book (as discussed later).

Since 1982, the average annual increase in consumer prices has been declining. Between 1985 and 1990, the index of consumer prices increased more slowly in France than in any of the other countries discussed in this book except Germany and Japan. The French inflation rate—3.6 per cent in 1989 and 3.4 per cent in 1990—was one of the lowest in western Europe.

As in most of the other countries, unemployment in France has increased significantly since the 1960s. It rose from 1.4 per cent in 1960 and 2.4 per cent in 1970 to 4.1 per cent in 1975, 6.3 per cent in 1980, and 10.5 per cent in 1987. It fell in the late 1980s, but was increasing again in the early 1990s.

In line with the international trends, since the 1970s the forms of employment in France have been changing substantially. By 1988, temporary employment represented about 7 per cent of the labour force, while about 11 per cent were in part-time employment. Female employment has continued to grow. The participation rate of women increased from 46 per cent in 1963 to 58 per cent in 1990.

Before the advent of the Fifth Republic in 1958, French politics were more volatile than in most of the other eight countries discussed. There are four political parties in France. The Gaullists and the Independent Republicans (who are part of the *Union pour la Démocratie Française)*, together with the Centre Right Party are broadly towards the Right of the political spectrum, while the Communist Party and the Socialist Party are to the Left of centre.

Between 1958 and 1981, France was governed by Right-of-centre governments. The Socialists made a decisive gain in 1981, when a Socialist president was elected: M. François Mitterrand. Initially his government was a Socialist–Communist coalition, but the Communists left the coalition in 1984. Although Mitterrand's first term as President was not due to finish until 1988, the Socialists were replaced by a Right-wing government in 1986, under the Prime Minister M. Jacques Chirac. In 1988, Mitterrand was re-elected for a second presidential mandate by a large majority vote. Though the parliamentary election results were slightly less favourable to the Left, a Socialist government was formed under Prime Minister M. Michel Rocard, which included a few centrist ministers. By 1992, there had been two further Prime Ministers after Rocard.

The industrial relations parties

Industrialisation and urbanisation emerged in France during the mid-nineteenth century, rather later than in Britain. Strikes were not permitted until 1864, but even then unions were still illegal. However, many informal unions were organised in this period on a local level. There were some parallels with the origins of unions in the English-speaking countries. Craftsmen were the first to organise, but craft unions were soon displaced by industrial unionism. The early unions were often involved in violent clashes with state agencies and employers, who tried to suppress them. Unions were eventually legalised in 1884.

The present features of French unions derive partly from their early history and their ideological complexion, from the traditional lack of mutual recognition between the industrial relations parties (the social partners) and from the important interventionist role of the French state in industrial and social matters, which tends to detract from the support of union and employer organisations.

The unions

The French union movement has been characterised by pluralism, rivalry and fragmentation on the one hand, and paucity of financial and organisational resources on the other. Since the 1970s, these structural weaknesses have been particularly apparent. Union density has traditionally been low in France. It was around 23 per cent in the mid-1970s (see Table A.20; see also Adam 1983). It fell to about 16 per cent by 1985 (Mouriaux 1986), and dropped to about 12 per cent or even less in the late 1980s (Rosanvallon 1986). These percentages are researchers' estimates; membership numbers reported by union confederations are inflated as they include members who do not pay their monthly dues regularly. Moreover, there is no equivalent of the *check-off* system for union dues that operates, for example, in most English-speaking countries.

There are five national union confederations as summarised in Table 7.1. One study provides the following estimates of membership: around 600 000 for the *Confédération générale du travail* (CGT); 470 000 for the *Confédération française démocratique du travail* (CFDT); between 400 000 and 500 000 for *Force ouvrière* (FO); around 300 000 for *Fédération de l'éducation nationale* (FEN); 100 000 for *Confédération française des travailleurs chrétiens* (CFTC); and less than 100 000 for the CFE–CGC (Noblecourt 1990). The official figures reported by the unions themselves also show there was a decline in membership during the 1980s.

The CGT, the oldest French confederation, was established in 1895. With the 1906 Charter of Amiens, the CGT adopted an anarcho-revolutionary program, wary of political parties and political action. (Interestingly, in the same year, the British unions turned in the opposite direction, by forming the Labour Party.) The coexistence of Marxists, with anarchist and social-reformist elements, led to a major split in the CGT in 1921, with an expulsion of the Marxists, following the split in the Socialist Party after the Russian Revolution. The two wings reunited during the 1936 Popular Front. There was another split in 1939 after the Russo–German pact. Then a further reunification took place during the 'resistance' and another

Table 7.1 Official membership figures of the main union confederations

	1976	1983 (thousands)	1986–88	
CGT	2 074	1 622	1 031	(1987)
FO	926	1 150	1 108	(1987)
CFDT	829	681	600	(1988)[a]
FEN	526	493	394	(1988)
CFE–CGC	325	307	241	(1986)
CFTC	223	260	250	(1987)

Note: a estimate.
The full name of each confederation is included in the text, also see List of abbreviations.
Source: Bibes and Mouriaux 1990.

split in 1948, when the minority group rejected Marxism and established the current FO (see later). Since the 1940s, most of the CGT's leaders have been Communist Party members, both at the top and intermediate levels. However, many of the CGT's members did not belong to the Communist Party. The CGT's membership has changed in four phases since the 1940s. After having reached a peak in 1947, it declined until 1958; it then grew between 1959 and 1975; and declined again after the mid-1970s. Between the late 1970s and the mid-1980s the CGT membership fell from over 2 million to about 1.5 million in 1983 and 1 million in 1987, and if we exclude retired members from its membership, the decline in working members was 50 per cent in the 1980s. As with the other confederations, the CGT is organised in industry federations, and in geographically based local unions. It draws its main strength from skilled manual workers. Its strength is the metal, building and chemical industries, and in municipal and health services. The CGT has an important technical, managerial and professional staff section, the *Union générale des ingénieurs, cadres et techniciens* (UGICT).

The FO was born in 1948 as a reaction to Communist interference in the CGT. It claims to be the true heir of the CGT's old policy of political independence and is staunchly anti-Communist. By the mid-1980s, the FO claimed to have become the second largest confederation with nearly 1 million members. It sees collective bargaining as the main element of union action, and aims to defend workers' job interests, independently of any political party. It is strongest among white-collar workers, technical and professional groups in the public sector, but has also been growing in the private sector. By 1979, the FO claimed that as many as 55 per cent of its members were from the private sector. The FO has also a small *cadre* (managerial) section, the *Union des cadres et ingénieurs* (UCI).

Confessional unionism began in 1919 with the formation of the CFTC. Its main objective was to promote peaceful collaboration between capital and labour, according to the social doctrine of the Catholic Church. The CFTC split in 1964, when the minority group retained the religious orientation and kept the name CFTC. Its centres of strength are among miners, Christian school teachers and health workers. Its total membership is around 250 000. The CFTC has a tiny *cadre* section, the UGICA (*Union générale des ingénieurs, et cadres*).

Following the CFTC's 1964 split, the majority group formally abandoned the Catholic connection and formed the CFDT. The CFDT used to be the second-largest union confederation as its membership between 1948 (old CFTC) and 1976 had nearly doubled to over 800 000 members, but it declined from 1977 onwards to about 600 000 by the late 1980s. In 1970, it adopted elements of a socialist-Marxist ideology with elements of Gramscism and it favoured self-management. The radicalisation of its ideology put it in closer competition with the CGT. But after 1979, the CFDT played down its former ideological emphasis. It is strongest in the metal, chemical and oil industries, health service, banking and insurance. The CFDT has a small *cadre* section, the *Union confédérale des ingénieurs et cadres* (UCC). However, UCC membership is restricted to 'senior' *cadres*, which explains partly why it is smaller than other unions' *cadres* sections.

The *Confédération générale des cadres* (CGC) was formed in 1944. In 1976 its membership was around 325 000 (engineers, executives, salesmen, supervisors, technicians), but from 1977 it declined by nearly a third of its members to about 240 000 in 1986. It is strongest in the metals and chemical industries and among salespeople. Its goals focus on issues such as winning more participation for *cadres;* maximising their pay differentials; and protecting their interests in relation to tax and social security. It claims not to be associated with any political parties. In 1981, this confederation changed its name to CFE–CGC (*Confédération française de l'encadrement–confédération générale des cadres*) given that about half of its members were not really management staff, but were supervisors, technicians and commercial agents (i.e. travelling salespeople).

All these five confederations are known as 'representative unions' at national level. This is a legal attribute granted on the basis of five criteria (the most important is proving that the union is totally independent from the employer). This confers on them some exclusive rights, for instance in collective bargaining; the nomination of candidates in the system of employee representation within the firm (see later); and in terms of representation on numerous governmental and other consultative bodies.

Except for the CGC, unions from all these five confederations recruit across all industries and trades and across all categories of employees. Thus they compete with each other. However, they each have their traditional strength in their own specific sectors, professional groups and regions.

The FEN is another important specialist union which is also 'representative', but only on a sectorial level (i.e. the education sector). The FEN decided to remain independent at the time of the CGT split. It recruits staff in most types of state educational institutions, and had slightly less than 400 000 members in 1988. Its membership declined subsequently. Measured by membership density in its own sector, the FEN is, nevertheless, one of the strongest French unions.

There are also several other 'autonomous' unions in specific sectors (the automobile industry for instance) or organising certain groups of employees such as the air traffic controllers, train drivers, lorry drivers, and journalists.

The employers

French industry includes a high proportion of small firms. In the post-1945 reconstruction, in the face of the increasing international competition within the incipient EC, there was extensive corporate rationalisation involving many mergers. Nevertheless, 36.2 per cent are still employed in firms of less than 50 employees. Such small firms are usually family businesses and often have a strong Catholic tradition of paternalism.

In contrast to the plurality of unionism with the various union confederations, at national level the employers are more united in their main confederation, the *Conseil national du patronat français* (CNPF). The CNPF embraces more than three-quarters of all French enterprises. Unlike its counterparts in Britain and Germany, the CNPF does engage in collective bargaining, though not on wages, as the basic minimum rates of pay are determined at an industry-wide level. The CNPF was established in 1945, though employers were already organised in a range of industry-level federations from the early nineteenth century, and at national level from 1919 onwards in a forerunner to the CNPF.

The post-1973 economic crisis stimulated important changes in the employers' strategy; they aimed to convince the government, the unions and public opinion more generally that there was a crisis and that business was vulnerable.

The employers' objective at the micro-level was to increase the flexibility of the workforce, a choice which they preferred to drastic employment reductions. At that stage the employers did not see flexibility being achieved through training. Flexibility was reached partly through 'quantitative *external* flexibility', that is, by intro-ducing shorter-term contracts of employment and more temporary work. Employers were especially enthusiastic about such employ-ment practices as they disliked the constraints imposed by the 1976 law on economic redundancies introduced by the Chirac govern-ment. (This law, requiring prior administrative permission before implementing redundancies, was abolished in 1986, also under a Chirac government.)

Another method used by the end of the 1970s and throughout the 1980s was 'quantitative *internal* flexibility' of working time.

(The average length of the working week could vary and could be calculated on a yearly basis; thus there were developments in terms of weekend work, shift-work, flexi-time, etc.). More recently, in the mid-1980s, the CNPF launched a campaign in favour of *wage* flexibility.

As to *functional* flexibility (new job content and work autonomy for specific groups of workers), there have been many experiments since the mid-1970s, but they depend on long-term training efforts, and it is not yet practicable to fully evaluate their scope and diffusion.

Since 1977, the CNPF has exhorted managers to pursue 'an active social policy at plant-level and take more initiatives', in order to facilitate the implementation of this whole range of flexibility practices. Managers have been encouraged to abandon their old autocratic behaviour, to by-pass traditional union channels and enter into direct dialogue with employees. Some employers enhanced the status of supervisory staff by letting them deal directly with grievances at a lower level in the managerial hierarchy than hitherto.

The state

State intervention is very important in French industrial relations. This reflects the traditional reluctance of unions and employers to use voluntary collective agreements. In periods when the Left has been in ascendancy, unions have pressed for new laws: in 1936 with the Popular Front, in 1945 with the Liberation, in 1968 following the May events, and in 1981 with the advent of the Socialist government.

Since the late 1960s, there have been closer links between the law and collective bargaining. Certain laws are based on the results of previously negotiated agreements or on earlier discussions between the industrial relations parties and the state. The state, then, does not play an authoritarian role in labour relations. Moreover, the state has tended to enhance the social partners' autonomy by transforming the legal framework for collective bargaining in 1971 and 1982.

The state is also a major employer, with about a quarter of civilian employees working in the public sector. The French public sector embraces a wider range of nationalised industries than is usual in most Western countries. As an employer, the state exerts great influence on pay settlements in the private sector too. It also influences wages through the legal increases and index-linked adjustments of the national minimum wage (SMIC). The SMIC is adjusted according to the price index of consumer goods when the latter has risen by 2 per cent. Moreover, the government can also raise the SMIC independently whenever it wishes. This was the case, for instance, in 1981 when the Left came to power. From a legal point of view, the SMIC should not constitute a basis for remuneration packages as a whole, but inevitably it exerts a general lever effect on all wages. However, since 1981, successive governments (Left and Right) have tended to avoid using the SMIC to raise average wage levels. According to a Ministry of Labour survey, there were approximately 1.7 million workers receiving the SMIC, that is 9.7 per cent of workers in 1988.

In the early 1980s the government intervened to fight growing unemployment. However, it managed to stabilise unemployment essentially through social policy rather than through economic action or job creation. The Socialist government launched youth employment programs and new opportunities for employers and unions to negotiate 'solidarity contracts'. The latter policy was either to encourage employers to recruit new workers at the same time as it organised early retirement plans, or to encourage employers to hire new workers following the reduction of weekly working time. Training and retraining schemes were also increased in order to boost youth employment. Moreover, the government training policy was linked to industrial restructuring both in the nationalised and the private sectors (e.g. in steel, coal mining, automobile manufacture and shipbuilding). The Socialist government's policy of reducing work time did not appear to be effective in creating new jobs.

When the Right was in power (1986–88) its main preoccupation was to introduce more flexible labour relations rules for employers by amending the laws, for example, on redundancy, working hours, and fixed-term and part-time hiring. Rather than dismantling all the policies of its predecessor, the Socialist Rocard government (elected in 1988) opted for a policy whereby employers and unions would engage in central enabling agreements in order to amend the laws enacted under the Right (see Conclusion). A series of initiatives and measures were launched rapidly in an attempt to fight unemployment.

In 1989, the Rocard government announced a second wide-ranging and ambitious 'social program' aiming to modernise the public service (with the idea of a 'growth pact' for this sector). It also redesigned some employment policies in an attempt to reduce the proliferation of temporary jobs, to integrate into society such excluded groups as immigrants, to link tax with social security expenditures, to encourage employee participation and to foster profit-sharing. This was followed by the adoption of social measures to improve the multitude of training and other policies in favour of the unemployed, especially the long-term unemployed and young unemployed.

The government also initiated a variety of economic and fiscal measures to encourage employers to create employment. A novel measure, adopted in 1988, was the establishment of 'a minimum integration income' designed to guarantee a basic wage for the most deprived, provided that they agreed to join state-funded schemes for improving their labour market prospects. In 1989 the government tried to discourage the use of *overtime* and to promote reductions in working time linked to the advent of more flexible hours.

The 1986 legislation which had abolished official controls on *redundancies*, was also reformed in 1989 to enhance works councils' rights to information and consultation with regard to redundancy matters. Whatever their size, all companies, then, had to prepare a 'social plan' before implementing economic redundancies. However, the government did not reinstate official controls over redundancies.

The government introduced a Bill on *precarious* (temporary) *employment*. This was based on a previous collective agreement which was reached by some of the social partners in March 1990, even though the FO and CGT had refused to sign it. In short, the reforms restricted the basic maximum length of fixed-term contracts to 18 months, redefined the circumstances in which they could be used and provided for greater disclosure of information about them to employee representatives.

As to wages, the government asked the social partners to open negotiations at sector level to improve the earnings of low-paid workers. This was accepted by the CNPF.

Employee representation within the enterprise

At plant level, there is a range of representative bodies set up by particular political institutions or in response to particular social events. Employee delegates (*délégués du personnel*) were instituted by the Popular Front in 1936; works committees (*comités d'entreprise*) in 1945 following the Liberation; and workplace union branches (*section syndicale*) in 1968. As a generalisation, employee delegates deal with individual employee grievances, works committees deal with workplace consultation, while union branches and stewards represent their union and participate in collective bargaining at the workplace. There is a legal framework for all these bodies.

Unlike shop stewards or workplace delegates in the English-speaking countries, who are union representatives, French employee delegates are not union representatives. However, in practice 70 per cent of them are elected from a union slate. Delegates must be elected every year by the total workforce in all enterprises which employ more than ten people. The 1982 Act stipulates that delegates

could also be elected in those workplaces with less than ten employees, where several firms operate on a common site (such as a
building site or commercial centre), and if there is a total of at least
50 employees. Most of the private sector is covered by this Act.

Employee delegates deal with individuals' claims on wages,
working conditions, the implementation of labour law and collective
agreements. They may also call upon the Labour Inspector in cases
where there is disagreement. The number of delegates elected varies
according to the size of the firm. The employer must meet them
collectively at least once a month. To fulfil their duties, they are
allocated 15 hours paid working time per month.

Delegates are elected by proportional representation. Manual
workers and lower clerical staff vote separately from technicians
and *cadres*. The election procedures must be agreed between the
employer and the unions. There is no exclusion of foreign 'guest
workers' from voting or from being candidates.

Unlike those of other countries, under these election procedures
there is a two-round secret ballot. In the first round, candidates can
be nominated only by one of the main union confederations, or by
any other affiliated union which is recognised as 'representative'
within the firm. If less than half of the electorate votes in the first
round, then any employee may stand as a candidate for the second
round. In practice, however, a second round is rarely required.

Works councils are supposed to be established in all firms
employing at least 50 employees. They use election procedures
similar to the ones summarised above. These committees have little
real decision-making power, except in relation to welfare issues.
They do have the right, however, to be informed and consulted at
specific periods on the general management of the business, particularly in relation to the number and organisation of employees, their
hours of work and employment conditions.

Each quarter, the employer is required to inform the works
committee about the general progress of orders, output and finances.
Employers should also provide employment data including details
of any short-term contracts and subcontract work. The employer
must justify the use of such measures. Once a year, the employer
has to submit a general report in writing to the works committee,
covering the business's activities, turnover, losses or profits, the
production achievements, substantial capital transfers, subcontracting, the allocation of profits, subsidies from the state or other public
authorities and their use, investments, and salaries. To help it to
examine the annual accounts, the works committee may choose an
expert accountant. Further, on an *ad hoc* basis, the committee must
be informed and consulted on all changes in the economic or legal
organisation of the business, in cases such as sales or mergers, for

instance. Moreover, under the October 1982 Act, the committee has to be informed and consulted before any large project involving the introduction of new technologies, whenever there may be consequences related to employment, qualifications, pay, training and working conditions. In firms with at least 300 employees, an expert can be coopted to study the situation (Rojot 1983).

The works committee does not only have to give its opinion, but its agreement is required on such issues as profit-sharing arrangements and changes in working hours. If the employer requests it, the representatives have to maintain confidentiality about the employer's information on production processes and finances. The works committee is composed of the employee representatives and the employer (or a deputy). The employer chairs the meeting, which takes place at least monthly. Each representative union can appoint a union observer to the committee. To fulfil their duties each employee representative can use 20 paid working hours per month. The works committee can create sub-committees to examine specific problems. Health, Safety and Improvement of Working Conditions Committees are compulsory in firms with at least 50 employees. Firms with at least 300 employees have to set up an employment-training committee. Many employers initially resisted works committees, but most have gradually come to accept them as having a legitimate role.

Since 1968, there have also been workplace union branches in parallel to the representative bodies. Before 1968, unions had no legal right to establish such branches. In firms of a certain size, branches can have an office and other facilities, and can appoint their own stewards. They can collect dues during working hours, use notice boards, distribute leaflets, and organise monthly meetings (outside working time). The Mitterrand government improved union rights by increasing the number of paid hours allocated to employee representatives for union duties and allowing them to circulate freely within the workplace. All employee representatives are legally protected against dismissal. Hindering a representative or the various bodies is unlawful.

The representative bodies are not a coherent system, but have grown in an *ad hoc* way. Moreover, with the complex and occasionally imprecise legal framework, there is some confusion of functions among the various bodies, not least because individual representatives frequently fulfil several functions. Often there is a lack of candidates to fill the various elected positions. In the larger firms, these representatives often coordinate the activities of the works committees as well as being employee delegates. Although this may be accepted by managers in big firms, in smaller firms managers may resent what they see as union interference.

A major innovation of the 1982 Act was to set up a *group/combine committee* within large multi-plant companies whose registered office is in France. The function of such committees is to receive, at least once a year, information about the financial and employment situation within the group or combine. As these French group committees developed, several multinationals of French origin later concluded agreements that provided information and consultation structures also at a European level (Jobert 1990).

A government-commissioned report (*rapport Bélier*) found that existing provisions for representation work poorly in smaller firms. Some 64 per cent of firms with between 11 and 49 staff do not have any union delegates. About 60 per cent of those with between 50 and 100 employees have no union delegates, and in the same size-category around 30 per cent have no company works committees. This finding led the government to propose legal as well as negotiated changes on the issue for 1991, but the initiative was postponed.

Employee participation and collective bargaining

The Employee Participation Act of February 1982 gave employees the right to stop working if they considered the job to be dangerous, but not to stop the machinery. The Act was further extended in August 1982 to give employees the right to have a say on the content and organisation of their work and, more generally, their working conditions. The Act prescribed that employees' views should be expressed 'directly' and 'collectively' on these matters. The law was innovative in two ways. First, it was intended to decentralise collective bargaining in all enterprises with at least 200 employees. However, while it was compulsory for employers to *initiate* negotiations with employees over arrangements for participation, they were not compelled to *conclude* the negotiations. Second, the Act was to be experimental. After a two-year trial period, the government evaluated the impact of the Act. An amended Act was introduced in 1986. This enlarged the range of issues subject to participation to include most production activities. It also allowed managerial staff to be represented directly in employee participation committees.

A Ministry of Labour report in 1985 concluded that nearly half the firms covered by the Act (45 per cent) had reached agreements with unions on employee participation. But in addition there were several hundred agreements reached in smaller firms where collective bargaining remained optional. Most unions had signed such agreements when they were represented in a firm. The incidence of agreements signed by unions, as a percentage of the firms in which they were present were: CGT (76 per cent), CFDT (78 per cent), FO (62 per cent), CFTC (84 per cent), and CGC (87 per cent).

The Report noted discrepancies between the views expressed by union officials at the national level and those of shop stewards at the level of the enterprise or workplace. Furthermore, while CGT and CFDT officials were firm in their support for employee participation, the FO was against any schemes which might enable the employer to manipulate employees and reduce their role as the representative of employees. The CGC (representing executive staff) feared that employee participation might jeopardise the power of the managerial and supervisory staff within the enterprise.

Most employee participation groups were based on workgroups with 15 to 20 members, and met for one or two hours on two to four occasions per year. Most agreements contained feedback procedures which required the employer to respond to requests from groups within a specified time period. The major achievements of the participation groups were in improving working conditions and work organisation. Employers were criticised for not dealing with employees' requests satisfactorily. Hence, many groups faded away. Nevertheless, by 1990, the Ministry of Labour estimated that between 10 000 and 12 000 enterprises had signed participation agreements, which covered some 3.5 million employees (Goetschy 1991).

The statutes on collective bargaining (1919, 1936, 1946, 1950, 1971, 1982) illustrate a recurrence of typically French labour law prescriptions. These attempt to compensate for the unions' organisational weakness and the lack of effective collective bargaining. For example, all employees, whether or not they are unionised, may benefit from a collective agreement. Furthermore, French labour law reinforces union pluralism and in some ways even favours the minority organisations (such as the CFTC, CGC and formerly the FO). Thus, a collective agreement is valid even if only one representative union has signed it. To what extent has this provision divided the union confederations? Traditionally (before the mid-1970s), the most radical ones (CGT and CFDT) tended to adopt an uncompromising approach during the negotiation process, while the reformist ones (FO, CFTC, CGC) were usually more willing to compromise and sign agreements. In many instances, however, such a division seems to have suited both categories of unions. The CGT and CFDT members could thus benefit from an agreement, even though their leaders had not compromised themselves by signing it.

Collective bargaining has traditionally taken place at industry level. Employer and union organisations preferred such bargaining for ideological as well as tactical reasons. This practice also reflected the lack of mutual recognition between unions and employers at plant or company level. Industry agreements covered the maximum number of employees, which was an advantage to the unions when their membership was low. The employers have favoured industry agreements which establish only minimal standards for a given industrial sector. Furthermore, for a long time this spared employers from having to recognise unions at plant level.

After 1968 there was a significant development in multi-industry bargaining and plant-level bargaining. Both practices were reinforced by the 1971 amendments to the 1950 Collective Bargaining Act. Innovative multi-industry bargaining dealt with such issues as job security, vocational training, the introduction of salaried status for manual workers, unemployment benefits following redundancies, and working conditions. Such national agreements provided a framework which aimed to encourage collective bargaining at lower levels (in a specific industry or firm).

The increasing number of plant-level agreements resulted from: first, the demands from employees after May 1968; second, new strategies used by employers to reduce labour turnover by granting employees specific company benefits; and third, the 1968 Statute, which legalised union delegates at plant level and gave them a legitimate function within collective bargaining. The plant level agreements were generally not innovative, but rather they improved on or adapted higher level agreements to local conditions. In practice, such domestic bargaining was generally confined to larger firms.

Following the 1973 energy crisis, there was a decline in the number of plant-level agreements. Multi-industry enabling agreements were less often followed by agreements at lower levels. There were significant difficulties, for instance, in implementing the 1975 multi-industry agreement on working conditions. However, during this period the parties could still conclude multi-industry agreements which were not 'enabling', but which settled precise conditions, especially about employment issues such as redundancy.

In the 1980s, the election of the Socialist government induced a different political and legal context for collective bargaining. A major objective of the Mitterrand government was the reform of workplace relations. It was outlined in the *Report on the Rights of Workers* by the Minister of Labour, M. Jean Auroux. This Auroux Report aimed to provide employees with real 'citizenship within the firm' and to create new opportunities so that 'employees may become actors of change within the enterprise'. The Report was not completely new; it adopted a gradual rather than a radical approach and partly reflected the 1975 Sudreau Report. Though the Report paid heed to the unions' platforms (especially the CGT's and CFDT's), it followed the government's own industrial relations policy and thus met varying receptions by the different union and employer organisations (Goetschy 1983).

The Auroux Report enumerated the following deficiencies of the French system of collective bargaining. First, many wage earners were not covered by any collective agreements, whether at industry or plant level (i.e. 11 per cent of wage earners in firms of at least ten employees). Such 'excluded workers' were particularly concentrated among temporary employees, for example, in the distributive trades and in hotels and restaurants; second, many agreements lacked job classification structures; third, there was a large gap between basic minimum wages and actual pay (an average of 30 per cent); fourth, collective agreements were highly fragmented (40 of the 1023 national or regional-level collective agreements covered more than half of the total number of wage earners); fifth, only a quarter of wage-earners were covered by a plant agreement; lastly, the low density of unionism and the divisions between unions undermined the 'legitimacy' of agreements.

The 1982 Collective Bargaining Act followed the Auroux Report. The 1982 Act included many prescriptions, most of which aimed to improve the existing system, but some of them were innovative. For instance, in firms which had union branches, employers were obliged to open negotiations every year on pay and working hours. However, there was no obligation to reach an agreement and the employer had the final say. Unlike in the USA, there was no requirement to bargain 'in good faith'.

Such provisions aimed to foster collective bargaining within the firm. The intention was to induce more 'integrative' attitudes, whereby employers would become more aware of their social responsibilities and unions more attentive to economic constraints.

As another innovation, non-signatory unions could veto a plant-level agreement. For example, if an agreement included derogatory clauses in relation to shorter working hours. Before using a veto, the non-signatory opponents had to win more than half of the votes in the works council or employee delegates' elections. Granting such veto rights to the largest opposition unions was expected to lead to more legitimate agreements.

Further, in national industry agreements, the obligation to meet once a year to negotiate wages and every fifth year to discuss possible job classification revision, should bring the agreed basic minimum pay rates and other conditions closer to actual practice. At the firm or industry level, the frequency of meetings (for a compulsory 'social dialogue') was expected to strengthen the negotiators' sense of responsibility in collective bargaining and to make them more responsive to their constituents.

After the 1982 Collective Bargaining Act, employers raised fierce criticisms of the novel obligation on them to negotiate at company level. However, their criticisms seemed to fade as the Act was implemented.

There were also several prescriptions which aimed to enlarge unions' rights to information and to provide expert help in the bargaining process. The Act further improved the existing procedures whereby the Minister of Labour could extend certain collective agreements to non-signatory firms. These extension procedures were very important, given that the employer might initially refuse to sign an agreement.

Both the Act and some other 1982 ordinances gave priority to collective bargaining rather than the law. The search for a new balance between state intervention and collective bargaining was the hallmark of Mitterrand's post-1981 strategy of social reform. However, this strategy was based on the 1969–71 industrial relations policy of the then Right-wing government, when Delors was the adviser to Prime Minister Chaban-Delmas.

The attempts by the early Mitterrand government to promote collective bargaining became entangled with its 'austerity plans' of 1982 and 1983. Nevertheless, plant-level bargaining was subject to a new boost, not only by the Auroux laws, but also because it suited employers' interests. Since 1987, on average, 6000 agreements have been made each year. In 1989, of the total number of agreements signed, 57 per cent were pay settlements and 35 per cent related to work time issues. This distribution has not changed much since 1986. About 30 per cent of wage agreements at enterprise level contained individualised pay-increase clauses, most often linked to a general increase. Moreover, there was a development of profit-sharing agreements linked to the firm's results (performance-related pay). More than 7000 such agreements were signed in 1990 covering 1.5 million wage earners.

However, in 1989 plant-level bargaining covered only about 20 per cent of all wage earners, as it did not cover smaller firms without unions. Such a restricted coverage is because collective bargaining remains essentially an industry-level activity. Most wage earners are covered, then, by an industry agreement, which was one of the objectives of the Auroux laws. Around 80 per cent of industry agreements concern pay issues.

After a decline of multi-industry bargaining in the late 1970s and early 1980s, it was revitalised again by the beginning of the 1990s. The development of multi-industry bargaining was supported both by the government and the CNPF which favoured a 'consensus approach' for achieving the modernisation of French enterprises. Among the unions, the CFDT has been most prominent in supporting such an approach. In 1988, a national orientation agreement on *technological change* was signed, with the aim of encouraging negotiations on this issue. The consensus approach also inspired the 1989 national framework agreement on the *flexible organisation of worktime*. There have been similar agreements on such issues as equal employment opportunities and the working environment. In 1990, the parties concluded an inter-industry *occupational training* agreement which later became law.

In 1990, employers' statutory contributions to vocational training were 1.2 per cent of the total wages bill. In practice, French companies spend around 2.7 per cent on employees' training.[2] Whereas the CGT has opposed such 'enabling' arrangements, the CFDT and CGC have supported these arrangements being agreed with the CNPF. By contrast, the FO and the CFTC have been critical and have refused to sign some of the agreements.

Representative elections

Besides their formal membership, then, unions' support can also be assessed on the basis of the results from 'social' elections such as the representatives to works committees, social welfare boards (*Sécurité Sociale*) and industrial tribunals (*Prud'hommes*).

The works committee election results for 1990 show that, in total, the five representative unions obtained around 70 per cent of the votes (see Table 7.2). Thus the unions have a much higher degree of support than might be inferred from their low membership. However, between 1977 and 1989 there was a significant increase for non-union representatives as shown by the voting results. This trend is further confirmed if we take into account the results in terms of the seats obtained. For example, as shown in Table 7.3, in 1987, with less than 25 per cent of the votes, the non-union representatives obtained 44 per cent of the seats. The disparity between the results in percentage of the votes and percentage of the seats reflects not only the peculiarities of the electoral system, but also the large proportion of small firms which are not unionised.

The participation rate for the works committee elections remains fairly high, though it has been declining (70.5 per cent in 1977, 65.4 per cent in 1989). As Table 7.2 shows, the support obtained by the CGT (in percentage of votes) declined from 37.4 per cent in 1977 to 25.1 per cent in 1989. For the first time ever, in 1989, in terms of the percentage of the votes the CGT was in second position, after the non-union representatives. Support for the CFDT seems to be stabilising after a steady decrease between 1981 and 1985. The

Table 7.2 Results of works committee elections (as percentage of votes cast)

Year	CGT	CFDT	FO	CFTC	CFE –CGC	Others	Non- union
1977	37.4	20.2	9.0	3.0	5.4	5.7	19
1979	34.4	20.5	9.7	3.1	5.8	4.8	21
1981	32.0	22.3	9.9	2.9	6.1	4.1	22
1983	28.5	21.9	11.1	4.0	6.5	4.7	23
1985	27.7	21.2	12.6	5.0	6.2	5.8	22
1987	26.8	21.3	11.3	4.8	5.9	6.0	24
1989	25.1	21.0	11.2	4.6	5.5	6.3	26

Source: Liaisons Sociales (25 July 1990).

FO and the CFTC have increased their share of the vote slowly over the last 15 years. In regard to the FO, however, its works committee election results have been increasing less than its membership. Altogether, the CFE–CGC remained fairly stable, but it registered a slight decrease from 1987 onwards.

Turning to industrial tribunals (see Table 7.4), it appears that although the CGT has remained the leading confederation, its support declined severely after 1979. The support for the CFDT remained stable, whereas the FO's support increased.

Despite their low membership, the support unions obtain through 'social' elections is relatively important. However, in general the various election results indicate that there has been declining support for the unions.

Table 7.3 Results of works council committee elections (in percentages of the seats obtained)

Year	CGT	CFDT	FO	CFTC	CFE –CGC	Others	Non- union
1987	18.3	15.9	9.1	3.6	5.1	4.6	44

Source: Liaisons Sociales (23 February 1989).

Why is union density low and declining?

Why has French unionism declined since the 1970s, even though the political environment has apparently been beneficial to unions (as the Left has been in power most of the time except between 1986 and 1988)?

First, major changes took place in the French economy. There was restructuring from traditionally well-organised industrial sectors

Table 7.4 Elections for industrial tribunals (percentages)

Year	CGT	CFDT	FO	CFTC	CGC	Others
1979	42.3	23.2	17.3	7.2	5.2	4.8
1982	37.0	23.5	17.7	8.5	9.6	3.7
1987	36.5	23.0	20.4	8.3	7.4	4.5
1992	33.3	23.8	20.4	8.5	6.9	6.8

Source: Bibes & Mouriaux 1990.

(coal, steel, metals, shipbuilding) to new industrial sectors, and a shift of jobs from industry to the service sector. The increasing number of small firms also led to a loss of union members.

Second, major changes in the labour market were detrimental to unionisation: unemployment rose in the 1980s. Furthermore there were changes in employment contracts and employment practices which meant an increase in the number of people who worked part-time (by half a million during the 1982–86 period), and on a temporary basis; both these categories are difficult to unionise. In 1989, there were approximately 600 000 people working under fixed-term contracts (i.e. 70 per cent of new employment) plus around 280 000 from temporary agencies. This corresponds to a rise in the use of temporary workers from about 2.5 per cent of all employment in 1977 to around 7 per cent in 1989. Besides, the development of the French equivalent of the British Youth Training Schemes (*travail d'utilité collective*, and *stage d'initiation à la vie professionnelle*) also hindered unionisation.

Third, young people's changing attitudes to unions (i.e. increasing scepticism about the efficiency of unions' action, versus their own individual capacity to negotiate; see Linhard & Mallan 1988). The decline in unionisation also appears to have been higher among women than among men.

Fourth, employers' social policies have been changing a great deal since 1977 (Morville 1985). The CNPF sought to establish a direct dialogue with employees and pursued a more active social policy by mobilising middle managers. Employers, then, were increasingly aiming to communicate with the workforce outside the formal employee representation system. Therefore unions were often by-passed and this tended to diminish their role even further. Employers developed a more participative style of management and introduced many innovations. This led, for instance, to an increase in the number of quality circles (30 000), which spread to a greater extent than in most other European countries. In practice, and though the CNPF had expressed some initial ideological fears, employers welcomed the Auroux law granting employees the right to direct participation (Goetschy 1991). Moreover, employers initiated a whole range of flexibility practices, for example in regard to working time (such as flexible hours), recruitment (short-time, part-time work), which often met employees' wishes, but which led to the individualisation of employment relations within the firm. In 1987, the CNPF issued guidelines promoting the individualisation of pay (de-indexation of wages and development of merit payments) which impinged on unions' wage bargaining function.

Fifth, there was increasing self-criticism by unions due to their ineffective strategies in the face of new challenges. On the one hand, the gap between the union leadership and the rank-and-file appears to have been increasing. This is due to the unions' work load, including the numerous duties resulting from the Auroux laws (see below), their increasing participation in welfare state bodies (social security, unemployment insurance, training, employment and administrative committees in the public sector) and to the developing trend of multi-industry bargaining. Such an 'institutionalisation' of unionism seems to have isolated unions from those they were supposed to represent (Adam 1983; Rosanvallon 1986).

On the other hand, union fragmentation was exacerbated during the 1980s due to intra-confederal conflict and increasing animosity between unions. Rivalry between CGT and CFDT led to the breaking-up of their Union of the Left in 1977. After the Left's 1978 electoral failure, the CGT and CFDT both initiated a process of self-criticism. The CFDT admitted that it had been too dogmatic and that it had been insufficiently attentive to workers' daily preoccupations. The CGT was less self-critical and did not question its fundamental strategies or links with the declining Communist Party, which had exacerbated its own decline. Inter-union rivalry became even more acute when confronted with the socialist government's austerity, modernisation and flexibility policies. The CGT was isolated whereas the CFDT continued to follow its reformist back-to-the-centre strategy (*recentrage*) that had begun in 1979, and launched the idea of the merger of non-communist unions.

In 1990, leaders of the CFDT and the FEN called for a 'labour axis' plan, that is, a possibility of a united front between non-communist confederations (excluding the CGT). This call has not yet generated great enthusiasm among the other unions. Part of the aim of such an axis would be to counterbalance the influence of large national groups such as the DGB (see ch. 8) or TUC (see ch. 2) within the unified EC. This represented a move away from the 'unity of action' practices of the 1970s, when CGT and CFDT managed to agree on a range of issues. Tensions emerged between various federations. There was considerable intra-confederal turmoil in December 1984 with the failure of the national multi-industry negotiations on flexibility of employment. Whereas the top negotiators of FO and CFDT were ready to accept the package deal, they faced tough opposition from elements within their own organisations. But it was especially between 1986 and 1988, with the strikes in the public sector and the setting up of informal 'coordination' groups outside the unions, that official union practices were challenged. In short, the decline of unionism is explicable in terms of several factors, including unions' work overload, their fragmentation, the disappointing results of the CFDT's *recentrage* strategy and the Left unions' policy disarray when confronted with a Left government in power.

Following the Left's 1981 electoral success, an increase in the CGT and CFDT membership might have been expected (as was the case in 1936 and 1945), but throughout the 1980s these unions continued to lose members.

Even before the problems of declining support in the 1980s, the weakness of the French union movement was a major issue. Among the *traditional* explanations of the low union density, we offer the following summary. First, closed shop practices were prohibited to safeguard individual freedom to choose whether to join a union (though there are some *de facto* closed shops in sectors such as the docks and printing). Second, as a legacy of their anarcho-syndicalist roots, French unions have traditionally put more emphasis on having an active core of 'militant' organisers, rather than recruiting a stable mass membership. This explains also why they have rarely built up bureaucratic organisations on the scale of those in Germany, for instance. Following this early ideological choice, militants tended to see their role as fostering strikes and political action, rather than engaging in collective bargaining with employers, which made it difficult to demonstrate clear bargaining results to their members. Third, all wage earners benefit from any improvement won by the unions; after it is signed, a collective agreement applies to all employees whether unionised or not. Fourth, in general, no specific welfare benefits accrue to a union member, as may be the case in other countries. Fifth, employers have often opposed any extension of union influence, and have long used paternalistic practices, particularly in the numerous small firms. Sixth, it was only in 1968 that unions obtained the right to establish workplace branches. Seventh, the fragmentation of unions on ideological and political grounds hampered the recruitment and retention of members.

The low union membership created other problems such as poor financial resources and small organisational infrastructures in comparison to many other European unions. Their financial resources remain all the more modest given that dues are paid irregularly; on average, a union member pays only half the required dues per year

(Mouriaux 1983) and union dues are relatively low (on average less than 1 per cent of wages).

Nevertheless, unions do have more political and industrial influence than their low density implies. They play an important role in collective bargaining and in representative elections. They also play a role in public tripartite or bipartite bodies transforming unions into a 'public service agency' (Rosanvallon 1986).

Industrial disputes

The right to strike is guaranteed by the French Constitution, but as with any other right, it is qualified. In the public sector since 1963, the unions have had to give five days' notice before a strike. But there is little legal regulation of strikes in the private sector. The distinction between legal and illegal strikes is drawn by the courts. In the private sector, a strike is legally defined as a stoppage of work. Hence other action such as industrial sabotage, working to rule or slowing-down is unlawful. A lawful strike has to concern 'industrial relations issues'. Despite legal constraints on sit-ins, such action is permitted when its primary aim is to seek negotiations, rather than merely to disrupt production. Nevertheless, excessive disruption of production through strikes is illegal and lock-outs are generally illegal.

Although there is little legislation on strikes, there are elaborate procedures for the settlement of disputes, including conciliation, mediation and arbitration, but these procedures are rarely used in practice. Mediation was used successfully in 1982 for ending disputes in the car industry, but was less effective in other instances such as the 1988 strike in SNECMA (a nationalised enterprise in the aeronautical sector).

Industrial disputes tend to be unpredictable in France, but, as in Australia, they are usually short lived (see Appendix). Strikes tend to be short because, as a legacy of the anarcho-syndicalist tradition, French unions have few financial reserves and generally do not grant strike pay. Moreover, France loses relatively few days due to stoppages compared with Italy and the English-speaking countries (see Table A.22).

Between 1979 and 1988, the number of days lost per annum was about a third of the annual average registered between 1970 and 1979 (1 199 000 days lost on average per year in the 1980s against 3 559 000 on average per year for the 1970s). However, both in 1982 and 1984, there were increases in the number of working days lost in France, induced by the Working-hours Ordinance (1982), the disputes in the car industry and to a lesser extent by the incomes policy. But the most salient factor is the relatively high proportion of strikes in the public sector from 1986 onwards. In 1986, 44 per cent of the total number of days lost were in the public sector (e.g. railways, the Parisian metro, gas and electricity workers). In 1987, a third of the total number of days lost annually were at SNCF (railways). Other categories such as school teachers, airline traffic controllers, pilots and journalists also undertook strike action. In 1988 the nurses engaged in a major strike, which spread throughout the hospital sector. There were also stoppages by prison warders, postal workers, television employees and in aeronautical manufacturing (SNECMA). In 1989 there were serious stoppages in the finance sector.

Most of the recent public sector strikes were a combination of claims for increases in pay (which was low in comparison to the private sector) and specific claims, for example, to improve the poor working conditions of the railway drivers and nurses, the lack of career possibilities, and the absence of modern personnel policies in the public sector. An important characteristic of some of these strikes was the setting up of 'coordination groups' to organise strike action (e.g. the railway strike) either by rank-and-file employees themselves or by stewards, in opposition to the union leadership. Sometimes they were acting against official union representation channels (e.g. the nurses' strike). As a result of the coordination groups' initiatives, unions have tended to consult their members to a greater extent than hitherto about the bargaining priorities, as well as about the ways to conduct the strike and the negotiations.

The 'coordination groups' share some common features: most of them are in the public sector; they mobilise young employees; address their claims directly to the state; question the traditional and often bureaucratic negotiation practices of the union confederations; and are led by charismatic (and often Left-wing) leaders. However, there are important variations between different coordination groups. The railways are characterised by the occupational identity and industry culture of the employees as well as by high union density and traditional industrial relations practices. This contrasts with the hospitals which have not displayed such features (Visier 1990).

After a series of strikes by civil servants, there were talks about limiting the right to strike in the public sector. However, they were inconclusive.

Conclusion

Although France has had a socialist president since 1981, and despite labour legislation tending to reinforce their position, French union confederations have continued to decline. This decline seems unlikely to be reversed in the near future, largely due to changes in the labour market, employers' policies and unsatisfactory union strategies.

A major feature of the 1980s was the active role played by the successive socialist governments in employment matters. They aimed to reshape the industrial relations rules towards greater flexibility to enable the modernisation of enterprises as well as to encourage job creation. Through the Auroux laws, they also aimed to foster collective bargaining practices at plant and industry level. The relative importance of various bargaining levels has been subject to debate and conflicts both between the social partners and political parties. As in Australia and elsewhere, the Right and employers favoured the decentralisation of bargaining, whereas the Left and the unions have been anxious to preserve the industry-level nexus.

The rhetoric of the 1986–88 Chirac non-socialist government included an aim to deregulate French industrial relations and to diminish the degree of legal prescription. It did reduce the legal constraints on redundancies and on working time flexibility, and it initiated an extensive privatisation program. However, in practice, this government did not revoke the main changes to labour law which had been introduced in the five previous years.

At the end of the 1980s, the Rocard government gave a boost to multi-industry bargaining, with the intention of developing a more consensual approach to the major human resources and industrial relations issues. This strategy won support from the CNPF and some of the reformist unions (especially the CFDT).

The Socialist government formed in 1991 under Madame Cresson meant a change of style rather than of content. Her major priorities were combating unemployment by immediate measures such as: encouraging household jobs; restructuring the management of the national employment office for the unemployed (*Agence Nationale Pour l'Emploi*); changing work organisation to increase the autonomy, level of skills and responsibility of employees; and reforming the French training system along the lines of the German model.

Altogether, as in Australia and most European countries, there has been a trend towards the decentralisation of bargaining and the advent of more practices to promote greater labour market flexibility. More fundamentally, the Left has, paradoxically, helped to improve the employers' image as providers of jobs and creators of wealth. In other words, the traditional view of the enterprise as a locus for class struggle has been withering away.

In comparison with other countries, the single European market and its social implications have not been subject to such extensive debates either in the unions or in the broader public arena. On the contrary, some French leaders were very active in promoting a Social Europe, including President Mitterrand, who was keen on a 'social dimension' and the setting up of a Social charter. (In spite of the advent of the Right-wing Balladur government in 1993, at the time of writing it appears that Mitterrand may retain responsibility for such EC issues, possibly until the 1995 presidential elections.) Moreover, some major French multinationals initiated information and consultation group committees at the European level, while the CFDT has played a key role in some of the EC's institutions.

A chronology of French industrial relations

1791	Le Chapelier law forbad strikes and unions, but not employers' associations.
1821	Building industry employers' association established.
1830s–40s	Many illegal combinations of workers and some collective agreements.
1864	Abolition of Le Chapelier law.
1871	Paris Commune.
1884	Unions were entitled to organise on a craft or industry basis, but not at the enterprise or plant level.
1895	Anarcho-syndicalist Amiens Charter asserted the CGT's independence of political parties.
1919	The CFTC established following the Pope's 1891 encyclical (see Chronology, chapter 6). First national industrial employers' confederation founded.
1920	Peak of union density (c. 25–30 per cent).
1921	CGT split, following Russian Revolution.
1934	General strike called by the CGT.
1936	Election of the Popular Front coalition of socialists, communists and radicals. Many strikes and sit-ins. Agreements between the employers' association and the reunited CGT heralded major social reforms including the introduction of employee delegates.
1944	The CGC established.
1945	The Liberation government initiated works councils within enterprises.
1946	The CNPF established as the main employers' association.
1948	Creation of the FO after a split within the CGT.

1950	Law on collective bargaining and the establishment of a minimum wage system.
1958	Multi-industry unemployment insurance agreement introduced the principle of national agreements.
1964	CFDT established as a secular breakaway from CFTC.
1965	Multi-industry four-week holiday agreement.
1966	Works committees' role extended in relation to training and profit sharing.
1968	Events of May precipitated a general strike; workplace union branches permitted.
1970	Multi-industry job security agreement; a multi-industry *mensualisation* agreement granted 'single status' for blue-collar workers.
1971	Amendment to 1950 Act to permit plant-level bargaining.
1974	A multi-industry redundancy agreement, including a continuation of 90 per cent of previous job's pay levels.
1981	Mitterrand's Socialist–Communist coalition formed the government.
1981	39-hour working week Ordinance.
1982	Auroux laws enacted; prices and incomes policy initiated; retirement age reduced from 65 to 60.
1983	Major strikes in the car factories.
1984	Abortive multi-industry negotiations to introduce more flexibility in employment protection laws (initiated by CNPF); Communists left 1981 coalition.
1986	Socialist government replaced by a Right-of-centre government.
1987	New Redundancy Act repealed the earlier requirement for administrative approval before redundancies; new flexible worktime law.
1988	Socialist government returns to power and announces its first social program.
1988	Bill on minimum integration income (*Revenu minimum d'insertion*).
1989	Socialist government announces its second social program.
1990	Important multi-industry agreements are reached.
1991	Restructuring of the national employment office.
1992	The government launched significant job-creation programs to counter long-term unemployment.
1993	Socialist government overwhelmingly lost the legislative elections. A Right-wing coalition government took office under Prime Minister Balladur, but President Mitterrand continued in his post.

8 Industrial relations in Germany
Friedrich Fuerstenberg

Modern German industrial relations history can be divided into at least three periods: first, the pre-Hitler period, before 1933; second, the Hitler period between 1933 and 1945; third, the post-Hitler period of 1945–90, when there was a political division between West and East Germany. Most of the following discussion focuses on the third period in West Germany. Developments in East Germany in this period are outside the scope of this chapter. It is too soon to make much comment on the post-1990 period of re-unification, except in the conclusion. This chapter starts by putting German industrial relations into context. It discusses the unions' and employers' roles before considering the main processes of industrial relations: collective bargaining and co-determination.

West Germany (The Federal Republic) was founded in 1949 within the western territories of the former German Reich. Almost a quarter of the population originally entered the country as refugees. Before re-unification, West Germany had a total population of 63 million people; 44 per cent of them were in civilian employment and 7.4 per cent of the labour force were foreign workers (1987). Relatively more people were employed in industry (40 per cent) than in any other OECD country. The services sector employed 57 per cent, while 3.4 per cent were in the agricultural sector (see Appendix; *Statistisches Jahrbuch* 1989:94). The most substantial shift has been from the agricultural sector which employed 25 per cent in 1950 (*Statistisches Jahrbuch* 1967:138). These shifts also had a profound impact on the structure of the labour force, as shown in Table 8.1. The female participation rate (54 per cent) is lower in Germany than in other countries discussed in this book except for Italy (41 per cent). Germany has a lower birth rate (about 10 per 1000) than any of the other countries, but it is already more densely populated (246 people per square km) than any of the others except Japan (325 people per square km).

Table 8.1   Status categories of the German labour force

	1950[a]	1961[a]	1970[b]	1983[c]	1988[d]
			(percentages)		
Blue collar	51	49	47	40	38
White collar (incl. civil service)	21	29	36	47	51
Independently employed	14	12	10	9	9
Assisting family member	14	10	7	4	2
Total	100	100	100	100	100

Sources: a Statistisches Jahrbuch (1967:138).
        b Wirtschaft und Statistik (1982:11–735).
        c Wirtschaft und Statistik (1984:5–170).
        d Statistisches Jahrbuch (1989:90).

The reconstruction of industry after the Second World War has been termed the 'economic miracle'. However, this country has experienced a relatively greater *increase* in unemployment since 1970 than in any of the other countries covered in this book (1970, 0.6 per cent; 1985, 8.3 per cent). Some saw this dramatic rise in unemployment as signalling the end of the economic miracle, but there are indications that economic growth will be resumed again, especially once re-unification has been digested. By the early 1990s, however, unemployment had fallen again to less than 5 per cent. West Germany was, and the re-united Germany is even more, clearly the most powerful economy in Europe, even though the unification process is difficult and Germany is experiencing some set-backs.

Between 1985 and 1991, there was a 13 per cent increase in consumer prices. This was less than in all the other countries except Japan (11 per cent). In the 1989–90 period there was a 3.8 per cent annual increase in consumer prices, the same rate as Japan (see Table A.12).

According to OECD statistics, the level of German government revenue is about 44 per cent of GDP (1988), which is slightly above the average for all OECD countries. But Germany has been the only OECD country with constantly decreasing levels of government revenue since 1980. Nevertheless, due to high social insurance contributions, the average take-home pay in German manufacturing industry is only 73 per cent of gross earnings (about the same as in Britain).

West German politics have been dominated by three political parties since the Second World War:

1 the Christian Democratic Union (CDU) with its sister party in Bavaria, the Christian Social Union (CSU);
2 the Social Democratic Party of Germany (SPD); and

3   the Free Democratic Party (FDP).

At regional and local levels, the Green Movement and the Republicans have some impact. In view of the system of 'personalised proportional representation', it is extremely difficult for one party to win an absolute majority in elections. Only in 1957 did the CDU–CSU succeed in so doing. Otherwise, at the Federal level in West Germany, there has always been a Coalition government, with the FDP playing an important role in spite of its small share of votes. Before 1966 and since 1982, the CDU–CSU has had the majority in cabinet. From 1969 until 1982 the SPD had the majority, while from 1966 until 1969 there was a Great Coalition between CDU–CSU and SPD. In 1990, for the first time in the re-united Germany, Federal elections took place. The CDU–CSU and FDP were the winners, while radical parties dwindled away. The rate of participation in elections has been slightly declining and 'floating voters' have been increasingly important.

As they are 'integrative' parties opposing radicalism, both CDU–CSU and SPD have strong factions representing workers' interests. From 1987 till 1990, within the Federal *Diet*, 2 per cent of CDU–CSU (and 8.9 per cent of SPD) deputies are *employees* of unions or other workers' organisations, while 35 per cent of CDU–CSU and 99 per cent of SPD deputies are union members. Following the principle of 'bargaining autonomy', the Federal government abstains from direct interference in industrial relations; there is no definite pro- or anti-union policy, despite frequent controversies regarding social and labour legislation. Thus, for example, co-determination was introduced in 1951 under a government dominated by the CDU–CSU, led by Adenauer.

The industrial relations parties

Industrialisation in Germany began later than in Britain, but earlier than in Sweden. German industrialisation took off relatively quickly in the closing decades of the nineteenth century. Unlike Britain the factory system developed within a society which retained a legacy of paternalism. Notions of a 'vertically-bonded works community' grew in this context (cf. Fox 1985).

Unions

The German labour movement grew out of the 1848 revolution (see Chronology at end of chapter). German unions were mainly occupationally based with strong ideological affiliations. They were strongly opposed by the state and employers at the beginning of

Germany's Imperial era, but later won significant social and political
roles, especially in the post-1918 Weimar Republic. However, the
unions were all abolished by Hitler under national socialism in 1933.
Following this traumatic experience, after the Second World War,
the surviving union leaders aimed to establish a more unified union
movement as an important way of fostering democracy.

There are four major union confederations: the German Trade
Union Federation (*Deutscher Gewerkschaftsbund*, DGB) with 17
affiliated unions (7.9 million members), which is the most influential; the Confederation of German Civil Service Officials (*Deutscher
Beamtenbund*, DBB) with 799 000 members; the German Salaried
Employees' Union (*Deutsche Angestelltengewerkschaft*, DAG) with
573 400 members; and—with no role in collective bargaining—the
Confederation of Christian Trade Unions of Germany (*Christlicher
Gewerkschaftsbund Deutschlands*, CGB), operating in some regions
(309 400 members). The relative density of organisation is shown
in Table 8.2.

There is also a much smaller confederation: the Union of Senior
Executives (*Union der Leitenden Angestellten*, ULA). It does not
generally identify itself with the labour movement and aims to
represent senior executives. However, in 1990 it had only 43 000

Table 8.2 Union density^a

		Employees				
		Civil service	White-collar	Blue-collar	Total	Women
Employees	total (millions)	2.4	10.2	10.1	22.7	8.8
	% of all employees	10.7	44.2	45.1	100.0	38.4
Percentage of unions share among organised employees	DGB	50.3	73.1	97.3	83.0	78.7
	DBB	43.7	2.8	0.3	8.4	8.9
	DAG	—	20.4	—	5.3	9.3
	Total %	100.0	100.0	100.0	100.0	100.0
Union density (Percentage of union members)	Total %	66.1	23.7	52.8	41.1	25.8
	DGB	33.3	17.3	51.4	34.1	20.3
	DBB	28.9	0.7	0.1	3.5	2.3
	DAG	—	4.8	—	2.2	2.4
	CGB	3.9	0.9	1.2	1.4	0.8

Note: a 1987 data.
Source: Institut der Deutschen Wirtschaft, Köln 1988 (figures rounded).

members and only two of its affiliates were recognised for collective bargaining.

Under its Federal structure, the real power within the DGB lies with the industrial unions. The three largest among them are the Union of Metal Industry Workers (*IG Metall*) with 2 727 000 members, the Union of Public Service, Transport and Communications Workers (*Gewerkschaft Öffentliche Dienste, Transport und Verkehr*) with 1 252 600 members and the Union of Chemical, Paper and Ceramics Industry Workers (*IG Chemie-Papier-Keramik*) with 676 000 members. They also dominate the triennial congress of the DGB. The DGB mainly performs coordinating and representative functions for the union movement. It also maintains a major research institute (*Wirtschafts und Sozialwissenschaftliches Institut des DGB*), which regularly publishes survey results and monographs about the issues of working life.

With the exception of the CGB, German unions are based upon an ideological pluralism which, of course, leaves scope for internal competition among factions; the social-democratic group is the most influential. Thus far, radical factions have attained influence only at local levels. The internal structure of the unions is characterised by representative democracy. But there is still an important element of direct member participation. With the exception of the union of printing workers, a union may call a strike only after having won a 75 per cent majority in favour, in a secret ballot. On the whole, however, union policy is highly centralised due to the following three factors. First, collective bargaining is conducted mainly at industry and regional levels; second, unions pursue policies which embrace wider social issues; third, industrial relations are highly bureaucratic and legalistic, which has induced the involvement of experts.

It is important to note the broad scope of the DGB's policies. These aim to safeguard and improve workers' rights, not only at the workplace and enterprise levels, but also at the level of the industry and wider society. Union activity thus transcends the realm of working conditions to embrace, for instance, concern about technological change. The unions also participate actively in adult education activities through their well-equipped training centres.

Union policy is 'cooperative' insofar as the unions receive information and are consulted about all major areas of social and economic policy. This extends to practically all public policy relating to the quality of life of the working population and their dependents. Technically, the unions are neutral in party politics; nevertheless, their political presence is obvious. Thus, the German unions are not only powerful partners in collective bargaining, but they also exert great influence on political and social life. Their structural power gained from institutionalised participation (see below), was augmented in the 1970s by an increase in unionisation, due to favourable labour market conditions and the politicisation of younger, especially female, employees. (Density of the DGB unions increased between 1970 and 1985 from 30 to 35 per cent.) Unlike the position in most of the other countries, the economic recession of the early 1980s did not precipitate a steep decline in union density (see Table 8.2).

Employers

There is considerable industrial concentration in the economy. In 1989, more than 39 per cent of those in employment worked in establishments with more than 1000 employees (compared with less than 1 per cent who worked in establishments with less than 20 employees). Nevertheless, small and medium-sized enterprises shape the employment structure in several important sectors.

Unlike the English-speaking countries, for instance, in Germany corporations have a two-tier board structure. It is the lower, managing board (*Vorstand*) which runs the firm, designs long-term policy and which implements most decisions. However, the bigger decisions are formally endorsed by the upper, supervisory board (*Aufsichtsrat*) which controls managerial performance. The supervisory board appoints the top managers, but generally meets only four times per year, so cannot interfere directly in management (as discussed later).

Employers' associations began for defensive purposes as a response to the growth of unions in the second half of the nineteenth century (Bunn 1984). Neither unions nor employers' associations were allowed under the Third Reich period. After 1945, the employers' associations re-emerged, following the unions. Employers' interests were organised centrally in parallel to those of the unions. The Confederation of German Employers' Associations (*Bundesvereinigung Deutscher Arbeitgeberverbände*, BDA) represents 46 national branch federations and 12 regional federations, comprising about 80 per cent of all enterprises (1985). The Confederation has 21 committees and working groups, which provide expert opinions and prepare political platforms. For this purpose, the employers' federations also operate jointly two research institutes (*Institut der Deutschen Wirtschaft and Institut für Angewandte Arbeitswissenschaft*).

Neither the BDA nor DGB participate directly in collective bargaining, but they coordinate and provide information. The member organisations, however, are the real centres of employers' power. They have substantial 'strike protection funds' and are the partners of unions in collective bargaining, except where there is company bargaining (e.g. at VW, which is an unusual case). Unlike their equivalent associations in the English-speaking countries, the German employers organise lockouts of workers in response to industry-wide strikes, especially in major metalworkers' disputes (Owen Smith 1981:199). In common with most other countries, the employers' organisations are ideologically conservative and act as an employers' voice to the state.

In spite of the large variety of enterprises, differing in size, production and market situation, the employers try to maintain solidarity during industry-wide negotiations. However, there is increasing flexibility provided by the system of enterprise- or plant-centred negotiations between works councils and management. These negotiations implement and augment collective agreements at industry level (see below).

There are different organisations in the public sector. At municipal level, the Federation of Local Government Employers' Associations (*Vereinigung der kommunalen Arbeitgeberverbände*, VKA), and at state government level, the German State Government Employers' Association (*Tarifgemeinschaft der Deutschen Laender*, TDL) have operated since 1949. At national level, since 1960 the Federal Minister of the Interior has been 'the employer' in negotiations.

The role of government

Germany has an extensive framework of labour law. The Federal Constitution (1940) grants the freedom of association and right to organise. Employer–employee relations are generally regulated by statutory law. There is a division of labour between local courts, regional appeal courts and a Federal labour court.

There is extensive legislation, for example, on labour standards, hours of work, sick pay, protection against summary dismissals and establishing employment rights for young workers, women and disabled people, as well as expectant or nursing mothers. In addition there are health and safety laws, which are implemented by Industrial Injuries Insurance Institutes (self-governing public corporations under state supervision). Labour and management are equally represented on the decision-making bodies of these institutions. Under the Occupational Safety Act (1973) there are about 60 000 trained safety experts in industry, supported by about 25 000 safety representatives at plant level, nominated by the employer in accordance with the works council. In recent years, special attention has been given to improve both the quantity and quality of workplace medical practitioners (at present about 10 000, 2500 of them on a full-time basis).

A comprehensive social security system has developed since the first introduction of social insurance in the 1880s. It is administered by self-governing agencies with either bipartite or tripartite boards. There is a Federal Institute for Labour at Nuremberg which administers the Federal Employment Service, the Unemployment Insurance Fund as well as Unemployment Assistance and Family Allowances. It also operates a large research institute on all matters of labour market policy.

There is a high level and wide coverage of vocational training in Germany. In 1982, 60 per cent of all employees had completed a three year period of such training and/or vocational school attendance after having finished full-time education. Further, 6.6 per cent had completed technical college training, 2.7 per cent had graduated from professional schools and 5.9 per cent were university graduates.[1] Moreover there is a continuing trend towards higher qualifications in the upper grades of the labour force.

The attempt to create a form of 'concerted action' aiming at a kind of national incomes policy failed, due to disagreement about the goals (cf. Clark et al. 1980). On the other hand, the main strategies of employers and unions cannot succeed without taking government action into consideration (e.g. in the case of policy options for or against state-financed additional employment). Government policy on industrial relations, however, is not to interfere, thus respecting the principle of bargaining autonomy (*Tarifautonomie*), limiting state influence to setting a normative framework and publishing basic pay data, especially on socio-economic targets, and on trends in planning the Federal budget, etc.

The main processes

Governmental interference in collective bargaining is rare. There is no governmental mediation, as the parties provide their own voluntary conciliation system. Nevertheless, in major disputes the government usually becomes involved, informally.

Collective bargaining

German industrial relations has a dual structure. At workplace and plant levels there is no direct bargaining between unions and employers. Instead, works councils and employers negotiate on a statutory basis. It is at industry-wide and regional levels (and less often at enterprise levels) that unions and the employers' federations enter into negotiations, which usually result in collective agreements. Out of more than 32 000 registered collective agreements in 1988, only 25 per cent were enterprise agreements (which are different from the plant agreements between work councils and management). The Collective Bargaining Law (1952) grants legal enforcement of agreements only to union members. However, most agreements apply to all employees in the particular sector of the economy. Distinctions between unionised and non-unionised workers are not allowed in collective agreements (following a Federal labour court decision in 1967).

There is a distinction between master agreements, which have a relatively long duration, and ordinary agreements, which usually last for a year and regulate major conditions of work (pay, working time, leave of absence etc.). In contrast to the latter ones, the majority of master agreements (1988, 64 per cent) are enterprise agreements. However, they cover only a small fraction of the workforce, mostly employed in firms that do not belong to an employers' association. As can be seen from Table 8.3, a wide range of special provisions may become the subject of collective agreements. There is a growing tendency to cover wage regulations for white- and blue-collar employees jointly.

Procedures in collective bargaining are highly formalised and

Table 8.3 Some contents of collective agreements

	1963	1978	1988
Total of valid registered collective agreements	12 647	36 705	32 000
Enterprise agreements	4 495	13 216	8 000
Framework agreements	2 044	3 685	2 800
Enterprise master agreements	930	1 822	1 800

	1974 %	1978 %	1988 %
Fringe benefits			
holiday pay	79	93	94
annual bonus	60	76	92
profit/capital sharing	77	92	95
Social security			
job security	32	52	—
wage guarantees	40	62	—
protection in case of rationalisation	45	48	55
additional unemployment compensation	21	—	—
sickness pay	30	42	—

Source: Boedler and Kaiser (1979:26); Clasen (1989:17).

even ritualised, as illustrated in the following example of a typical set of *IG Metall* negotiations:

1 The claim is discussed at plant level by the members and officers and then screened by negotiation committees which make recommendations about the form and extent of the claim to the union board. Four weeks before termination of the collective agreement, the union informs the employers about the claim.
2 A negotiating committee is established. Bargaining starts two weeks before the expiry date of the current collective agreement.
3 There is a peace obligation which continues to apply for four weeks after the expiry date. After this period, the workers may initiate demonstrations and other sanctions.
4 A new collective agreement is negotiated or, in case of a failure to agree, one or both parties may declare a breakdown of the negotiations; then the union negotiating committee may propose a strike ballot.

Under stage 4, after a failure to agree, the parties may jointly appeal to a conciliation board within two working days; after another working day this may be done by either party, unilaterally; the other would then have to join after two more working days. Then the independent chair of the conciliation board (usually a well-known retired politician or public servant) has to be nominated without delay. The board must convene within three working days and present a proposal within five working days. After six more working days, the parties in dispute have to decide whether or not to accept this proposal.

Unlike the position in Britain or Australia, for instance, such procedures are usually followed strictly. Moreover, there are relatively few stoppages (see Appendix), in spite of the lack of legislation concerning strikes or lockouts. However, there are many legal constraints on industrial action, partly deriving from court decisions. Thus, legal strikes are strictly limited to industrial relations topics. It is generally illegal to call a strike about a political issue.

However, there have been some major disputes. There were stoppages in 1984, both in the printing and the metal industries. In the latter, for example, the union wanted a reduction in the basic working week from 40 to 35 hours, with no loss of pay. This was part of the union's strategy to counter high levels of unemployment. But the employers insisted that such a reduction in hours would render German goods less competitive in international markets. Following a nine-week stoppage, therefore, as an alternative to reducing hours, the employers proposed to introduce more flexible working hours. The government did not support the union's campaign, though it proposed to introduce early retirement provisions from the age of 58.

The outcome of this dispute was a compromise. The average basic week would become 38.5 hours in 1985, but this could vary between 37 and 40 hours for different groups of workers in a plant. Such variations were to be negotiated at plant level. This represents a decentralisation of collective bargaining and increases the role of works councillors. The 1984 dispute revealed a new set of union tactics, called 'the new flexibility'. These tactics included local strikes, for example, in component-making firms, which in effect would stop production in much of the car-manufacturing industry, without the unions calling a general industry-wide stoppage.

The toughest subsequent industrial dispute was in 1992 when the public service union assumed leadership in the annual sequence of collective bargaining, and demanded a general wage increase in spite of the government's increasing difficulties in financing German re-unification. The public service union members returned to work in May 1992 after an 11 day strike which brought chaos to the nation's transport system and left garbage in the streets. A general wage increase of 5.4 per cent was agreed with the government, but did not win the support of the rank-and-file. As a consequence, the position of the union's top leaders was severely weakened and there were moves to decentralise the union's power structure. Another potentially disruptive strike in the metal industry was narrowly averted two weeks later when the employers agreed to an increase of 5.8 per cent (compared with the union's original demand of a 9.5 per cent increase).

Although for Germany these were uncharacteristically controversial disputes, there is still a widespread consensus that stoppages should be a last resort and only about fundamental issues.

Co-determination

There is a long tradition of attempts to introduce industrial democracy in Germany. Works councils were first established by law in 1916, in industries which were important for the economy in the First World War. They became obligatory under the Works Councils Act of 1920.

Since the Second World War, union influence at the enterprise level has been enlarged by the various laws on co-determination, in particular:

1 the Works Constitution Act (1952–72) enlarged the legal rights of works councils in private enterprises;
2 the Co-Determination Act (1951) established full parity co-deter-

mination within the supervisory boards of the coal and steel industries, and a labour director as full member of the managing board;

3   the Co-Determination Act (1976) established countervailing parity in supervisory boards of limited liability companies with more than 2000 employees; and

4   the Personnel Representation Act (1974), provided for the election of staff councils in public services and enterprises.

The main instrument for implementing co-determination is the works council, elected by all employees of a firm regardless of their union affiliation, and operating on a defined legal basis (see Table 8.4). However, works councillors usually cooperate closely with union officers or hold union office themselves. Works councils cannot call a strike, but they have the right to sue management in a case of alleged breach of contractual rights. In such rare cases, the issue is referred to an arbitration tribunal.

Works councils have many rights to information, consultation and co-determination. The 1972 Works Constitution Act, for example, requires works council consent on: works discipline, daily working hours and breaks, temporary short time or overtime work,

Table 8.4   Results of works council elections (percentages)

	1975	1978	1981	1984	1987
participation rate (total)	79.1	81.3	79.9	83.68	83.30
participation rate blue collar	82.6	81.9	79.9	82.59	82.50
participation rate white collar	72.7	80.8	79.3	82.53	83.60
re-election works councillors	72.3	72.8	65.6	70.28	68.38
re-election works council chairpersons	69.9	75.9	75.4	73.11	71.51
1st election works councillors	27.8	27.2	34.4	29.72	31.62
1st election works council chairpersons	30.1	24.1	24.6	26.89	29.44
Organisation density:					
DGB works councillors	67.9	58.6	63.2	63.9	65.39
DGB works council chairpersons	78.8	71.84	79.9	75.10	74.81
DAG works councillors	10.4	14.6	8.5	8.9	5.56
DAG works council chairpersons	2.6	14.38	5.2	6.81	3.56
CGB works councillors	2.6	0.7	3.7	0.8	1.04
CGB works council chairpersons	0.0	0.06	0.5	0.14	0.26
ULA works councillors	NA	NA	0.4	0.3	0.14
ULA works council chairpersons	NA	NA	0.5	0.04	0.01
others works councillors	1.6	2.8	0.9	0.7	0.36
others works council chairpersons	0.6	0.66	3.4	0.87	1.22
non-organised works councillors	17.5	23.3	23.3	25.4	27.51
non-unionised works council chairpersons	1.5	13.06	10.5	17.04	20.09

Note: NA No data available.

Source: Institut der Deutschen Wirtschaft 1975–87. (The data include firms with no union candidates nominated for election.)

the fixing of job piece rates, pay systems, suggestion schemes, holiday schedules, any monitoring of employee performance, safety regulations, welfare services in the establishment, and the administration of works housing for employees.

Works councils can also co-determine any changes to the pace of work or the working environment. In such cases, works councils may demand ergonomic data at the expense of the employer. They can also co-determine the process of personnel selection and occupational training. In the event of any major operational changes in the enterprise, the employer and the works council shall negotiate over the change and, in the case of any economic disadvantages for employees, agree on adequate lay-off and compensation arrangements.

A representative system of co-determination always poses the problem of adequately representing all the different interests in a constituency. Works councils do reflect the relative strength of blue-collar and white-collar interests. Some groups tend to be proportionately under-represented, however (e.g. younger workers, the unskilled, women and foreign workers) but there is a trend towards increasing the proportion of women and foreign workers.

The relations between works councils and the unions are usually close. In most enterprises, union officers participate in works council meetings from time to time. They regularly address works assemblies. Communication between works councils and unions varies according to the degree of unionisation of the employees.

Labour directors were first established in the coal and steel (*Montan*) industries in 1951. They are appointed in the same way as other members of the managing board, but they cannot be appointed against the wishes of the employees' representatives on the supervisory board, who usually initiate such an appointment. Usually these directors are highly qualified and experienced union members (but not officials). Labour directors have a special concern with personnel and social policy, but also participate fully in the shaping of general company policy, which has to be jointly agreed by the members of the managing board. Thus a dual allegiance is established: the labour director is responsible both for effective management and for effective representation of the workers' points of view.

In other industries, labour directors are not institutionally linked with unions and have clearly defined managerial functions. Therefore, there is no question of a dual or conflicting loyalty. In dealing with co-determination in supervisory boards, two types of legal provisions have to be considered. In the case of a minority representation, members elected by the workforce cannot determine decisions against the will of shareholders' representatives. Outside the coal and steel industry, such situations are typical. For companies with less than 2000 employees, only one-third of the supervisory boards have to be employee representatives, nominated by the works councils.

Parity of workers' representation has been achieved only in the coal and steel industries. There, since 1951, representatives of capital have been nominated by the shareholders' meeting, while the labour ones have been nominated by works councils and unions. The parties choose a chair by co-opting a 'neutral' person. In 1976, this system was extended to all German companies with more than 2000 employees. There are, however, two major differences between the 1951 and 1976 laws. Outside coal and steel, at least one employee representative is nominated by the *Leitende Angestellte* (senior executives). Furthermore, in impasse situations, the chair (nominated by the shareholders) has a casting vote.

From the employers' point of view there are five problems with the 1976 Co-Determination Act: the contradiction between parity and the property principle, the endangered autonomy of collective bargaining, the representation of middle managerial employees below the senior executive level, the election procedures for nominating workers' representatives for the supervisory board, and the position of the labour director.

By contrast, the unions see other problems, especially the evasion tactics of some firms. By reorganising, altering the capital composition and changing the legal form of the enterprise, in 1978 alone about 30 companies tried to avoid extended co-determination in supervisory boards. Some other companies tried to change their statutes. In the following years, however, the situation stabilised. Between 1985 and 1988 the number of co-determined companies increased from 476 to 500. Unions were also concerned about their secrecy and the lack of information, and about procedures which gave advantages to shareholders' representatives, such as the double vote for the chair in committees with a non-parity composition. In spite of such problems for unions, co-determination at supervisory board levels has generally led to a gradual modification of entrepreneurial goals, towards more socio-economic goals, e.g. by introducing social planning and by implementing more re-training strategies in the face of technological change.

Current and future issues

Co-determination fosters a strategy of 'cooperative unionism', for several reasons. The unions were re-established after the Second World War as integrative associations, representing the interests of workers with different political and ideological affiliations jointly. The resulting concentration on social and economic issues and the independence from political parties marks a decisive difference when compared with industrial relations in France or Italy, for example. Traditionally, German unions never considered themselves merely as labour market institutions or 'business unions', unlike those in North America. The German unions always aimed at settling larger issues in the wider society. There are still minorities of radicals and reformers who have different orientations, but most of them hold that the design and realisation of reforms is possible only by getting involved in decision-making processes. In the course of implementing the different co-determination laws, thousands of new functions and positions for union officials have been created, thus establishing a network of influence which cannot easily be abandoned. They have also acquired much knowledge which has increased union concern with new types of problems. Gradually the unions have developed an infrastructure matching their claim for co-determination and enabling them to deal with the employers on many more issues than traditionally defined by the scope of collective bargaining.

The relative success of co-determination was possible only because the employers and the managers became convinced that such a system provided an efficient way of managing employment relationships. The relatively low number of stoppages in Germany reflects its alternative means for preventing and settling disputes. Works councils provide an efficient grievance machinery within the plants. Co-determination in supervisory boards is a form of conflict management; it provides for discussion of all major issues and possible problems for the workforce before final decisions are taken. Consultation and negotiation starts before the two sides become entrenched. The unions have an involvement at the early stages of social, technological and economic change. Strikes as an ultimate means for pressing workers' claims become necessary only in rare cases of fundamental dissent. As a consequence, however, bureaucratic procedures and oligarchic structures develop. These may exclude the shop floor from direct participation. Thus the co-determination institutions at a higher level may lose touch with the rank and file.

Those who plead for more militancy and direct democracy in industrial relations usually deplore strong union involvement in managerial affairs. But, putting ideological considerations aside, the growth of a segmented internal labour market in large companies calls for new union strategies. Co-determination is a pragmatic approach towards influencing working conditions. The effects of investment policy, for instance, on the organisation of work, qualifications and skills cannot be influenced by traditional bargaining techniques. Instead, the whole process of making investment decisions and implementing them by technological, economic and possibly social planning needs to be accompanied by continuous communication and consultation in order to avoid outcomes detrimental to workers' interests. It is precisely this communication and consultation structure, combined with the opportunities for greater influence, that co-determination provides. Its greater efficiency, however, is offset by complaints about the lack of direct participation. Thus, demands for more at workplace-level democracy are an inherent dynamic factor in German industrial relations.

Technological change

In the 1980s, the German economy was faced with structural changes. Their impact upon industrial relations can be illustrated by the current changes in technology. The union strategies focus upon protection against an increase of work load and stress, against deskilling and on the reduction of working time as a protection against loss of jobs. There has not yet been a general policy of job creation by reducing working time. Hence, the possible consequence—an equivalent reduction of workers' income—is still an unsettled issue, despite the 1984 metal industry dispute (see earlier discussion).

Demands for government action usually focus on employment stabilisation, the improvement of job security, and the maintenance of skills and qualifications. Unions are demanding a greater conceptual linkage between the government's labour market and educational policies on the one hand and its measures to improve the economic structure on the other hand. They advocate a streamlining of all policies directed towards influencing technological change. The research program for the 'humanisation of work life' administered by the Federal Ministry for Research and Technology, is supported in principle by all unions. However, as a prerequisite for this support the unions want to be involved in the design of research projects through their representatives in advisory boards and works council participation in their implementation at plant levels. Thus far, there have been many such action research projects, though they have mainly been pilot studies. There is still a need to foster a wider application of results.

Employers and their associations also assume some social responsibility for technological change. The great challenge for them is to develop and utilise new technologies in order to foster productivity and competitiveness, whilst also providing more humane forms of job design. It is not easy for employers to find workable

Table 8.5 Government regulations on humane work design

Regulation	Year	Contents
Safety of Machines Act	1963	Obliges all users of machines and equipment to ensure that all safety instructions and technical rules are observed.
Works Constitution Act	1972	Regulates cooperation between works councils (i.e. shop committee) and managements; contains special information rights and participation of workers in job design (workplaces, processes, technologies, the environment).
Occupational Safety Act	1973	Regulates the employment of security staff (medical and engineering) and the application of research findings on work humanisation.
Workplace Decree	1975	Contains minimum requirements for the work environment (noise, lighting, climate etc.).
Decree on Toxic Substances	1986	Sets maximum workplace concentrations of toxic substances to be observed.

Source: Projekttraeger Humanisierung des Arbeitslebens (1981:20ff).

compromises between social, economic and technological considerations. Nevertheless, there is considerable scope for them to discuss such matters with unions and works councils. There are numerous cases of management, union and works council participation in the humanisation of work programs.

Government strategies to improve industrial relations in view of technological change primarily focus upon adjusting the legal framework. (Recent government regulations are listed in Table 8.5.) As a result, the socio-economic environment for introducing technological change has been profoundly restructured. In particular, the 1972 Works Constitution Act provides considerable information, consultation and co-determination on plant-level industrial relations issues, including those associated with technological change (see Figure 8.1).

Such regulations help the parties to cope successfully with the problem of innovative applications of technology while maintaining consensus between the industrial relations parties. Nevertheless, there are also other relevant factors. Perhaps the most important is job security. By 1986, unemployment had risen to about 8 per cent—the highest level since the 1930s. Between 1980 and 1989 the potential labour force increased by 2.1 million people, while the number of people employed remained stable. Most West Germans

Figure 8.1   Regulation of issues associated with technological changes under the Works Constitution Act[a]

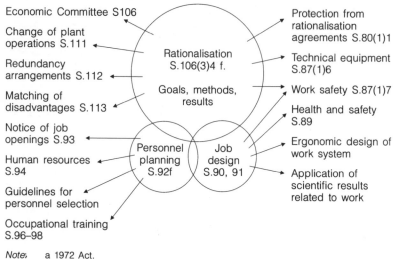

Economic Committee S106

Change of plant operations S.111

Redundancy arrangements S.112

Matching of disadvantages S.113

Notice of job openings S.93

Human resources S.94

Guidelines for personnel selection

Occupational training S.96–98

Rationalisation S.106(3)4 f.

Goals, methods, results

Personnel planning S.92f

Job design S.90, 91

Protection from rationalisation agreements S.80(1)1

Technical equipment S.87(1)6

Work safety S.87(1)7

Health and safety S.89

Ergonomic design of work system

Application of scientific results related to work

Note: a 1972 Act.

Source: Adapted from Wiesner (1979:46) S = refers to paragraphs of the *Works Constitution Act.*

seemed to accept that new technology was not generally destroying jobs; rather, its impact on employment depends on how it is introduced and on the market conditions.

Reduction of and flexibility of working time

The German Confederation of Unions (DGB) hopes that the gradual introduction of a 35-hour week will have a lasting, positive effect on employment. Taking an opposite view, the employers advocate the notion of a 'new policy on working hours', which allows for individual flexibility in working time, to be attained by a more economically efficient deployment of labour. The employers argue that this will result in the creation of new jobs. This trend towards a reduction in working time has led to a difficult situation, in which employers, employees and their representatives are faced with a very complex challenge.

1   Appropriate working-time arrangements must take account of specific work situations. In other words, a distinction should be made between sectors (branches of industry), levels (plant, enterprise, industry), categories of workers (shift workers, etc.) and

the scope of regulations (weekly working time, holidays, retirement).

2   This distinction raises the question of the extent to which collective and individual working-time arrangements are effective in attaining general employment policy objectives, a question which is currently seen as important. Linked to this is the unions' basic problem of trying to ensure that individual, flexible working-time arrangements do not irreversibly lead to unduly flexible and individualistic working conditions.

3   The unions' strategy has always been to neutralise the adverse effects of productivity increases on employment by the reduction of weekly working hours, in particular. Today, however, this approach, when combined with claims for a full wage adjustment, is leading to an imbalance. The employers' strategies to restore their cost-benefit advantage have proved effective in the past. Once again such strategies could overcome the unions' initial successes.

4   It is difficult to coordinate objectives linked to working time with a general employment policy. As the organisation of working time affects workers' whole way of life, as well as that of their families, it cannot be reduced to a single dimension, which is simply the subject of employment policy considerations. This is apparent, for instance, from the unions' concern about a possible increase in the work intensity as a result of a reduction in working hours.

One possible way to resolve these difficulties would be to review and to try to relate the competing interests within a general framework. The outcome of the labour disputes in the metal and printing industries have led to a fairly general introduction of the 38.5 hour week. This has shown that a realistic reorganisation of working time must allow both for a general reduction in working time and flexible implementation, depending upon the individual contexts. However, the only system likely to be acceptable to all would have to be economically viable and feasible from the employers' standpoint. From the workers' standpoint, it would have to guarantee that their right of co-determination and their influence in collective bargaining would not be reduced.

This problem has to be tackled at several levels: at the level of the national economy, changes need to be made to the overall system of working hours; at sectoral or regional levels, new regulations must be incorporated into collective agreements; and new works agreements must be signed at the level of enterprises and plants. Flexibility in working hours may be attained in particular enterprises provided that it is not at the expense of workers' interests and, at the same time, that it remains within the framework of overall regulations.

Conclusion

The German industrial relations system is facing major challenges due to both internal and external structural changes. Internally, the growing number of collective agreements containing provisions related to the introduction of new technology demonstrates a continuing degree of flexibility in the German model of industrial relations. Externally, the establishment of a Single European Market is posing the problem of maintaining the post-1949 West German traditions of cooperation, in spite of increased transnational pressures upon labour markets, which are precipitating further organisational innovations. But the most important issue is the re-unification of East and West Germany.

Within the former German Democratic Republic, free and independent unions did not exist. The FDGB, 'Free German Trade Union Federation', with 9.6 million compulsory members and, therefore, a density of 98 per cent, in its constitution recognised the leadership role of the Communist Party (SED). Its main functions were cooperation in implementing centralised economic planning and administration of fringe benefits and welfare agencies. There was no experience with collective bargaining and freely elected works councils. As a consequence, the FDGB had no share whatsoever in the opposition to and overthrow of the old regime. In September 1990 the FDGB dissolved and since October 1990 the DGB has claimed the coverage of the whole re-united Germany. West German legislation (especially the Collective Agreements Act and the Works Constitution Act) has been introduced. Works council elections have taken place and some collective agreements (e.g. for post and railway employees) have been concluded. New unions have been established and are inclined to merge with their West German counterparts.

The employers' side has been following a similar path. In a joint statement, the DGB and BDA expressed their intention to cope in a socially acceptable way with the employment crisis in what was East Germany. More than one third of workers in the former GDR lost their jobs following the re-unification. Furthermore, it was estimated that nearly all of the former GDR's 8.5 million workers would require new qualifications or refresher courses to raise their skills to the standards of the west (McCathie 1992:16). But restructuring the Eastern provinces' economy will also affect the former West Germany through the continuing immigration from the Eastern provinces and possibly from Eastern European countries, which are also suffering from the collapse of their planned economies.

The future development of industrial relations in Germany, therefore, will not only reflect internal adjustment processes, but increasingly also the challenges from economic reorganisation in Europe as a whole.

Generally, there are good prospects of maintaining and further developing the post-1949 innovations in industrial relations if attention is given to the need for increasing flexibility and participation, especially at workplace levels.

A chronology of German industrial relations

1832	Secret association of German craftsmen in France, Switzerland and Britain.
1844	Silesian weavers' revolt.
1846	*Gesellenverein* (journeymen's association) founded.
1848	Year of revolutions.
1848–54	General German Workers' Fraternity, comprising 31 workers' associations and three workers' committees.
1848–53	Association of cigar-producing workers.
1849–53	Printers' association formed.
1863	Foundation of the General German Workers' Association.
1865–67	First national associations of cigar workers, printers and tailors.
1869	Foundation of Social Democratic Workers' Party.
1869	Prussian Trades Law grants freedom of coalition.
1873	First collective agreement (in the printing trade).
1878–90	Anti-socialist legislation.
1891	First industrial union: German Metal Workers' Association.
1892	First trades union congress.
1894	Foundation of first large Christian trade union (coal miners).
1899	Congress of Free Trade Unions recommends collective agreements.
1904	Main employers' association founded.
1905	First long strike by the German miners' union.
1913	Association of German Employers' Federations established. 3 million union members; 10 885 collective agreements cover 1.4 million employees.
1914–18	First World War.

1916	Law to enforce works committees in all production establishments with more than 50 workers.
1918	Law on collective agreements
1918–24	Central Working Commission of employers and workers in manufacturing industries and trades.
1919	Foundation of General German Trades Union Federation (ADGB).
1920	General Strike against rightist riot (*Kapp-Putsch*).
1920	Works Councils Act.
1921	Foundation of *Akademie der Arbeit* (Academy for Labour Studies).
1927	Law on Labour Courts.
1928	Law on collective agreements.
1928	Thirteenth ADGB Congress discusses co-determination.
1933	Unions abolished by National Socialist government.
1939–45	Second World War.
1945	Decision to found the DGB
1949	Founding congress of DGB.
1951	Co-determination Act for coal and steel industries.
1952	Works Constitution Act.
1955	Personnel Representation Act (for employees in the public sector).
1963	Foundation of Christian Trade Union Movement.
1963	Lockout of metal workers.
1967	'Concerted action' begins.
1972	New Works Constitution Act.
1974	New Personnel Representation Act.
1976	Co-determination Act for firms with more than 2000 employees.
1978–79	Steel strike: dispute about shorter working week.
1984	Metal workers' dispute about a shorter working week.
1989	Amendment of the Works Constitution Act, including minority protection, definition of managerial employees, and consultation in technological change.
1990	Re-unification of West and East Germany. Dissolution of FDGB.
1992	Public services strike.

9 Industrial relations in Sweden
Olle Hammarström

Sweden became an industrial society later than most of the other countries covered in this book. At the turn of the century, Sweden was a poor agrarian society with high emigration. Sweden has 29 per cent of its civilians employed in industry; 3.3 per cent are still in agriculture, while 68 per cent are in services, partly as a result of the very strong growth of local and regional government since the 1960s.

Swedish industrial relations have long fascinated foreign observers. With a total population of 8.6 million and with 4.5 million in the labour force, Sweden is the smallest of the countries discussed. However, 84 per cent of its women are in the labour force, which is the highest female participation rate of any OECD country. In comparison with the other countries, Sweden tends to lose fewer working days in stoppages (apart from Japan and Germany) although recent years have witnessed a rise in strike activity.

After the 1991 election, there were seven political parties represented in the Parliament. The percentage of the popular vote which they each received is given in brackets. Four of them are liberal conservative *(bourgeois)* parties: the Moderate/Conservative Party (22 per cent); the Centre/Agrarian Party (9 per cent); the People's/Liberal Party (9 per cent); and the Christian Democratic Party (7 per cent). These four parties form a minority conservative Coalition government. At the 1991 election a new party, the New Democrats (7 per cent)—a populist Right-wing party—entered the Parliament. The small Communist Party (6 per cent) has never been part of any Swedish government, but it has fairly often been an ally to the much more important Social Democratic Party (38 per cent), which has formed the government for 53 years in the 59 year period 1932–91, including a continuous period of 44 years between 1932 and 1976. During this period, Sweden became known as a country of high taxes and a highly developed welfare state. In the 1980s, the average *take-home* pay in Swedish manufacturing industry was only 66 per cent of *gross earnings* (after tax and social security contributions, but excluding family benefits), which was a lower percentage than in any of the other countries. In the period 1985–91, there was an increase in the consumer price index in Sweden of about 50 per cent, higher than any of the other countries except for Australia (51 per cent) (see Table A.12).

After a marked shift in economic policy in 1990–91, the inflation rate has fallen below the EC average. At the same time the very low level of unemployment (1.5 per cent in 1990) is rising rapidly and had passed 7.5 per cent by early 1993. Nevertheless, in the post-war period, Swedish unemployment has consistently been less than in most of the other countries discussed in this book. Some years it has been even lower than in Japan (see Table A.5).

Political and economic context

Following its relatively late industrialisation, Sweden also became unionised somewhat later than other countries. The trade union movement started to develop during the 1880s. At first, the Social Democratic Party, which was established in 1889, functioned as a union confederation, but then the Swedish Trade Union Confederation (LO) was formed in 1898. The employer organisations developed as a response to the growth of the unions. The Swedish Employers' Confederation (SAF) was established in 1902.

The Swedish union movement began with craft unions but by 1910 the concept of industry unions was dominant. Several factors explain this shift. Social democratic union organisers worked hard to have industrial unionism accepted by the union movement but craft training was also poorly developed at the time when the first unions were formed. Furthermore, industrialisation occurred to a large extent in the form of *'bruk'* or one-company towns or villages, where it was natural to form one union against the one employer.

The right to organise and bargain collectively had no legal basis at first and was strongly contested by the employers. The first industrial disputes were combined struggles for the right to organise and for higher pay in the 1870s. These struggles intensified around the turn of the century; for example, in a lockout in the engineering industry in 1905.

These conflicts led to the recognition of union rights in the so-called 'December compromise' of 1906. In an agreement with LO, the SAF acknowledged the unions' right to organise and bargain collectively. For its part, LO accepted that all collective agreements were to include a clause giving the employer 'the full right to hire and fire and to organise production'. The agreement was seen as a major step forward by the union side. The right to organise had been achieved, even though employers' rights were then commonly seen as natural. This was the first example of a major agreement reached by the central organisations on behalf of their affiliated unions and employer associations.

However, the 'December compromise' was not fully recognised by all employers; therefore, some of them continued to implement anti-union policies. The first nationwide dispute was in 1909. The legendary 'great strike' started as a lockout by employers as an attempt to weaken the unions. The dispute ended with the workers returning to work without an agreement. It was a heavy defeat for the unions whose membership declined from 162 000 members in 1908 to 85 000 members in 1910.

Industrial relations legislation developed slowly. It was reactive rather than promoting reform. In 1906 an Act on voluntary mediation was passed and a small mediation office was established. From 1910–20, employers and conservative politicians tried on several occasions to introduce legislation that would restrict unions' rights to strike. These attempts were blocked by socialist and liberal interests. As strikes continued to be seen as a major social problem, Acts on Collective Bargaining and the Labour Court were passed in 1928 despite union opposition. These Acts were the first legal recognition of union rights.

In 1932, after the election of the first Social Democratic government with a workable parliamentary majority, the situation changed. The unions adopted a new strategy as they no longer saw the government as a natural ally of the employers. The new relationship between capital and labour led to the Basic or 'Saltsjöbaden' Agreement of 1938, which laid the foundation for labour–management cooperation and consultation. This spirit of cooperation became known as 'The Swedish Model' during the 1950s and 1960s.

There are no official definitions of 'The Swedish Model'. Different writers have given it different meanings. Common to all definitions is, however, the philosophy that unions and employers should take full responsibility for wage formation and industrial peace whereas the government should take responsibility for upholding full employment. The interests that brought unions and employers together to form the Swedish Model was the common interest to stimulate rationalisation and productivity growth and the desire to avoid government interference in collective bargaining.

The cooperative spirit of the Swedish Model was codified into the Basic or Industrial Peace Agreement of 1938 (the Saltsjöbaden Agreement, named after the place where the negotiations took place). After that followed other agreements that together formed the collective bargaining base for the Swedish Model. They were the Industrial Welfare Agreement of 1942; the Vocational Training Apprentices Agreement of 1947; the Time and Motion Studies Agreement of 1948; and the Works Council Agreement of 1946.

During the pre-war years, the Social Democratic government largely followed a Keynesian economic policy, which used the budget deficits to fight unemployment. After the war, a significantly modified version of Keynesian policy was developed. In 1951, the LO Congress adopted a policy based on the so called 'Rehn–Meidner' model, named after two prominent LO economists who proposed a new approach to economic policy. The LO took the view that trade unions should take into account the government's economic policy when formulating their wage demands. In exchange for union support, the government agreed to pursue a policy of full employment. Economic growth was secured by union commitment to rationalisation and technical development. This government also gave support to an 'active labour market policy' which encouraged both geographical and skill mobility for displaced workers. The Labour Market Board (AMS) was established in 1948 and has ever since had a strong position in developing labour market policies.

In adopting this program, the unions assumed partial responsibility for the national economic performance, thereby changing their policy from the early 1930s. Industrial conflict, then, was partly transferred to the political arena with the state taking an active part in income redistribution through taxation and social security legislation.

The period from 1950 to the end of the 1960s was one of stability in the labour market. Steady economic growth, particularly through the 1960s, meant that wage disputes could be settled without great difficulties. Unions accepted management's right to 'hire and fire' and to rationalise the production within the expanding sectors of the economy. This transition process was facilitated by the government's active labour market policy. The main emphasis of union demands during this period was for improved social security.

Major reforms in the old age pension system (the 'AP Funds') were introduced in 1960 along with other social benefits. The political controversy over the pension system (compulsory system or voluntary system) dominated the political debate for almost ten years and contributed to a continuation of the political domination by SAP.

During this period, LO implemented its policy of 'solidaristic' wage policy which was an essential element of the Rehn–Meidner model. The policy had two ingredients. One was 'equal pay for equal work' regardless of industry or company. That meant that company profit levels were not the main target for negotiations. Subsequently, poor economic performers were forced out of business, while the profits in the most successful companies were not challenged by the unions. The other dimension of the 'solidaristic' wage policy was the narrowing of the gap between the lower-paid and the higher-paid workers. The gap was attacked by both a progressive taxation system and by pay contracts which gave extra wage increases to low-income earners.

The harmonious pattern of industrial relations that emerged in Sweden during the 1950s and 1960s was facilitated by steady economic growth. The industrial development of Sweden was originally based on natural resources: iron, timber, and hydro-electrical power. In addition, some important innovations allowed a number of Swedish firms to become major players on the world markets such as AGA (lighthouses), SKF (ball bearings), Nobel (explosives), Ericsson (telephones), Electrolux (refrigerators), Atlas Copco (rockdrilling) and Alfa-Laval (separators). Sweden became the home base for multinationals, rather than merely a host country. The number of people employed by Swedish multinationals outside of Sweden is nearly three times as many as the number of Swedes working in foreign-owned multinationals. Industrial relations in Sweden has thus developed on a national basis without any strong influence from other countries.

Sweden is more dependent on international trade than any of the other countries discussed in this book. Around 28 per cent of Sweden's GDP is exported. Approximately half of the production of the engineering industry, which is dominant in the Swedish economy, is exported. The figures are even higher for such other sectors as the iron, steel and wood industries. The strong dependence on international competition has also been a factor that has inclined Swedish unions in the private sector to accept productivity improvements. Both technical as well as administrative rationalisation have traditionally been accepted, and often welcomed by Swedish unions.

The main participants in industrial relations

Unions

Unlike the position in Australia, the establishment of a union in Sweden does not require any registration or acceptance by government authorities or courts. Any group of employees is free to form its own union and will be automatically covered by industrial relations legislation. The more advanced union rights are, however, reserved for unions holding contracts. The most significant of these rights is access to company information and the right to initiate bargaining on any major changes before they take place. There are very few newly-organised unions in Sweden, mainly because the existing unions appear to serve their members effectively and they protect their area of interest from competing unions.

There are three main union confederations: the LO (The Swedish Trade Union Confederation) and TCO (The Swedish Confederation of Professional Employees) dominate the blue- and white-collar sectors respectively. A third confederation, SACO (The Swedish Confederation of Professional Associations), consists of professional unions organising employees who generally possess an academic degree.

LO's 20 affiliated unions have a total membership of 2.3 million people including retired members. This means that the LO covers more than 90 per cent of blue-collar employees—a very high density by international standards. The majority of affiliated unions are organised on an industrial basis with one union in each company or site. The largest unions are the Swedish Municipal Workers' Union (640 000 members) and the Swedish Metal Workers' Union (470 000 members). The LO represents its affiliated unions in the areas of social and economic policy. Traditionally, it also bargained collectively on behalf of all members in the private sector. In the public sector, however, the two major unions bargain directly, without the direct involvement of LO.

TCO was formed in 1944 by the merger of two organisations, one covering private sector employees and the other covering public sector employees. The 19 unions affiliated to TCO have 1.3 million members. It does not take part in collective bargaining, but is active in training and represents its unions in negotiations with the government on general economic and social policies. The largest member unions are SIF, the Swedish Union of Clerical and Technical Employees in Industry (300 000 members), SL, Teachers' Union (193 000 members) and SKTF, Swedish Union of Local Government Officers (185 000 members). The largest member unions are 'vertical' industry unions, which means they organise all white-collar employees at all levels in an enterprise. They make up three-quarters of total TCO membership. The other member unions are organised on an occupational basis. For the purpose of collective bargaining, the TCO-affiliated unions were organised into two bargaining cartels: PTK for the private sector and TCO–OF for the public sector. However, PTK also includes unions outside TCO which are affiliated to SACO.

SACO is the smallest of the three confederations. The 25 member unions of SACO have around 300 000 members. The unions are organised primarily on the basis of common academic background. The largest unions are those which organise teachers in secondary education and graduate engineers. SACO has bargaining cartels for the state and local government sectors. In the private sector most SACO unions are affiliated to PTK.

The links between LO and the Social Democratic Party (SAP) are traditionally very strong. LO's financial support to the party is of prime importance, particularly in election campaigns. A significant part of the local electoral work is also carried out by union activists. The strong links between the LO and SAP are also demonstrated through the recently abolished system of collective membership. The close relationship is also reflected in the party's leadership and in the government. During the long period of Social Democratic government (1932–76), approximately half the cabinet was recruited from the union leadership.

Most employees in Sweden are members of unions (see Appendix); more than 90 per cent of blue-collar employees and some 80 per cent of white-collar employees. This exceptionally high union density by international standards is explained by several factors. One is that the unemployment benefit system is administered by the unions. Most workers regard it as natural to belong to a union for protection against possible unemployment. Other benefits offered by the unions also help them in recruiting members. However, perhaps the most important reason is the degree of union influence achieved during the long period of Social Democratic government. The close relationship between successive Social Democratic governments and LO helped the unions to establish themselves as a significant and well-established force in society. Thus, for most Swedes it is almost automatic to join a union when they enter the labour market. In contrast to LO's affiliation with the Social Democratic Party, TCO and SACO have no formal political affiliation. Union membership, as a total, has not fallen in recent years but membership as a proportion of the labour force fell marginally in the 1988–90 period.

Employers' organisations

Employers in Sweden are as well organised as the employees. There are four employer confederations: one for the private sector and three for the public sector. The Swedish Employers' Confederation (SAF) organises employers in the private sector. SAF acts for more than 45 000 affiliated companies organised in 36 sectoral associations. The SAF-affiliated companies employ some 1.3 million people. For the national government authorities there is the National Agency for Government Employers (SAV) and for the local government sector there are two organisations. The municipalities collaborate through the Swedish Association of Local Authorities and the county councils through the Federation of County Councils. These organisations act on behalf of 278 municipalities and 23 county councils. The public sector has more than 1.5 million employees, of whom more than half a million are national government employees.

Characteristics of the social partners

Swedish unions and employers' organisations (the 'social partners') are large and well-funded by international standards, in view of their high density of membership and their relatively high level of subscriptions. Union subscriptions are normally in the range of 1 to 2 per cent of gross earnings. In addition to subscriptions, the social partners also enjoy some government funding, particularly for training. The unions accumulate funds to meet the costs of industrial disputes. The size of funds varies, but is large by international standards. Most unions can compensate their members from two to four weeks on full pay. The employers' associations also accumulate such funds.

Another feature of Swedish unions is the high degree of centralisation in decision-making. Decisions about strikes and accepting collective agreements are normally taken by central bodies such as the executive committees. Even in cases where centralisation in decision-making is not formally regulated in the statutes, members usually follow the recommendations of their leaders. Although Swedish unions are centralised, this does not mean that they are weak or inactive at the local level. On the contrary, in comparison with unions in other countries, the level of local activity is high. Wherever there are ten or more members, it is usual that a local branch of the union will be formed. Approximately 10 per cent of union members hold an elected position in their union organisation and 15–20 per cent of the membership receive some form of union training each year. Participation in union meetings, however, is usually low. It is common to find only 5–10 per cent attendance at regular meetings. Attendance of 50 per cent or more is common only for annual meetings or when decisions are to be taken on collective agreements or strike action.

The role of the government

The Swedish state is a large employer. Usually there is a government Minister for Wages, who is ultimately responsible for the state's employment policies, which are implemented by at least two agencies. Pay negotiations are handled by the National Agency for

Government Employers (SAV). The permanent head of the Ministry of Wages usually chairs the SAV board.

The private sector has been the traditional pace-setter in Swedish pay negotiations. It is also widely accepted that the production costs and productivity of the export sector is of prime importance in pay determination. However, there are cases where the public sector takes the lead and reaches agreements ahead of the private sector. In non-pay issues it has been common for SAV to break new ground, ahead of the private sector. One example is the area of industrial democracy (discussed later).

The government exerts its main influence on industrial relations through its political role. Traditionally, industrial relations has been left to the employers and unions. However, during the 1970s a number of new laws were introduced, constituting a new framework of industrial relations. These laws deal with issues such as industrial democracy, the work environment, security of employment, and union rights. These laws generally limit the rights of employers and strengthen those of employees and their unions.

The main processes of industrial relations

Every union has its own statutes, including rules about how to enter into collective agreements. It is common practice that the right to conclude agreements is entrusted to a union's executive committee. A union may give its mandate to a central union council or a bargaining cartel to bargain on its behalf. Central agreements were the general practice between 1956 and 1982. A central agreement is normally a recommendation that has to be endorsed by each participating union before it is binding.

Such central agreements include a peace obligation, whereby the employers agree to increase economic rewards in exchange for a guaranteed period of labour peace. Once an agreement is ratified, the detailed applications are worked out through industry-wide and local agreements. Any disputes must be referred to the central level rather than settled by industrial action.

Central agreements usually include several pay components. It is common to have a general pay increase (either in percentage or absolute terms) as well as specific increases directed towards special groups such as low-income earners, women, shift workers, and tradesmen. Agreements may also include guarantee clauses which permit an adjustment of pay according to changes in the consumer price index or wage increases in other sectors. This means that the central agreements are supplemented by industry-, plant- or company-level agreements before the individual wage increases are finally determined. Central agreements generally cover a period of one to three years. During this period, there may also be local bargaining. Where piece-rate pay systems are in use, there may be a great deal of local bargaining. Increases in pay outside of the central agreement is called 'wage drift'. Wage drift has traditionally been in the range of 25–50 per cent of the centrally agreed wage increase. During the 1980s, wage drift increased and in some instances equalled the increase provided for by the central contract. This was caused partly by market forces and partly by employers' aims to widen wage differentials.

In addition to the pay agreement, there are other central agreements. They cover such subjects as working hours, the working environment, joint consultation and equal opportunities for women. Central agreements may also be supplemented by local agreements which specify how the rules are to be applied in particular situations. Collective agreements sometimes replace or supplement the law in regard to non-pay issues.

Local bargaining

Although the structure of local bargaining differs markedly from one workplace to another, we will describe the process in a typical medium-sized private-sector company with 300–400 employees. The employees would be organised in three or four local union 'clubs'. All manual workers would belong to an LO-affiliated union. The first-line supervisors would belong to SALF (the supervisors' union) and most of the rest of the white-collar employees would belong to SIF (the main white-collar union in private industry).

SALF and SIF would cooperate in the bargaining cartel PTK. The local unions would be represented on the company board with one LO and one PTK representative, and their deputies would also attend. There would be a work environment committee with a majority of union representatives. The economic performance of the company would be regularly discussed in the economic committee, where the LO and PTK representatives would meet with management. There would be regular meetings every month in which management would report about production and investment plans, among other things. The unions would indicate if they wished to take an issue further, in which case separate negotiations about that issue would be organised. The unions would initiate negotiations about grievances, as requested by the members. Most of the contacts between management and unions would be informal. Formal labour–management contacts would be limited to four or five board meetings, three or four meetings of the work environment committee and four to six cases of collective bargaining, besides the pay negotiations.

Public sector

Union–management relations in the public sector are similar to those in the private sector. However, some differences should be mentioned. There are usually more unions among salaried employees, as professional unions are more strongly represented in the public sector where there tends to be larger concentrations of employees. Another difference is the greater degree of formalisation in union–management contacts. The employer fulfils the 'primary duty of negotiation before deciding on a change of the operation' by sending a written proposition in the form of 'draft minutes' which describe the proposition. The union representatives confirm that they accept by signing the minutes. A formal document confirming the agreement is completed, but no meeting is ever held. This greater formality in the public sector can, in part, be seen as a reflection of the more bureaucratic traditions in the public sector, but can also be explained by the large size of most public sector organisations.

Dispute settlement

The Swedish government plays only a limited role in settling disputes. The Swedes differentiate 'interest' disputes and 'rights' disputes (see ch. 1). In the case of interest disputes, parties have the right to engage in industrial action after giving proper notice (usually one week). A small state agency provides mediation. However, the mediator has only an advisory role and there is no formal obligation for the parties to accept the mediator's proposal or to withhold industrial action if requested by the mediator. In most years there are 30 or 40 cases of mediation. Parliament can in theory legislate to seek an end to an industrial dispute, but such action is very unusual.

In the case of rights disputes, there should be no industrial action. Disputes about the interpretation of laws or agreements must be referred to the National Labour Court or, in some cases, to regional lower civil courts or magistrates. Verdicts of the lower courts may be appealed to the Labour Court, which is the final arbiter for all labour disputes. The Labour Court hears around 250 cases per year, including individual grievances.

The right to engage in industrial action includes lockouts as well as strikes. In addition, there are milder forms of industrial action such as bans on overtime and new recruitment, as well as 'black bans' on certain jobs. However, industrial action is only allowed when contracts have either expired or been properly terminated. Industrial action undertaken during a contract period is prohibited by law. Actions in support of other unions (secondary conflicts) are, however, always allowed. If a union engages in an illegal strike, either at the local or central level, the employer may sue the union for damages. To avoid responsibility for an illegal strike, union officials must actively discourage their members from taking part. Only in this way can they avoid being fined or sued for damages. Individual union members who take part in unlawful industrial action can also be fined by the Labour Court. These fines have traditionally been limited to a maximum of SEK200 but this was increased to SEK5000 in 1992.

Issues of current and future importance

During the 1960s, when Sweden experienced a period of high economic growth and continuous industrial peace, the concept of the 'Swedish Model' became well known internationally. The model can briefly be described as having relatively few well-organised and strong employers' associations and unions. The unions have positive attitudes to rationalisation and rely upon the government to pursue an active labour market policy in order to absorb technological and structural unemployment. The Swedish Model is normally traced from 1938 when, as noted earlier, the LO and SAF reached the first so called Basic Agreement which regulates procedures of collective bargaining and matters of cooperation. Under the Basic Agreement, decisions about what to produce and how to organise production were managerial prerogatives. Pay and conditions have always been subject to bargaining, with the right to take industrial action when the contracts are to be renewed.

The first Basic Agreement was reached after a long period of sustained conflict. Throughout the 1920s and 1930s Sweden had one of the highest levels of industrial disputation in Europe. Then, there were strong demands for legislation that would restrict the rights to strike, to hold lock-outs, and engage in free collective bargaining.

The 'Swedish Model' worked well until the early 1970s, and then came under increased strain. The unions' radical demands for economic and industrial democracy met with strong employer resistance. The political and economic scene changed when 44 years of Social Democratic government came to an end in 1976. At that time, Sweden was engulfed in economic crises. The employers felt that it was both politically and economically necessary to fight back. The unions' demands for 'economic democracy' in the form of Wage Earner Funds, were strongly opposed by the three liberal conservative political parties and by the SAF, which has played an increasingly visible role in politics since the late 1970s.

In 1980 there was the biggest ever industrial dispute in Sweden. A strike was met by an employer lock-out of 80 per cent of the workforce. The dispute was settled after two weeks on the basis of a mediated proposal. Some commentators claimed that this conflict symbolised the end of the 'Swedish Model' and its spirit of cooperation. The dispute symbolised the end of an era of relatively peaceful central collective bargaining. However, the Swedish Model had never precluded the possibility of industrial disputes.

The 1980 dispute can be attributed partly to the role of the government in the pay determination process. Throughout the 1970s, government had sought to influence this process in various ways. Public statements on what was acceptable were issued and adjustments of the taxation system were frequently used. Furthermore, the government's intervention in the 1980 pay round was ill-timed. The pay settlements in 1981 and 1983, however, were achieved without disputes. During 1983 and 1984 agreements were reached, in the main, without assistance of mediators.

An important new element in Swedish industrial relations is the move towards decentralised bargaining. Following the failure of their 1980 lock-out, the private employers realised that such tactics would no longer be effective in opposing union power. The employers gradually adopted the view that wage solidarity had gone too far and that employers were losing ground with the existing central model. They decided to break up the centralised bargaining arrangement. The first step was taken in 1983 when the influential Engineering Employers' Association and their counterpart unions reached agreements outside of the central round of negotiations. Since then the Engineering Employers' Confederation and the Metal Workers' Union have continued to negotiate outside of SAF. Increasingly, the other employers' associations and unions followed suit. By 1990 SAF had decided that it would no longer take part in any wage bargaining with LO.

Another new element in the 1980s was the introduction of profit-sharing systems and employee stock-ownership systems. Such systems were strongly advocated by management but met with scepticism or outright opposition by certain unions. By 1989 one-quarter of private-sector employees were covered by profit-sharing systems and almost one-third by employee stock-ownership systems.

Industrial democracy

Industrial democracy is a broad term which refers to the influence of employees on their working lives or, more precisely, 'what and how they produce'. The debate in Sweden has concentrated on two areas: first, work organisation and the individual's influence over his or her job; and second, union influence over top management decisions via collective bargaining and through representation on company boards.

As in many other countries, industrial democracy has been part of the debate on the radical Left in Sweden for many years. Towards the end of the 1960s, demands for increased employee influence were raised in the unions. The debate has been influenced by the effects of technological change in the workplace, the growing awareness of work environment issues, health hazards and the wave of radical political ideas that swept through Europe. Some union demands were heeded in the political arena and a number of reforms were introduced.

In a simplified form, the union strategy on industrial democracy can be described as follows. Mobilisation of interested members and union activists was achieved by focusing on problems of health and safety at work. This created a political climate in which laws and regulations in support of industrial democracy could be introduced, which culminated in a revision of the industrial relations legislation, in an Act on Co-determination at Work (MBL). These laws were supplemented by financial support for training and research which, to a large extent, was channelled through the unions.

The MBL has become the legal framework for industrial democracy in Sweden. Since 1977, the MBL has prescribed that management should be a joint effort by capital and labour—i.e. managers and union representatives. Both sides should have equal rights to information, which means that unions should be able to obtain all the relevant information available in the company. Further, the MBL stipulates that management has to consult the unions before any decision is taken on major changes in the company (such changes range from reorganisation to the introduction of new technology). Although management is not obliged to reach agreement, it has to allow time for unions to investigate the matters for decision and consult at either local or central level before it implements decisions. MBL also gives the unions priority rights in interpreting agreements in some cases. They also have rights of veto over the hiring of subcontractors if they suspect that their use might violate laws or agreements. By law, the local union has the right to appoint two directors (and two deputies) to the board of most private companies which employ at least 25 people. This right is commonly used in large and medium-sized companies but less commonly used in small companies.

The introduction of MBL and other laws which constitute the legal base for reform of working life was very controversial in the

1970s. The employers strongly opposed most of the laws and predicted that reforms would lead to inefficiency, higher costs and inhibit the decision-making process. The employers also argued that this legislation would be preferable if it promoted individual employee involvement, rather than union activity. On the union side, there were high expectations that the reforms would lead to an improved work environment, greater job satisfaction, better control for individuals over their daily life at work and a stronger say for the local unions in the development of the enterprises in which their members work.

The outcome of the reforms so far has proved both sides wrong. Their results have had limited impact. Problems that were expected by the employers have, by and large, not materialised. Management has continued to operate without undue difficulties and few negative effects have been recorded. From the unions' perspective, there is a general feeling of disappointment about the reforms. No significant change in the power situation at the workplace has taken place. While the reforms are seen as a definite step forward, the step is too short and much too slow for most union activists.

It is generally accepted that MBL has led to improved provision of information by management to the local unions. Consultation with the unions before deciding on changes has become standard procedure. It is also reported that the operation of the board has improved in some companies as the result of participation by union representatives at this level.

There are many possible explanations as to why the reforms did not have greater impact. One explanation is the economic situation. When the MBL was formulated, the thinking of policy-makers was still dominated by the economic expansion of the 1960s. The assumption was that the economy was still expanding and that the process of management involved deciding about new investments, recruitment and similar issues. However, by the time the reforms were introduced in 1977, the situation had changed and Sweden was in the grip of a worldwide economic crisis. Instead of discussions about new investments, the unions found themselves involved in negotiations about plant closures, retrenchments and shortening of the working week. The new union influence and co-determination tended not to involve positive plans about the expansion of enterprises, but controversial decisions about how to survive in a recession. Within the public sector, negotiations were focused on cuts in government spending and their effects. Thus, the relationship between management and unions became increasingly strained.

In spite of these strains, in 1982 SAF reached a new basic agreement on efficiency and participation, with LO and the Federation of Salaried Employees (PTK). This agreement was an attempt to implement MBL in the private sector by setting up a joint Development Council which would promote efficiency and participation in individual firms. Significantly, this agreement provided for considerable adaptation depending on local circumstances; for instance, in relation to technological change.

Technological change

During much of the 1970s, industrial democracy was a focal point of debate. During the 1980s, however, the call for industrial democracy has gradually receded and been replaced by a debate on new technology, concerning the use of microprocessors in all shapes and forms. In common with their counterparts in other advanced industrial societies, Swedish employers support the introduction of new technology on the grounds of economic necessity. To stay competitive, they argue, there is no choice but to introduce technological change. Although such changes may have negative effects on the level of employment, in the short run failure to keep abreast of technological developments will mean failure in the long run.

Swedish unions have traditionally sympathised with economic rationalisation and technological development. The success of several large Swedish multinational enterprises in the engineering industry, such as Volvo, Saab-Scania and Ericsson, has had considerable influence on the thinking of the unions. One debate within the union movement has been whether computer technology represents 'traditional' technological change or should be regarded as a new and different phenomena which requires a different strategy. By and large, Swedish unions have favoured the former approach. Computer technology may have far-reaching consequences for the nature and level of employment. However, Swedish unions feel that their traditional policies and practices can be applied to most forms of new technology.

Union strategy on computer technology has been developed in three broad phases. The first phase can be described as 'fact finding'. This involves obtaining basic information about the technology. What systems are being marketed, sold and installed? What are the consequences of these installations? In the first phase, unions have been hesitant observers rather than adopting a highly active role.

The second phase of union strategy has involved the negotiation of 'technology agreements'. The emphasis of this phase has been on putting demands on employers. It is argued that unions should not get involved in detailed negotiations about what equipment to buy and how to install it. The unions' role should be to make demands on the management in terms of desired outcomes. Typical union aims are to regulate the number of jobs or to obtain agreements on no lay-offs. They may also seek to regulate noise levels, ergonomic standards and exposure times in front of VDUs. Computer technology has been regarded as a 'black box'. Unions should not get involved in the content of the box but get guarantees of the uses through collective agreements. They should say 'no' to the installation of computer technology unless specific criteria are met.

The technology agreement strategy has resulted in several technology policies at both central and local levels and in some collective agreements. However, the success of these agreements has been limited. In many cases, management has expressed sympathy for the union demands but found no means of meeting them. Economic realities have forced unions to accept new technology even when their criteria have not been met. This experience has led the unions to the third phase: the union alternative to computer technology.

The third phase has involved unions becoming active in research and development. This strategy is derived from the insight that unions cannot exert sufficient influence on those who are designing and marketing computer technology by putting pressure on the buyer (that is, the management). To ensure that new technology is in compliance with their demands, unions must deal directly with the producers (of hardware and software) and seek to influence the product-development process. This is a very recent stage of development and so far, there is only limited experience. During the 1980s there were a handful of projects in which unions were involved in research and development. The most advanced attempt was one where the Nordic printing unions collaborated with researchers to develop software systems for newspaper production.

Economic democracy—wage-earner funds

Economic democracy has been a dominant issue in the Swedish political debate since the 1971 decision of the LO Congress to investigate this matter. The concept has included two ideas: profit sharing and collective ownership. The arguments in favour of these developments have been both economic and power related. Employees should get a share of the profits, but part of the wealth which is generated should be reinvested in Swedish industry through a system of collective ownership. The LO saw economic democracy as a necessary complement to the 'solidaristic' wage policy, whereby wages are not related to the profits in an individual company but the economy as a whole. The argument in favour of expanding workers' power through wage-earner funds was put forward in view of the limitations of industrial democracy. Employees would exert influence, it was argued, if they were part-owners of their firms through the funds.

The first radical proposal for wage-earner funds, the Meidner Plan, was adopted by LO in 1976. It aimed, in the long run, to make the unions the majority shareholders in all major industries in Sweden. It was based on a compulsory issuing of new shares based on company profits. These shares would then be transferred to funds controlled by the unions.

The plan met unprecedented opposition from the employers. The Social Democratic Party was largely positive in its support, but had some reservations. The Liberal–Centre political parties acknowledged the need for such reforms but favoured individual rather than collective arrangements.

The wage-earner fund proposal was discussed at length by the LO and the Social Democratic Party but they had difficulties finding a proposition that was radical enough to satisfy the LO, yet practical enough to be politically feasible. The whole issue became a political burden to the Social Democratic Party and it lost the elections in 1976 and 1979 partly on this issue. However, it managed to win the election in 1982, despite controversy surrounding the wage-earner fund issue. Following the long and intensive counter campaign by the employers, the three non-socialist parties did not promote their own separate propositions. Instead, they all focused their campaign on criticising the LO/Social Democratic Party proposals. Those supporting the wage-earner funds and the employers were totally opposed to each other. Unions made several different proposals, but the coalition of employers and the non-socialist parties used the same argument against all.

Although the issue had become a political burden, the Social Democratic Party was re-elected in 1982 on a policy committed to implementing a form of wage-earners' funds. In October 1983, the opponents of these funds mounted a massive protest demonstration in Stockholm, when more than 100 000 members of the business community marched on Parliament. Nevertheless, in November 1983, the new government introduced a diluted version of the original proposal, which included the establishment of five regional funds which would receive money in two ways: firstly, through an increase of 0.5 per cent of the pension fee, payable by employers; secondly, through a profit-sharing system whereby 20 per cent of profits exceeding a set proportion ('excess profits') would be paid into the funds. Each of the regional funds would be administered by a separate board appointed by the government after consultation with the unions. The parliamentary decision on the funds included a provision that contributions would be paid up to 1990 but not thereafter. LO wanted the system to be extended into the 1990s.

However, the opposition parties declared that, should they get elected to government, they would terminate the funds and stop the whole system.

The five regional funds began operation in 1984. Following a general boycott by the employers, no established business leaders accepted nomination to the fund boards. In the absence of such representatives, the boards were comprised of politicians, leaders of public-sector organisations, union representatives and academics. The range of interests represented on the fund boards was not as wide as intended by the supporters of the fund concept, but each region was able to assemble a board.

The first investments made by the funds were shares in established Swedish industries listed on the Stockholm Stock Exchange. The engineering industry was the main area of interest. It is also clear that the funds were attempting to buy into industries in their own region. There were some examples of companies issuing shares direct to a fund, but the majority (90 per cent) of placements were on the open market.

The five wage-earner funds operated in the same manner as insurance companies and pension funds. There were few signs of their precipitating a 'fundamental change of the economic system in the direction of state socialism' as had been predicted by earlier opponents of the funds. The funds were used for research and for incentives for savings. A proportion of the funds were invested in a new venture capital fund. Following the defeat of the Social Democratic government in 1991, the new Conservative–Liberal coalition government decided to abolish the wage-earner funds.

Conclusion

Industrial relations in Sweden has passed through three broad stages. The first stage was from the beginning of the union movement in the 1890s up to the mid-1930s. During this period the unions were established. The relationship between capital and labour was antagonistic and there was a high level of industrial disputes. The government was either passive or supported the owners of capital.

The second stage lasted for most of the 44 years of Social Democratic government from the mid-1930s to the early 1970s. The 'Swedish Model' was established during this period with a low level of industrial conflict, a 'solidaristic' wage policy, an active manpower policy and labour–management cooperation. An economic policy reliant on economic growth subsumed many of the pay-related problems for the unions and paved the way for a pattern of labour–management relations with few industrial disputes.

A third stage emerged in the 1970s. More radical union ambitions, the election of a non-socialist government in 1976, severe economic problems and a strategy based on free enterprise and a market economy on the employer side, represented significant changes. The 1980 dispute symbolised these new developments. Wage-earner funds were introduced after a bitter and drawn-out conflict, but were not seen as a complete victory by the unions. The wage-earner fund system became a political burden for the Social Democratic Party and did not constitute a basic change in Sweden's economic system. The employers tried to reverse the trends as far as they could. Their prime objective was to deregulate Sweden and allow for more market influence. Fragmentation of the bargaining structures, more flexible working-time arrangements, profit sharing, and payment-by-results systems became examples of initiatives advanced by their associations.

During the 1980s a new collective bargaining structure emerged. The centralised bargaining structure that dominated during the 1960s and 70s was replaced with a more fragmented structure. This development was led by the Engineering Employers' Association against the ambitions of most unions and some of the employers' organisations. In 1983 and 1984 it looked as if industry-wide bargaining would become the dominant pattern. The wage rounds of 1986, 1988 and 1989 showed a partial return towards centralised bargaining. The last two wage rounds were comprised of central frame agreements covering the three main bargaining sectors and a separate structure for the engineering industry with the Engineering Employers' Association having separate agreements with the four unions (*Metall*, SIF, SALF and CF). The SAF 1991 decision to withdraw from central bargaining marked the end of the bargaining pattern that had started in 1956. The 1991–93 agreement was reached after pressure from a special government commission. However, the 1993 wage round is expected to begin with a series of company-level agreements in the leading engineering firms.

The 1980s also included a return to the cooperative efforts by unions and employers. The cooperative approach was concentrated on work organisation, technical development and skill formation. Two programs financed by the Work Environment Fund—the Development Program and the program on Leadership, Organisation and Co-determination, (LOM)—can be seen as examples of a new generation of joint union–management efforts. However, cooperative arrangements in the non-wage areas were hampered by disagreements between employers and unions about the locus of wage negotiations.

With the return of the Social Democratic government in 1982 the economic policy was changed. A large devaluation was the initial step towards an expansionist export-led recovery that proved successful for some years, but also postponed the tougher structural decisions that the government started taking after 1989. Sweden reduced its deficit in the state budget and restored balance in its foreign trade. The unemployment rate, that was already low by international standards (3.7 per cent in 1983), was brought down to a historically very low level (1.2 per cent in mid-1989). The government gave high priority to measures to restructure industry and stimulate flexibility of the labour force. By 1990, fighting inflation had become the government's main priority and unemployment increased dramatically in the early 1990s.

Industrial conflicts during the 1980s were slightly higher than previous decades. A new element was that white-collar workers accounted for the majority of the working days lost in industrial stoppages. White-collar unions have more often been involved and particularly public-sector employees. Notable groups that have taken part in major conflicts are nurses, fire-fighters and physicians. The involvement of public-sector employees in industrial conflict does bring the government a new role in industrial relations. But the Social Democratic government did not attempt to change or interfere with the basic industrial relations rules. It was still unions and employers who carried full responsibility for industrial conflicts.

Despite the change of government in 1991, does the Swedish Model still exist? That question has been debated on several occasions since the great conflict of 1980. Several commentators announced the death of the model after the conflict. The model is no longer the same, as the employers are distancing themselves from it.

However, the basic common values between employees and employers still exist: a joint interest in efficiency and rationalisation of production and a commitment to place the responsibility for industrial peace on unions and employers. The Swedish government still accepts responsibility for an active labour market policy and gives high priority to maintaining relatively full employment. All parties agree that good wages and security of employment presuppose structural changes and technical development. Nevertheless, since the change of government there have been strong disagreements about wage policies. Employers want wage setting to be more market-related, while the unions seek to maintain a solidaristic wage policy related to social as well as economic concerns.

One new feature is the role of the employers. Through the 1980s they were more interested in changing wage relativities and increasing wage differences than limiting the total employment costs. This put pressure on governments to fight inflation without the support of employers. Other new elements in the industrial relations scene are the increasing prominence of white-collar unions and the growth of the service sector.

It is no longer possible for blue-collar unions to dominate the unions' agenda. The existence of more than one union confederation has complicated the industrial system. The Swedish Model has, however, not managed to solve the conflict between inflationary wages and full employment. The pay determination machinery has demonstrated its inability to control wage drift. This inability is a serious threat to the Swedish Model.

In 1991, the Social Democratic government applied to join the EC. The major changes in Central and Eastern Europe since 1989 have paved the way for neutral Sweden to enter the EC. If economic crises continue and if the non-Socialist government prevails in Sweden for some years, it is likely that labour–management relations in Sweden will move in a 'continental European' direction, especially once Sweden becomes a full EC member. This would be likely to lead to fragmented bargaining structures, more government intervention, and a consequent weakening of the unions. On the other hand, if a SAP government is returned to office before long, there may be a return to a modified version of the Swedish Model.

A chronology of Swedish industrial relations

1898	LO founded.
1902	SAF founded.
1906	December Compromise Agreement. Employers accepted the right for workers to organise.
1909	General strike of 1909 followed by a severe decline in union membership.
1928	Establishment of Labour Court and a Collective Bargaining Act.
1936	Law regulates unfair dismissal for union activity, and the social partners' rights to negotiate.
1938	SAF–LO Basic Agreement at Saltsjöbaden, which set a cooperative 'spirit' for labour relations.
1944	TCO founded.
1946	SAF–LO–TCO Works Councils Agreement revised in 1966 and ended in 1977 by MBL.
1956	Beginning of LO–SAF central bargaining.
1971	LO and TCO adopt policies for industrial democracy.
1972	LO–SAF Rationalisation Agreement on productivity, job satisfaction and job security.
1973	Initial law on board representation for local unions.
1974	Law makes it difficult to dismiss employees, and for

	companies to hire workers on probation without union approval. Law gives local union representatives time off for union work with pay.
1975	The wage-earner fund debate begins. Law to give employees educational leave.
1976	Non-Socialist Coalition government replaces the Social Democratic Party.
1977	Co-determination at Work Act (MBL) implemented.
1980	Lock-out/strike throughout most of the private sector. Largest labour market conflict.
1981	LO and Social Democratic Party congresses approve principles for wage-earner funds.
1982	Social Democratic Party re-elected. SAF–LO–PTK Agreement on Efficiency and Participation.
1983	Wage-earner funds implemented. Industry-wide bargaining replaces the 1956–83 centralised pattern.
1984	Government initiative to introduce new three party model for central wage fixation based on 'social contract'.
1985	Widespread introduction of profit-sharing system and employee stock-ownership system in the private sector.
1986	Major public sector conflict. Leading to a break up of traditional, rigid wage structure in the public sector.
1989	New leadership in SAF seeking a final break-away from centralised wage formation models.
1990	SAF decides that it will no longer take part in wage bargaining. A new form of wage commission (*Rehnberg-gruppen*) manages to establish a two-year wage agreement covering almost the entire labour market.
1991	SAF decides that it will no longer nominate representatives to decision-making state authorities including the Labour Market Board (AMS). Change of government to a four-party Conservative–Liberal coalition.
1992	The new government changes the composition of boards and statutory organisations. Representatives from union and employer groups are replaced by members of parliament and independent experts.
1993	Unemployment rises to a post-war record high level.

10 Industrial relations in Japan
Yasuo Kuwahara

This chapter starts by putting Japanese industrial relations into context, sketches some historical background, then discusses the roles of unions and employers and the Japanese approach to collective bargaining and labour–management consultation. The current issues discussed include: job security, labour shortages, foreign workers, technological change, and small and medium-sized enterprises.

In terms of its population of 124 million people and of its GDP of $2891 billion (see Appendix), Japan is the second largest economy of the nine countries discussed in this book (the USA is the largest). Japan's economy had a higher growth rate than any of the other countries in the 1980s. In terms of GDP *per capita* on a nominal basis, Japan ranks second, after Sweden. But if we consider a basis of 'purchasing power parties', Japan ranks third, after the USA and Canada (see Table A.6). Evidently, Japan is a very powerful economy.

Japan's labour force is 65 million and the labour force participation rate is 64 per cent. Some 78 per cent of the labour force are employees. About 7 per cent of the labour force work in primary industries, i.e. agriculture and fisheries. Manufacturing, mining and construction industries employ 34 per cent, while 58 per cent work in the tertiary industries, i.e. services, wholesale and retail, finance, utilities and government.

Japan is in many respects the most distinctive of the nine countries. On average, the Japanese enjoy the longest life span (82 years for women and 76 years for men). The Japanese ageing ratio (population of those 65 years old and over, divided by the total population) will be the highest among the major developed countries in the year 2025, according to an estimate by the Ministry of Health and Welfare (Koseisho 1989). The structure of Japan's population will change substantially from the pyramid-shape of the 1950s to a

Figure 10.1 Changes in the population pyramid

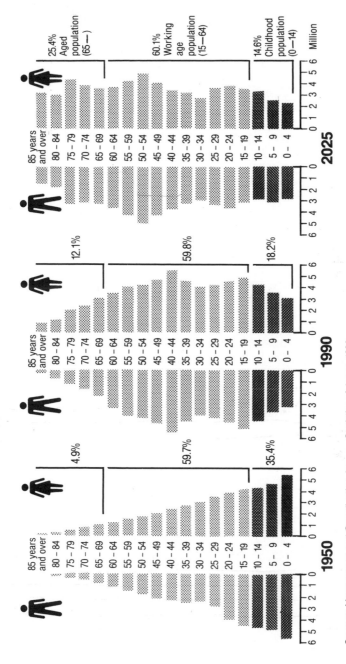

Sources: Management and Coordination Agency, *Statistics of Japan, 1990*
Ministry of Health and Welfare, *Estimates of Future Population, June 1991*.

top-heavy shape towards 2025. They work for more hours and lose relatively fewer working days in industrial disputes. Their population density of 326 people per square kilometre is higher than in any of the other countries discussed in this book. The unemployment rate, at less than 3 per cent, has been lower than in the other countries (except, in some years, Sweden).

Since the end of the Second World War, with the exception of a short period just after the war, Japanese politics have been dominated by what is now called the Liberal Democratic Party (LDP), which is a Conservative party. The opposition parties have exerted influence from time to time; however, none of them has obtained enough power to hold office in national politics. In this context, a remarkable change was seen in the election of the House of Councillors (*sangiin*) in 1989 when the Japan Socialist Party (JSP) and other opposition parties won more seats than the LDP. But in the more important House of Representatives (*shugiin*), the LDP maintained its majority. Both the LDP and JSP substantially increased their members at the elections of 1990, while the other parties declined.

Depending on their dominant ideology, unions are associated with various opposition parties such as the JSP, Democratic Socialist Party (DSP), and the Japan Communist Party (JCP). Successful candidates of the opposition parties may be either recommended and supported by a union, or may be those who have been associated with unions in the past. Despite these relationships between parties and unions, rank-and-file members of unions tend to vote for candidates of their choice. A recent notable change is the increased votes for the LDP by union members.

The Japanese model of industrial relations

Since the mid-1970s, Japan has attracted much attention for its favourable economic performance and its 'cooperative' industrial relations, which allegedly support this economic performance. The growing international interest in Japanese management and industrial relations has been perplexing to the Japanese themselves, since throughout the twentieth century Japan has tried to follow models derived from the West (for example, Britain, the USA and Germany). Before the 1973 oil crisis, the Japanese tended to see such countries as much more advanced, so that various management techniques and technologies were imported from them.

However, many of the Western countries which once led Japan in economic prosperity, have had sluggish economies for some time. By contrast, the economy of Japan has developed steadily (though it too has problems on the horizon to solve). Thus, these other countries have lost their legitimacy as models. Moreover, the former models are now looking for a new model themselves, and, ironically, Japan is frequently the source of inspiration. Many people in other countries, both developed and developing, want to 'import' the Japanese model, but to what extent is it transferable to other countries?

To begin to answer such a question, we need some historical background. Japan's feudal era ended with the Meiji Restoration of 1868. Hitherto, Japan had little contact with Western countries. Industrialisation began in the following decade—a century later than in Britain. Japan's early factories in major industries were begun by the state, but in 1880 it sold most of them to a few selected families. These were the origin of what later became the powerful _zaibatsu_ groups of holding companies, which were based on these groups' commercial banks.

Although some unions (e.g. for printers and for ironworkers) began in this period, the familial basis of industrialisation continued well into the twentieth century. Many factories had their own dormitories, especially in the textiles industry. In many industries, they had master workers (_oyakata_) who were subcontractors, like the early British foremen. Following the First World War, there was an acute shortage of skilled workers. Firms wanted to recruit workers directly. Hence many large firms intervened in the _oyakata_'s prerogative to recruit. With the rapid development of industries, the system of skill formation through apprenticeship was absorbed into internal training within firms.

As the paternalist tradition developed in the 1920s and 1930s, the unions did not exert much sustained influence. With the increasing pressure of a militaristic regime, unions were dissolved between 1938 and 1943 and the employers' associations were absorbed into the mobilisation for war production.

After Japan's unconditional surrender in 1945, the Allied powers' General Headquarters (GHQ) tried to reshape the organisation of work and industrial relations as part of the post-war reconstruction. The main elements of the present model, then, were established after the war under American influence.

Unions

The Japanese labour movement developed rapidly under GHQ's democratisation program. Although much of Japan's industrial base was destroyed during the war, only four months after its end, union membership had reached pre-war levels and by 1949 there were 6.6

Table 10.1   Number of unions and their membership density

Year	Labour unions[a]	Union membership[b] (persons)	Estimated union density (%)
1935[c]	993	408 662	6.9
1940[c]	49	9 455	0.1
1945[c]	509	380 677	3.2
1949	34 688	6 655 483	55.8
1950	29 144	5 773 908	46.2
1955	32 012	6 285 878	35.6
1960	41 561	7 661 568	32.2
1965	52 879	10 146 872	34.8
1970	60 954	11 604 770	35.4
1975	69 333	12 590 400	34.4
1980	72 693	12 369 262	30.8
1982	74 091	12 525 619	30.5
1983	74 486	12 519 530	29.7
1984	74 579	12 463 755	29.1
1985	74 499	12 417 527	28.9
1986	74 183	12 342 853	28.2
1987	73 138	12 271 909	27.6
1988	72 792	12 227 223	26.8
1989	72 605	12 227 073	25.9
1990	72 202	12 264 509	25.2
1991	71 685	12 396 592	24.5

Notes: a Based on *Tan-i rodo kumiai* (unit labour unions). This is the basic
organisational unit for unions in Japan and is comprised of workers in the
factory, office site, etc. or an enterprise.
b Based on *tan-itsu rodo kumiai* (enterprise labour union) which, in most
cases, are comprised of the unions of a single enterprise.
c The numbers are as at 30 June, except for 1935, 1940 and 1945 which
are for the end of year.

Sources: Ministry of Labor, *Basic Survey on Trade Unions*; *Year Book of Labor
Statistics & Research, 1948, 1950, and 1992.*

million union members, a density of 56 per cent. There were,
nonetheless, some setbacks for the unions. For instance, their plans
to hold a general strike in 1947 were countermanded by GHQ.
However, the unions continued to grow and recorded a peak membership of 12.6 million members in 1975, a density of 34 per cent.

After this peak, both the membership and the density of unionisation stagnated. Membership density fell to a low of 24 per cent
in 1991. What was responsible for this decline? One of the main
causes has been the change in industrial structure, especially the
shift towards the service sector.

During the decade after the 1973 oil crisis, there was substantial
rationalisation in the manufacturing sector, which was highly
unionised. Since a union shop clause is usually adopted, union

membership varies with the rise and fall of the unionised firms or industries. When the firm is expanding, union membership generally increases and vice versa. Although there has been an increase in the number of employees in the service sector, the average size of firms in terms of employment tends to be relatively small, and of course it is generally more difficult and costly for unions to organise in small firms than in large ones. Another cause is the general improvement in living standards, which has tended to make employees less enthusiastic about union activities.

Japanese unemployment was about 1.1 per cent at the end of the 1960s, when the economy enjoyed high growth. Although the level of unemployment in Japan has remained less than in most Western countries, it has more than doubled since 1970 (see Appendix). In the recessionary period after the 1973 oil crisis, many companies adopted a tougher stance towards unions, claiming public support for such policies. Employees have become more concerned about the competitive position of the companies for which they work and seem to have a high degree of commitment to the firm.

This reflects their expectation of 'lifetime employment' and seniority based wages; such practices were consolidated after the Second World War. Permanent manual and non-manual staff are employed not for specific jobs or occupations, but as *company* employees. Companies prefer to employ new school leavers rather than experienced workers who have been trained in other firms. Their induction program is designed to encourage them to conform to the norms of the enterprise.

Young recruits start at a comparatively low level of pay, which is based on their educational qualifications. Their pay increases in proportion to their length of service in the firm. Promotion is largely based on length of service, which is supposed to correlate with the employee's level of skill developed within the organisation. Therefore, it is disadvantageous for workers to change employers and for employers to lay-off employees who have accumulated specific skills required in that particular company. Typically, in the so-called primary labour market (e.g. permanent or regular employees working for large organisations), there is a tacit understanding about the long-term commitment between employer and employee. However, this is not confirmed in a written contract.

Most unions in today's Japan are organised not by occupation or by job, but by enterprise or establishment. An enterprise union consists solely of regular employees of a single firm, regardless of their occupational status. (Since enterprise unions usually include blue-collar and white-collar workers as members, the union density among white-collar workers is relatively high in Japan.) These employees are expected to stay in the same company until their mandatory retirement age, unless they are made redundant or leave voluntarily.

An increasing number of companies are raising the retirement age from 55 to 60 years old, in accordance with the lengthening average life span of the Japanese. Many workers remain in work even after reaching their mandatory retirement age. They find other jobs in subsidiaries or similar enterprises by recommendation of parent companies, or they start small business by investing their retirement allowances and other financial resources. Many employees who have been promoted to supervisory and/or managerial positions were often previously union members and some were even union leaders.

Only about a third of all employees comprise the core of genuinely regular employees. (This is a rough estimate of the percentage of employees working for the big organisations listed in the major stock exchanges and the public sector.) Many of the other employees work in smaller businesses or on a temporary or part-time basis and are often excluded from unions. Therefore, union density among female workers (who constitute the majority of part-time workers) has been lower than among male workers. The density is generally low in small and medium-sized enterprises (SMEs). However, in SMEs which are stable or expanding, there are many regular employees who stay in the same company for most of their working lives. In practice, therefore, it is difficult to draw a clear line between the primary and secondary labour markets in Japan.

Since enterprise unions include non-manual staff and manual workers of the same enterprise, a worker leaving the company would lose union membership automatically. The same is true for employees who are promoted to managerial positions. In spite of its name, an enterprise union not only functions for the benefit of the enterprise. It has legal protection against an employer's interference into its affairs as well as against other unfair labour practices.

Many enterprise unions grew sporadically in the period of turmoil after 1945. Some of them evolved from the factory- and company-based war-time production committees. Since most Japanese unions are organised for individual enterprises or plants, there are many unions: more than 71 600 according to one authority (Rodosho 1991). Unionism is strongest among regular employees in large organisations. In 1989 about 97 per cent of enterprise union members worked in firms which employed more than 100 employees (Rodosho 1989). Although there are other types of union organisation, such as industrial, craft and general unions, these are exceptions. *Kaiin*, the Seamen's union, is a rare example of an industrial union.

Most of the enterprise unions within the same industry join an industrial federation of unions. There are more than 100 such federations. The major functions of the industrial federations are: coordinating the activities of the member enterprise unions with the aim of increasing wages and improving working conditions; dealing with problems common to a whole industry; guiding and assisting member unions in specific disputes; and political lobbying in the interest of workers. These industrial federations themselves belong to the national centres, of which *Rengo* (JTUC, Japan Trade Union Confederation) is the largest.

After the two 1970s' oil crises, unions at industrial and national levels waged what they called a 'policy-oriented struggle' with the aim of ensuring stable employment and maintaining their members' standard of living. In the course of such labour activities, another movement 'to unite the labour front under the initiative of private sector unions' emerged in December 1982: *Zenminrokyo*, the Japanese Private Sector Union Council. It was formed by the labour federations in the private sector and reflected their enthusiasm for further consolidation of their unity and strength. This organisation developed into a larger union centre, *Rengo*, which would integrate the public sector unions. The new *Rengo* was established in 1989, when it had 78 industrial federations with nearly 8 million members. Public sector unions used to have more power compared with those in the private sector. However, in general, union membership has decreased since 1978 and the leading edge of unionism has shifted towards unions in the private sector.

Although the national confederations have important roles, the enterprise unions have more resources and are more powerful. The latter are autonomous in running their organisations and in promoting their members' interests. Furthermore, they are financially independent and self-supporting. Most union activities occur at the enterprise level, rather than at federation level.

As the company's success greatly influences members' working conditions and employment opportunities, enterprise unions generally have a cooperative attitude toward management. Employees generally identify with their employer in making decisions which would, for instance, enhance the employer's competitiveness. Thus, a key aspect of the work environment in the Japanese company is this interdependence and the belief that the company is a 'community of fate' (i.e. 'everyone is in the same big family'). In addition, the relatively modest wage differential between managers, white-collar and blue-collar workers tends to reinforce the worker's sense of identification with the firm. This is quite different from some Western countries where there is a more rigid class structure.

It is generally believed that the advantage of enterprise unionism lies in its policies being adapted to each enterprise rather than reflecting any broader craft or political issues. Labour–management relations based on enterprise unionism tend to be more flexible than those based, say, on craft unionism. On the other hand, there are disadvantages from a union's point of view: newly-employed workers automatically acquire union membership and their union dues are 'checked-off' from their pay automatically; thus their 'union consciousness' is generally less than their 'enterprise consciousness'.

Employers

During the period immediately after the Second World War, there were many violent labour disputes in Japan as a result of the economic disorder and the shortage of food and daily necessities. At that time, neither the employers nor workers had much industrial relations experience. To cope with this labour offensive and to establish industrial peace and order, employers organised regional and industrial associations. However, partly because of the so-called 'democratisation' policy of GHQ, employers were often obliged to yield to union pressures, thus facing an erosion of their managerial prerogatives.

Although most bargaining takes place at the enterprise level, some industries engage in collective bargaining at industry level; for example, in private railways, bus services and textiles. Apart from these few examples, none of the other national or regional employers' organisations engage in collective bargaining.

Nikkeiren, the Japan Federation of Employers' Associations, was founded in 1948. It is the most important employers' organisation from an industrial relations point of view and it has many functions. It coordinates and publicises employers' opinions on labour problems, selects employer representatives to the various government commissions, councils and ILO delegations, and provides its member organisations with advice and services on labour conditions and employment practices. Every year at the time of the *Shunto* (the Spring Labour Offensive), *Nikkeiren* releases guidelines to be followed in dealing with demands from the various unions during collective bargaining. Thus although most of them do not have a direct role in bargaining, the employers' associations seem to have an important role behind the scenes (Levine 1984:318ff). The main determinant of the outcome of collective bargaining is the individual company's business performance.

Figure 10.2   A model of a typical large Japanese company

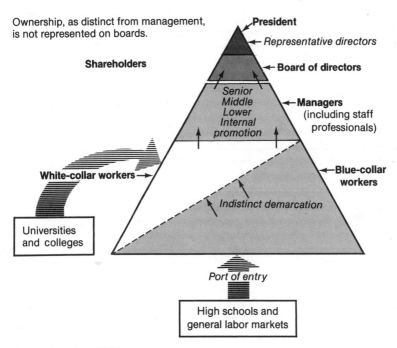

Source: Kuwahara (1989)

Employee-managed firms?

The basic structure of Japanese companies, particularly the large ones, is quite different from the structures found in North America and most European countries. The corporate structure of large Japanese companies may be closer to a model of 'employee-managed firms', unlike large companies in Western countries which are often characterised as 'shareholders' prerogative firms'. The structural characteristics of Japanese companies should not be seen as barriers to competition; the Japanese corporate system is quite legitimate, even though it is different.

The economic literature on labour-managed, or employee-managed, firms usually distinguishes them from other firms by assuming them to have a distinct functional objective. It is assumed that employee-managed, or *Illyria* firms, seek to maximise the dividend or net income per worker, while capitalist firms seek to maximise total profit (Ward 1958).

In addition, an employee-managed or a labour-managed firm implies a type of participatory management. Although various definitions could be formulated, a generally acceptable one would be that an employee-managed firm is a productive enterprise where ultimate decision-making rights are held by member-workers on an equal basis regardless of job, skill-grade, or capital contribution. Using this definition, the typical Japanese firm might be called 'quasi employee-managed', even if, strictly speaking, it is not truly run by all the workers. Although board directors are not officially elected or nominated by employees, and outside directors representing large shareholders such as banks, insurance companies, and parent companies are sometimes included as members of the board, most decisions and operations are executed by board directors who were promoted from within the corporation.

In Japanese companies, board directors are usually promoted from among the senior managers who have worked for the company for a long time, often 25 to 30 years, after graduating from university, college or high school. Many of these people had been leaders of enterprise unions when they were rank-and-file employees. Indeed, many employees who have been promoted to supervisory and/or managerial positions were often previously union members and some were even union leaders. When promoted from senior managerial positions to board directors, individuals are asked to adopt a different role as members of the top management group. However, this change takes place quickly. Directors who have been promoted internally after a long career might be expected to place the interests of the enterprise community, consisting of executive members and employees, above the interests of stockholders. (However, even if there are few outside directors, the interests of large shareholders are rarely neglected. Firms generally consult them before making important decisions. In general, larger shareholders are interested in capital gain rather than increasing dividends.)

Since internal promotion is the usual path for advancement, most employees have a strong commitment to the firm. In the Japanese company, the word *shain*, which literally means 'member of the company', is often used. This word contains unique nuances that do not have an equivalent in Western terminology. It means more than a mere hired worker, but implies membership of an organisation or community formed by people with the same interests. There is a sense that a Japanese corporation is a social entity of its own.

Under this system, employees often participate in the various stages of the decision-making process. Small-group activities such as Quality Control Circles (QCC) or Total Quality Control (TQC) are widely spread throughout Japanese firms. With a reduction in the degree of explicit industrial conflict and the increasing development of 'internal labour markets', the difference between collective bargaining and joint consultation is becoming less distinct.

Most blue-collar workers are paid on a monthly salary basis, as are white-collar workers. Another important issue in Japanese firms is the performance-related remuneration system. Besides wages or salaries, most Japanese workers receive large seasonal bonus payments worth about 4.2 months' salary a year (the industry average in 1989). This practice originated from the employers' consideration of the extra expenditure required for the Buddhist 'bon festival', a kind of ancestor worship ritual observed in summer, and for the end-of-year and New Year celebrations. The amount of bonus fluctuates according to the performance of the company or industry and according to the merit of employees. However, it does not fluctuate much, and workers assume that the bonuses are an integral part of their annual income. Despite the relative stability of the amount, employees do relate any small changes to variations in the company's profit. This increases employees' interest in the operation and performance of the company for which they work. The bonus system has attracted the interest of some Western economists as an effective measure to conquer stagflation (Weitzman 1984).

Collective bargaining

Pay agreements may be concluded separately from agreements on other matters. Most unions conduct pay negotiations during the Spring Labour Offensive in April and May each year, while negotiations on more comprehensive labour agreements may be conducted at other times. However, an increasing number of unions also make other claims during the Spring Labour Offensive; for example, for increases in overtime rates, revisions of allowances, shorter working hours, raising the retirement age and expanding private pensions.

The structure of enterprise unions usually corresponds to the organisation of the enterprise (i.e. plant, department or divisional groupings). Grievances are often settled informally; formal procedures are rarely used. Management often attempts to subdue tensions and conflict and to reinforce a feeling of community, following the pre-war tradition of paternalism. This does not mean that industrial disputes are unheard of; there were many large-scale and long disputes in mining and major manufacturing industries in the 1940s and 1950s. Some strikes were led by radical leaders. Most of these disputes left deep wounds on industrial relationships which would not easily heal.

Such disputes taught the unions and employers some important lessons. Although there were many stoppages in 1974, there was a substantial reduction subsequently. Disputes are usually settled directly between the parties concerned, but sometimes a third party conciliates. Conciliation machinery for the private and public sectors is provided by the central and local labour relations commissions. Special commissions act for public-sector employees and for seamen. Nearly all the disputes brought before these commissions are settled either by conciliation or mediation; few disputes go as far as arbitration.

Contemporary Japanese industrial relations are relatively stable and relations between the parties can be characterised as cooperative. Some see this in a positive light. Others have a more negative view, arguing that enterprise unions are too dependent on employers, and that the relationship is one of collaboration and incorporation. However, given that the corporate structure of large Japanese companies is akin to 'quasi employee-managed firms' where the interests of employees are well represented, enterprise unions may be more appropriate than the traditional occupationally-based unions, for instance, in terms of decision-making and in fostering workplace democracy and employee morale. However, it is open to question to what extent Japanese firms fulfil this; the pursuit of company profits tends to come before consideration of the individual employee.

Unions represent sectional interests, and enterprise unions are no exception. Since most people are expected to work for many years as employees in the same enterprise, they tend to place much emphasis on the improvement of their working conditions, but do not pay so much attention to the interests of the temporary workers at the same establishment. This may be an unfortunate characteristic of quasi employee-managed firms, where regular employees want to maintain their stable positions even if this is at the expense of non-regular employees, such as part-time workers and temporary workers (who are disproportionately likely to be women).

Why has the relationship between unions and employers changed so fundamentally since the 1950s? There has been increased competition among firms, improved standards of living, a shift towards a service-oriented economy and also public opinion is more conservative than it was in the 1950s. But are cooperative industrial relations desirable under all circumstances? These relations may come under severe stress when labour and management have to face a serious economic depression, which may precipitate redundancies.

Issues of current and future importance

The social and economic environment in Japan is still changing rapidly. There is an ageing population, an increase in the proportion of highly educated workers, growing participation by women in the labour market, increased immigration of foreign workers, and moves towards an 'information society'.

Job security and employment practices

In the midst of the post-1973 recession, many countries experienced increases in unemployment. Unemployment in Japan was 1.1 per cent in 1964 and remained less than 1.5 per cent until 1974. Since then, the unemployment rate had increased to 2.0 per cent in 1980 and 2.8 per cent in 1986–87—the highest rate since these statistics were first collected in the early 1950s. Unemployment had increased particularly among those less than 24 years old and those over 40 years old. Unemployment subsequently declined, but rose again in 1992–93.

Total employment has continued to increase, despite the increase in unemployment. In the 1975–80 period, overall employment rose by 3 million, from 34.7 million to 37.7 million employees. The industries which created most jobs were retailing and wholesaling, business services, construction and medical services. The new high-technology industries also expanded. Heavy-manufacturing industries contracted, however, including textiles, shipbuilding, steel and nonferrous metals, lumber and industrial machinery. In such declining industries, many unions, especially the federations at the industrial level, participated (possibly for the first time) in the reorganisation of industry by asking the government to establish industrial policies which took the unions' viewpoint into account.

The stagnation following the oil crisis taught employers some important lessons, for example, about the difficulties of laying off redundant workers. Companies generally do not dismiss permanent employees, since there is no institutionalised lay-off system comparable to that of the USA. Moreover, if firms did lay off people, this could destroy the 'high trust relations' which currently exist between managers and employees. Instead, one of the strategies adopted in Japan was to increase flexibility by minimising the number of permanent (regular) employees, and by employing temporary and part-time workers instead. On the other hand, raising the mandatory retirement age from 55 to 60 or even to 65 is expected to increase the commitment of employees to particular organisations. Since the retirement allowance and private pensions are generally related to length of service, employees want to stay in companies for as long as they are allowed.

Many companies are modifying their traditional employment and pay system to introduce more flexible HRM practices. The innovations include 'plateauing' the age-wage profile after a certain age, say 45 (an automatic seniority pay increase is not expected after such an age) and introducing selective career paths which induce early retirement. Some firms have reduced their total number of employees by 'natural wastage' or attrition.

Labour shortages

Since the latter half of 1986, there has been a remarkable shift in the supply–demand relationship in the labour market. The increase in the value of the yen led to a threat of a recession, in particular among export industries. Japanese industry responded positively to this situation by reorienting itself towards developing domestic demand and the economy began to grow again. With firms showing a greater propensity to recruit more workers each month, the number of employees increased sharply.

From 1987, the job-offers to job-seekers ratio (the number of job offers divided by job seekers) increased as the Japanese economy overcame the yen's appreciation and returned towards a steady growth path. Furthermore, the unemployment rate declined again from the first quarter of 1988, after having temporarily risen to 3 per cent in 1987. In 1986–87 the Japanese economy had been plagued by fears of unemployment in the midst of the recession induced by the soaring yen. Therefore, there was much discussion about the dramatic changes that had taken place in only two years.

In June 1988 the job openings-to-applicants ratio exceeded 1.0 for the first time in 14 years. The October 1989 ratio was 1.03. It increased to 1.4 in October 1991. Thus, the employment situation improved from the macro viewpoint, but the labour shortages were not necessarily uniform throughout all sectors of the labour market.

The labour shortages in the early 1990s gradually spread to many industries, and were especially serious in construction, retailing and other elements of the service sector as well as in the machinery and metals segments of the manufacturing sector. Many of these industries offered working conditions that were not attractive to young workers and many firms encountered difficulties caused by the acute shortage of young people. How did industries deal with the shortage of workers? Strategies used by employers included: technological innovation, flexible use of workers, and the employment of foreign workers.

Technological innovations

There was much concern in the 1950s and also in the 1970s that technological innovation would lead to decreased employment opportunities and worsening unemployment through improved pro-

Figure 10.3   Trends in number of new job offers and seekers (seasonally adjusted)

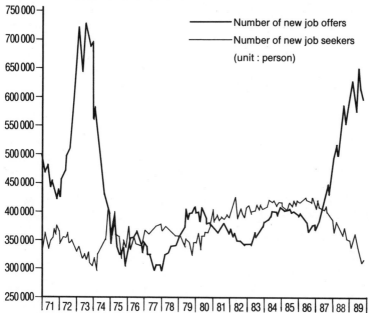

Number of new job offers
Number of new job seekers
(unit : person)

Source: Employment Security Bureau, Ministry of Labour, *Statistics on Employment Security,* Tokyo

ductivity (i.e. that there would be a labour-saving effect). However, subsequent developments have diminished such concerns. Unlike the popular view in many other countries, the move towards a service-based economy and the introduction of new technologies are not generally seen as causing a reduction in job opportunities in Japan.

Japan is leading the world in the diffusion of labour-saving technologies. A variety of technologies, known as factory automation and office automation, have been introduced in many areas. According to a survey by the Association of Industrial Robot Producers, in 1987 Japan was ahead of the other major market economies in terms of its having more than a 60 per cent share of all the industrial robots in the OECD.

New technologies, particularly micro-electronics, were used to create many new products including videotape recorders, word processors and personal computers, which in turn expanded employment opportunities to a great extent. Many labour-saving technologies have also been introduced to cope with the shortage of labour. This, however, has posed problems in other respects. With the proportion of new school graduates declining, along with the ageing of the labour force, restructuring through technological innovation may prove difficult for some groups in the years ahead. Middle-aged and older persons, for example, are not well prepared to respond to new technologies, while it is less of a problem for younger members of the workforce. It has long been advocated that older people should be assisted in terms of retraining and redeployment, but this has not been easily accomplished.

Flexibility

Another way to cope with the shortages of labour is to introduce greater labour market flexibility. Since the late 1970s, there has been a considerable expansion in the employment of part-time workers and those available from temporary agencies. The job-opening to job-applicants ratio for part-time workers was 4.0 in 1990. Most part-time workers are female, and particularly middle-aged married women. The percentage of part-time female workers who work less than a 35-hour week had risen to more than 29 per cent by 1991. In addition, the average length of service for part-time workers with one employer has gradually become longer. In 1988 they worked an average of 4.1 years. The rate of turnover among part-time workers has remained stable in recent years.

In contrast, the rate of turnover of young workers has tended to rise. Furthermore, it remains high against the backdrop of the tight labour market. Approximately 20 per cent of young workers with high school diplomas left their initial place of work within a year and 40 per cent left within three years. An increase in the number of young workers (known as *freeters*) who do not want to stay with a single firm, is contributing to such changes. Simultaneously, the average length of service among 'core-workers' (regular employees) is getting longer; in 1987 it was 12.4 years for men and 7.1 years for women (Rodosho 1987). Notable changes, then, are taking place in Japan's so-called 'lifetime' employment practices.

The foreign labour issue

When faced with a serious shortage of labour, many employers have employed foreign workers who are often 'illegal labourers' from developing countries in Asia and elsewhere. Until the mid-1980s, there was little discussion about the employment of foreign workers. However, the subsequent appreciation of the yen and tight labour market widened more than ever the wage differentials between Japan and developing countries.

Partly due to the government's slow response to the foreign

labour issue, there has been an increasing number of foreigners who entered Japan with tourist or student visas, but then, unlawfully, entered the labour market. This includes those who are engaged in activities not allowed by law, or who have stayed in Japan for longer than permitted by their visa. It is estimated that, by 1991, at least 210 000 foreign workers were employed unofficially in construction and some aspects of manufacturing and the service sector. They are especially engaged in those jobs which are considered demanding, dirty and dangerous.

In the construction sector, for instance, foreign labourers are employed through personal connections with a subsidiary firm's boss, through employment agencies, including brokers or syndicates. They are also employed on a daily basis in the day-labourer market. Regrettably, an undercover network of syndicates or brokers has been established which provides bridges between Japan and the foreign workers' countries of origin. Many immigrants who look for employment opportunities in Japan depend on such a network. The 'trade' in foreign workers often involves the use of professional smugglers who extract exorbitant fees for transport and for providing false documents (e.g. visas and Japanese passports). Often, workers who find employment opportunities through these channels are exploited and are forced to work in substandard conditions for low wages. A substantial number of cases involving illegal foreign workers is reported each year.

Under these circumstances, the Japanese government introduced an amendment to the Immigration-Control and Refugee-Recognition Act, with effect from June 1990. The amendment expanded the categories of legal residence and employment under which engaging in professional or occupational activities is authorised, while introducing penalties against employers and brokers who employ illegal workers or who facilitate such employment. The Japanese government's policy is to prohibit unskilled (or 'workers for "simple" jobs') from seeking work in Japan. The amendment has not changed this. This policy is rationalised by arguing that if there is an abundant supply of cheap labour, it will obstruct the progress of rationalisation and industrial restructuring in desirable directions such as high-value-added industries or high-technology industries. Unless there is strong support for the maintenance of fair working conditions for foreign workers, it may be necessary to continue to prohibit the inflow of unskilled workers for the time being.

The pressure from the Asian developing countries to supply the required labour is very strong. However, Japan must develop a long-term policy to accommodate the increasing number of immigrants who are attempting to adapt to Japanese society. Such a policy should cover not only working conditions but also broader areas such as housing, education, social security, regional issues and political rights, so that foreign workers are satisfactorily absorbed into Japanese society for the mutual benefit of all concerned.

Small and medium-sized enterprises

The stereotypical Japanese employment practices mentioned above (e.g. long-term commitment and enterprise unions) are usual for most *large* employing organisations, but are also found, albeit to a lesser extent, in SMEs. Some 94 per cent of all Japanese employees work in SMEs, defined as establishments with less than 100 employees.

There are wide differences in wages and working conditions, depending upon a firm's size. These differences reflect different capital–labour ratios and other factors resulting in higher value-added productivity in large firms. SMEs are not an inefficient and declining sector. SMEs account for a wide range of economic activity and increasing support for them is emerging today from many diverse quarters, because they can be innovative and more flexible.

It is difficult to generalise about the characteristics of HRM and industrial relations in SMEs because of their wide variety. Subcontractors are one type of SMEs which play an important role in manufacturing industries (but the percentage of subcontractors is low in other industries). Although it is hard to obtain an exact picture, about 66 per cent of manufacturing firms are subcontractors of one type or another. Industries which have many subcontractors are: the car, textiles, clothing, general machinery, electrical machinery and metal industries. The percentage of subcontractors had increased in each of these industries in the 1970s. However, as

Table 10.2   Private establishments and number of people employed by size of establishment and by industry

Size of establishment	Number of establishments (distribution %)		Number employed (distribution %)	
All sizes	6 559 381	(100.0)	55 014 018	(100.0)
1–4 persons	4 221 069	(64.3)	9 199 536	(16.7)
5–29	2 052 790	(31.3)	21 116 549	(38.4)
30–99	233 597	(3.6)	11 525 293	(20.8)
100–299	42 487	(0.6)	6 673 059	(12.1)
300 or more	9 438	(0.1)	6 599 671	(12.0)

Source: Prime Minister's Office *Census of Establishments* (1987); Management and Coordination Agency *Establishment Census of Japan* (1991).

a firm increases in size, it tends to be less dependent on other firms (Chusho Kigyo Cho 1983).

The independent firms constitute another type of SME; they compete with each other in the market. In this category, there are a growing number of SMEs based on high technologies. This category of firm typically combines advanced technology with high levels of business acumen and technical ability. There are still relatively few of these firms compared with the traditional type of SMEs; however, they are expected to have a great impact on their product and labour markets.

Since union density is low in SMEs, the terms and conditions of employment are generally determined by market factors. In the case of the very competitive subcontractors, profit margins are low. Wage levels determined in the primary labour market do not correspond with the wage levels in SMEs, although there is a spillover effect.

As mentioned earlier, there has been a growing number of workers who work part-time. About 29 per cent of women workers were part-timers in 1991. Such workers have become more likely to be mobile, in the sense that they enter and leave the labour force. The motivation of such employees is changing. Increasing numbers of them are entering the labour market not only for economic reasons but also for socio-cultural reasons: for example, to escape from the tedium of being a 'housewife'. Employers are also increasingly seeking to employ more part-time workers in order to gain greater flexibility in their labour force.

When considering these recent changes—the dynamic role of SMEs and the characteristics of Japan's part-time or temporary workforce—the simple stereotype of a dual labour market should not be automatically applied to the Japanese situation. Japanese labour markets are complex and segmented. Even the so-called primary labour markets in the manufacturing sector have stagnated since the oil crises, especially in basic industries such as steel, nonferrous metals and chemicals. On the other hand, many SMEs have emerged as more dynamic and profitable, though they are often characterised as being in the secondary labour market.

SMEs are playing a larger role. The growth of the service sector has led to an increasing diversity of workers' conditions being dependent upon their employer's specific business conditions. By the mid-1990s, 60 per cent of civilian employees will be in the service sector. The future of unionism in Japan greatly depends on whether unions can recruit such employees.

Conclusion

The pre-war paternalist traditions still influence the views and behaviour of older people in Japan, but these are being questioned by the younger generation. Before the 1970s, some union leaders and Left-wing academics saw the main characteristics of the Japanese model (e.g. lifetime employment, seniority-based wages and enterprise unions) as feudalistic practices which should be abandoned. There was, however, a dramatic change of view during the mid-1970s when such characteristics came to be seen as increasingly important explanations of the post-war Japanese economic miracle.

In comparison with most other OECD countries, Japan has enjoyed high rates of economic growth. This may be an unexpected result of the war which destroyed almost all of the special interest organisations, which, as Olson (1982) argued, may hinder the growth of an economy. Various bottlenecks in the supply of oil and other raw materials have impeded Japan's growth, particularly since 1973. By the mid-1980s, then, Japan had entered a stage of slower growth, though it continued to grow more rapidly than most other developed countries.

One of the most important characteristics of Japanese society, which is also reflected in its HRM and industrial relations, has been its adaptability. There are various other characteristics of Japanese HRM and industrial relations which help to maintain flexibility, and thus, to facilitate adaptation to change. Some examples of these are: the relatively vague and wide job descriptions and flexibility of workforce allocation in organisations; lack of rigid work rules which are often found in other developed countries; widespread use of bonus systems; and long-term merit-rating for both managers and employees.

Increasingly, such constraints as lower rates of economic growth and the ageing of the population have induced some rigidities into Japanese society. The narrowing of promotion opportunities for managers is becoming a serious issue among a prime age group (i.e. those who are 35–45). The position of white-collar workers is also a major concern. Their status in enterprises and society is undergoing substantial changes. However, unlike some countries in Europe, Japan is not likely to see the emergence of radical white-collar unionists.

The future of the Japanese model of industrialisation depends upon its ability to continue to adjust to change by eliminating barriers to economic growth, with the help of various innovations. The model is changing, as there is continuing structural change in the face of strong international competitive forces. New technologies are being used widely as a means to thwart rigidities in the labour market and in the wider society. Hitherto, the process of 'creative destruction' has generally had a positive impact on the Japanese labour market and has had favourable consequences for employers and most workers.

Japan's economy has long been looked upon as 'fragile' or 'precarious', despite its overwhelming success, particularly after the first oil crisis. It has overcome the many difficulties of the post-war period including oil crises and the appreciation of the yen. Japanese economic- and corporate-policy makers have demonstrated their flexible but tough characteristics.

Japanese management is regarded in other industrialised and industrialising countries as a model, suitable for surviving keen competition in the global market. Japanese styles of management are being transferred through direct foreign investment by Japanese firms. Such direct foreign investment increased greatly in the late 1980s.

As Japanese firms move their operations overseas, local employees have promotion opportunities in such international enterprises. About 10 per cent of the employees of Japanese companies outside Japan are managerial and white-collar staff. It makes sense for the Japanese to train and promote non-Japanese employees for senior managerial positions overseas. But for this to happen successfully, both sides have to accept considerable changes in their expectations and their deeply-held values.

Blending into a Japanese company overseas presents challenges typical of any cross-cultural adaptation. Rather than merely creating new management strategies in a foreign country, a learning process is involved. It is not a one-way transplant of technology; the recipient's interests must be considered. The continued viability of Japanese management strategies will be tested in this process to create a new international hybrid best-practice approach to management.

A chronology of Japanese labour–management relations

1868   *Meiji* Restoration ended the feudal era.
1880   Early government factories sold to family groups, the genesis of *zaibatsu*, holding companies.
1887   Unionisation movement among printers, iron-workers and other craft workers (which soon disappeared).
1892   Formation of National Federation of Chambers of Commerce.
1894–95   Sino–Japanese War.

1897   Founding of *Rodokumiai-kiseikai*, the first successful
            union in Japan. Ironworkers' union and Japan Railway
            Union (*Nittetu Kyoseikai*) organised.
1900   Enactment of *Chian-iji-ho* (Maintenance of the Public
            Order Act) with provisions to prohibit workers' right to
            organise.
1901   Government-owned Yawata Ironworks opened.
1903   Ministry of Agriculture and Commerce issued 'Status
            of Factory Workers'.
1904–05   The Russo–Japanese War.
1906   Japan Socialist Party organised.
1907   Violent strikes at Ashio and Besshi copper mines.
1911   Factory Law promulgated.
1912   Founding of *Yuaikai* (Friendly Society).
1914–18   First World War.
1920   Great Depression. Large-scale labour disputes at
            Yawata Ironworks. First May Day.
1921   Founding of *Nippon Rodo Sodomei* (Japan Labour
            Foundation).
1922   Japan Communist Party organised.
1925   General Election Law promulgated. Public Peace Main-
            tenance Law promulgated.
1927   A large-scale strike at *Noda Shoyu*.
1929   Lifting of the gold embargo. *Showa* panic.
1931   Pre-war record for the number of labour disputes. The
            Manchurian Incident started.
1937   Sino–Japanese War started. Founding of *Sangyo-
            hokokukai* (Association for Services to the State
            through Industry)—a labour–management cooperative
            association.
1940   Organisations of workers and farmers dismissed.
            Dainihon Sangyo Hokokukai (The Great Japan Federa-
            tion of Patriotic Industries) inaugurated. *Taisei
            Yokusankai* (The Imperial Rule Assistance Association)
            organised. It merged with *Dainihon Sangyo Hokokukai*
            in 1942.
1941–45   Second World War.
1945   Hiroshima and Nagasaki reduced to ashes by atomic
            bomb explosion. The Potsdam Declaration accepted.
            Japan's unconditional surrender. The Trade Union Law
            promulgated.
1946   Workers' control of Tsurumi Works, *Nippon Kokan K.K.*
            Six labour unions, including the labour union of
            Tsurumi Workers, *Nippon Kokan* and the labour union
            of Toshiba Corporation, started production control.

Labour disputes at the *Yomiuri Shimbun*. Japanese Confederation of Labour (*Sodomei*) organised. Labour Relations Adjustment Law promulgated. The Constitution of Japan promulgated (came into effect on May 3, 1947). *Nichirokaigi* (Congress of Labour Unions of Japan) organised.

1947   The General Headquarters ordered the suspension of 1 February general strike. The Constitution of Japan came into effect. *Densan* (Japan Electric Industry Workers' Union) and *Tanro* (Japan Coal Miners' Union) organised. Ministry of Labour set up.

1948   The Japan Federation of Employers' Association (*Nikkeiren*) organised. Revised National Public Service Law and Public Corporation and National Enterprise Labour Relations Law promulgated. Trade Union Law and Labour Relations Adjustment Law revised. Dodge Line introduced. The Korean War broke out. Conference for organising General Council of Trade Unions of Japan (*Sohyo*). Red purge. The Peace Treaty with Japan signed. The Japan–US Security Treaty signed.

1952   The Third May Day. Bloodshed at the Palace Plaza. Third labour law revised.

1954   Human rights disputes at Ohmi Kenshi Co., Ltd. All Japan Federation of Labour Unions (*Zenro*) organised. *Sohyo* consolidated five industry level offensives into a united wage increase in spring.

1956   Japan joins the United Nations.

1958   Labour disputes at Oji Paper Co., Ltd.

1959   Minimum Wages Law passed by the Diet. United movement to stop the revision of the Japan–US Security Treaty. Labour disputes at Miike Coal Mines.

1964   Japan joins the OECD. Federation of IMF–JC.

1965   Japan ratified ILO's Convention 87.

1973   First oil crisis.

1974   The biggest strike in the history of the Spring Offensive—about 6 million participants.

1980   UAW (International Union, United Automobile, Aerospace and Agricultural Workers of America) asked for the Japanese automobile manufacturers direct investment in the US.

1982   Japanese Private Sector Trade Union Council (*Zenminrokyo*) formed.

1987   Japanese Private Sector Trade Union Confederation (*Rengo*) formed.

1989	Start of new *Rengo* (Japan Trade Union Confederation) which merged the public sector unions.
1988	Revision of Labour Standard Act (promotion of shorter working hours).
1990	Revision of the Immigration and Refugee Recognition Act.
1992	Law of Child-Rearing Leave for Parents introduced. Japanese economy slows down.
1993	Skill Training System for Foreign Workers established.

11 Conclusions: Towards a synthesis of international and comparative experience of nine countries

Oliver Clarke

The discussion in this book, up to this point, has concerned the nature of international and comparative industrial relations and explained the differing experiences of nine industrialised market economies (IMEs). This chapter attempts to provide a comparative analysis of the development of industrial relations in these countries—with occasional references to the experience of other countries—and to identify the more important trends.

Post-war industrial relations systems

It is useful to start by noting some of the factors which helped shape the different industrial relations systems after the Second World War. The war itself was obviously of key importance. For war-devastated Germany and Japan a completely new start had to be made. In Italy and France, where free unions had led a shadowy underground existence during the war, some elements of the pre-fascist, pre-war pattern carried forward but there were significant new features (see chs 6 & 7). In the USA the exigencies of wartime production helped the Wagner Act procedures to mature, and if the strike wave of 1946 led to what unions saw as the repressive Taft–Hartley Act of 1947, there was no strong movement to replace the New Deal system (see ch. 3). Canada had only recently adopted arrangements deriving from the US New Deal model and was building on them (see ch. 4). In Britain, where the industrial relations system was seen as outstandingly effective, the industrial relations parties saw no need to effect major changes (see ch. 2). In Australia, though industrial relations were often turbulent in the 1940s, none of the parties were moved to seek major changes (see ch. 5). On the other hand, Sweden (the only one of the nine countries discussed that had not been at war), which had laid a new foundation for its industrial relations in

245

the late 1930s, did an exceptionally effective job during the war and its aftermath in ensuring that its industrial relations were well adapted to the post-war world (see ch. 9). It was then that the active labour market and solidaristic wage policies were designed, that centralised collective bargaining evolved, and that the Swedes conducted a fruitful debate on the relationship between wages and full employment.

An important feature of the post-war industrial relations systems in nearly all of the countries was the new prominence of unions. If such an expression can be applied to these organisations—some of which had already had a continuous life of nearly a century—the unions had 'come of age'. Their contribution to the war effort in the victorious countries, their role in resistance movements in occupied countries, and as a potential democratic force in defeated countries, everywhere ensured their place in the post-war polity. They had become valued partners of governments.

In rebuilding their economies, the continental European countries showed some similarities in their approach to industrial relations. The model chosen was broadly one in which pay and working conditions were determined by collective bargaining at the industry level, whether nationally or regionally, and in which matters of shared interest to the employer and workers were dealt with by works councils or works committees. Such bodies became compulsory for all but small firms, either by law or by central collective agreement in Germany, France, Italy and Sweden (and in Belgium, Denmark, the Netherlands and Norway). By this division conflict was largely—though not, of course, entirely—kept out of the individual enterprise. Interestingly, the types of institution constructed did not adopt the format of the joint consultative or joint production committees which attracted so much attention in Britain in the 1940s, but accorded specific rights to the representative bodies in relation to managerial decisions.

Changes to the post-war orthodoxy

By 1952 the post-war systems of industrial relations were broadly in place in forms which would remain unchanged in essentials for, in some cases, around two decades, in others until the 1990s. Up to the late 1960s nothing occurred to necessitate a fundamental change in industrial relations structures; however, their operation was notably influenced by two factors: the changing attitudes of workers and a growing conflict between the outcome of pay determination processes and the needs of the economies as perceived by governments.

First, a new generation of workers came into the labour force: better—and less conservatively—educated; confident of their bargaining power in a situation (in most countries) of unprecedentedly low unemployment and confident that thanks to apparently endless economic growth they could count on regular improvements in wages and working conditions without extra effort on their part. The acceptance of a subservient role which had characterised earlier generations now gave place both to a growing militancy, to a demand for more say in decisions within the enterprise, and to less willingness to accept boring, repetitive, or otherwise unpleasant jobs. Workers flexed their muscles in manifestations which seemed to herald a new era—the French 'events' of May 1968, the 'hot autumn' of 1969 in Italy, the wildcat strikes in peaceful Germany, Belgium and Sweden in 1969–70, and the Lordstown strike at General Motors in 1971 in the USA. In Britain, in 1969, unions forced a Labour government to withdraw its own industrial relations proposals and, in 1974, a miners' strike hastened the end of Heath's Conservative government and its Industrial Relations Act 1971 (see ch. 1).

A major factor associated with the change in attitudes and in the economic environment was the new propensity, at least in peacetime, for pay increases to outstrip what could be afforded from higher productivity and any improvement in the terms of trade, thereby adding to inflationary pressures. The severity of the tendency varied considerably. In Germany and Japan it was rarely a serious problem, nor was it a problem in Austria and Switzerland, but it was frequently a problem in Britain and Italy and at times in the USA and Canada. Where the problem was troublesome, although governments came to place increasing reliance on monetary and fiscal policies, some also tried to rely on what came to be known as incomes policies which could be statutory or voluntary, bilateral, multilateral or unilateral.

Where the need for checking the growth of wages was immediate and obvious, a temporary wage freeze might be acceptable; otherwise pay moderation tended to become a factor which unions would seek to trade off against government promises to adjust their policies in other fields to take more account of union aspirations. The advantage of an incomes policy was, of course, that if excessive pay growth could be restrained, monetary policies could be less harsh, thereby avoiding consequential reduction in business activity and hence increased unemployment. There were successful incomes policies but they were few and mainly shortlived. The chief disadvantages were that it was difficult to ensure continued compliance over time; that the price of union cooperation tended to be too high; that it was difficult to ensure that the policy bore equitably on different groups of the working population; and that such advantage as might be gained could be lost in the free-for-all which tended to follow termination of a policy.

The impact of recession

The late 1960s and early 1970s, then, were a period of worker militancy which seemed set to continue, at least in some of the countries under discussion. What would have come of it we cannot know for in 1973–74 the economic environment deteriorated sharply, notably on account of the massive increase in oil prices by the Organisation of Petroleum Exporting Countries (OPEC). That increase was in effect a tax on the non-oil producing countries, which, if recompensed by equivalent pay increases, would simply add to inflation. In the event, the behaviour of collective bargainers varied between countries. In Germany relatively little inflation ensued. In Japan there was major inflation, but only for one year. In Britain and Australia pay increases were generally seen as unjustifiably high. Canada adopted an incomes policy in 1975–78. In Italy, and in other countries where indexation of wages on prices was an important component of wage fixing machinery, there was no avoiding the inflationary effects.

It took time for industrial relations systems to adjust to the new and tougher economic environment, and some of them had not fully done so at the end of the 1970s when OPEC induced the second massive rise in oil prices. This time, however, although the impact on collective bargainers again varied between countries, several governments were determined to use non-accommodating monetary policies—i.e. stronger measures which would make it more difficult for employers to concede wage increases—to lessen wage pressures. These policies proved effective, though they also had a discouraging effect on industrial activity in a world which was already moving into the worst recession since the 1930s: the recession of 1980–82.

The recession of 1980–82 was not just a cyclical phenomenon but marked a shift in the world economy. The long-term competitive advantage of the old industrialised countries had been wearing away over the post-war years. Multinational enterprises had been globalising production, both to expand markets and to make use of low labour costs in some countries. Some of the newly industrialising economies, notably South Korea, Taiwan, Singapore and Hong Kong, had managed their own economies exceptionally well and were outperforming the old IMEs. Also, new technology was facilitating the internationalisation of production.

For several of the nine countries under discussion this recession also marked a new phase in industrial relations. A phase of union growth, of relatively full employment, of moves towards industrial democracy, and of regular annual improvements in wages and working conditions, was giving way to a phase of difficulty for unions, of much higher levels of unemployment, and of concession bargaining (especially in the USA) and hard-to-get improvements. How the various actors and elements of industrial relations fared in the early-1980s' recession and subsequently is the subject of the next part of this chapter.

The unions

The immediate evidence of the changing fortunes of the unions is to be found in membership data.[1] Across our nine countries the development has been uneven, though in almost all cases membership density failed to keep pace with the growth of the labour force. In the USA membership density has declined practically continuously since 1955, though membership numbers peaked as late as 1979, since when they too have declined. Membership density in Canada, on the other hand, has borne up relatively well, at least until recently. In Japan, density declined slowly but steadily from 1975 onwards. Australian union membership dropped from 51 per cent in 1976 to 41 per cent by 1990, while French and Italian membership densities fell substantially in the 1980s and British membership fell from 51 per cent in 1980 to less than 40 per cent by the early 1990s. On the other hand, Swedish membership density increased steadily from the 1960s until recently and German density remained fairly steady (see Appendix).

That unionisation should fall in the conditions of the 1980s is hardly surprising; unemployment rose in most countries—and unemployed workers are more likely to drop out of than to join unions. Union membership has always been particularly strong in the old manufacturing and extractive industries, but these industries were among those most severely hit in the 1980s. Employment growth was usually in the service sector, much of which is hard to organise. It is usually thought that unionisation is relatively easy to achieve in large establishments with a stable full-time male workforce; however, the size of establishments has been tending to fall and there has been a considerable influx of women workers and workers on atypical conditions—part-time, temporary and fixed-term workers—with a lower propensity to organise. Also, in the harsher conditions of the 1980s and 1990s, unions were less able to attract members by achieving large improvements in wages and working conditions. It is, perhaps, surprising in the circumstances that, in total, union membership has held up as well as it has.

But what, then, accounts for the considerable differences in the fortunes of unions between countries? What common elements emerge, for example, from looking at the countries where membership has held up well or even improved—Canada, Germany and Sweden in the present sample, to which could be added Belgium, Denmark, Finland, Iceland, Luxembourg, and Norway? It is difficult to see any factors common to these countries—though all the Nordic countries are in this group—but there are some elements that seem relevant. In these countries, excepting Canada, it can be said that unions are deeply involved in day-to-day public affairs. In some, for instance, they are concerned with the administration of social security, though as the French experience shows, this does not guarantee maintenance of membership.

Comparison of the US and Canadian experience is particularly interesting. The two countries have comparable labour legislation and most of their bargaining is at enterprise level. Further, despite some defections, in 1986 36 per cent of Canadian (unionised) workers were still affiliated to US unions (Lipsig-Mumme 1989:251). Yet whereas in 1965 membership density was a little higher in the USA than in Canada, by 1989 a unionisation rate of 16 per cent in the USA was less than half of the Canadian rate (33 per cent). The explanation would seem to lie in the more favourable union recognition procedures of Canadian legislation; the more union-accommodating stance of Canadian employers (who, anyway, have no 'sunbelt' in the south to go to); and the more vigorous strategies of Canadian unions including, or so Lipsig-Mumme (1989:254) suggests, political strategies (see chs 3 & 4).

The particularly substantial drop in membership density in the UK is easy to explain. Aggressive union behaviour in the 1970s, culminating in the 'winter of discontent' of 1978–79, did considerable harm to the public image of unions, thereby reducing propensity to join. Also, the decline of the unions' traditional heartlands of steel, engineering, coalmining, the docks, and rail transport lost many members. The series of laws bearing on unions and their activities enacted by the post-1979 Conservative governments also had a negative impact on union membership (see ch. 2).

Unions' political influence

Where membership was lost (coupled with the colder economic climate and high unemployment in several countries) bargaining power in relation to employers was reduced and, to some extent, influence on governments lessened. Unions' political activities and influence do, of course, vary across our countries. Most US union leaders prefer political power to be in the hands of the Democrats; nonetheless, most US unions formally maintain a neutral stance, while applying the electoral test of 'reward your friends and punish your enemies'. The Reagan administrations of the 1980s were seen as hostile to labour, the major exception being their substantial labour–management cooperation program. The subsequent Bush administration showed a few signs of a more positive approach and the unions were reassured to some extent by the Democrats' strong position in both the Senate and the House of Representatives, though initially that achieved little for them in terms of legislation beyond raising the minimum wage. The unions' hopes were raised, however, by the advent of the Clinton administration in 1993.

In our sample of countries, the British unions suffered the worst reverses of political influence. Under the Labour governments of 1974–79 union influence on government policies reached a higher level than ever before, but it vanished with the accession to power of Mrs Thatcher's government in 1979. Closely linked with the Labour Party—as the British Trades Union Congress and most of its large constituent unions are—the unions have been associated with electoral policies which were found unconvincing at four successive general elections. (However, under Mr Major's Conservative government, unions continue to play a substantial, if diminished, part in Britain's multifarious tripartite bodies, not to mention their continuing influence in local government.)

The French unions, long divided into factions of differing political viewpoints, fared unevenly, though all of the central bodies tended to lose ground as measured by such indicators as elections to enterprise committees. The CGT, though still by far the biggest union centre, was weighed down by its close association with the increasingly unpopular Communist Party. In the earlier part of the 1980s the CFDT suffered from identification with the governing Socialist Party at a time when the government was forced to adopt austerity measures. FO's 'business unionism', however, retained popularity (though FO has become much more militant). But despite their overall fall in membership, political influence of the French unions, while not as great as in some former times, endured, as indeed did the influence of the Italian unions as witnessed by the success of their campaigns against government proposals concerning tax and health service charges in 1989.

In Sweden, though strains developed in its relationship with the employers' confederation, the manual workers' union centre, LO, retained a powerful influence on the Social Democratic Party, which was in continuous government—except for 1976–82—from 1932 to 1991. In the 1970s, LO persuaded the Party to adopt the electorally unpopular wage-earner funds proposal, and through the 1980s and into the 1990s the unions, despite government pleas for moderation, successfully secured wage increases which were often difficult to reconcile with price stability. If Swedish experience is an example of the durability of union influence, Australia shows the most remarkable transformation. Australian unions have long had a political role, but with the Accord of 1983, the ACTU—then a relatively weak central body in comparison with, for example, its Swedish and German equivalents— came to have a strong influence on a broad range of Australian economic and social policies, an influence which continued into the early 1990s, despite the decline in membership already mentioned.

The employers

From the period of post-war reconstruction until the end of the 1970s, for most of the nine countries it was the active pressure of workers and their unions which led to the majority of the initiatives with regard to the structure and operation of industrial relations systems. Employers and their organisations found it difficult to cope with workers' demands and claims for improvements in pay and conditions at the level of the enterprise and with legislative moves to strengthen workers' rights. Nevertheless, employers generally devoted little priority to seeking reform of industrial relations systems. When employers were faced with a choice between making concessions and resisting a strike, their market position, in the years of sustained economic growth, often inclined them to concede. The economically rational behaviour of employers then came into conflict with the efforts of governments to ensure price stability; every inflationary increase in labour costs achieved by workers and unions was also an inflationary concession on the part of the employer. Employers were also expected to shoulder much of the mounting cost of social security and various advances in worker protection in the form of payroll taxes and strengthened legislative requirements.

With the recession of 1980–82, employers in the IMEs were faced with new challenges and new opportunities. Many industries had to restructure and competition became increasingly fierce; hence, there was a greater need to ensure efficient working and to restrain labour costs. Governments saw that industries' struggle for survival precluded adding to their cost burdens and, indeed, sought to lighten their load. At the same time, growing unemployment sapped the bargaining strength of workers and their unions. Thus there was a tendency in most countries for employers to take a tougher stance both in collective bargaining and in increasing the efficiency of management and working practices. Employers made more use than in the past of HRM techniques which discouraged unionisation. There were, however, interesting differences in employers' policies between countries.

In the USA, union gains in the prosperous years and widespread cost-of-living clauses induced a substantial number of employers to take aggressive action to lower existing labour costs, while at the same time, in a political climate favourable to them, employers' resistance to union recognition intensified. The attack took the form of concession bargaining, involving some mixture of pay reductions, reduction of holidays, and cutbacks in fringe benefits, and, in some cases, the introduction of 'two-tier' structures with new workers being engaged on less favourable terms than those applied to existing employees. A substantial number of US employers moved to parts of the south where unionisation was low (see ch. 3). Interestingly, Canadian employers were much less aggressive than US employers, despite the prevalence of US-owned firms and the many similarities between the industrial relations systems of the two countries. Of all our sample of countries it was only in the USA that a large number of employers took an anti-union stance. Elsewhere, employers tended to pursue cost reduction by improving productivity, reducing employment levels and enhancing operational flexibility rather than attacking pay, working conditions and unionisation. Perhaps the key factor dictating the tougher stance of US employers was the extent to which labour costs, particularly in the unionised sector, had grown out of line with costs in other countries. Such differences had been supportable when American industrial and technological superiority had been unchallenged, but as other industrialised countries moved towards American levels of efficiency such high labour costs were no longer sustainable.

Economic growth was more rapid in Japan than in any other of the countries under discussion and on the whole was somewhat less affected by the recessions of the early 1980s and the early 1990s, though sectors like shipbuilding, coal and steel suffered considerably. There is little evidence of aggressive anti-unionism being adopted by Japanese employers, even where an industry did enter difficult times. Some Japanese enterprises responded to the changed market conditions by expanding their operations in low labour cost countries, but at home they continued to pursue efficiency coupled with workplace harmony. Unemployment continued at lower levels than in any of the other countries except Sweden.

In Australia some employers aligned themselves with the New Right, but in general the major focus of interest of employers was in making the best of the Industrial Relations Commission's arbitrated awards, following the successive stages of the Accord (though by the 1990s these were encouraging less centralised enterprise bargaining). The employers' organisations, for their part, were disadvantaged in the face of the strong union–government partnership. Their disadvantage was magnified by their multiplicity—the Australian Chamber of Commerce and Industry, the Business Council of Australia and the important, independent-minded Metal Trades Industry Association among others, represented a variety of viewpoints (see ch. 5).

In continental Europe many employers undoubtedly strengthened their resistance to union claims and their insistence on efficient working, but there were very few widespread attacks on unions; employers generally still saw their relationship with unions as a continuing one. There were no significant changes in the role of the employers' associations or in their influence on governments. Nor was there any substantial shift in the policies they followed except in Sweden where, under new leadership, SAF—the central organisation of private employers—moved away from the centralised tripartism which for so long characterised Swedish industrial relations (see ch. 9).

Developments in continental Europe were broadly similar to those in Britain, but there were some differences. Work-groups had not achieved such a strong position in manufacturing workplaces in any other country considered here; and especially after the favourable legislation of 1974–76, in few countries did unions have so much bargaining power and such a strong legal position. However, in Britain the early 1980s' recession coincided with the advent of a Conservative administration which saw the unions as a major cause of the country's industrial malaise and which, through a series of laws, effectively weakened the ability of unions to resist change—though the high level of pay increases through the 1980s and into the 1990s suggests that, in some contexts, they may have retained considerable bargaining power. It seems clear that in the 1980s British employers effected more reform of workplace practices than most (arguably they had more need to do so). Nevertheless, though there were a few cases of withdrawal of union recognition and more determination in beating strikes, there was no widespread anti-union activity. When faced with problems where they could have used the new legislation against the unions, most employers—though by no means all—preferred not to go beyond drawing workers' attention to the legal position.

Regarding the position of British employers' associations, there was only one notable shift. In Britain, as in continental Europe, pay and working conditions in the early post-war years were mainly determined by industry-wide collective bargaining. But though there was some erosion in several European countries of such bargaining, only in Britain was it largely superseded by enterprise or workplace bargaining. This clearly reduced the bargaining role of the employer associations. Significantly, early in 1990 the Engineering Employers' Federation, long regarded as the most important of the industry associations, announced that it did not intend to carry on national bargaining on wages and working conditions in the future, thereby ending 92 years of negotiating history at industry level. (Admittedly, national bargaining in the engineering industry had been decreasing in importance for more than twenty years.)

Collective bargaining

In all of the countries covered here except Australia, collective bargaining has long been the generally preferred way of determining wages and working conditions. In the post-war years the practice became more and more widely used, extending particularly to cover more white-collar and public service workers and to cover elements of the employment relationship which had earlier been regarded as the prerogative of management. The growth continued in nearly all of the countries up to the 1980s. It is difficult to assess recent changes in coverage, but in those countries where union membership has fallen significantly there has probably been some accompanying decline in the extent of collective bargaining.

Currently, there is no uniformity as to the level at which collective bargaining is customarily conducted. In North America, multi-employer bargaining is very much a minority practice with enterprise or workplace (plant) bargaining as the norm (see chs 3 & 4). In Japan too, bargaining is mainly at the enterprise level (see ch. 10). At a national level, the *Shunto* establishes union objectives and influences bargaining strategy but the outcome is determined within the enterprise. German collective bargaining remains basically at the national or regional industry level, although workplace negotiation has been increasing steadily over the years and was given further impetus by the important metal industry agreements in 1984 which required several aspects of working time to be determined at the workplace. Moreover, the works councils also play an important role (see ch. 8). French bargaining levels, traditionally at national or regional industry level, were affected by the law of November 1982 requiring unionised enterprises to negotiate each year on pay and working hours—though it did not require them to reach agreement. The law has certainly shifted collective bargaining towards the enterprise but has not fundamentally changed workplace relations (see ch. 7).

Bargaining levels have long been an issue in Sweden. In the

1950s collective bargaining between SAF and LO, the peak private-sector employer and manual worker union bodies, began to be conducted centrally (i.e. for all industries) though there was controlled flexibility in the application of the central agreement in different industries and firms. The flexibility was not, however, considered sufficient in the important metals sector and, in 1983, that sector opted out of the central negotiations. In the next year's bargaining round, decentralisation was general and, though there were subsequent central agreements, there was uncertainty at each round about which level would prevail. In the 1990s, however, the moves were unmistakably towards enterprise bargaining (see ch. 9).

Despite the arbitration machinery—which to an extent incorporates collective bargaining—in Australia there are also direct negotiations (see ch. 5). These have tended to be most prevalent when the Australian Industrial Relations Commission has had least involvement in the pay determination process, as in 1974 and 1981–82. However, under the post-1983 Accord, direct negotiations on pay and working conditions generally amounted to little in comparison with the adjustments awarded by the Commission. The Accord held because there was an increasing amount of flexibility in its successive stages, and Commission awards in the late 1980s and early 1990s provided for significant adjustments to be worked out within enterprises, having regard to their productivity and other issues. This process was described as 'managed decentralism'.

The most clearly defined shift in the level at which wages are determined has undoubtedly been downward, from industry-wide to enterprise or workplace. But there has also been a perceptible shift in some countries to central national discussions, if not bargaining, involving governments. Australia is a clear example of this, with the key negotiations being between the Labor government and the ACTU. In Sweden, where the traditional model required the government to keep out of collective bargaining, governments in the 1980s were increasingly drawn into trying to solve the country's bargaining difficulties. Indeed, it was an unsuccessful attempt by the government to check what it deemed to be excessive wage growth that led to the temporary resignation of Prime Minister Carlsson in February 1990. In Italy, governments have been embroiled with the unions and employers on a number of issues with relevance for industrial relations. In Japan, frequent discussions take place between government, unions, employers and independents in the framework of the Labour–Management Round Table, though such discussions should not be described as bargaining and are a continuing process of creating understanding, rather than specific negotiations.

Possibly all of these bargaining shifts result from increased

competition, which induces demands for more flexible and efficient
workplace practices. This draws negotiation to the enterprise or
workplace. At the same time, the continued tendency in some
countries for the level of increases in labour costs to be of concern
to the national economy incurs government attention and sometimes
intervention (Bamber & Córdova 1993).

Industrial conflict

In all the countries where collective bargaining is established, strikes
and lockouts are accepted as the logical continuation of a dispute
when bargaining fails. There were no major national changes in the
1980s in the conduct or treatment of strikes in the countries examined here, except for the British legislation since 1980 which substantially limited the wide immunities granted to the unions by the
Trade Disputes Act of 1906 (see ch. 2). The Italian government
considered restricting strikes, and in early 1990 the Swedish government made an unsuccessful attempt to ban strikes until the end
of the following year. There were also some regional examples, such
as strong anti-strike legislation in Victoria (Australia) and British
Columbia (Canada) (see chs 4 & 5).

Some countries mediate their industrial conflicts much more
successfully than others (though it does not follow that a high-strike
country is necessarily a country with 'bad' industrial relations). In
Australia, though strikes are technically illegal, disputes are supposed to be resolved by the arbitration machinery without a stoppage
of work; however, in practice, although its strike rate declined after
the early 1980s, Australia still has a relatively large number of
strikes, albeit far fewer than hitherto (see Appendix).

The incidence of working days lost through disputes fell in most
countries in the 1980s (except in Sweden); by the early 1990s the
losses were much less than in the period of militancy which started
in the late 1960s. This is what we would expect in a recession. But,
as shown in the Appendix, there is a great deal of variation in the
experience of different countries. Using average data for the decade
1980–89 as a whole, Germany, France, Japan and Sweden appeared
to lose relatively few working days, while Canada and Italy were
relatively strike-prone, with Australia, the UK and the USA occupying intermediate positions (see Figure A.1).

Relative positions in any such league table of strikes may vary
from one year to another. For example, there was an unusually high
number of days lost in France in 1968, in Sweden in 1980 and in
Germany and the UK in 1984 (the year of the major strikes in
Germany by metalworkers and in Britain by mineworkers). Gener-

ally, in the medium-term, there is stability in the relative position of most countries. Japan, however, has changed its position. In the 1950s there were more working days lost per 1000 employees in Japan than in Britain. Also, in the early 1950s France was more strike-prone than Australia, while Sweden was one of the most strike-prone countries before its long period of Social Democratic government which began in the 1930s. If the analysis were extended to include all IMEs, Switzerland and Austria would usually be at the bottom of a league table. The *total* days lost in 1987, for instance, were 72 in Switzerland, and 4822 in Austria. (The corresponding figure for Canada that year—admittedly a much larger country—was almost 4 million days.) The Appendix gives a further indication of differences and trends.

Labour–management cooperation and industrial democracy

Relationships between labour and management contain elements of both conflict and cooperation. Though there are no measures of the extent of cooperation, we can note trends from new legislation and reported developments. The Second World War and post-war reconstruction elicited a high level of cooperation and this became institutionalised, at least in Western continental Europe, in works councils and similar bodies. The Japanese achieved similar results, without such formal institutions, through their consultative/participative management styles.

In the mid-1960s, debate flourished concerning workers' participation and industrial democracy; usually this was seen in terms of giving workers or unions seats on the board of directors of enterprises, or strengthening works councils. The movement peaked with Sweden's Board Representation Act 1972 and Codetermination at Work Act 1976; the German Works Constitution Act 1972 and Codetermination Act 1976; and legislation in, for instance, Austria, Denmark, Ireland's public sector, the Netherlands and Norway. In Britain the ambitious proposals of the Bullock Committee on Industrial Democracy 1977, met with little support and tough opposition; after the Callaghan Labour government left office in 1979 the subject was no longer discussed by policy-makers, at least not in terms of institutional change. In Australia, the 1973–75 Whitlam Labor government was keenly interested in the issue of industrial democracy, though little came of that interest. At the State level the South Australian government of Don Dunstan held a major international conference and set up an agency for promoting industrial democracy, but these initiatives too bore little fruit.

Though there has been minor legislation since the 1970s (e.g.

the Swedish amendment of 1987 extending the possibilities for board representatives, the German works council legislation of December 1988, and also the more substantial Auroux laws in France in 1982), it is clear that the movement to enhance workers' participation by statutory means has 'run out of steam'. Nevertheless, there has been continued interest in enhancing the involvement of workers in their enterprises. In several countries, as part of their HRM programs, employers are adopting schemes to elicit higher degrees of employee commitment, at least in relation to their core workforce. The apparent success of the Japanese economy has been linked by many with Japan's consensual pattern of enterprise labour–management relations. This has led to many attempts at emulation. In the USA the well known cases of Saturn and NUMMI are worthy of note. In Canada too, in the late 1960s and 1970s there was interest in improving cooperation, with much discussion of European practices, but no great change eventuated. Since 1986, Australia has produced both a governmental and a joint employer–union statement on increasing industrial democracy, both stressing employee involvement rather than institutional changes. In forms of cooperation, as in bargaining, the enterprise level has become more important in all nine countries. This is due to the increased need for enterprise competitiveness, and the collaboration between management and workers in maximising productive use of capital and labour and in ensuring uninterrupted work.

Parallel with the interest in industrial democracy came an increase in critical attitudes towards work which, often accompanied by shortage of labour, led to a new look at work organisation. It was found that many jobs could easily be made much more satisfying to the worker and that operating efficiency might even gain thereby. A series of major enterprises, like Volvo and Saab-Scania in Sweden, Olivetti in Italy, and ICI in Britain and Australia, led the way in reorganising work and much was done—and still is being done—through diffusion by public or private agencies and programs which sprang up in several of the countries in the 1970s. Examples include the Humanisation of Work Program in Germany, the National Agency for the Improvement of Working Conditions in France, the Centre for Working Life in Sweden, the Work Research Unit in Britain, the Work in America Institute in the United States and the Working Environment Branch of the Australian Federal Department of Employment and Industrial Relations. (The earlier work by the Tavistock Institute in Britain and the Work Research Institutes in Norway was also particularly notable in promoting new thinking about work.)

The role of the government and the legal framework

In the aftermath of the Second World War, governments almost everywhere took on an unprecedentedly active role in regard to industrial relations. The role of governments in industrial relations may be categorised in terms of five components: maintaining protective standards; establishing the ground rules for the interaction between the parties; ensuring that the product of that interaction is consistent with the needs of the economy; providing services for labour and management; and as a major employer.

Across the years of economic growth all of these roles extended. Protective legislation became more detailed, adding appreciably to production costs. The volume of legislation concerned with the relations of the parties, including industrial democracy, increased too, though less so than protective legislation and in different ways and at different times in different countries. Services to employers and workers expanded—notably in the field of work organisation and the quality of working life in the 1970s. Collective bargaining became more important to economic policy-makers because of the new (in peacetime) propensity to produce results which put pressure on price stability. Incomes policies were often tried as a remedy—in Britain, Canada and the USA, for instance—but rarely had lasting success. There was widespread extension of the right of public service workers to organise and to have what sometimes amounted to collective bargaining rights.

In the 1980s there was a clear shift in these functions. Governments became cautious about extending protection, and some even started to review existing protection to see if the need still justified the costs. France abolished the need for administrative authorisation for dismissals, and several countries relaxed rigid rules about working time and the rules about the employment of women on nightwork. With regard to the governmental roles in setting the rules for industrial relations in the 1980s, there were two important attempts to shift the pattern through legislation. First, in Britain a Conservative government sought, through a series of new laws, to reduce the volume of unofficial strikes and to strengthen the members' control of unions. Some argue that the legislation has helped to fundamentally change British industrial relations; it has certainly made workers and their unions more hesitant about going on strike (see ch. 2). Second, in France the Auroux reforms of 1982 sought to establish more cooperative labour–management relations at the workplace. There too, though the legislation effected a number of changes, it hardly had the hoped for result in transforming workplace relations (see ch. 7). A third case was the Australian

Industrial Relations Act of 1988, which followed the Hancock Report. However, this Act involved a tidying up of existing legislation rather than an attempt to effect radical change (see ch. 5). In the 1980s, there was no appreciable change in the provision of conciliation, mediation and arbitration services or of the newer advisory services concerning work organisation. The outcome of collective bargaining continued to create problems for economic policy-makers in Sweden, Italy and Britain, and was also difficult to deal with in Australia (which did, however, go against the trend with its relatively successful and durable incomes policy, the post-1983 Accord). In the early 1990s, the situation became difficult in Germany because of the problems arising from unification. In other countries, the pressure of wages on prices became less intense, due partly to high unemployment and partly to governments following non-accommodating monetary policies. Even so, in the early 1980s several countries found it necessary to resort to temporary wage freezes, or to dampen the effects of pay indexation arrangements. Italy abolished its long-established indexation system in 1992.

In their role as employers, governments, which had consistently followed practices equivalent to those of recognised 'good' private employers, faced with rapidly rising costs and restricted income, found it necessary, as recession bit, to cut their labour costs, both by reducing numbers and by limiting salary increases. There were some standstills on salaries and, in the USA and Japan, governments rejected proposals made by established independent bodies concerning the adjustments to be applied to civil service pay. Another development was the privatisation of some publicly owned industries and enterprises, which took workers out of the public and into the private sector.

International aspects of industrial relations[2]

As they have been touched on in relation to several countries, it is appropriate to discuss the international institutions concerned with industrial relations.

In industrial relations in the past, international activity has rarely impinged visibly on day-to-day workplace relations, and not very much on national legislation or collective bargaining. There was the standard-setting work undertaken by the ILO, but otherwise, in government, employer (except multinational employer) and union circles alike, international affairs have usually been marginal activities. Nevertheless, the above-mentioned international elements have been growing in importance, more so in some respects than in others.

Multinational enterprises

Several factors have been influential in promoting the internationalisation of industrial relations. The growth of multinational enterprises has eroded the significance of national boundaries and weakened the ability of governments, local firms and unions in a single country to insulate themselves from external influences. Multinational enterprises have often played an important role in 'exporting', or trying to transfer, HRM policies and practices from one country to another, especially from their home country to various host countries in which they operate (Dowling & Schuler 1990).

In some countries, particularly those which are competing for capital investment by providing cheap labour, employment laws may be changed to attract multinationals. Although it is often argued that multinationals provide good pay and working conditions for their employees in less developed economies (LDEs) and newly industrialising economies (NIEs), some of these firms have used 'offshore' manufacturing locations to evade the higher pay and stricter regulation of working conditions which have been achieved by unions in their home country. There are, of course, considerable differences in the degree to which a multinational can impose its will on a host country. As Blanpain (1993) notes: 'the entities of a multinational enterprise located in various countries are subject to the laws of these countries . . . (and have to) manage their business within the framework of law, regulations and prevailing labour relations and employment practices, in each of the countries in which they operate'. Thus, there is a two-way influence between a firm and the countries in which it operates. A multinational must adapt to the local laws and practices, yet it may also use its influence to change these in accordance with its own self-interest.

By the 1970s, the post-war growth of multinational enterprises led governments—only partly on the urging of unions—to establish, through the Organisation for Economic Co-operation and Development (OECD) (1976) and the ILO (1977), international codes (instruments) concerning the operations of such enterprises, including guidelines regarding employment and industrial relations.[3] The guidelines were voluntary and there was no provision for possible individual transgressions to be judged. Consultation facilities were provided by the international organisations for unions and employers. Ever since the promulgation of the instruments, the unions have pressed for the guidelines to have more force and have submitted cases of alleged infringement to the relevant authorities in the OECD and the ILO. The unions' representations had some impact, particularly in the early days, but the results fell far short of their hopes. The employers' organisations, for their part, have made efforts to ensure adherence to the guidelines but have argued against any strengthening of them. In recent years governments have shown little enthusiasm for any tightening up or extension of the instruments.

International union organisations

For many years unions have made links across national boundaries in an attempt to counter the influence of international capital. There are three main international union confederations: the International Confederation of Free Trade Unions (ICFTU), the World Federation of Trade Unions (WFTU) and the World Confederation of Labour (WCL). The demarcation between them is mainly in terms of political ideology.

The ICFTU is anti-communist in its orientation. The American Federation of Labor–Congress of Industrial Organizations (AFL–CIO) rejoined in 1981 after an absence of twelve years, and most of the main union confederations in the nine countries discussed in this book belong to the ICFTU. The ICFTU plays a major role in organising the workers' group at the ILO. Most ICFTU activities fall into one of three categories. First, in its representational activities, the ICFTU calls attention to injustices committed by governments or employers. Second, its services, and especially its organisational activities, are largely directed to LDEs and NIEs where unionism is weak. Third, the ICFTU has fairly self-sufficient regional organisations for Asia and for North and South America. Since the 1970s it has become rather stronger in Africa than it was formerly. Its regional organisation in Europe was disbanded in favour of a more all-inclusive European Trade Union Confederation (ETUC, see below).

The WFTU, which brought together the official trade union movements in the former communist countries and communist-inclined unions in some market-economy countries, such as the French *Confédération générale du travail*, has been in disarray since the widespread collapse of communism. The WCL now has few major members among unions in the western market economies and is much smaller than the other two world confederations. The WCL formerly had a Christian identity, but now has a secular radical socialist ideology. The *Confédération française démocratique du travail* (CFDT), the second largest French confederation, used to be a major constituent, but it no longer belongs to the WCL. There is another small confederation in Europe—the *Confédération internationale des cadres* (CIC)—which aims to represent executive and professional staffs as a 'third force' between capital and labour (Bamber 1986).

There have been international trade (union) secretariats (ITSs) for particular crafts, occupations or industries since 1889 (Northrup & Rowan 1979). The ITSs bring together individual national unions in particular sectors of industry. They are sometimes referred to as the industrial internationals, since they focus on particular industries or occupations and concentrate on sectors or major companies rather than on wider political issues. For instance, they coordinate research on health and safety hazards and technological change in their sectors. They also aim to gather information and to maintain international union solidarity in relation to certain large multinationals. Nevertheless, the latter is an almost impossible task, as workers' interests in one country may seem to conflict with those in another. The ITSs are autonomous organisations, but most of them generally follow the ICFTU on broad policy issues. Mergers and recruitment have considerably increased the size of the main ITSs in recent years and they have also increased their activity, particularly as a response to the growth of multinational enterprises and the internationalisation of production. The largest ITS is the International Metalworkers' Federation (IMF) with 168 affiliated unions in 70 countries. The IMF has established 'world councils', mirroring particular major manufacturers, to provide a forum for representatives of workers employed by those firms in different countries. Other large ITSs include the Commercial and Clerical Workers (FIET), the Public Service Employees, the Chemical Workers, the Textile Workers, and the Transport Workers. A General Conference of ITSs meets about once a year to review common problems and interests.

The moves towards market-based economies in Eastern Europe have significant implications for the demarcations between the international union confederations. In particular, the WFTU has been under severe strain following the decline of communism. However, the ICFTU, the ETUC and several of the ITSs have forged links with the new unions in the former communist countries of Eastern Europe.

In spite of the activities of these and many other international union organisations, the labour movement has found it extremely difficult to exercise much influence over the activities of multinationals. However, most unions are concerned about the growing power of multinationals, and consequently their international activities are increasing.

Supranational governmental organisations

The ILO is the major forum for international industrial relations activities by governments, employers and unions. The ILO was founded in 1919 under the First World War peace treaty and was associated with the League of Nations. Unlike the League, the ILO

Figure 11.1 The structure of the International Labour Organisation

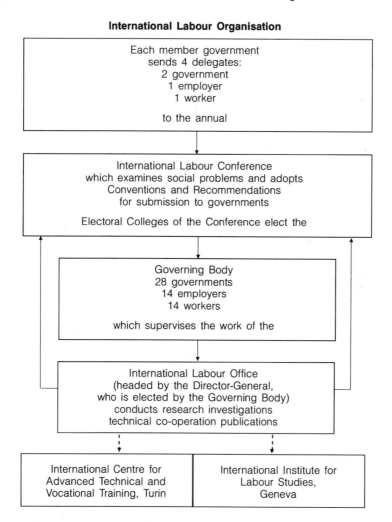

International Labour Organisation

Each member government
sends 4 delegates:
2 government
1 employer
1 worker

to the annual

International Labour Conference
which examines social problems and adopts
Conventions and Recommendations
for submission to governments

Electoral Colleges of the Conference elect the

Governing Body
28 governments
14 employers
14 workers

which supervises the work of the

International Labour Office
(headed by the Director-General,
who is elected by the Governing Body)
conducts research investigations
technical co-operation publications

International Centre for
Advanced Technical and
Vocational Training, Turin

International Institute for
Labour Studies,
Geneva

Source: Reproduced, with minor modifications, from Smith (1984:23).

survived the Second World War and became associated with the United Nations. By 1992, the ILO had 159 member states; its structure is illustrated in Figure 11.1.

The ILO has been an important agency for the development of international labour standards. As the major source of international labour law and of data on international and comparative industrial relations, it has adopted over 170 conventions and around 180 recommendations, which have had more than 5500 ratifications.

> These conventions deal with a wide range of issues, including:
> (i) fundamental human rights such as freedom of association,
> equality of treatment, and abolition of forced labour;
> (ii) occupational health and safety; (iii) working conditions;
> (iv) social security and workers compensation; (v) labour
> administration; (vi) migrant workers, and (vii) the specific
> needs or circumstances of particular occupational groups . . .
> Collectively, these standards are referred to as the 'International
> Labour Code'. (Creighton 1992:37)

The ILO is also an important source of information on personnel policies and practices throughout the world (Johnston 1970; Galenson 1981). Although it constitutes 'a gigantic exercise in transplantation' (Kahn-Freund 1976), like most other international agencies, the ILO is cautious about offending its members, so its recommendations are drafted carefully. Hence, the obligation on members to promote collective bargaining is tempered by the terms 'by measures appropriate to national conditions' and 'only where necessary'. It is significant that many of the ILO's conventions and recommendations relate to issues which are seen as not directly impinging upon the power relations between labour, capital and the state, such as: protective standards, discrimination in employment and general conditions of work. The ILO cannot compel its members to adhere to particular standards and it is left to governments to decide which ones they will ratify. Furthermore, the ratification of ILO conventions by a government does not necessarily mean that it will enforce them and governments may subsequently denounce them (e.g. Britain, see ch. 2).[4] As one observer puts it:

> It would be idle to pretend that the ILO is not confronted by a
> number of major problems. Some of these relate to matters
> which are largely outside its control—notably the severe
> budgetary constraints under which it has been forced to operate
> for a number of years. Others are of its own making—for
> example an over-elaborate and inflexible bureaucracy, and a
> conservative and self-interested (especially on the part of the
> social partners) attitude to standard-setting and to the reform of
> established procedures and structures.
> On the more positive side, there is abundant evidence to

suggest that the ILO can and does play an important role in protecting basic human rights and in combating the exploitation of the economically and socially disadvantaged.

It is, for example, widely recognised that the ILO played a major part in protecting union rights in Poland in the 1980s, when the authorities in that country were intent upon suppressing the Solidarity union. It is now very actively involved in helping the emerging democracies of Eastern Europe, Africa and Latin America to adopt labour laws and systems of labour administration which conform to accepted international standards.

(Creighton 1992:39)

Moreover, the ILO can have a considerable impact, for instance, through its freedom of association standards (especially in relation to the right to strike and to engage in autonomous collective bargaining). Furthermore, these are standards which cannot be avoided simply by non-ratification. Respect for the principles of freedom of association (which are for all practical purposes identical to the freedom of association conventions) is an obligation associated with ILO membership.

A change in the employment practices in one country, which results in improved wages or conditions, can become a precedent used by unions to demand similar reforms. This is especially likely within trading blocks such as the European Community (EC). Though there were generalised references to promoting improved working conditions and living standards for workers in the instrument setting up the Communities—the Treaty of Rome 1957—the Treaty included little specific detail on industrial relations. There were, however, general references to the harmonisation of laws and, amongst binding provisions, some concerning: freedom of movement for workers; equal pay for equal work; and the establishment of a European Social Fund to facilitate employment and labour mobility. The EC has an Economic and Social Committee which is consulted on relevant matters, and also has consultative arrangements with the ETUC, the private employers' confederation, the Union of Industrial and Employers' Confederations of Europe (UNICE), and the European Centre for Public Enterprises (CEEP) (both organisations are known by their French acronyms). Nonetheless, the EC provides another example of the limits to transferability of industrial relations regulations and processes, as the member countries have generally preserved their separate approaches to industrial relations, despite their attempts to move towards similar social and economic policies in other spheres.

The European Commission, the EC's executive arm, has always monitored industrial relations developments and across the years has promoted a number of directives concerning, for instance: collective redundancies (1975); the rights of workers when the enterprise is transferred to another owner (1977); and protection of workers in cases of insolvency. It has also been interested, without much impact so far, in the possibilities of international collective bargaining. Also, from the mid-1960s, proposals were drafted concerning: the creation of a European Company; the harmonisation of company law; and informative and consultative arrangements in large national and multinational firms. Of these, the first two failed to gain acceptance largely due to the problem of the position of workers in the company structure, with the Commission insisting on some measure of codetermination and consultation on an international basis. All three proposals met determined opposition from the employers and some governments and were effectively put aside until a more propitious time. The Commission put forward modified proposals for the European Company in 1988, and some of the concepts of the third proposal re-emerged in a draft directive under the Social Charter's Action Program.

In 1986 the Single European Act set the target of a 'free movement of goods, persons, services and capital' in a more closely integrated Europe by the end of 1992. The single European market is breaking down the barriers between national labour markets, but perhaps more importantly it is precipitating greater competition in product markets, which also has implications for labour markets. Both developments are of considerable concern to unions. The new Europe should also, it was considered, have a 'social dimension'. In 1988 the European Company proposal was again brought forward, this time in a much more flexible form, and in 1989 the Commission presented a Draft Charter of Fundamental Social Rights which, at the Strasbourg summit of December 1989, became the subject of a 'solemn declaration' by eleven of the twelve states, the British dissenting. By this time, after much criticism, the Charter was fairly weak and permissive (its weakness aroused more criticism from the unions and the European Parliament), but it was accompanied by an Action Programme of 47 proposals envisaging various directives and other instruments and touching on, among other things: introduction by member states of an equitable wage; regulation of working time; a labour clause in public contracts; the role of unions and employers in collective bargaining; information, consultation and participation by workers of European-scale enterprises; and equity-sharing and financial participation by workers (see *Free Labour World*, September 1992, p. 3).

The apparent determination of the Commission and most Community governments (with the notable exception of Britain) to legislate in respect of industrial relations and working conditions has led UNICE to the view that it might be better off seeking to reach understandings with the unions on an international basis so as to discourage European legislation—a departure from the longstanding conviction among most employers that workplace matters should on no account be dealt with internationally. The Commission has long favoured such employer–union dialogue at European level and this was allowed for in the Single European Act of 1986 which incorporated the possibility in a new Article (118B) inserted in the EC Treaty.

The position was further complicated by the unprecedented intergovernmental agreement on social policy in the 1991 Maastricht Treaty. The British refusal to accept a stronger Community social policy led to agreement that the eleven member states other than Britain might have recourse to the Community institutions and procedures to pursue certain social objectives with widened provisions for the use of qualified majority voting in the Council without British participation. Britain was not to be bound by instruments adopted under this procedure, thus opening up a prospect of some uniform arrangements applying in eleven member countries with different arrangements being operative in Britain.

Whatever is the outcome of these varied developments, there are going to be significant developments in the European dimensions of industrial relations. Although full transnational bargaining is still on the remote horizon, a few companies have already set up joint consultative arrangements where they meet union representatives from different countries (Gold & Hall 1992). In September 1990 the European public-sector employers' confederation, CEEP, made an agreement with the ETUC setting up dialogue on training matters, health, safety and labour mobility, rail transport and energy supply. Moreover, some national unions, like the airline pilots, are strengthening their relationships on a European basis.

The establishment of the EC and OECD prompted the unions to form permanent organisations to represent their interests at each forum. A notable activity of the ETUC, and particularly of the Trade Union Advisory Committee (TUAC) to the OECD, has been to formulate views on the desirable form of international economic and social policies which they have put before heads of government at their various summit meetings. The union officials involved in this work come from a variety of national and international collectivities—for instance, an official from one of the Swedish union centres might also be active in the Nordic Trade Union Council, the ICFTU, the ETUC, TUAC, and the workers' group in the ILO, and, indeed, other bodies. The international unions have consultative rights with a range of international organisations as well as with those mentioned.

International employers' associations

International employers' organisations corresponding to the general and regional international union bodies—mainly the International Organisation of Employers (IOE) in Geneva, the UNICE in Brussels, and the Business and Industry Advisory Committee to the OECD (BIAC) in Paris—have also been increasingly busy in recent years. Unlike many employers' organisations at the national level, those at the international level began less as a response to the growth of unions and more as a reaction to the growth of supranational governmental agencies (Oechslin 1985). Hence international employers' organisations generally have a shorter history and play a less general role than their union counterparts. The origins of the IOE, the most prominent employers' group, can be traced back to the first ILO conference in 1919. The IOE's role has grown since the Second World War, although its main activities are still focused on representing employers' interests at the ILO (Windmuller & Gladstone 1984; Upham 1990).

As a parallel to the situation in many individual countries, another employers' confederation places more emphasis on trade and economic matters: the International Chamber of Commerce (ICC). There is a broad division of responsibilities between the IOE and ICC, with the former concentrating on industrial relations issues, but the division is not always clear. Both the IOE and ICC, for example, are concerned about the various attempts to constrain multinationals by unions, governments and international agencies. The employers are less prone than the unions to be divided in terms of political ideology, but, in the post-1945 period, the IOE did not admit members from Eastern Europe.

International migration of labour and capital

International migration of labour has steadily become more important since the 1950s for most of the countries discussed here. The US, Canada and Australia have historically been countries that welcome immigration, but the number of immigrants in France, Germany and Britain—where they are mainly Commonwealth and Irish immigrants—has risen until there are now several million in each. In Germany the position of the immigrants—mainly from Turkey and South East Europe, but recently from former communist countries—has been complicated by the problems of industry in the East. Italy, formerly a labour-exporting country, now has many African and Albanian immigrants. Even in Japan, one of the world's most ethnically homogeneous nations, there has been an influx of labour from other Asian countries which, if small by Western standards, has become a matter of public debate. Within the EC, free movement of labour was provided in the Treaty of Rome 1957, but movement between the twelve countries has been less than might have been expected. Though it has often created social problems and changed the composition of the labour force, immigration has not had a dramatic impact on industrial relations.

Capital migration also increased, particularly into the EC countries, as non-EC firms sought to ensure a European base in view of the post-1992 'Single Europe'. The influx of Japanese capital—not only into Europe—has been particularly marked and Japanese management has achieved some notable successes in building good and productive industrial relations in the European and North American plants of Japanese companies.

Eastern Europe

A notable international factor in industrial relations has been the sudden collapse, since 1989, of the centrally planned economies of Eastern Europe. The details are outside the scope of this book but clearly have implications for our sample of countries, notably the European ones. The unification of Germany has, for most practical purposes, simply spread the former West German system of industrial relations, including the union structure, to the whole of Germany (see ch. 8). Unification is unlikely to change the system fundamentally, but it has brought problems in reconciling different levels of productivity and different levels of wages, and, of course, in coping with the exodus of workers from the East to the West. By 1993 these problems had led to serious unemployment in what used to be East Germany.

Whatever systems of industrial relations the other East European countries design, they are unlikely to induce any structural change in West European systems. Their economies, however, if they are successful in modernising their industries, will provide competition, as well as markets, for the West, and, as their unions and employers become more closely linked with those of the West, they will introduce new ways of thinking.

Further challenges

The main challenges faced by industrial relations systems in IMEs in the 1980s and early 1990s sprang from the need to adjust to a changing economic and industrial environment and a new and far-reaching wave of technological change; the two were, of course, interrelated. Technological change of itself was readily accommodated in all of the countries (Bamber & Lansbury 1989); there were only a few cases of serious opposition. Workers realised that the enterprises for which they worked needed to utilise the latest technology to stay in business and welcomed the feeling of being in the front line of technological advance. In any case, reduced union bargaining power impaired their ability to resist, even had they wished to do so.

The new economic and industrial environment posed more difficult problems. The redistribution of world production and trade and the accompanying substantial contraction of industries like steel, shipbuilding and textiles, plus technological change and the shift from manufacturing to services, added up to a considerable loss of jobs and change in skill requirements. Although there was considerable creation of new jobs, there were many cases where a large number of jobs disappeared in areas in which there was little alternative employment available. Again, however, there was relatively little major disruption to the established industrial relations systems. There were some major upsets—such as the disturbances when certain French steelworks and shipyards[5] were closed, and the long strike by the British mineworkers' union in 1984–85—but on the whole closures and reductions were effected without serious industrial conflict. In part, of course, workers—and their union leaders in particular—recognised the inevitability of such closures. Also, the laws, social policies and collective agreements built up over the post-war era helped to cushion the severity of redundancy.

Different countries have dealt with job security in different ways. The USA, long dedicated to the principle of 'employment at will', reluctantly enacted the fairly mild Worker Adjustment and Retraining Notification Act 1988. The ease of dismissal in the USA is matched by that nation's capacity for creating new jobs and the mobility of much of its working population. In Japan, great efforts are made to help workers whose services are no longer required. In Germany, the law requires that a Social Plan be drawn up where sizeable reductions of the workforce are involved, making provision for helping displaced workers. France has similar arrangements; help includes extended notice, redundancy payment, facilitated early retirement, training and retraining arrangements, and relocation allowances. In Britain, legislation originating in the 1960s provided for extended notice of dismissal and redundancy payments. And in Italy laid-off workers can be helped through the *Cassa Integrazione Guadagni*, a public fund guaranteeing up to 80 per cent of pay during lay off. Sweden, with the help of its Active Manpower Policy and the Labour Market Board, experienced remarkably little difficulty in running down its shipyards (Stråth 1987). And in Canada, federal law requires employers planning to terminate 50 or more workers to establish a joint planning committee, which attempts to make the best of the situation. The changes discussed in this section have had another effect which is only slowly making itself felt. Pre-war workplaces typically experienced less change than is usually the case in the 1990s, and usually had a more stable employment structure. There were managers, supervisors, technicians, clerical and administrative staff, skilled, semi-skilled and so-called unskilled manual workers, nearly all employed on the basis of a full working week. However, several of the divisions between these groups have become blurred, not least the distinction between manual and non-manual workers. The need for workforce flexibility to deal with rapid product changes and fluctuating order books has often, coupled with new technology, led to a gradually increasing segmentation of the enterprise labour force—a core group of functionally flexible, skilled workers, enjoying good pay, regular conditions and a relatively high job security; and a secondary labour force of less skilled and less advantaged workers, often part-time, fixed term or temporary workers.

Conclusion

After an unprecedented period of economic growth, the post-1945 Keynesian consensus fell apart and there was a period of militancy followed by several uneasy years of adjustment as major economic changes impinged on the IMEs. Then a recession in the early 1980s induced a realisation that the world was not going to return to the expansive days of, broadly, from 1950 to the mid-1970s. This realisation was confirmed by the recession of the early 1990s. Meanwhile, nearly all the material gains and most of the institutional advances made by workers and unions in the expansionary period were preserved. There have been surprisingly few major changes in the structure of the industrial relations systems of our countries (and most of these changes were in the least effective systems) since the 1970s. Rather, what happened was that the forces at work changed the *output* of the systems without necessitating *systemic* change. Nonetheless, significant changes seemed to be emerging in the early 1990s, for instance, in Australia, where the role of the Industrial Relations Commission appeared to be in decline, and in Sweden, where the right-of-centre government came to power in 1991 and new policies were adopted by the employers' confederation.

The dominant general external forces acting on industrial relations since the 1970s have been the redistribution of world trade, investment and production, technological advance and, consequent on a change in dominant ideological views about their relative merits; a shift from: collectivism to individualism; state ownership to privatisation; and regulation to deregulation. These forces seem set to continue. But though they may bring forth similar responses from countries, there is little to suggest that these forces are inducing a convergence in industrial relations systems.

It would be wrong to see industrial relations systems as passing through a period of crisis; rather, we are seeing what Baglioni (1989:248) has called a 'return to normalcy', after a long period of exceptional circumstances. This does not mean that industrial relations will not change.[6] They will continue to adapt, and they will continue to be imperfect—there will always be conflict and need for adjustment at places of work. However, it seems unlikely, at least in the light of the situation prevailing in the early 1990s, that there will be significant structural change in industrial relations systems in the near future, except perhaps in one or two of them which have shown themselves least well-adapted to their present environmental conditions. Improvement in some countries would probably require political changes as well as greater motivation to change amongst employers and union leaders.

Appendix
Employment, economics and industrial relations: comparative statistics[1]
Greg J. Bamber and Gillian Whitehouse

The collection of international statistics presented in this Appendix provides a context for the themes covered throughout the book. It helps to meet the increasing demand for cross-nationally comparable statistics from researchers and practitioners in industrial relations and related fields. The aim is to display and review selected data for the nine countries covered in the preceding chapters over a time period which allows patterns of continuity and change to be demonstrated.

There are many difficulties associated with this task. For example, methods of collecting data and definitions used may vary a great deal between countries. While some of our tables are based on hitherto unpublished statistics, we rely, wherever possible, on the standardised data published by agencies such as the International Labour Organisation (ILO), Eurostat—the statistical office of the European Community (EC)—the Organisation for Economic Cooperation and Development (OECD)[2] or the US Department of Labor's Bureau of Labor Statistics (BLS). Each of these organisations attempts to some extent to standardise data from individual countries. The ILO, for example, sets standards (through the International Conference of Labour Statisticians). Although there is a time lag before such data become available, they are generally more reliable for cross-national comparison than most national sources.

Where our data are inconsistent with national sources, it is usually due to our use of standardised figures. Ultimately, however, the quality of such data depend on the collection and processing of figures at national level, where there is always some risk that political expediency might interfere with the procedures—for example, where rates of unemployment, inflation or industrial stoppages are being reported. In several countries, including Australia, the government statistical offices follow international standards and

275

have statutory independence so that politicians should not be involved in changing the definitions or publication dates of statistics.

As most tables cover a lengthy period of time, another problem encountered is series breaks in data sets. The UK, USA, Canada and other countries have breaks in important data series. Allowing for such breaks, in most tables time-series data are reasonably valid for comparisons within a country, but comparisons between countries generally have less validity, due to major international differences of definition and methods of calculation, despite the attempts at standardisation. Furthermore, there is a delay before time series reflect major political changes such as the reunification of Germany. While the former German Democratic Republic (East Germany) joined the Federal Republic of Germany in 1990, most available data for Germany do not yet include the former East Germany.

Any work in this field dates, but the data are useful to draw broad comparisons over time and between countries, rather than to focus on the very latest statistics. We cite details of our sources so that readers can update such data and analyse them further. In the following pages the data chronicle the broad context for each of the nine countries discussed in this book—for example, in terms of population, the structure of the economy and unemployment— before we then turn to such more specific industrial relations issues as unionism and disputes.

Total labour force and civilian employment

To illustrate the importance of definitions, note that Table A.1 cites data on the total labour force, while Table 85
4 refers to civilian employment. The relationship between these two concepts is as follows:

Total labour force = civilian employment + unemployment + armed forces.

Civilian employment includes all those above a specified age in self-employment (own account), as well as employees in paid employment. Also included are unpaid family members and those temporarily absent due to factors such as illness, holidays, bad weather or industrial disputes (but US employment data omit unpaid family workers working less than 15 hours in the reference week). Thus many part-time workers are included, but not calculated as full-time equivalents. To simplify this Appendix, we do not include full definitions. For precise definitions, which vary slightly over

Table A.1 Population and labour force[3]

	Population (millions)					Total labour force (millions)				
	1963	1973	1983	1988	1990	1963	1973	1983	1988	1990
Australia	11	14	15	17	17	4.5	6.0	7.1	8.0	8.5
Canada	19	22	25	26	27	6.9	9.4	12	13	14
France	48	52	55	56	56	20	22	24	24	24
Germany	57	62	61	61	63[a]	27	27	27	30	30
Italy	51	55	57	57	58	21	21	23[b]	24	24
Japan	96	109	119	123	124	47	53	59	62	64
Sweden	7.6	8.1	8.3	8.4	8.6	3.7	4.0	4.4	4.6	4.5
UK	54	56	56	57	57	25	26	27	29	28
USA	189	212	234	246	252	74	91	113	123	126

Notes: In most tables, numbers less than 10 are rounded to one decimal place; numbers greater than 10 are rounded to the nearest whole number, which is appropriate in view of the imprecision of most of them.
a 80 for unified Germany.
b Data after 1980 have been revised.

Source: OECDb; d (various years).

time and between the various agencies, see the official ILO, OECD and BLS publications (e.g. ILO 1984; OECDb; e; US BLS 1985).

Labour force participation

Participation rates for each country are shown in Table A.2. The participation (or activity) rate is the total labour force divided by the population of working age (in most countries 15–64, but in some countries there is no upper limit).

In all of the nine countries, the long-term trend is towards a lower participation rate for men, which reflects the expansion of tertiary education and the increasing level of incomes and pensions which enable men to retire earlier. By contrast, the trend is towards higher participation rates for women, except in Japan, where, although many young women enter the labour market, few take up permanent jobs. Moreover, there has been a sharp drop in the number of female family workers in Japanese agriculture (ILO 1984:55).

The longer years of schooling and increasing levels of incomes and pensions (leading to earlier retirements) also influence women's participation levels, but the influence of these factors has been overridden by the increasing role of women in the world of paid work. Decreasing birth rates, changing social attitudes and structural changes in labour markets are factors conducive to the higher participation rates of women.

Table A.2 shows that the participation rate for men is reasonably similar among the nine countries, varying only between about 75 per cent (France) and 89 per cent (UK). The differing total participation rates largely reflect the differing levels of female participation in each country. These vary quite markedly across countries, ranging from 44 per cent (Italy) to 84 per cent (Sweden). The Scandinavian countries generally have high total participation rates, partly because they have a high proportion of part-time workers, most of whom are women (see Table A.3), who are supported by the widespread availability of childcare. The low rate in Italy may reflect the relatively large informal economy of 'clandestine employment' there. It is possible that people may be 'discouraged' from engaging in 'active search for work' and it can be difficult for the authorities to measure the size of the labour force accurately, particularly in the large rural sector in such southern European countries.

Although we do not present participation rate data analysed by age, it is worth noting that there are significant differences between the participation rates of people in different age categories. For

Table A.2 Labour force participation

	Men (percentages)					Women (percentages)					Total (percentages)				
	1963	1973	1983	1989	1990	1963	1973	1983	1989	1990	1963	1973	1983	1989	1990
Australia	94[a]	92	86	85	86	39[a]	48	52	61	62	67[a]	70	70	73	74
Canada	88[b]	86	85	87	86	40[b]	47	60	68	69	63	67	72	78	78
France	87[c]	85	78	77	73	46[c]	50	54	58	58	68	68	66	67	65
Germany	95	89	80	82	NA	49	50	50	54	NA	71	69	65	68	69
Italy[d]	92	85	80	77	77	37	34	40	44	44	63	59	60	60	60
Japan	90	90	89	87	88	57	54	57	59	60	73	72	73	73	74
Sweden	92	88	86	89	88	55	63	77	83	84	74	76	81	86	86
UK	97	93	88	89	89	47	53	58	68	68	72	73	73	78	79
USA	89	86	85	88	88	43	51	62	69	70	66	68	73	78	78

Notes: a 1964 data.
      b 1966 data.
      c 1968 data.
      d Population data 14–64 years, data after 1980 have been revised.

Source: OECDa; b (various years).

example, in 1966, the male participation rate in Australia was 96 per cent for the 45–54 age group, but only 79 per cent for the 60–64 age group. Such differences tend to be magnified in periods of economic recession. By 1979, the rate was 92 per cent for the 45–55 age group, but it had fallen to 54 per cent for the older age group. This suggests that such groups may become 'discouraged job seekers' and take up the option of early retirement particularly when there are fewer jobs available (Carter & Gregory 1981:Table A.1; see also ILOa and OECDb, which include detailed data on labour force participation by age and OECDa (1992) which includes a chapter on the participation of older workers).

Part-time employment

Part-time employment has grown in most of the countries in recent years. The definition of part-time working varies greatly between countries, so inter-country comparisons are difficult. Nevertheless, we can infer from Table A.3 that part-time working is much more usual in Sweden and the UK than in France and Italy (but it seems likely that there are also many part-timers in the informal economy in Italy).

In all the countries, a large majority of part-timers are women. In Europe and Japan, part-time work is associated with the life-cycle phase when women are most likely to be involved in child-bearing and care. Particularly in Canada and the USA, however, part-timers tend to be younger than full-timers and are often single people who are combining employment with education.

Besides such supply side factors, there has been a changing demand. The shift towards labour-intensive services with weekly and daily peak demands tended to increase the demand for part-timers. Many employers are seeking greater labour market flexibility, for example, from full-time towards casual and part-time employment. Part-timers often are not covered by the same degree of labour market regulation nor are they necessarily entitled to as many fringe benefits, so they may be easier to dismiss and cost proportionately less than full-timers (Thurman & Trah 1989:5). Alternatively, some employers may choose to use overtime for full-time employees to avoid incurring the extra overhead costs of taking on additional employees.

Structure of employment

Structural shifts in employment are illustrated in Table A.4. The

Table A.3 Part-time employment

	Part-time employment as a percentage of:															Women's percentage share of part-time employment				
	Total employment					Male employment					Female employment									
	1973	1978	1983[a]	1989	1990	1973	1979	1983[a]	1989	1990	1973	1979	1983[a]	1989	1990	1973	1979	1983[a]	1989	1990
Australia	11	16	17	21	21	3.4	5.1	6.1	7.8	8.0	27	34	36	40	40	80	79	78	78	78
Canada	11[b]	12	15	15	15	5.1[b]	5.7	7.6	7.7	8.1	20[b]	23	26	24	24	70[b]	72	71	72	71
France	7.2	8.2	9.7	12	12	2.6	2.5	2.6	3.5	3.5[c]	15	17	20	24	24	78	82	85	83	83
Germany	10	11	13	13[d]	NA	1.8	1.5	1.7	2.1[d]	NA	24	28	30	31[d]	NA	89	92	92	90[d]	NA
Italy	6.4	5.3	4.6	5.7	5.7[e]	3.7	3.0	2.4	3.1	3.1[e]	14	11	9.4	11	11[e]	58	61	65	65	65[e]
Japan[f]	7.9	9.6	10	18	18[e]	4.6	5.2	4.8	8.0	8.0[e]	15	18	21	32	32[e]	61	64	71	73	73[e]
Sweden	18	24	25	24	23	3.7	6.5	6.3	7.2	7.3	39	46	46	42	40	88	85	87	84	84
UK	16	16	19	22	22	2.3	1.9	3.3	5.0	5.0	39	39	42	44	44	91	93	90	87	87
USA[g]	17	14	20	17	17	9.4	7.4	12	10	10	28	24	29	26	25	66	70	67	69	68
USA[g]			*14*	*18*	*18*			*7.2*	*10*	*11*			*24*	*28*	*28*			*68*	*67*	*70*

Notes: a The number of non-declared persons in the 1983 data for the EC countries is distributed proportionately between full-time and part-time employment.
  b 1975.
  c Includes conscripts contrary to earlier years.
  d 1988.
  e 1989.
  f Data refer to employees at work during the survey week in non-agricultural industries.
  g Since 1985, the USA defines part-timers as all those who *usually* work less than 35 hours per week; this thereby includes those who, for economic reasons, usually work part-time. Data in italics show the results of excluding this group in the calculations.

Source: OECD[b]; d (various issues).

structure of employment is conventionally divided into three broad categories: agriculture (including hunting, forestry and fishing); industry; and services. Industry is broader than manufacturing, as it also includes mining and construction. The distinctions between these three sectors are defined by the United Nations (UN) (1971). These distinctions are becoming outdated, however, especially as the agricultural and industrial categories are tending to contract, while services are expanding in most of the nine countries. The services category is now extremely heterogeneous as it includes all the industries which do not fit one of the first two categories, including public administration, finance, property and business services, community services, recreation, personal and other services and many more. Therefore, some commentators suggest that it would be appropriate to subdivide services into further categories such as: tertiary, consisting of tangible economic services; quaternary, comprising data processing; and quinary, covering unpaid work, homework where pay is secondary, and professional services of a quasi-domestic nature (e.g. Jones 1982). However, as yet the authorities do not provide a sufficiently comprehensive set of such data, nor do we have a sufficiently well developed conceptual framework within which to gather and analyse it.

As an additional complication, the distinctions between categories are not always precise due to classification difficulties and because some people work in more than one sector. Moreover, the trend towards subcontracting and the growth of employment agencies have tended to distort the data and so have exaggerated the growth of services.

Unemployment

The unemployed comprise all people above a specified age who during the reference period were: (a) without work, i.e. were not in paid employment or self-employment; (b) currently available for work, i.e. were available for paid employment or self-employment; and (c) seeking work, i.e. had taken specific active steps to seek paid employment or self-employment (OECDb). With regard to comparative measures of unemployment, the OECD generally uses standardised unemployment rates. However, on a national basis, in most countries discussed, unemployment statistics are measured directly (as in Australia) through the monthly labour force survey which uses international concepts and standards, but in others unemployment statistics are compiled as an administrative by-product of a system for registration for unemployment benefits or job placement assistance (as in the definitions adopted by Germany and

Table A.4 Civilian employment by sector

	Civilian employment (millions)					Agriculture (percentages of civilian employment)					Industry					Services				
	1963	1973	1983	1988	1990	1963	1973	1983	1988	1990	1963	1973	1983	1988	1990	1963	1973	1983	1988	1990
Australia	4.3[a]	5.8	6.3	7.4	8.4	10	7.3	6.6	5.9	5.5	38	35	28	26	25	52	57	65	68	69
Canada	6.5	8.8	11	12	14	12	6.5	5.5	4.5	4.2	33	31	26	26	25	56	63	69	70	71
France	19	21	21	21	24	20	11	8.0	6.8	6.1	40	40	34	30	30	40	49	58	63	64
Germany	26	26	25	27	29	12	7.3	5.6	4.0	3.4	48	47	42	40	40	40	45	52	56	57
Italy[b]	20	19	20	21	24	27	18	12	9.9	9.0	38	39	36	32	32	35	43	52	58	59
Japan	46	53	57	60	61	26	13	9.3	7.9	7.2	32	37	35	34	34	42	49	56	58	58
Sweden	3.7	3.9	4.2	4.4	4.6	13	7.1	5.4	3.8	3.3	41	37	30	30	29	46	56	65	67	68
UK	24	25	23	26	28	4.4	2.9	2.7	2.3	2.1	46	42	34	30	29	49	55	64	68	69
USA	68	85	101	115	125	7.1	4.2	3.5	2.9	2.8	35	33	28	27	26	58	63	68	70	71

Notes: a OECD secretariat estimate.
b Data after 1980 have been revised.

Source: OECDb; d (various issues).

Table A.5 Unemployment

Year	Australia	Canada	France	Germany	Italy	Japan	Sweden	UK	USA
				(percentage of the labour force)					
1960	1.4	6.4	1.4	1.0	5.5	1.7	1.7	1.3	5.4
1965	1.5	3.6	1.2	0.5	5.3	1.2	1.2	1.2	4.4
1970	1.6	5.6	2.4	0.6	5.3	1.1	1.5	2.2	4.8
1975	4.4	6.9	4.1	4.0	5.8	1.9	1.6	3.2	8.3
1980	6.0	7.4	6.3	3.3	7.5	2.0	2.0	5.6	7.0
1981	5.7	7.5	7.4	4.6	7.8	2.2	2.5	9.0	7.5
1982	7.0	10.9	8.1	6.7	8.4	2.4	3.1	10.4	9.5
1983	9.8	11.8	8.3	8.2	9.3	2.6	3.5	11.2	9.5
1984	8.9	11.2	9.7	8.2	9.7	2.7	3.1	11.2	7.4
1985	8.2	10.4	10.2	8.3	9.9	2.6	2.8	11.5	7.1
1986	8.0	9.5	10.4	8.0	6.2	2.8	2.7	11.6	6.9
1987	8.0	8.8	10.5	7.6	11.8	2.8	1.9	10.4[a]	6.1
1988	7.1	7.7	10.0	7.6	11.8	2.5	1.6	8.3	5.4
1989	5.7	7.5	9.4	6.8	11.8	2.3	1.3	6.1	5.2
1990	6.9	8.1	8.9	4.9	10.3	2.1	1.5	6.9[b]	5.4
1991	9.6	10.3	9.6	4.3	11.0	2.1	2.7	8.3	6.7
1992[c]	10.4	10.4	9.8	4.7	11.2	2.2	4.5	9.8	7.1
1993[c]	9.9	10.0	9.8	4.8	11.5	2.3	5.2	9.7	6.5
1993[d]	10.9	11.0	10.5	7.5	9.7	2.4	7.5	10.6	7.1

Notes:
a Series break 1986–87.
b New series based on EC labour force surveys.
c OECD projections (not standardised).
d The Economist 6 March 1993; 27 March 1993. Jan. 1993 figures. All data seasonally adjusted except for Sweden.

Sources: OECDb; d; e (various years) except for the last row.

the UK), which will be affected over time by changes in legislation and eligibility criteria.

Unemployment levels are a crucial influence on the relative power of workers and employers. Table A.5 shows that unemployment rates have generally been lower in Japan and Sweden than in the other countries and that these two countries maintained low levels of unemployment throughout the 1970s and 1980s recessions, in marked contrast to most other countries. Before the 1970s, Australia and Germany also had comparatively low rates. The 1973 oil crisis was a turning point that was associated with an increase in unemployment in most countries. Unemployment generally fell in the mid-1980s, but did not return to the relatively low levels that prevailed in the 1950s and 1960s. In the early 1990s the trend is for unemployment to increase; however, significant cross-national differences are still evident. Some of the recent data in Table A.5 are based on OECD projections; these have been consistently over-optimistic. This is illusrated by the last row of recent data, though these are from a different source whose definitions may vary from those of the OECD.

Gross domestic product

Gross domestic product (GDP) is a measure of the total sum of final goods and services produced by an economy at market prices. GDP includes the cost of capital goods consumed in production processes. Intermediate products are not counted separately, as their value is already included in the prices of final goods and services. Income from abroad is excluded; hence the term gross *domestic* product. (Gross *national* product (GNP) equals GDP plus net property income arising from foreign investments and possessions.)

Like most of the other indicators we discuss, measuring GDP is fraught with difficulties. Apart from the inherent limitations of such measures of national output and income as indications of a country's economic well-being (e.g. see Waring 1988; Clark 1989:36), there is also a degree of variation between countries in how GDP is measured. For instance, Italy includes an estimate of GDP from its 'underground economy', its informal sector, but such estimates are inevitably crude. Nevertheless, most of the national authorities use internationally agreed conventions, which include a notion of the 'economically active population', and define GDP in a narrow economic sense. Although far from perfect, it is the best available indicator of relative economic prosperity because it is measurable and comparable. We need to keep in mind its limitations, however, and also to refer to other complementary measures such as those developed by the OECD and United Nations Development Programmes (see also Anderson 1991).

Table A.6, columns 3 and 4 show that Japan had by far the most rapid annual rate of growth of GDP in the 1980s, while column 5 shows that in nominal terms (i.e. converted at exchange rates) Sweden, Germany and Japan have overtaken the USA's GDP. This reflects an upward movement in dollar prices inside these countries relative to actual US prices. It does not mean, for example, that Japanese citizens are necessarily richer than US citizens.

To make more realistic comparisons of productivity or living standards, an attempt should be made to eliminate price differences between countries. In view of the vagaries of currency exchange rates, various organisations attempt to calculate purchasing power parities (PPPs). These are alternative rates of conversion which try to equalise the purchasing power of different currencies—i.e. make it possible to buy the same basket of products everywhere. To calculate PPPs, detailed comparisons are made between the prices of individual goods and services in different countries. Special price surveys have been conducted for this purpose by the OECD and Eurostat. Some initial results are shown in Table A.7, column 6 (see also Table A.6 and A.11).

Conversions of GDP figures by means of PPPs (as in Table A.6, column 6) show that, in *real* terms, the US per capita GDP continues to be ahead of that of the other countries. Canada has the second highest level (about 90 per cent of the US level).

Comparisons of PPPs are more valid between similar countries but there are some circumstances when PPPs may give a misleading indication of comparative standards. If taxes are high, purchasing power is low; but this ignores the fact that there may be commensurately high public provision of non-traded (free) *services*. So the rankings change dramatically, for example, between the USA and Sweden depending on whether nominal exchange rates or PPPs are used; Sweden appears richer if the former, the USA appears richer if the latter.

Exchange rates and purchasing power parities

Official annual average market exchange rates are summarised in Table A.7. Unlike the other tables, this one also includes Switzerland for reference, as Swiss francs are sometimes used as a basis for international comparisons (e.g. Table A.11). Note how exchange rates fluctuate considerably, even when averaged over a whole year. On a daily basis these rates are much more volatile. There has been greater stability among those countries that have joined the Euro-

Table A.6 Gross domestic product per capita and by sector

| | GDP[n] (billion US $) | | Average annual GDP change | | GDP per capita (1000s US $) | | Sectoral contributions to GDP (%s) by: | | | | | |
| | | | | | | | agriculture | | industry | | services | |
	1990	1989	1990–89	1989–79	1990[n]	1990[p]	1990	1980	1990	1980	1990	1980
Australia	298	282	2.2	3.2	17	16	4.2[a]	5.2	31[a d]	36	65[a d]	58[e]
Canada	579	546	1.2	3.1	21	19	2.9[b]	3.8	30[b]	33	68[b]	63
France	1192	958	2.6	2.1	21	17	3.5	4.2	29	34	67[b]	62
Germany	1490	1189	4.2	1.8	24	18	1.7[a]	2.1	39[a e]	43[f]	59[a e]	55[e]
Italy	1089	866	2.7	2.5	19	16	3.1	5.8	33	39	64	55
Japan	2891	2819	5.5	4.1	24	18	2.6[a]	3.7	42[a]	42	56[a]	54
Sweden	230	189	0.9	2.0	27	17	2.9[a]	3.4	30[a]	31	67[a]	66
UK	978	838	1.6	2.3	17	16	1.3[c]	1.7	30[c f]	37	69[c f]	62
USA	5330	5132	-0.2	2.8	21	21	2.0[b]	2.6	29[b g]	34[g h]	69[b g h]	64[g h]

Notes:
a 1988.
b 1986.
c 1987.
d Sewage services included under industry.
e Publishing included under services.
f Repair services of consumer durables other than clothing included under services.
g Sanitary and similar services included under services.
h Includes government enterprises.
n Nominal current prices and exchange rates.
p Using purchasing power parities (PPPs).

Source: OECDd.

Table A.7 Exchange rates

	Official exchange rates per US$					Exchange rate adjustment (%) for comparing pay, reflecting purchasing power
	1975	1980	1985	1989	1990	1989
Australia	0.76	0.88	1.4	1.3	1.3	+12.9
Canada	1.0	1.2	1.4	1.2	1.2	+6.7
France	4.3	4.2	9.0	6.4	5.4	+5.4[a]
Germany	2.5	1.8	2.9	1.9	1.6	—
Italy	652	855	1909	1372	1198	+14
Japan	297	226	238	138	145	—
Sweden	4.1	4.2	8.6	6.5	5.9	-19.2
UK	0.45	0.43	0.77	0.61	0.56	+12
USA	1.0	1.0	1.0	1.0	1.0	+19
(Switzerland)	2.58	1.68	2.45	1.64	1.39	-18[b]

Notes: a 1988.
b According to German consumption pattern only.
Source: US BLS (1991b) for columns 1–5; IMF (1991:63), using German data for column 6.

pean Exchange Rate Mechanism, though it suffered considerable
strain in 1992.

Purchasing power parities may differ significantly from the
official exchange rates, as noted above. Table A.7, column 6 shows
the percentage adjustment of the official exchange rate for comparisons of *pay* based on purchasing power. This adjustment is based
on an analysis of differing national consumption patterns conducted
by the German Federal Statistics Office. The analysis embraces
some 350 goods and services, but reflects merely consumer expenditure, excluding direct taxation and employees' contributions to
social insurance (IMF 1991:62).

Hourly labour (remuneration/compensation) costs

Hourly labour costs vary a great deal between countries. Table A.8
presents an index of the relative costs per hour of production work
in manufacturing, compared to those in the USA. These compensation costs include: pay for time worked; other direct pay; levies for
insurance, pension, contractual and other benefits; and for some
countries, labour taxes. The index shows that, in comparison to the
USA, these total costs were significantly lower, in 1991, in the UK,
Japan and Australia. Marked contrasts in pay levels between countries can be inferred from Tables A.8 and A.9. Such comparisons
should be undertaken with caution due to the vagaries of nominal
exchange rates. For example, it might be inferred that Canadian
wages were less than those in the USA in 1985, but higher in 1991.
But this apparent change of relativities is largely (though not

Table A.8   Hourly labour costs

	Hourly labour costs (index USA = 100)					
	1975	**1980**	**1985**	**1989**	**1990**	**1991**
Australia	87	86	63	86	87	86
Canada	91	85	83	103	108	112
France	71	91	58	88	102	99
Germany	100	125	74	124	145	143
Italy	73	81	57	95	110	111
Japan	48	57	49	88	85	93
Sweden	113	127	74	122	141	143
UK	52	75	48	73	84	87
USA	100	100	100	100	100	100

Source: US BLS (1992:5). These data relate to production workers in manufacturing.
Costs are converted from national currency units to $US at prevailing annual
average exchange rates, as in Table A.7.

entirely) an exchange rate phenomenon rather than a reflection of an enormous increase in Canadian wages since 1985.

Hourly labour costs can be divided into two broad components: pay for time worked; and all the other above-mentioned costs. In most countries, these other compensation costs have increased more rapidly than pay for time worked. The largest relative shift was in Sweden, where the other costs rose from 31 per cent in 1975 to 41 per cent in 1986. There was an exception to the trend in Italy, where social insurance rates have been partially subsidised since 1977. Although they are not cited in Table A.8, it is worth noting that in the newly industrialising economies of Hong Kong, Korea, Singapore and Taiwan, compensation cost levels in 1990 ranged between 20 and 30 per cent of US levels.

Changes in labour costs

Changes in labour costs are particularly significant in labour-intensive industries. But compensation per employee (Table A.9, columns 1–6) is less significant than unit labour costs (columns 7–12). *Unit labour costs* reflect changes in productivity as well as hourly labour costs. Table A.9 also summarises some comparative unit labour cost data on a US dollar basis. It shows that unit labour costs rose most in Italy and least in Japan during the 1977–87 period.

Increases in labour costs tend to be associated with low or falling rates of unemployment. This is one basis for the economic forecasting on such issues conducted by international organisations. For instance, following a slowdown in economic activity since the second half of 1990 and rising unemployment, the OECD projects that remuneration growth will fall in the next two years as inflation slows. The most recent data in Table A.9 are based on OECD projections which, in relation to inflation rates, have been consistently over-pessimistic. As illustrated in Table A.9, the OECD infers that there will be a rise in remuneration in the USA between 1991 and 1992, but not in the other countries.

With a sharp slowdown in employment growth in the early 1990s, labour productivity growth should increase as economic activity increases. Consequently, it is expected that there will be a slower rate of growth of unit labour costs in most countries, with the sharpest falls in those countries where there is the largest rise in unemployment (OECDa 1991:5ff).

Table A.9 Changes in labour costs in the business sector[a]

	Compensation (remuneration) per employee (percentage changes from previous period)						Unit labour costs (percentage changes from previous period)					
	1977–87	1989	1990	1991	1992[b]	1993[b]	1977–87	1989	1990	1991	1992[b]	1993[b]
Australia	9.0	8.3	7.9	4.7	3.7	4.1	7.3	8.6	8.0	4.3	0.6	2.0
Canada	7.0	5.6	6.6	5.4	3.7	3.3	5.7	5.1	6.8	4.7	2.0	0.9
France	10.3	4.6	5.0	4.1	4.0	3.8	7.4	1.1	3.6	3.1	1.6	1.3
Germany	4.6	3.0	3.9	6.2	6.2	5.4	2.9	0.4	2.3	4.5	4.7	3.2
Italy	14.4	9.5	8.2	8.9	6.2	5.7	11.9	6.0	7.0	8.2	4.7	3.5
Japan	4.6	4.0	5.0	4.2	2.9	3.3	1.5	1.0	1.5	1.5	2.3	1.1
Sweden	8.8	11.4	10.3	7.6	4.3	3.8	6.5	9.9	11.1	6.5	0.3	1.0
UK	10.7	8.8	10.6	8.0	6.4	5.0	8.0	9.7	10.0	7.2	3.3	1.8
USA	6.2	3.2	4.5	3.6	4.1	3.9	5.7	3.1	5.0	3.6	2.4	2.5
EC	9.6	5.8	6.5	6.8	5.8	5.2	7.2	3.4	5.1	5.4	3.7	2.7
Total OECD	7.2	4.6	5.6	5.1	4.5	4.2	5.4	3.1	4.6	4.0	2.8	2.3

Notes: a Aggregates are computed on the basis of 1987 values expressed in 1987 US dollars.
b Secretarial forecasts.
Source: OECDa (1991:9; 1992:8).

Table A.10 Output

	GDP per employed person (thousands of $US)	GDP per hour worked ($US)
Australia	28.9	14.8
Canada	37.1	18.4
France	33.9	16.9
Germany	32.0	15.4
Italy	34.1	16.9
Japan	27.2	12.7
Sweden	26.7	13.4
UK	28.1	12.8
USA	39.8	18.7

Source: Blandy and Brummitt (1990:31), based on OECD *Economic Surveys* 1989/90 which use 1987 data.

Output

Output can be measured in terms of GDP per employed person and GDP per hour worked. Although these measures relate output to the number of people employed and the number of hours worked, they do not measure the specific contribution of labour as a single factor of production. Rather, they reflect a range of other influences, including the use of new technologies, capital investment, capacity utilisation, energy efficiency, and the skills and efforts of management as well as workers. Like many of the other indicators, this one is only an approximation, because the type, quantity and quality of the output vary greatly from one country to another, and between industries and firms (Smith et al. 1982). Nevertheless, we can infer from Table A.10 that in 1987 productivity was relatively high in North America and relatively low in Japan and the UK. This accords with BLS unpublished data on real GDP per employed person, but, unfortunately, the BLS series excludes Australia.

Purchasing power

Comparative purchasing power calculations provide a way of overcoming some of the problems in comparing living standards. Such calculations aim to evaluate the relative purchasing power of workers' pay in different countries, as discussed with reference to GDP per capita at purchasing power parities (see Tables A.6 and A.7).

The International Metalworkers' Federation (IMF) publishes surveys of metalworkers' purchasing power, based on average hourly net wages (i.e. after deduction of workers' social security contribu-

Table A.11 The purchasing power of working time

	Bread (per kilo)	Coffee (per kilo)		Men's shoes (per pair)		1 litre petrol (super)	Rent 3–4 rooms[a] (monthly)		Colour TV (0.5m screen)	Income tax[b] (annual)	Net earnings (hourly)
	mins	hrs	mins	hrs	mins	mins	hrs	mins	hrs	hrs	Swiss francs
Australia	7.75	2	47		615	3.5	92	30	85	303	12.58
Canada	4.75		38		300	2.0	34	15	44	390	19.64
France[d]	17	1	27		1915	8.5	153	15	145	107	8.96
Germany	10.75		57		545	4.0	30	45	85	353	16.66
Italy	15.25	1	27		715	7.8	65	15	118	304	13.42
Japan	13.5	3	29		600	4.5[c]	67	45	52	186	18.57
Sweden	22		40		615	3.8	34	30	82	NA	17.55
UK	9.5	2	39		545	4.8	28	00	47	447	13.17
USA	6.75		29		400	1.5	36	15	26	191	20.73

Notes: a Plus kitchen and bathroom.
b For a metalworker with two dependent children and an unemployed wife.
c Ordinary, not super.
d 1988.

Source: IMF (1991:50ff) using 1989 data.

tions), expressed in working time required for the purchase of selected consumer items. In an attempt to obtain comparable data, the price levels used are for medium quality goods in a major industrial town. Table A.11 presents such an analysis for the automobile industry.

This table is reproduced to illustrate an interesting approach. We do not necessarily endorse the IMF data as reliable, for these calculations are particularly difficult, so may not always accurately reflect reality, even though much of the data are derived from the German Federal Statistics Office which aims to take into account the cost of living and the different patterns of consumption in the various countries. Nevertheless, these data show that there are wide differences in the cost of living, earnings and tax between countries.

One of the IMF's objectives in undertaking a regular international comparison of net earnings is to determine differences in standards of living between workers performing the same quantity and quality of work—differences resulting from gaps in the purchasing power of their incomes.

> Using the method of purchasing power parities therefore makes it possible to obtain a comparison of earnings which is closer to reality than does a simple comparison based on official rates of exchange (IMF 1991:62).

Consumer prices

Cost of living increases are a major influence on pay settlements, union growth and other aspects of HRM and industrial relations. Table A.12 shows that Italy experienced a 'double digit' rate of increase in its cost of living (consumer-price inflation) in the early 1980s. By contrast, the rate was less than 3 per cent in both Japan and Germany. In all the countries except the USA the inflation rate was less during 1987–88 than in the first half of the 1980s. The 1985 index (column 5) shows that Australia experienced a higher rate of inflation in the second half of the 1980s than any of the other countries, but by early 1993 it had declined almost to zero.

Hours of work

Hours of work are also difficult to compare between countries because the data are not consistent, but generally include part-time workers. In brief, some countries collect data on (a) average hours *actually worked*, while others' data refer to (b) average *hours paid for*. Hours actually worked include normal hours of work, overtime,

Table A.12 Consumer prices

	Percentage annual increase	Percentage annual changes			Consumer prices index 1991
	1981–86	1986–87	1987–88	1989–90	(1985 = 100)
Australia	8.2	8.5	7.2	6.9[a]	151
Canada	5.8	4.4	4.0	5.0	132
France	7.4	3.1	2.7	3.4	122
Germany	2.6	0.2	1.2	3.8	113
Italy	11.3	4.7	5.0	6.4	144
Japan	1.8	– 0.2	0.5	3.8	111
Sweden	7.4	4.2	5.8	10.9	150
UK	5.5	4.2	4.9	9.3	144
USA	3.8	3.7	4.1	6.1	128

Note: a Fourth-quarter of 1989 cf. fourth-quarter of 1990.
Sources: OECDe; d: BLS 1991b.

stand-by hours at place of work and short rest periods at the workplace including tea or coffee breaks. Hours paid for comprise hours actually worked and, depending on national practices, may also include factors such as paid annual leave, paid public holidays, paid sick leave, meal breaks and time spent on travel from home to work and vice versa. These broad differences are indicated by the summary notes against each country in Table A.13. Apart from the USA, in most countries in the post-1945 period there has been a general reduction in the number of hours worked per year. The reduction largely reflects an increase in holiday entitlements, as well as a fall in the length of the basic working week.

Table A.13 illustrates, nevertheless, that the general long-term trend towards a reduction in the average working week was not sustained over the 1980s in manufacturing (but this may not necessarily reflect the trends in other sectors). There were increases in hours per week during the decade in all the countries except France and Germany. One explanation of this is that, for men, the trend towards a reduction in formal hours worked may be being counteracted by an increase in overtime. Women's average hours have decreased in some countries, but increased along with those of men in Sweden and the UK. However, the difference between men's and women's hours of paid work remains marked in all countries for which a gender breakdown is available, and has increased over the 1980s in Australia and Japan.

In 1989, among the countries for which we have reasonably comparable data in manufacturing industry (total), the Australians appeared to work on average the least hours *per week*, while the Japanese, Americans and British appeared to work the most. Although the Japanese and the Americans have a similar formal holiday entitlement (column 7), the Japanese are much more likely to forego part of their entitlement, so, in total, they tend to work most hours per year, even longer than the Americans and British. This illustrates that it is more appropriate to compare working hours on an annual, rather than on a weekly, basis.

On an annual basis, we can infer from Table A.13 (column 8) that Japanese and American industrial employees are contracted to work significantly longer than their counterparts in Europe. For example, 'based on a notional 40-hour week, Japanese workers have contractual hours which represent the equivalent of an additional 11.5 weeks per year' compared with those in Germany (Blyton 1989:134). If paid absence from work is taken into account (column 9), the difference between Japan and Europe is even greater; it exceeds the European average by some 500 hours per year. This underlies the pressure on the Japanese to reduce their working hours.

Table A.13 Hours of work

	Men 1980	Men 1990	Women 1980	Women 1990	Total 1980	Total 1990	Holidays[f]	Annual hours of work 1990 Agreed hours[p]	Annual hours of work 1990 Hours worked[j]
Australia[a]	38.6	39.9	33.8	33.2	37.4	38.1	31[q]	NA	NA
Canada[b]	NA	NA	NA	NA	38.5	38.2	NA	NA	1734
France[a]	NA	NA	NA	NA	40.7	38.8	35	1763	1678
Germany[b]	42.2	39.8	40.0	38.4	41.6	39.5	42	1708	1589[e]
Italy[b]	NA	NA	NA	NA	38.6[d]	40.1[e]	39[g]	1776	1764[m]
Japan[a]	42.4	42.5	38.4	37.1	41.2	40.8	22	2226	2078[n]
Sweden[b]	39.2[c]	40.0	32.8[c]	34.5	37.6[c]	38.5	36	1800	1480
UK[a]	41.9	42.6	37.3	38.3	39.6	41.6	35	1763	1647[p]
USA[b]	NA	NA	NA	NA	39.7	40.8	22	1912[h]	1782

Notes:
a Hours actually worked.
b Hours paid for.
c Eleven months average.
d Calculated on a daily basis.
e Dependent employment.
f Annual leave, extra holidays (averages) and public holidays.
g Includes average reduction of working time by 100 hours.
h 1984.
j Adjusted for absence from work due to illness, accidents, maternity, convalescence and other personal reasons.
m 1983.
n 1988.
p 1985.
q *Workplace: The ACTU magazine*, Summer, 1992: 29.

Sources: ILOa; BLS unpublished data, 4 April 1986; Federal Union of German Employers' Associations (BDA), cited by ILO (1987:30); Blyton (1989:136); OECDa 1992:280 except as shown by note q. Most of these data are for manufacturing.

Columns 8 and 9 underestimate the actual working time of full-time workers because they exclude overtime. Like absence from work, overtime varies considerably among countries, industries and occupations. In the mid-1980s, levels of overtime in manufacturing include 2.9 per cent of hours worked in Sweden, 3.3 per cent in Italy, 4.1 per cent in Germany, 7 to 8 per cent in Japan, 8 per cent in the USA and 8.8 per cent in the UK.

The same annual length of working time can be reached in different ways. For example, relatively long annual hours in the USA are due mainly to annual leave entitlements which are nearly three weeks shorter than the European average, combined with a relatively low level of absence from work (ILO 1987:29).

Besides the weekly or annual basis, hours of work can also be measured on a lifetime basis. The typical age of entry into the labour force varies. Also, there are considerable international differences in periods of withdrawal from employment in the formal labour market. Furthermore, normal retirement ages vary between 55 and 65 in the nine countries. However, more people are retiring earlier, especially those who experience ill health. Also, on average, women still retire earlier than men. Early retirement tends to be more prevalent in economic recessions. A current trend in Australia and Europe is towards lower retirement ages—a trend associated with relatively high levels of unemployment. By contrast, in Japan, there is a trend towards the retirement ages moving up from 55 to 60; and in the USA, formal retirement ages have been abolished. In most countries there is a move towards more flexible retirement ages.

Women's earnings

Women's earnings remain a matter of contention in all nine countries. The objective of equal pay for women is included in the ILO constitution adopted in 1919 and 1946, and its 1951 Equal Remuneration Convention (no. 100), which has been ratified by well over 100 member countries. The notion of equal pay is also endorsed by many other national and international authorities, including the EC's Treaty of Rome. Nevertheless, women's earnings remain significantly below those of men. Table A.14 shows the substantial gap between men's and women's earnings in manufacturing. In 1975, this gap was narrowest in Sweden and widest in Japan. In subsequent years the gap narrowed further in Sweden, but widened in Japan, though the rate of change slowed in all the countries in the latter half of the 1980s. Since public policies to promote 'equal pay' often seem to have had little impact, it has become apparent that

Table A.14   Women's earnings

	Women's earnings as percentage of men's (hourly earnings in manufacturing)		
	1975	1985	1990
Australia	78	79	80[a]
Canada[b]	60	66	NA
France	76	79	79[c]
Germany	72	73	73
Italy	NA	NA	NA
Japan	51	49	49[d]
Sweden	85	90	89
UK	66	68	68
USA[b]	60	64	NA

Notes: a 1989.
   b Data for 1975 and 1985 are estimates and refer to annual earnings for year round full-time workers, average earnings for Canada and median earnings for USA. US statistics include self-employed workers. Data for the USA and Canada are not comparable with figures from the other countries.
   c 1987.
   d 1986.

Sources: ILOa (Australia, France, Germany, Sweden, UK); OECDa 1988 (Canada, USA, Japan).

change requires the application of processes to 'revalue' jobs in which women are concentrated. The USA, for example, has moved towards a notion of 'comparable worth' in an attempt to close the earnings gap between men and women, and many countries have developed job evaluation schemes in the pursuit of equal pay for work of equal value.

Table A.14 presents hourly earnings, so the fact that women, on average, work fewer hours than men does not contribute to the earnings gap identified. The difference in earnings does, however, reflect factors such as the likelihood that more men will engage in paid overtime and receive bonuses. Furthermore, a major cause of the earnings gap is the segregation of women into low paying occupations (and into low status jobs within them). This segregation is often explained as a consequence of the fact that women still shoulder most of the home-making responsibilities and therefore are more likely than men to have broken career patterns. But processes within the labour market also contribute to the persistence of this pattern (see Walby 1988).

Segregation and unemployment of women

Segregation between and within occupations and industries is extremely difficult to measure for the purposes of cross-national comparison. The best data available are those reported by the OECD based on 'dissimilarity indices' (for methodological details see OECDa 1988:208). Table A.15 sets out dissimilarity indices of male and female employment distribution by major occupational groups for the nine countries. The indices are designed to take a maximum value of 100 if the distributions of men and women across major occupational groupings are completely dissimilar, or a value of zero if they are the same (that is, if the ratio of women to men within each employment category is the same as the ratio of women to men in employment as a whole).

Several factors limit the value of these indices. They are based on highly aggregated data. They are also complicated by differences in occupational classifications between nations, and definitions may change over time. Furthermore, the measures give no indication of status segregation within occupations. Nevertheless, the data reported in Table A.15 suggest that a high level of segregation across occupational groups exists in all nine countries and they provide no evidence of a convergence in employment distributions associated with the increased participation of women in the labour force in recent decades. Detailed studies at national level reinforce these conclusions, and show that the use of narrower occupational divisions brings to light an even greater level of dissimilarity between male and female employment distributions (e.g. see Jonung 1984).

The caveats raised above indicate that it is inappropriate to draw firm conclusions from the cross-national contrast displayed in Table A.15, although the data do imply a high degree of variation between countries. Relatively low levels of occupational segregation recorded in Japan need to be qualified, however, because within occupations women rarely pursue sustained careers. Few women in Japan are recruited into management, and low participation rates of married women indicate that short working careers are common (OECDa 1988:214).

Table A.15 also shows that there is a higher level of unemployment among women than men in most of the countries. These data understate the reality, because more women than men are generally 'discouraged' from 'active search for work' or from registering as unemployed. In 1982, there were about 1 million women in the USA in this category (nearly 1 per cent of the labour force). Also, much female unemployment is 'hidden' in part-time working. Although many women choose to work part-time, some part-timers would prefer to work full-time. In 1983, in the USA, there was a total of at least 6.5 million non-agricultural workers involuntarily on part-time schedules (ILO 1985:216; see also Table A.3).

While unemployment rates for women have consistently been

Table A.15 Dissimilarity indices[a] of occupational segregation and unemployment by gender

	Occupational segregation			1989 unemployment rate (percentage)	
	1970 (or nearby year)	1980 (or nearby year)	1985	Women	Men
Australia	47.2	49.0	47.8	6.2	5.3
Canada	48.7	42.4	41.0	7.9	7.2
France	38.9	38.3	NA	12.6	7.0
Germany	35.1	36.4	37.8[b]	8.2	5.9
Italy	23.4	24.6	NA	18.6	7.9
Japan	25.3	25.1	22.4	2.3	2.2
Sweden	44.3	43.1	38.8	1.4	1.3
UK	42.4	44.4	NA	4.0	7.7
USA	44.0	41.4	37.8	5.3	5.0

Note: a Dissimilarity indices of male and female employment distribution by major occupational groups.
       b 1984.

Sources: OECDa (1988:209); OECDb.

higher than those for men in all the countries (with the exception of the UK where there have been definitional changes which may have excluded more women from being counted as unemployed), this gap has tended to narrow in recent years. Two processes are important in explaining this change: the impact of recession which has resulted in many women withdrawing from the labour market altogether; and structural changes which have led to greater job losses occurring in traditional areas of male employment, particularly heavy industry.

Training

Training, development and skill formation are increasingly recognised as vital issues, not least as sources of competitive advantage. Australia, for instance, has conducted surveys of training expenditure and of how workers get their training. International agencies are increasingly focusing on training issues. Yet, unfortunately, systematic international and comparative data are scarce and unreliable (cf. US GAO 1990). This is unfortunate, as current debate over product and process flexibility and the impact of training on individuals' pay and labour market careers (see OECDa 1991:141ff) could be advanced through comparative analysis.

The *output* of competencies and skills is a most important indicator. However, most countries define and measure skills in different ways and training institutions vary greatly between countries. Moreover, most of the available data relates to the training *input*, for example, expenditure by governments, enterprises or individuals; or time expended by employees (such time may be either on-the-job or off-the-job; pre-employment, during employment or between employment; structured or unstructured). Therefore, the OECD has made a preliminary effort to collect comparative data on training (see Table A.16) which summarises public expenditure on labour market programs.

We might infer from Table A.16 that Japanese public expenditure on the three categories of training is less than that of any other country. However, Table A.16 should be interpreted with caution, because from other sources we can also infer that Japanese employers conduct a great deal of training, both on-the-job and off-the-job (Dore & Sako 1989; JIL 1991:65). Hence although the publicly funded provision that is measured may be less than in most other countries, the total provision may be more than elsewhere. In Japan, on-the-job training, in particular, is part of well established processes of induction, work organisation, team-working and supervision.

Table A.16   Public expenditure on labour market programs as a
             percentage of GDP

	Training for unemployed adults and those at risk	Training for employed adults	Youth training
Australia	0.06	—	0.04
Canada	0.22	0.04	—
France[a]	0.27	0.04	0.14
Germany	0.35	0.03	0.01
Italy[b]	0.03	—	0.43
Japan	—	0.03	—
Sweden	0.45	0.01	—
UK	0.19	0.03	0.18
US	0.09	—	—

Notes: a 1989.
         b 1988.
         — Nil or less than half of the last digit used.

Source: OECDa (1991:238ff), after Lynch 1992.

Public sector

In the post-1945 period, one of the most notable trends was the expansion of the public sector in almost all modern societies. This expansion occurred in numbers employed in the public sector and in levels of public expenditure. Table A.17 shows, however, that there are marked differences between countries. Government employment as a percentage of total employment ranges from 6.3 per cent in Japan to 32 per cent in Sweden. The same pattern is evident in expenditure levels with general government expenditure accounting for 27 per cent of GDP in Japan, compared with 57 per cent in Sweden.

Expenditure on social welfare is also highest in Sweden. Table A.17 presents only part of the picture, however, as it refers only to government expenditure, while in some countries private schemes such as company pension funds and insurance play an important role in welfare. The total government final consumption expenditure included in column 3 of Table A.17 also embraces expenditure on health. This also varies considerably between countries. For instance, the USA does not have a comprehensive public medical care scheme (though it does have schemes for the aged and particular needy groups), Australia re-introduced a 'Medicare' scheme in 1984, while the UK has had a National Health Service since the late 1940s.

Cross-national differences in public expenditure on education are

Table A.17 Public sector

	Government employment[a] (% of total employment) 1990	Current general government expenditure (% of GDP) 1990	Government final consumption expenditure (percentage of GDP 1990)		
			Total	Education	Social security and welfare
Australia	17[b]	32[d]	17[d]	3.8[d]	0.7[d]
Canada	19[b]	42[d]	NA	NA	NA
France	23	46	19[c]	4.8[c]	1.5[c]
Germany	15	42[d]	20[b]	3.7[b]	2.1[b]
Italy	16	48	17	4.9	0.7
Japan	6.1[b]	26[d]	9.3[d]	3.2[d]	0.5[d]
Sweden	32[b]	57[d]	26[b]	5.1[b]	4.8[b]
UK	20	38[d]	20[d]	3.7[d]	1.4[d]
USA	14[d]	35[d]	18[d]	4.6[d]	0.6[d]

Notes: a Producers of government services, except for Australia, Canada and France which are general government.
b 1988.
c 1987.
d 1989.
Source: OECDd.

not as marked as those on other measures reported in Table A.17. Sweden's expenditure is the highest at 5.3 per cent of GDP, while the UK spends least on education (3.6 per cent of GDP) among the nine countries. Once again, the data refer only to government expenditure and do not account for contributions to education and training from other private sources such as industry.

Public expenditure and taxation

International comparisons in levels of public expenditure reflect different levels of taxation. The relative balance in provision of services between the public and private sectors in areas like health, education, welfare, and post-retirement income are relevant factors that affect levels of taxation.

While it is difficult to compare rates of taxation between countries, given the range of means by which taxes are collected, Table A.18 shows that total tax receipts as a percentage of GDP varied from 30 per cent in Australia and the USA to 56 per cent in Sweden. The table illustrates that little change occurred over the 1980s, with the USA, Australia and Japan consistently having the lowest levels of tax receipts among the nine countries. The contribution of personal income tax to total tax receipts was highest in Australia and lowest in France, while taxes on goods and services were highest in the UK and lowest in Japan and the USA.

International trade

Exporting, importing and the pattern of world trade do not tend to change dramatically from year to year, but there have been major changes during the post-1945 period. These changes are especially due to the emergence of the newly industrialising economies and the growing importance of the oil trade. For example, when Britain became a substantial oil producer after 1975, oil became an 'import substitute'. The decline in its oil imports tended to mask the increase in its imports of manufactured goods.

In absolute terms, the USA was by far the biggest exporter in 1953, even though Europe had largely recovered from the Second World War by then. By the 1980s, however, the USA was no longer so dominant. Germany and Japan, in particular, had greatly expanded their exports. Of the top 20 exporters in 1953, only 14 were still in the list in 1984. Australia was among the departures. The newcomers were led by Saudi Arabia, Taiwan and South Korea (see *The Economist*, 18 Jan. 1986:91; see also *Economist* 1991: 28). International trade is proportionately more important in some

Table A.18 Taxation

	Total tax receipts percentage as percentage of GDP		Tax structure as percentage of total tax receipts[a]					
			Personal income tax		Corporate income tax		Taxes on goods and services	
	1986	1989	1986	1989	1986	1989	1986	1989
Australia	31	30	47	45	9.0	13	30	28
Canada	33	35	37	38	8.1	8.5	30	30
France	44	44	13	12	5.1	5.5	29	29
Germany	38	38	29	30	6.0	5.5	25	26
Italy	36	38	28	27	11	10	26	27
Japan	29	31	25	25	21	24	13	13
Sweden	54	56	38	39	4.7	3.8	25	24
UK	39	36	28	27	10	12	31	31
USA	29	30	35	36	7	8.5	18	16

Note: a These columns do not add to 100 per cent as miscellaneous taxes and social security contributions by employers and employees are
not included.

Source: OECDd.

Table A.19 International trade and tourism

| | International trade | | | | International tourism | |
| | Imports | | Exports | | | |
	As a % GDP (current prices) 1987	Annual average % growth 1982–87	As a % GDP (current prices) 1987	Annual average % growth 1982–87	Expenditure as a % of imports[a] (goods & services)	Receipts as a % of exports[b] (goods & services)
Australia	14	1.7	14	7.1	6.3	6.5
Canada	21	11	23	8.4	6.3	4.2
France	18	3.7	16	3.1	3.6	5.9
Germany	20	5.0	26	3.7	6.6	2.1
Italy	16	6.4	15	4.3	5.3	6.4
Japan	6.4	6.1	9.7	5.6	6.2	0.8
Sweden	26	5.1	28	6.1	7.3	3.7
UK	23	7.2	20	5.1	4.4	3.5
USA	9.1	11	5.7	2.0	5.4	5.8

Notes: a 1990.
b 1989.
Source: OECDd (1989, 1991).

countries than others. Table A.19 shows that, as a percentage of GDP in our nine countries, imports and exports are greatest for Sweden and least for the USA and Japan. These differences reflect the small home market in Sweden and the huge ones in the USA and Japan. Nevertheless, international trade is vital for all nine countries. Exporting and importing of goods and services may be reflected in the traffic of HRM and industrial relations policies and practices.

International trade comprises commodities, goods and services. Tourism is an increasingly important form of international trade. Column 6 shows that international tourism was least significant for Japan, but it was a more important source of export earnings for Australia than for any of the other countries. Tourism has become Australia's largest source of foreign currency earnings, having overtaken Australia's traditionally dominant exports of such commodities as wool and coal. Therefore, there has been a growing public-policy focus on the HRM, industrial relations and other aspects of Australia's tourism industry.

Union membership

Union membership is a crucial variable for practitioners and students of industrial relations. In some countries it can be more appropriate to consider the coverage of collective bargaining agreements or arbitration awards which can be estimated more accurately. However, it is more usual to consider comparative union membership (density) data, though perhaps there are even more limitations with these than with most other comparative data. Union density is given by the formula:

$$\frac{\text{actual union membership}}{\text{potential union membership}} \times 100$$

The numerator may be based on survey data, but is usually based on membership figures supplied by the unions themselves. Many unions simply report estimates, as they do not collect precise membership details centrally. Some include unemployed and retired members. For various purposes, moreover, they may either wish to exaggerate or understate their membership. The numerator also depends on the working definition of a union. Does it include employee associations (USA), staff associations (UK) and professional organisations of doctors and lawyers, for instance, which may have some union functions?

The denominator depends on the definition of potential union membership. This raises many questions. Several countries have more than one series of union density data. For instance, certain series are based on population surveys that may be limited to civilian employment, which excludes the armed forces, but such surveys also tend to understate density in comparison with those based on union returns. Some series exclude other groups who rarely belong to unions, such as employers, the self-employed, the retired, the unemployed and those employed in agriculture, forestry and fishing in most countries. In Australia in 1990, for instance, according to the series based on union data (ABS 1990a) there was a 54 per cent total union density (though only a 50 per cent density of paid-up 'financial' members), but according to household survey data (ABS 1990b) there was only a 40 per cent total density of employees in their main job. While these sources report differing levels of union density, the trend movements over time between these measures have generally been consistent. It is also important to note that within each country, the aggregate union density data conceal enormous variations between men and women, and between different occupations and sectors (see Bain & Price 1980; Visser 1988; ABS 1990b; OECDa 1991:98ff).

Table A.20 primarily draws on an OECD study conducted by Visser (OECDd 1991:ch. 4). This table shows that union density is lowest in France and the USA, while it is highest in Sweden. During the 1980s there were significant declines in union density in several countries (Australia, France, Japan, UK and USA). Nevertheless, there was a reasonable consistency in the OECD rank order of each country in the 1970–88 period. Explanations for the diminution of union density usually refer to sectoral changes in employment away from traditionally highly unionised areas, though other factors are also important. Some authors (e.g. Bain & Elsheik 1976) explain the rise and fall of union membership in terms of the business cycle. However, widespread decline or stagnation in union density since the 1970s raises serious questions about such earlier explanations. For an explanation of union density in Britain, derived from the theory of social selection, which draws from 'Marxian' and 'industrial relations' schools, see Runciman (1991:697–712).

Bain and Price (1980) is an authoritative source; unfortunately, however, it covers only six of our nine countries and has little post-1976 data. Walsh (1985) is a good source on our four EC member countries and for useful discussions, see ILO (1985:5ff) and Chang and Sorrentino (1991).

Industrial stoppages

Industrial stoppages include strikes and lock-outs. What is the

Table A.20 Union membership

	Union density						OECD rank order[b]	
	1970	1975	1980	1985	1988	1989[m]	1970	1988
Australia	52	51[d]	50[eh]	46[fh]	42[h]	41[a]	NA	11
Canada[h]	31[j]	34	35	36	35	33	16	14
France	22	23	19	16	12	11	19	24
Germany	33	37	37	37	34	33	15	15
Italy	36	47	49	42	40	47	13	13
Japan[h]	35	34	31	29	27	26	14	17
Sweden	68	74	80	84	85	84	1	1
UK	45	48	51	46	42	41	11	12
USA	NA	23	23	18	16[k]	16	NA	22

Notes: a ABS (1990b) which relates only to union membership in an individual's main job, for employees aged 15–69.
b Rank order of 20 OECD countries in 1970, but 24 in 1988.
d 1976.
e 1982.
f 1986.
g 1982–88.
h Recorded membership (may include unemployed or retired members).
j 1971.
k 1989.
m This column uses a different source: (Chang & Sorrentino 1991:51) and is based on *adjusted* density, which appears to be significantly different for Italy and Australia; so in the latter case yet another source is used: ABS (1990b:5) which uses 1990 data; see note a.
Source: OECDa (1991:101).

relative incidence of industrial stoppages ('strike-proneness') in the nine countries? Given that studying industrial stoppages is so central to the field, we offer more comment on these data than in the earlier sections. We should be particularly cautious about making international comparisons, however, in view of the many idiosyncratic national definitional distinctions which are not adopted consistently across any two of the countries, let alone across all of them (see Table A.21; also Fisher 1973).

Canada, Germany, Italy, Japan and Sweden, for example, do not take into account the working days 'lost' by workers not directly involved in the dispute. In some countries (e.g. UK and USA), a distinction is made between stoppages about 'industrial' issues and those which arise over 'political' or 'non-industrial' matters. When attempting to make comparisons, such distinctions are more traps for the unwary. Before 1975, Italy did not count days lost due to political strikes, while France excludes certain industries from its statistics. Australia, on the other hand, includes stoppages which may last for only a few hours, as long as a total of 10 working days are lost. Thus Australia counts stoppages that would not be counted either in the UK or the USA. For such reasons, Shalev (1978) cautions against 'lies, damn lies and strike statistics'. Moreover, in 1981, the USA increased the minimum-size threshold for inclusion in its strike statistics to at least a full shift and from five workers to 1000. In 1987, Canada followed suit in an attempt to counter the criticism that it was more strike prone than the USA. Hence international comparisons became even more difficult (Edwards 1983:392). However, Canada subsequently resumed the publication of data on the pre-1987 basis (10 working days lost) and we have used this threshold in Table A.22. Nevertheless such distinctions make it very difficult to compare the patterns of work stoppages between countries (see ch. 11).

Work stoppages are only one form of sanction, of course. There are many others, including working-to-rule, working without enthusiasm, banning overtime working and so on, but there are no comparative data available on such forms of collective sanction. Nor are there any comparable data available on the many forms of individual sanction such as apathy, industrial sabotage and quitting.

There are various indicators of dispute-proneness, including the number of working days lost in stoppages per 1000 employees (which is reflected in Figure A.1), number of stoppages per 100 000 employees, number of workers involved per 1000 employees, and the average stoppage duration (Creigh et al. 1982). However, these indicators are not standardised. The above indicators can be calculated across all sectors, even though mining, manufacturing, construction, and transport and communication tend to account for a

Table A.21 Industrial stoppages: comparisons of coverage and methodology

	Minimum criteria for inclusion in statistics	Political stoppages included?	Indirectly affected workers included?	Sources and notes
Australia	10 or more days lost	Yes	Yes	Arbitrators, employers and unions
Canada	At least half a day plus 10 or more days lost	Yes	No	Manpower Centres, press, provincial Labor Departments, conciliation services
France	One work day. However, public sector and agricultural employees are excluded	Yes	Yes	Labour inspectors
Germany	More than 10 workers involved and more than one day's duration or 100 or more working days lost	Yes	No	Compulsory notification by employers to Labour Offices
Italy	No restrictions on size	Yes post-1975	No	Local police reports sent to Central Institute of Statistics
Japan	None. But excludes unofficial disputes	Yes	No	Compulsory notification to prefectorial labour policy section or Labour Relations Commission
Sweden	More than one working day's duration	Yes	No	Press reports compiled by State Conciliation Service are checked by employers' organisations and sent to Central Statistical Office
UK	More than 10 workers involved and of more than one day's duration, unless 100 or more working days lost	No	Yes	Local unemployment benefit offices which also check with press, unions and large employers
USA	Before 1982: more than one day or more than five workers; from 1982: more than one day's or shift's duration and more than 1000 workers involved	No	Yes	Reports from press, employers, unions and agencies, followed by questionnaires

Figure A.1   Working days lost per 1000 employees: all industries and services[a]

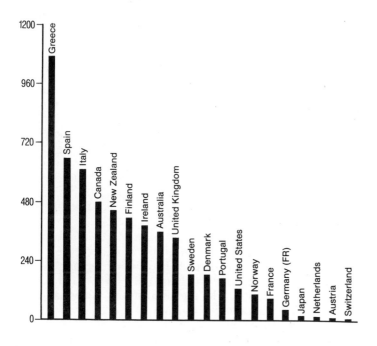

Note: a Annual averages 1980–89 (those for Greece and Portugal are based on incomplete data).

Source·   Adapted from Bird 1991:655.

large proportion of the working days lost in many countries. Furthermore, stoppages in these industries may have a particularly serious impact on an economy. Therefore the ILO also has a series of international comparisons based on these four sectors which reduces the effect of national differences in industrial structure. The number of working days lost in stoppages per 1000 employees in these four sectors is a useful international measure of dispute-proneness—probably the best of a rather dubious bunch of strike activity measures, therefore it is illustrated in Table A.22. This table does not reflect the tendency in some countries towards increasing militancy in other sectors, for instance, banking, education and health. In certain cases these have become relatively more prominent in terms of their propensity for industrial action. Also, in most countries the service sector in general has become increasingly important.

Hence Figure A.1 is also worth noting, for it includes all industries and services.

There appear to be huge differences in dispute-proneness between countries. Shalev (1980) considers three types of explanation for such differences: institutional; infrastructural; and political.[4]

Institutional explanations

Institutional explanations focus on the structure of union movements and bargaining machinery, as well as on links between unions and political parties. Ross and Hartman's classic study, for example, argued that 'the existence of a labor party with close trade union affiliations is perhaps the greatest deterrent to the use of the strike' (1960:68). They also argued on the basis of 1900–56 data that the use of strikes was 'withering away'. Both arguments have subsequently been discredited. Australia and the UK have labour parties and appear to be relatively dispute-prone, and in most other countries strikes have hardly withered away.

In an attempt to explain why the USA once appeared to be more dispute-prone than five other countries, Clegg (1976) uses three explanatory variables: the level of bargaining; the presence of disputes procedures; and the indirect effect of the level of bargaining through factional bargaining. He argues that the American-style decentralised (plant) bargaining structure promotes factionalism within the unions and hence recourse to unofficial strikes for internal political reasons. Moreover, American unions can call official strikes at particular plants at far less cost to themselves, in contrast with unions in countries which generally engage in industry- or regional-level bargaining.

However, 'collective bargaining arrangements are reflections of the distribution of power and the outcomes of conflicts between labour movements (unions and parties), employers and the state at the time these arrangements came into being' (Shalev 1980:29). Shalev admits that such institutions may subsequently acquire a degree of 'functional autonomy'. Nonetheless, they are no more than intervening variables in comparative theories.

Infrastructural explanations

The focus on the economic infrastructure in some Marxist theories attempts to move beyond an institutional framework. For instance, Ingham (1974), in his comparative study of strikes in Sweden and Britain, seeks explanations in the influence on the development of industrial relations systems of: industrial concentration, technological complexity and product differentiation. He concentrates on how these infrastructural factors influence the structure and strategies of

Table A.22 Working days lost per 1000 employees:[a] selected industries[b]

	1981	1982	1983	1984	1985	1986	1987	1988	1989	1990	1991	Average[d] 1974–78	1982–91
Australia	1730	810	620	530	520	570	530 *	640	370	530	590	1400	570
Canada[c]	1870	1410	600	940	580	1190	750	1140	470	1160	310	2140	850
France[c]	160	260	160	160	90	70	70	130	100	50	60	300	120
Germany	5	—	—	460	—	—	—	—	10	10	10	90	50
Italy[e]	140	280	210	110	420	400	490	310	370	610	NA	1650	(360)
Japan	20	20	20	20	10	10	10	10	10	10	NA	220	(10)
Sweden	60	—	10	20	10	—	10	790	40	20	10	20	90
UK	330	460	330	3240	660	190	330	440	200	180	40	760	610
USA[c]	470	300	590	160	140	370	100	110	530	170	130	1172	260

Notes:
a   Employees in employment (some figures have been estimated).
b   Mining and quarrying, manufacturing, construction, and transport, storage and communication.
c   Significant coverage differences referred to in the text and in Table A.21.
d   Annual averages for those years within each period for which data are available, weighted for employment.
e   Includes electricity, gas and water (estimates).
— Less than 5 days lost per 1000.
*   Break in series.
(Parentheses) indicate averages based on incomplete data.

Sources: Bird 1991; Bird 1992 after ILO and OECD data. For definitions, see Table A.21.

employer organisations and argues that, in Sweden, the powerful and cohesive employers' confederation negotiated centralised regulatory procedures with a similarly potent union confederation. This provided a means of settling disputes and a way of exerting control on both sides of industry.

Ingham's analysis, however, attributes too much importance to the employers in the formation of industrial relations institutions. It is more realistic 'to conceive of the development of worker and employer organisations dialectically, that is, as an ongoing process of challenge and response' (Shalev 1980:30). Also, examination of infrastructure alone cannot adequately explain differences in strike propensity between a wider range of countries, nor does it explain the dramatic change in the pattern of Swedish industrial disputes in the late 1930s.

Political explanations

Another school of thought (associated with notions of 'corporatism') offers an explanation in terms of political exchange. Thus in Sweden, the employers were faced with a highly unionised workforce holding a firm grip on political power in the late 1930s. This induced the employers to a policy of accommodation with the labour movement (Korpi 1981).

The fundamental difference between the earlier 'institutional' approaches and this political approach is that the latter emphasises that strikes are merely one working-class strategy, while political action is another. Thus political economists see the role of governments and labour political action as important independent variables. Since the unions have had a powerful position in the polity in Sweden, this provides an alternative to action in the industrial arena. This explanation appears also to apply to Germany, Austria and Norway, which lose a relatively low number of working days. The explanation also could apply to Italy, Canada and the USA, which have been dispute-prone and in each case the unions have relatively little power in the political arena, though arguably the unions have had some influence on governments in Italy and Canada (see ch. 11). It is less easy to explain in these terms the relatively low number of days lost in France and Japan in recent years. The unions have not consistently been powerful in the polity in these countries.

These summaries of competing explanations of variations in 'strike proneness' between countries highlight the complexity of the issues at stake and the need to look beyond mono-causal explanations. Furthermore it is not sufficient simply to compare the incidence of strikes, but variations in the length and types of disputes also need to be recognised.

Stoppage duration

While there are considerable difficulties in obtaining an accurate measure of dispute duration which is internationally comparable, an indication of the average length of stoppages can be obtained by calculating the number of working days lost per worker involved. Table A.23 presents this measure for the nine countries for 1980 and 1990. It highlights the different cleavage between countries in terms of stoppage duration compared with 'dispute proneness'. Australia, for instance, is near the top of the dispute-prone league table (Table A.22) but near the bottom of the average stoppage-duration league. A possible explanation for such differences lies in the variation between countries' institutional machinery for dealing with disputes. For example, in France and Australia there are statutory ways of dealing with grievances, 'where they concern failure to observe the law, or to observe regional agreements in France and arbitration awards in Australia' (Clegg 1976:74). Furthermore, in common with French unions, few Australian unions prescribe strike benefits in their rules.

Table A.23   Annual average duration of stoppages[a]

	1980	1990
Australia[b]	2.8	1.9
Canada[b]	20	15
France[d]	3.0	3.3[e]
Germany[h]	2.8	1.4
Italy	1.2	1.0[e]
Japan[c]	1.8	2.5[e]
Sweden	6.0	10.5
UK[h]	14.3	6.5
USA[k]	26	32

Notes: a Working days lost per worker involved.
       b Excluding stoppages involving the loss of less than 10 working days.
       c Excludes disputes lasting less than half a day.
       d Only localised disputes; excluding agriculture and public administration.
       e 1989.
       h Including disputes lasting less than one day or less than 10 workers only if over 100 working days lost.
       k Excluding disputes involving less than 1000 workers and lasting less than a full day or shift.

Source: Calculated from ILO (a) as cited by ABS 1991; for definitions see Table A.21.

Concluding comment

In any country, the current institutions, infrastructure and working-class representation in the polity reflect a mixture of economic, social and political variables. Therefore, as Creigh et al. point out 'it is not perhaps surprising that any attempt to relate developments to two or three explanatory variables can be faulted' (1982:20).

Although we can criticise most of the various theories which have been put forward, attempting to formulate comparative explanations is still worthwhile as a way of beginning to understand the complex differences between national patterns of industrial relations and HRM.

For many, the notion of convergence has been an especially attractive theory (see ch. 1). However, the pattern of industrial disputes and other indicators in the countries discussed in this book hardly lends support to the notion of convergence. If anything, it implies that there is a continuing divergence between these countries. For example, some of them are dispute-prone and others much less so. As a whole, this Appendix has summarised a wide range of indicators that relate to the nine countries. These data illustrate a considerable and continuing diversity between these countries.

Endnotes

Chapter 1 Studying international and comparative industrial relations

1 Readers can benefit from an initial foundation as provided by such a book, from which they can then move further towards a broader perspective; selected sources on the various issues and countries are cited in each chapter's list of references. For further reading, see the many relevant publications of: the International Labour Organisation (ILO), its International Institute for Labour Studies and the International Industrial Relations Association. Also, there is a range of books that provide valuable sources of references, including: Bennett & Fawcett (1985); Poole (1986); Dowling & Schuler (1990) and Bray (1991). The European Foundation for the Improvement of Living and Working Conditions has initiated a useful series, *European Employment and Industrial Relations Glossaries*, general editor Tiziano Treu (e.g., see Terry & Dickens (1991) in References: Chapter 2).

2 There are *comparative* studies that focus, say, on two industries or establishments within one country. Although such studies can be very insightful, they do not have an *internationally* comparative dimension.

Chapter 2 Industrial relations in Britain

1 Britain includes England, Scotland and Wales, whilst the UK includes Britain and Northern Ireland. Although Northern Ireland has much in common with Britain, some important elements of industrial relations are different. This chapter concentrates on Britain, although some of the cited statistics here and in the Appendix refer to the UK as a whole.

2 According to the most recent OECD data, this generalisation holds whether we use GDP per capita at nominal current prices and exchange rates or purchasing power parities (see Table A.6).

3 *Employment Gazette* 1990:259. According to WIRS, which excludes establishments with fewer than 25 employees, union density among

319

manual workers fell from 58 per cent in 1984 to 48 per cent in 1990 (Millward et al. 1992).

4 *Employment Gazette* 1990:403; the union density data in this and the next two paragraphs are based on a *new* question in the 1989 Labour Force Survey of individuals in employment, so are not strictly comparable with earlier data that were based on union sources.

5 A steward (also known as a shop steward or staff representative) is not a union employee, but usually has some time off work to represent fellow union members in the workplace where he or she is employed (see Goodman & Whittingham 1969; Terry & Dickens 1991).

6 There was a doubling in the membership of the Institute of Personnel Management (IPM) in the 1980s. However, there were indications of a decline in the proportion of corporate boards which included a director of personnel or HRM (Legge 1988; Millward et al. 1992).

7 An unofficial strike takes place without the official approval of the union hierarchy.

8 A 'convenor' is the senior steward in a workplace. The convenor is usually chosen by the stewards.

9 For a review of the debates about such flexibility and the core-periphery model, see IMS (1986) and Pollert (1991).

10 The NUM represents most of the manual workers. There are also three other unions in British Coal: the British Association of Colliery Management, representing middle and senior managers, the National Association of Colliery Overmen, Deputies and Shotfirers, which represents first-line supervisors and the Union of Democratic Mineworkers, which is based in the East Midlands. There is a range of publications on the miners' dispute e.g. Beynon 1985.

11 As one contrast, in Australia, although there was a decline in strikes, there appeared to be a simultaneous increase in the incidence of other forms of industrial action in the 1980s (see ch. 5), but in Britain there appeared to be a decline in the incidence of all forms of industrial action (Millward et al. 1992).

Chapter 6   Industrial relations in Italy

1 For an analysis of the impact of industrial relations on economic performance see Dell'Aringa & Lodovici (1990).

2 Sforzi (1990) has identified as many as 61 industrial districts and each one can have around 10–20 thousand employees. There may be as many as 1000 to 3000 firms with less than 20 employees. Small firms cooperate when their activities are complementary, but competition is great among those involved in similar activities.

3 For a full analysis from a comparative perspective, see Piore & Sabel (1982). For an analysis of the functioning of industrial districts, see Brusco (1982 and 1986); Solinas (1987); Perulli (1990).

4 At the 1992 election, the percentage of seats (630) won in Parliament by each party was as follows: Right: MSI–DN 5.4 (34); Centre: Liberal Party 2.7 (17), DC 32.7 (206), PSDI 2.5 (16), PRI 4.3 (27);

Left: PSI 14.6 (100), Green 2.5 (16), PDS 17.0 (107), Communist Refoundation 5.5 (35); Others: 4.1 (17). The growing voter protest has favoured *Lega Nord* (Northern League, 8.7 per cent and 55 seats), which advocates autonomy for the North within an Italian Federation. With 339 seats, the current coalition formed by DC, PSI, PSDI and PLI, has only a small majority.

5 For a more detailed analysis of unions' political strategies see Lange & Vannicelli (1982); Cella & Treu (1986). For a bibliography of studies on Italy see Lange (1977).

6 It is not easy to assess the actual union membership. In 1984 for the election of union representatives among 201 717 cast votes in all ministries the percentages were as follows: CISL 30.7, CGIL 24.1, UIL 17.4, Confsal 13.6, CISNAL 2.9, CIDA 2.1, others 7.

Chapter 7   Industrial Relations in France

1 We acknowledge that this is a revised version of the chapter from the 1987 edition of this book which was written by Janine Goetschy and Jacques Rojot; this version was edited and re-written in English by Greg Bamber.

2 For a classic comparative study of training arrangements in France and Germany, see Maurice et al. (1986).

Chapter 8   Industrial relations in Germany

1 These data are derived from the microcensus, in *Wirtschaft and Statistik* (1984 2:108); 28.9 per cent of those interviewed gave no response; most of them had no such training.

Chapter 11   Conclusions

1 See Appendix; in addition this section draws on Visser (1989); also his work as summarised in OECD (1991).

2 Much of this section was based on an earlier draft written by Greg Bamber.

3 On the OECD, see Appendix, note 2.

4 ILO conventions can be denounced only 'within the year following the expiration of ten years from the date upon which the convention first comes into force', and during every tenth year thereafter. Ratification remains operative even following withdrawal from the ILO, unless and until denounced in an appropriate year. (South Africa continued to report on ratified conventions even though it withdrew from the ILO in the early 1960s.)

5 An interesting comparison of different countries' rationalising their shipbuilding industries is in Stråth 1987.

6 For a discussion of change in industrial relations see Clarke and Niland 1991.

Appendix

1 This appendix is a point of departure, and we encourage readers to send us suggestions for improvement. For a longer though less up-to-date point of departure, see Bean (1989). We acknowledge that an earlier version of most of our tables was published in Bamber and Whitehouse (1992:347–70), and we are aiming to update and extend those tables in future issues of the *International Journal of Human Resource Management.*

2 Both the EC and the OECD conduct research and hold conferences on industrial relations issues that are relevant to their member countries, which are all IMEs. (However, the OECD has phased down its industrial relations work.) Four of the nine countries belong to the EC and Sweden has applied to join. Each of our nine countries belongs to the OECD, which includes 24 IMEs in total. It publishes useful data sets, projections and appraisals. The OECD was formed in 1960; it was based on an earlier group of eighteen European countries set up in 1948 to coordinate the distribution of Marshall aid after the Second World War. The OECD's aims include:

> to achieve the highest sustainable economic growth and employment and a rising standard of living in Member countries, while maintaining financial stability, and thus to contribute to the development of the world economy;
>   to contribute to sound economic expansion in Member as well as non-member countries in the process of economic development. (OECDa:ii)

In comparison with the United Nations, ILO, World Bank and other large international bureaucracies, the EC and OECD have an advantage, in so far as their members have much more homogeneous economies and embrace fewer different cultures and languages. Unlike the EC, the OECD has no formal power over its members. It is not a supranational organisation but a place where economic policy-makers discuss problems and experiences. It does not have the authority to impose policies, rather its power lies in its capacity to disseminate ideas.

The work of the OECD in respect of industrial relations, which is on a small scale, tends to be primarily concerned with those aspects of the subject which are most relevant to the major concerns of the organisation, such as economic and employment policy. Unlike the ILO, the OECD does not establish rules or conventions relating to the rights of labour which member countries are expected to follow. As indicated above, it is primarily an organisation where governments can discuss common problems and policy options for dealing with them (Clarke 1987).

3 In tables, when citing data that relate to a particular year, we are usually referring to an average for that calendar year.

4 For other points of departure, see Batstone (1985) and Jackson (1987).

References

Preface

Adams, R.J. (1991) 'An international survey of courses in comparative industrial relations' in M. Bray ed. *Teaching Comparative Industrial Relations* Sydney: Australian Centre for Industrial Relations Research and Teaching, University of Sydney

Chapter 1 Studying international and comparative industrial relations

Adams, R. (1981) 'A theory of employer attitudes and behaviour towards trade unions in Western Europe and North America' in G. Dlugos and K. Weiermair in collaboration with W. Dorow, eds *Management under Differing Value Systems* Berlin: de Gruyter, pp. 277–93
——(1988) 'Desperately seeking industrial relations theory' *International Journal of Comparative Labour Law and Industrial Relations* 4, 1, pp. 1–10
Bain, G.S. and Clegg, H.A. (1974) 'A strategy for industrial relations research in Great Britain' *British Journal of Industrial Relations* 12, 1, pp. 91–113
Bamber, G.J. (1986) *Militant Managers? Managerial Unionism and Industrial Relations* Aldershot: Gower
——(1990) 'Flexible work organisation: Inferences from Britain and Australia' *Asia–Pacific Human Resource Management* (J. Institute of Personnel Management Australia) Melbourne, 28, 3, pp. 28–44
Bamber, G.J., Boreham, P. and Harley, B. (1992) 'Economic and industrial relations outcomes of different forms of flexibility in Australian industry: An analysis of the Australian Workplace Industrial Relations Survey', in *Exploring Industrial Relations: Further Analysis of AWIRS*, Canberra: Department of Industrial Relations, Industrial Relations Research Series, no. 4, pp. 1–70.
Bamber, G.J. and Lansbury, R.D. eds (1989) *New Technology: International Perspectives on Human Resources and Industrial Relations* London: Unwin Hyman

Bamber, G.J., Shadur, M.A. and Howell, F. (1992) 'The international transferability of Japanese management strategies: An Australian perspective' *Employee Relations*, 14, 3, pp. 3–19

Barbash, J. and Barbash, K. eds (1989) *Theories and Concepts in Comparative Industrial Relations* Columbia: University of South Carolina Press

Bean, R. (1985) *Comparative Industrial Relations* London: Croom Helm

Bendix, R. (1970) *Embattled Reason* New York: Oxford University Press

Bennett, J. and Fawcett, J. eds (1985) *Industrial Relations: An International and Comparative Bibliography* London: Mansell/British Universities Industrial Relations Association.

Blain, A.N. and Gennard, J. (1970) 'Industrial relations theory: A critical review' *British Journal of Industrial Relations* 8, 3, pp. 389–407

Blanchflower, D.G. and Freeman, R.B. (1989) 'Going different ways: Unionism in the United States and other OECD countries' *Mimeograph* August

Blanpain, R. (1993) 'Comparativism in labour law and industrial relations' in R. Blanpain et al. (1993), pp. 3–25

Blanpain, R. ed. (1993) *Comparative Labour Law and Industrial Relations in Industrialised Market Economies* 5e. Deventer: Kluwer

Bray, M. ed. (1991) *Teaching Comparative Industrial Relations* Sydney: Australian Centre for Industrial Relations Research and Teaching, University of Sydney

Brown, D. and Harrison, M.J. (1978) *A Sociology of Industrialisation* London: Macmillan

Chamberlain, N.W. (1961) Book review of Kerr et al. (1960) *American Economic Review* 51, 3, pp. 475–80

Clarke, R.O. (1990) 'Industrial restructuring and industrial relations in continental European countries' *Bulletin of Comparative Labour Relations* 20, pp. 19–38

Clegg, H.A. (1976) *Trade Unionism Under Collective Bargaining: A Theory Based on Comparisons of Six Countries* Oxford: Blackwell

Cochrane, J.L. (1976) 'Industrialism and industrial man in retrospect: A preliminary analysis' in J.L. Stern and B.D. Dennis eds (1977) *Proceedings of the Twenty-ninth Annual Winter Meetings, Industrial Relations Research Association* Series, Madison: IRRA, pp. 274–87

Craig, A. (1975) 'The framework for the analysis of industrial relations systems' in B. Barrett et al. eds *Industrial Relations and the Wider Society* London: Collier Macmillan, pp. 8–20

Deyo, F. (1981) *Dependent Development and Industrial Order: An Asian Case Study* New York: Praeger

Doeringer, P.B. (1981) 'Industrial relations research in international perspective' in P.B. Doeringer et al. eds *Industrial Relations in International Perspective: Essays on Research and Policy* London: Macmillan, pp. 1–21

Dore, R. (1973) *British Factory, Japanese Factory: The Origins of National Diversity in Industrial Relations* London: Allen & Unwin

Dowling, P.J. and Schuler, R.S. (1990) *International Dimensions of Human Resource Management* Boston: PWS-Kent

Dunlop, J.T. (1958) *Industrial Relations Systems* New York: Holt, Rinehart & Winston

Flanders, A. (1970) *Management and Unions: The Theory and Reform of Industrial Relations* London: Faber

Freeman, R.B. (1989) 'On the divergence in unionism among developed countries', *Discussion Paper* No. 2817, National Bureau of Economic Research

Giles, A. (1989) 'Industrial relations theory, the state and politics' in J. Barbash and K. Barbash (1989) pp. 123–54

Giles, A. and Murray, G. (1988) 'Towards an historical understanding of industrial relations theory in Canada' *Relations Industrielles* 43, 4, pp. 780–810

Gill, C. and Krieger, H. (1992) 'The diffusion of participation in new information technology in Europe: Survey results' *Economic and Industrial Democracy* 13, 3, pp. 331–58

Gill, J. (1969) 'One approach to the teaching of industrial relations' *British Journal of Industrial Relations* 7, 2, pp. 265–72

Goldthorpe, J.H. (1984) 'The end of convergence: Corporatist and dualist tendencies in modern western societies' in J.H. Goldthorpe ed. *Order and Conflict in Contemporary Capitalism: Studies in the Political Economy of Western European Nations* Oxford: Clarendon, pp. 315–44

Gould, W.B. (1984) *Japan's Reshaping of American Labor Law* Cambridge, Mass.: MIT Press

Gourevitch, P. et al. (1984) 'Industrial relations and politics: Some reflections' in P.B. Doeringer et al. eds (1981) *Industrial Relations in International Perspective: Essays on Research and Policy* London: Macmillan, pp. 401–16

Gourevitch, P. et al. (1984) *Unions and Economic Crisis: Britain, West Germany and Sweden* London: Allen & Unwin

Hill, J.D., Ward, W.A. and Lansbury R.D. (1983) *Industrial Relations: An Australian Introduction* Melbourne: Longman Cheshire

Hyman, R. (1975) *Industrial Relations: A Marxist Introduction* London: Macmillan

——(1987) 'Strategy or structure? Capital, labour and control' *Work, Employment and Society* 1, 1, pp. 25–53

——(1980) 'Theory in industrial relations: Towards a materialist analysis' in P. Boreham and G. Dow eds *Work and Inequality Vol 2: Ideology and Control in the Labour Process* Melbourne: Macmillan, pp. 38–59

Kahn-Freund, O. (1974) 'On uses and misuses of comparative law' *The Modern Law Review* 37, 1, pp. 1–27

——(1976) 'The European social charter' in F.G. Jacobs ed. *European Law and the Individual* Amsterdam: North Holland, pp. 181–211

——(1979) *Labour Relations: Heritage and Adjustment* Oxford: Oxford University Press

Kerr, C. (1983) *The Future of Industrial Societies: Convergence or Continuing Diversity?* Cambridge, Mass.: Harvard University Press

Kerr, C. et al. (1973) *Industrialism and Industrial Man: The Problems of*

Labour and Management in Economic Growth Rev. e. London: Penguin

Kochan, T.A., McKersie, R. and Cappelli, P. (1984) 'Strategic choice and industrial relations theory' *Industrial Relations* 23, 1 (Winter), pp. 16–39

Kochan, T.A., Locke, R. and Piore, M. (1992) 'Introduction: Employment Relations in a Changing World Economy' Mimeo., Cambridge: Massachusetts Institute of Technology, Sloan School of Management

Korpi, W. (1981) 'Sweden: Conflict, power and politics in industrial relations' in P.B. Doeringer et al. eds (1981) *Industrial Relations in International Perspective: Essays on Research and Policy* London: Macmillan, pp. 185–217

Lange, P. et al. (1982) *Unions, Change and Crisis: French and Italian Unions and the Political Economy, 1945–1980* London: Allen & Unwin

Lansbury, R.D., Sandkull, B. and Hammarström, O. (1992) 'Industrial relations and productivity: Evidence from Sweden and Australia' *Economic and Industrial Democracy* 13, 3, pp. 295–330

Littler, C. (1982) *The Development of the Labour Process in Capitalist Societies: A Comparative Study of the Transformation of Work Organisation in Britain, Japan and the USA* London: Heinemann

Mandel, E. (1969) *A Socialist Strategy for Europe* Institute for Workers' Control Pamphlet No. 10, Nottingham: IWC

Mayo, E. (1949) *The Social Problems of an Industrial Civilization* London: Routledge

Mills, C. Wright (1959) *The Sociological Imagination* New York: Oxford University Press

Oswald, A.J. (1985) 'The economic theory of trade unions: An introductory survey' *Scandinavian Journal of Economics* 87, pp. 160–93

——(1987) 'New research on the economics of trade unions and labor contracts' *Industrial Relations* 26, 1, Winter, pp. 30–45

Parker, M. and Slaughter, J. (1988) *Choosing Sides: Unions and the Team Concept* Boston: South End Press

Peetz, D., Preston, A. and Docherty, J. eds (1992) *Workplace Bargaining in the International Context* Canberra: Australian Government Publishing Service

Piore, M.J. (1981) 'Convergence in industrial relations? The case of France and the United States' *Working Paper* No. 286, Department of Economics, Cambridge: Massachusetts Institute of Technology

Piore, M.J. and Sabel, C. (1984) *The Second Industrial Divide: Possibilities for Prosperity* New York: Harper & Row

Poole, M. (1986) *Industrial Relations: Origins and Patterns of National Diversity* London: Routledge

——(1992) 'Industrial relations: Theorising for a global perspective' in R.J. Adams and N. Meltz eds *Industrial Relations Theory, Its Nature, Scope and Pedagogy* Metuchen, N.J.: Scarecrow

Purcell, J. (1989) 'The impact of corporate strategy on human resource management' in J. Storey ed. *New Perspectives on Human Resource Management* London: Routledge, pp. 67–91

Ross, A.M. and Hartman, P.T. (1960) *Changing Patterns of Industrial Conflict* New York: Wiley

Schregle, J. (1981) 'Comparative industrial relations: Pitfalls and potential' *International Labour Review* 120, 1 (Jan.–Feb.), pp. 15–30

Servias, J.M. (1989) 'The social clause in trade agreements: Wishful thinking or an instrument of social progress?' *International Labour Review* 128, 4, pp. 423–32

Shalev, M. (1978) 'Lies, damned lies and strike statistics: The measurement of trends in industrial conflict' in C. Crouch and A. Pizzorno eds *The Resurgence of Class Conflict in Western Europe Since 1968, Vol 1: National Studies* London: Macmillan, pp. 1–20

——(1980) 'Industrial relations theory and the comparative study of industrial relations and industrial conflict' *British Journal of Industrial Relations* 18, 1, pp. 26–43

Shirai, T. ed. (1983) *Contemporary Industrial Relations in Japan* Madison: University of Wisconsin Press

Sisson, K. (1987) *The Management of Collective Bargaining: An International Comparison* Oxford: Blackwell

Strauss, G. (1992) 'Creeping toward a field of comparative industrial relations' in H. Katz ed. *The Future of Industrial Relations* Ithaca: Cornell University Press

Streeck, W. (1987) 'The uncertainties of management in the management of uncertainty: Employers, labor relations and industrial relations in the 1980s' *Work, Employment and Society* 1, 3, pp. 281–308

——(1988) 'Change in industrial relations: Strategy and structure' *Proceedings of an International Symposium on New Systems in Industrial Relations* 13–14 September, Tokyo: Japan Institute of Labour

Thurley, K. and Wood, S. (1983) *Industrial Relations and Management Strategy* London: Cambridge University Press

Van Liemt, G. (1989) 'Minimum labour standards and international trade: Would a social clause work?' *International Labour Review* 128, 4, pp. 433–48

Walker, K.F. (1967) 'The comparative study of industrial relations' *Bulletin of the International Institute for Labour Studies* 3, pp. 105–32

Walton, R.E. and McKersie, R.B. (1965) *A Behavioral Theory of Labor Negotiations: An Analysis of a Social Interaction System* New York: McGraw Hill

Womack, J., Jones, D. and Roos, D. (1990) *The Machine that Changed the World* New York: Rawson–Macmillan

Chapter 2 Industrial relations in Britain

ACAS (annually) *Annual Report* London: Advisory, Conciliation and Arbitration Service, Her Majesty's Stationery Office

——(1980) *Industrial Relations Handbook* London: Advisory, Conciliation and Arbitration Service, Her Majesty's Stationery Office

Ahlstrand, B.W. (1990) *The Quest for Productivity: A Case Study of Fawley after Flanders* Cambridge: Cambridge University Press

Armstrong, E.G.A. (1984) 'Employers associations in Great Britain' in

J.P. Windmuller and A. Gladstone eds *Employers Associations and Industrial Relations: A Comparative Study* Oxford: Oxford University Press, pp. 44–78

Bain, G.S. ed. (1983) *Industrial Relations in Britain* Oxford: Blackwell

Bain, G.S. and Price, R.J. (1983) 'Union growth in Britain: Retrospect and prospect' *British Journal of Industrial Relations* 11, 1, pp. 46–68

Bamber, G.J. (1986) *Militant Managers? Managerial Unionism and Industrial Relations* Aldershot: Gower

Bamber, G.J. and Lansbury, R.D. eds (1989) *New Technology: International Perspectives on Human Resources and Industrial Relations* London: Unwin Hyman

Bamber, G.J. and Snape, E.J. (1986) 'British routes to employee involvement' in E.M. Davis and R.D. Lansbury eds *Democracy and Control in the Workplace* Melbourne: Longman Cheshire

Basset, P. (1986) *Strike Free: New Industrial Relations in Britain* London: Macmillan

Beaumont, P.B. (1990) *Change in Industrial Relations: The Organization and Environment* London: Routledge

Berridge, J. (1992) 'Human resource management in Britain' *Employee Relations* 14, 5, pp. 62–92

Beynon, H. ed. (1985) *Digging Deeper: Issues in the Miners' Strike* London: Verso

Brown, W. (1981) *The Changing Contours of British Industrial Relations* Oxford: Blackwell

Certification Office (annually) *Annual Report of the Certification Officer for Trade Unions and Employers' Associations* London: The Office

Claydon, T. (1989) 'Union derecognition in Britain in the 1980s' *British Journal of Industrial Relations* 27, 2, pp. 214–24

Clegg, H.A. (1979) *The Changing System of Industrial Relations in Great Britain* Oxford: Blackwell

Daniel, W.W. (1987) *Workplace Industrial Relations and Technical Change: Based on the DE/ESRC/PSI/ACAS Surveys* London: Francis Pinter

Daniel, W.W. and Millward, N. (1983) *Workplace Industrial Relations in Britain: The DE/PSI/ESRC Survey* Aldershot: Gower

Davies, P. and Freedland, M. (1984) *Labour Law: Text and Materials* London: Weidenfeld & Nicolson

Department of Employment (monthly) *Employment Gazette* London: Her Majesty's Stationery Office

Donovan (1968) *Royal Commission on Trade Unions and Employers' Associations: Report* Cmnd 3623, London: Her Majesty's Stationery Office

Dunn, S. and Gennard, J. (1984) *The Closed Shop in British Industry* London: Macmillan

Edwards, P.K. and Scullion, H. (1982) *The Social Organization of Industrial Conflict: Control and Resistance in the Workplace* Oxford: Blackwell

Flanders, A. (1970) *Management and Unions: The Theory and Reform of Industrial Relations* London: Faber & Faber

Fox, A. (1985) *History and Heritage: The Social Origins of the British Industrial Relations System* London: Allen & Unwin

Goodman, J.F.B. and Whittingham, T.G. (1969) *Shop Stewards in British Industry* London: McGraw-Hill

Gospel, H.F. and Littler, C.R. (1983) *Managerial Strategies and Industrial Relations: An Historical and Comparative Study* London: Heinemann

Hyman, R. (1989) *Strikes* 4e. London: Macmillan

Industrial Relations Services (1988) *Industrial Relations in Britain: An Industrial Relations Services Guide* London: Eclipse

IMS (1986) *Changing Working Patterns: How Companies Achieve Flexibility to Meet New Needs* London: National Economic Development Office/Institute of Manpower Studies

Kessler, S. and Bayliss, F. (1992) *Contemporary British Industrial Relations* London: Macmillan

Legge, K. (1988) 'Personnel management in recession and recovery: A comparative analysis of what the surveys say' *Personnel Review* 7, 2, pp. 1–72

Lewis, R. (1986) *Labour Law in Britain* Oxford: Blackwell

Mackie, K.J. (1989) 'Changes in the law since 1979: An overview' in B. Towers ed. *A Handbook of Industrial Relations Practice: Practice and the Law in the Employment Relationship* 3e. London: Kogan Page

MacInnes, J. (1987) *Thatcherism at Work: Industrial Relations and Economic Change* Milton Keynes: Open University Press

McCarthy, W.E.J. (1964) *The Closed Shop in Britain* Oxford: Blackwell

McLoughlin, I.P. and Gourlay, S.N. (1992) 'Enterprise without unions: The management of employee relations in non-union firms' *Journal of Management Studies* 29, 4, September

Marchington, M. and Harrison, E. (1991) 'Customers, competitors and choice: Employee relations in food retailing' *Industrial Relations Journal* 22, 4, pp. 286–99

Marchington, M. and Parker, P. (1990) *Changing Patterns of Employee Relations* Hemel Hempstead: Harvester Wheatsheaf

Marginson, P., Edwards, P.K., Martin, R., Purcell, J. and Sisson, K. (1988) *Beyond the Workplace: Managing Industrial Relations in the Multi-Establishment Enterprise* Oxford: Blackwell

Marsh, A. (1979) *Concise Encyclopedia of Industrial Relations* Aldershot: Gower

Metcalf, D. (1989) 'Water notes dry up: The impact of the Donovan proposals and Thatcherism at work on labour productivity in British manufacturing industry' *British Journal of Industrial Relations* 27, 1, pp. 1–32

Millward, N. and Stevens, M. (1986) *British Workplace Industrial Relations 1980–1984: The DE/ESRC/PSI/ACAS Surveys* Aldershot: Gower

Millward, N., Stevens, M., Smart, D. and Hawes, W.R. (1992) *Workplace Industrial Relations in Transition* Aldershot: Dartmouth

Palmer, G. (1983) *British Industrial Relations* London: Allen & Unwin

Pelling, H. (1971) *A History of British Trade Unionism* Harmondsworth: Penguin

Pollert, A. ed. (1991) *Farewell to Flexibility?* Oxford: Blackwell

Poole, M. (1986) *Towards a New Industrial Democracy: Workers' Participation in Industry* London: Routledge & Kegan Paul

Purcell, J. (1987) 'Mapping management styles in employee relations' *Journal of Management Studies* 24, 5, pp. 534–48

Richardson, R. and Wood, S. (1989) 'Productivity change in the coal industry and the new industrial relations' *British Journal of Industrial Relations* 27, 1, pp. 33–56

Sisson, K.F. (1987) *The Management of Collective Bargaining: An International Comparison* Oxford: Blackwell

——(1990) ed. *Personnel Management in Britain* Oxford: Blackwell

——(1992) 'Change and continuity in UK industrial relations: "Strategic choice" or "muddling through"?' Paper presented to the International IR/HR Project, Paris: Organisation for Economic Co-operation and Development/Cambridge: Massachusetts Institute of Technology

Snape, E.J. and Bamber, G.J. (1989) 'Managerial and professional employees: Conceptualising union strategies and structures' *British Journal of Industrial Relations* 27, 1, pp. 93–111

Stevens, M., Millward, N. and Smart, D. (1989) 'Trade union membership and the closed shop in 1989' *Employment Gazette* November, pp. 615–23

Storey, J. (1992) *Developments in the Management of Human Resources: An Analytical Review* Oxford: Blackwell

Storey, J. ed. (1989) *New Perspectives on Human Resource Management* London: Routledge

Terry, M. and Dickens, L. eds (1991) *European Employment and Industrial Relations Glossary: United Kingdom* London: Sweet and Maxwell /Luxembourg: Office for Official Publications of the European Communities

Towers, B. ed. (1992) *A Handbook of Industrial Relations Practice: Practice and Law in the Employment Relationship* 3e. London: Kogan Page

—— (1992) *The Handbook of Human Resources Management* Oxford: Blackwell

Trevor, M. (1988) *Toshiba's New British Company: Competitiveness through Innovation in Industry* London: Policy Studies Institute

Turner, H.A. (1962) *Trade Union Growth, Structure and Policy: A Comparative Study of the Cotton Unions* London: Allen & Unwin

Wadhwani, S. (1990) 'The effect of unions on productivity growth, investment and employment: A report on some recent work' *British Journal of Industrial Relations* 28, 3, pp. 371–86

Wainwright, H. and Elliott, D. (1982) *The Lucas Plan: A New Trade Unionism in the Making* London: Allison & Bushby

Webb, S. and Webb, B. (1897) *Industrial Democracy* London: Longman

Wedderburn, K.W. (1986) *The Worker and the Law* 3e. Harmondsworth: Penguin

Wickens, P. (1987) *The Road to Nissan: Flexibility, Quality, Teamwork* London: Macmillan

Chapter 3 Industrial relations in the United States of America

Adams, R.J. (1980) *Industrial Relations Systems in Europe and North America* Hamilton, Ontario: McMaster University

Allen, R.E. and Keaveny, T.J. (1988) *Contemporary Labor Relations* 2e Reading, Massachusetts: Addison-Wesley Publishing Co.

Barbash, J. (1967) *American Unions: Structure, Government and Politics* New York: Random House

——(1981) 'Values in industrial relations: The case of the adversary principle' *Proceedings of the Thirty-third Annual Meeting, Industrial Relations Research Association* Madison, Wisconsin: IRRA, pp. 1–7

Bauman, A. (1989) 'Union membership in 1988' *Current Wage Developments, February, 1989* Washington: Government Printing Office

Bernstein, I. (1970) *The Turbulent Years* Boston: Houghton Mifflin

Bureau of the Census (1989) *National Data Book and Guide to Sources, Statistical Abstracts of the United States* 109e Washington: Government Printing Office

BNA (1992) *Collective Bargaining Negotiations and Contracts* Washington: Bureau of National Affairs

Cappelli, P. (1985) 'Plant-level · concession bargaining' *Industrial and Labor Relations Review* 29, 1, October

CCH (1987) *Unemployment Insurance Reports* Chicago: Commerce Clearing House

Commons, J.R. (1913) 'American shoemakers, 1648–1895' *Labor and Administration* New York: Macmillan

Cooper, W.J. and Terrill, T.E. (1991) *The American South: A History* New York: Alfred A. Knopf

Donn, C.V. and Lipsky, D.G. eds (1987) *Collective Bargaining in American Industry* Lexington, Mass.: Lexington Books

Elkouri, F. and Elkouri, E.A. (1973) *How Arbitration Works* 3e Washington: Bureau of National Affairs

Feuille, P. and Wheeler, H.N. (1981) 'Will the real industrial conflict please stand up?' in J. Stieber, R.B. McKersie and D.Q. Mills eds *US Industrial Relations 1950–1980: A Critical Assessment* Madison, Wisconsin: IRRA, pp. 255–95

Foner, P.S. (1947) *History of the Labor Movement in the United States, Vol. 1* New York: International Publishers

Forbath, W. (1991) *Law and the Shaping of the American Labor Movement* Cambridge, Mass.: Harvard University Press

Freeman, R.B. and Medoff, J. (1984) *What Do Unions Do?* New York: Basic Books

Geoghegan, T. (1991) *Which Side Are You On? Trying to be for Labor When It's Flat on Its Back* New York: Farrar, Strauss & Giroux

Gompers, S. (1919) *Labor and the Common Welfare* New York: Dutton

Hecksher, C. (1988) *The New Unionism: Employee Involvement in the Changing Corporation* New York: Basic Books

Heneman, H.G. III, Schwab, D.P., Fossum, J.A. and Dyer, L.D. (1980) *Personnel/Human Resource Management* Homewood, Illinois: Richard D. Irwin

Hession, C.H. and Sardy, H. (1969) *Ascent to Affluence: A History of American Economic Development* Boston: Allyn & Bacon

Kassalow, E.M. (1974) 'The development of Western labor movements: Some comparative considerations' in L.G. Reynolds, S.A. Masters and C. Moser eds *Readings in Labor Economics and Labor Relations* Engelwood Cliffs, New Jersey: Prentice-Hall

Katz, H.C. and Kochan, T.A. (1992) *An Introduction to Collective Bargaining and Industrial Relations* New York: McGraw-Hill

Kempski, A. (1989) 'Bargaining '89' *AFL–CIO Reviews the Issues* Issue No. 31, Washington: AFL–CIO

Kochan, T.A. (1980) *Collective Bargaining and Industrial Relations* Homewood, Illinois: Richard D. Irwin

Kochan, T.A., Katz, H.C. and McKersie, R.B. (1986) *The Transformation of American Industrial Relations* New York: Basic Books

Kochan, T.A. and Katz, H.C. (1988) *Collective Bargaining and Industrial Relations* 2e. Homewood, Il.: R.D. Irwin

Lebergott, S. (1984) *The Americans: An Economic Record* New York: W.W. Norton

Ledvinka, J. (1982) *Federal Regulation of Personnel and Human Resource Management* Belmont, California: Kent

Mills, D.Q. (1978) *Labor–Management Relations* New York: McGraw-Hill

Mitchell, D.J.B. (1983) 'The 1982 union wage concessions: A turning point for collective bargaining?' *California Management Review* 25, 4, pp. 78–92

National Treasury Employees Union v. Von Raab 489 US 656 (1989)

Perlman, S. (1970) *The Theory of the Labor Movement* New York: Augustus M. Kelly (first edition, 1928)

Piore, M.J. (1982) 'American Labor and the Industrial Crisis' *Challenge* March–April 1982, pp. 5–11

Scoville, J. (1973) 'Some determinants of the structure of labor movements' in A. Sturmthal and J. Scoville eds *The International Labor Movement in Transition* Urbana, Illinois: University of Illinois Press

Skinner v. Railway Labor Executives Association 489 US 602 (1989)

Stieber, J. (1980) 'Protection against unfair dismissal: A comparative view' *Comparative Labor Law* 3, 3, pp. 229–40

Sturmthal, A. (1973) 'Industrial relations strategies' in A. Sturmthal and J. Scoville eds *The International Labor Movement in Transition* Urbana, Illinois: University of Illinois Press

Taft, P. (1964) *Organized Labor in American History* New York: Harper & Row

Taylor, F.W. (1964) *Scientific Management* New York: Harper & Row (first edition, 1911)

Taylor, G.R. (1951) *The Transportation Revolution* New York: Rinehart

Wheeler, H.N. (1985) *Industrial Conflict: An Integrative Theory* Columbia: University of South Carolina Press

Chapter 4 Industrial relations in Canada

Abella, I. (1973) *Nationalism, Communism and Canadian Labour* Toronto: University of Toronto Press
Adams, G.W. (1985) *Canadian Labour Law: A Comprehensive Text* Aurora, Ont.: Canada Law Book
Anderson, J., Gunderson, M. and Ponak, A. (1989) *Union–Management Relations in Canada* 2e. Toronto: Addison-Wesley
Archer, K. (1991) *Political Choices and Economic Consequences: A Study of Organized Labour and the New Democratic Party* Montreal: McGill-Queen's University Press
Arthurs, H.W., Carter D.D. and Glasbeek, H.J. (1988) *Labour Law and Industrial Relations in Canada* 3e. Toronto: Butterworths
Brown, D.J.M. and Beatty, D.M. (1989) *Canadian Labour Arbitration* 3e. Agincourt, Ont.: Canada Law Book
Chaykowski, R.P. and Verma, A. eds (1992) *Industrial Relations in Canadian Industry* Toronto: Holt, Rinehart and Winston
Craig, A.W.J. (1990) *The System of Industrial Relations in Canada* 3e. Scarborough, Ont.: Prentice-Hall
Craven, P. (1980) *'An Impartial Umpire': Industrial Relations and the Canadian State* Toronto: University of Toronto Press
Finkelman, J. and Goldenberg, S. (1983) *Collective Bargaining in the Public Service: The Federal Experience in Canada* 2 vols Montreal: The Institute for Research on Public Policy
Hébert, G., Jain, H.C. and Meltz, N.M. eds (1989) *The State of the Art in Industrial Relations* Kingston: Industrial Relations Centre, Queen's University and Centre for Industrial Relations, University of Toronto
Kaplan, W., Sack, J. and Gunderson, M. eds (1991) *Labour Arbitration Yearbook 1991, Vols I, II* Toronto: Butterworths-Lancaster House
Katz, H.C. and Meltz, N.M. (1991) 'Profit sharing and auto workers' earnings: The United States vs Canada' *Relations Industrielles* 46, 3, pp. 515–30
Kealey, G.S. (1980) *Toronto Workers Respond to Industrial Capitalism, 1867–1892* Toronto: University of Toronto Press
Kumar, P., Arrowsmith, D. and Coates, M.L. (1991) *Canadian Labour Relations: An Information Manual*, Kingston, Ontario: Industrial Relations Centre, Queen's University
Lacroix, R. (1987) *Les greves au Canada* Montreal: Les Presse de l'Université de Montréal
Lemelin, M. (1884) *Les Négociations Collectives dans les Secteurs Public et Parapublic* Montréal: Editions Agence d'Arc
Maslove, A.M. and Swimmer, G. (1980) *Wage Controls in Canada, 1975–1978: A Study of Public Decision Making* Montreal: The Institute for Research on Public Policy
McKenna, I. ed. (1989) *Labour Relations into the 1990s* Don Mills, Ont.: CCH Canadian
Meltz, N.M. (1990) 'Unionism in Canada, U.S.: On parallel treadmills?' *Forum for Applied Research and Public Policy* 5, 4, Winter, pp. 46–52
—— (1990) 'The evolution of worker training: The Canadian experience'

in L. Ferman, M. Hoyman, J. Cutcher-Gershenfeld and E. Savoie eds *New Developments in Worker Training: A Legacy for the 1990s* Madison, Wisconsin: Industrial Relations Research Association, pp. 283–307

Palmer, B.D. (1983) *Working Class Experience: The Rise and Reconstitution of Canadian Labour, 1800–1980* Toronto: Butterworths

Riddell, Craig, W. (1986) *Canadian Labour Relations* Toronto: University of Toronto Press

Rose, J.B. (1980) *Public Policy, Bargaining Structure and the Construction Industry* Toronto: Butterworths

Sethi, A. ed. (1989) *Collective Bargaining in Canada* Scarborough, Ont.: Nelson Canada

Thompson, M. and Swimmer, G. eds (1984), *Conflict or Compromise: Public Sector Industrial Relations* Montreal: Institute for Research on Public Policy

Troy, L. (1990) 'Convergence in international unionism, etc.: The case of Canada and the USA' *British Journal of Industrial Relations* 30, 1, pp. 1–43

Verma, A. (1991) 'Restructuring in industrial relations and the role for labor' in M. Hallock and S. Hecker eds *Labor in a Global Economy: A US–Canadian Symposium* Eugene, Oregon: University of Oregon Books, pp. 47–61

Weiler, J.M. ed. (1981) *Interest Arbitration: Measuring Justice in Employment* Toronto: Carswell

Weiler, P. (1980) *Reconcilable Differences* Toronto: Carswell

Woods, H.D. (1973) *Labour Policy in Canada* Toronto: MacMillan

Woods, H.D., Carruthers, A.W.R. Crispo, J.H.G. and Dion, G. (1969) *Canadian Industrial Relations* Ottawa: Information Canada

Chapter 5   Industrial relations in Australia

ABS (1990a) *Industrial Disputes, Australia, Dec. 1989* Canberra: Australian Bureau of Statistics, Catalogue No: 6321.0

——(1990b) *Trade Union Statistics, Australia* Canberra: Australian Bureau of Statistics, Catalogue No: 6323.0

——(1989) *Trade Union Members, Australia, August 1988* Catalogue No: 6325.0

ACTU/Trade Development Council (1987) *Australia Reconstructed* Canberra: Australian Government Publishing Service

ALP–ACTU (1983) *Statement of Accord by ALP and ACTU Regarding Economic Policy* Melbourne: Australian Labor Party–Australian Council of Trade Unions

Automotive Industry Council (1990) *Labour Turnover and Absenteeism* Melbourne: Australian Manufacturing Council

Beggs, J.J., and Chapman, B.J. (1987) 'Australian strike activity in an international context: 1964–1985' *Journal of Industrial Relations* 29, 2, pp. 137–49

BCA (1989) *Enterprise-based Bargaining Units: A Better Way of Working* Melbourne: Business Council of Australia

—— (1991) *Avoiding Industrial Action: A Better Way of Working* Melbourne: Business Council of Australia

Blandy, R. and Niland, J. eds (1986) *Alternatives to Arbitration* Sydney: Allen & Unwin

Callus, R., Moorehead, A., Cully, M., and Buchanan, J. (1991) *Industrial Relations at Work: The Australian Workplace Industrial Relations Survey* Canberra: Australian Government Publishing Service

Castles, F.G. ed. (1991) *Australia Compared* Sydney: Allen & Unwin

Chapman, B.J. and Gruen, F.H. (1990) 'An analysis of the Australian consensual incomes policy: The Prices and Incomes Accord' *Centre for Economic Policy Research, Paper No. 221* Canberra: Australian National University

CAI and ACTU (1988) *Joint Statement on Participative Practices* Canberra: Australian Government Publishing Service

Committee of Review into Australian Industrial Relations Law and Systems (1985) *Report* Canberra: Australian Government Publishing Service

Cook, P. (1991) Address at the Launch of *Industrial Relations at Work* in K. Nash *Designing the Future: Workplace Reform in Australia* Melbourne: Workplace Australia, pp. 102–3

Creigh, S.W. and Makeham, P. (1982) 'Strike incidence in industrial countries: An analysis' *Australian Bulletin of Labour* 8, 3, pp. 139–55

Dabscheck, B. (1989) *Australian Industrial Relations in the 1980s* Melbourne: Oxford University Press

——(1990) 'Industrial relations and the irresistible magic wand' in M. Easson and J. Shaw, eds *Transforming Industrial Relations* Sydney: Pluto, pp. 117–30

Davis, E.M. (1990) 'The 1989 ACTU Congress: Seeking change within' *Journal of Industrial Relations* 32, 1, pp. 100–10

—— (1992) 'The 1991 ACTU Congress: Together for Tomorrow' *Journal of Industrial Relations* 34, 1

Davis, E.M. and Lansbury, R.D. eds (1986) *Democracy and Control in the Workplace* Melbourne: Longman Cheshire

——(1988), 'Consultative Councils in Qantas and Telecom', *Journal of Industrial Relations* 30, 4, pp. 546–65

Davis, E.M. and Pratt, V. eds (1990) *Making the Link: Affirmative Action and Industrial Relations* Canberra: Australian Government Publishing Service

Deery, S. and Plowman, D. (1991) *Australian Industrial Relations* 3e Sydney: McGraw Hill

Department of Employment and Industrial Relations (1986) *Industrial Democracy and Employee Participation* Canberra: Australian Government Publishing Service

Department of Industrial Relations (1990) *Women and Work* Canberra: Women's Bureau

Dufty, N.F. and Fells, R.E. (1989) *Dynamics of Industrial Relations in Australia* Sydney: Prentice Hall

Easson, M. and Shaw, J. eds (1990) *Transforming Industrial Relations* Sydney: Pluto

Eccles, S. (1982) 'The role of women in the Australian labour market' *Journal of Industrial Relations* 24, 3, pp. 315–36

Evans, A.C. (1989) 'Managed decentralism in Australia's industrial relations' *Eleventh Sir Richard Kirby Lecture* University of Wollongong, Sydney: Metal Trades Industry Association

Fisher, W.K. (1990) 'The Green Paper: A Failure in Consultation?' in M. Easson and J. Shaw *Transforming Industrial Relations* Sydney: Pluto, pp. 109–16

Ford, G.W., Hearn, J.M. and Lansbury, R.D. eds (1987) *Australian Labour Relations: Readings* Melbourne: Macmillan

Ford, G.W. and Plowman, D. eds (1989) *Australian Unions* Melbourne: Macmillan

Frenkel, S. (1990) 'Australian trade unionism and the new social structure of accumulation' Paper presented to the Asian Regional Conference, International Industrial Relations Association, Manila

Frenkel, S. and Peetz, D. (1990) 'Enterprise bargaining: The BCA's report on industrial relations reform' *Journal of Industrial Relations* 32, 1, pp. 69–99

Gregory, R.G. (1991) 'How much are Australia's economy and economic policy influenced by the world economy?' in F.G. Castles ed. *Australia Compared* Sydney: Allen & Unwin, pp. 103–23

Hancock, K. and Isaac, J.E. (1992) 'Australian experiments in wage policy' *British Journal of Industrial Relations* 30, 2, June, pp. 213–36

Howard, W.A. (1977) 'Australian trade unions in the context of union theory' *Journal of Industrial Relations* 19, 3, pp. 255–73

Hyman, R, (1989) *Strikes* 4e. London: Macmillan

Isaac, J.E. (1977) 'Wage determination and economic policy' *The Giblin Memorial Lecture* Melbourne: University of Melbourne

Kyloh, R.H. (1989) 'Flexibility and structural adjustment through consensus' *International Labour Review* 128, 1, pp. 103–23

Lansbury, R.D. (1978) 'The return to arbitration: recent trends in dispute settlement and wages policy in Australia' *International Labour Review* 117, 5 (Sept.–Oct.), pp. 611–24

——(1980) *Democracy in the Workplace* Melbourne: Longman Cheshire

——(1985) 'The Accord: A new experiment in Australian industrial relations' *Labour and Society* 10, 2, pp. 223–35

—— (1991) 'The harder edge of industrial relations' *Directions in Government* 5, 10, pp. 16–17

Lansbury, R.D. and Davis, E.M. (1990) 'Employee involvement and workers' participation in management: The Australian experience' *Advances in Industrial and Labor Relations* 5, pp. 33–57

Lansbury, R.D. and Macdonald, D. eds (1992) *Workplace Industrial Relations: Australian Case Studies* Melbourne: Oxford University Press

McDonald, T. and Rimmer, M. (1989) 'Award restructuring and wages policy' *Growth* CEDA, 37, pp. 111–34

Macintyre, S. and Mitchell, R. eds (1989) *Foundations of Arbitration* Melbourne: Oxford University Press

Moore, D. (1989) 'Industrial relations and the failure of the Accord' *Australian Bulletin of Labour* 15, 3, June, pp. 153–84

Nash, K. (1991) *Designing the Future: Workplace Reform in Australia* Melbourne: Workplace Australia

National Wage Case March 1987 Dec 110/87 M Print G6800

National Wage Case August 1988 Dec 640/88 M Print H4000

National Wage Case August 1989 Dec 530/89 M Print H9100

National Wage Case April 1991 Dec 300/91 M Print J7400

National Wage Case October 1991 Dec 1150/91 M Print K0300

Niland, J.R. (1976) *Collective Bargaining in the Context of Compulsory Arbitration* Sydney: New South Wales University Press

Peetz, D. (1990) 'Declining union density' *Journal of Industrial Relations* 32, 2 (June), pp. 197–223

Plowman, D. (1989) *Holding the Line: Compulsory Arbitration and National Employer Coordination in Australia* Melbourne: Cambridge University Press

Rimmer, M. and Zappalla, J. (1988) 'Labour market flexibility and the second tier' *Australian Bulletin of Labour* 14, 4, pp. 564–91

Sheehan, B. and Worland, D. eds (1986) *Glossary of Industrial Relations Terms* 3e Melbourne: Industrial Relations Society of Victoria

Singleton, S.G. (1990) *The Accord and the Australian Labour Movement* Melbourne: Melbourne University Press

Whitfield, K. (1987) *The Australian Labour Market* Sydney: Harper and Row

Women and Work (1990) Canberra: Women's Bureau, Department of Employment, Education and Training

Yerbury, D. (1980a) 'Collective negotiations, wage indexation and the return to arbitration: some institutional and legal developments during the Whitlam era' in G.W. Ford, J.M. Hearn and R.D. Lansbury eds *Australian Labour Relations: Readings* Melbourne: Macmillan, pp. 462–503

——(1980b) 'Industrial relations inquiries' *Industrial Relations Reform* Occasional Paper No. 6, Kensington: University of New South Wales, pp. 13–16

Yerbury, D. and Isaac, J.E. (1971) 'Recent trends in collective bargaining in Australia' *International Labour Review* 110 (May), pp. 421–52

Chapter 6 Industrial relations in Italy

Accornero, A. (1989) 'Recent trends and features in youth unemployment' *Labour: Review of Labour Economics and Industrial Relations* 3, 1, pp. 127–47

Altieri, G. et al. (1983) *La Vertenza sul Costo del Lavoro e le Relazioni Industriali* Milano: F. Angeli

Baglioni, G. (1991) 'An Italian mosaic: Collective bargaining patterns in the 1980s' *International Labour Review* 130, 1 pp. 81–93

Barbadoro, I. (1973) *Storia del Sindacalismo Italiano vol. 2* Firenze: La Nuova Italia

Beccalli, B. (1972) 'The rebirth of Italian trade unionism 1943–54' in S.J. Woolf *The Rebirth of Italy, 1943–50* London: Longman pp. 181–211

Bordogna, L. (1989) 'The COBAS fragmentation of trade union representation and conflict' in R. Leonardi and P. Corbetta eds *Italian Politics: A review vol. 3* London: Pinter, pp. 50–65

Brusco, S. (1982) 'The Emilian model: Productive decentralization and social integration' *Cambridge Journal of Economics* 6, pp. 167–89

—— (1986) 'Small firms and industrial districts: The experience of Italy' in D. Keeble and E. Weber eds *New Firms and Regional Development in Europe* London: Croom Helm

Cagiano de Azevedo, R. and Musumeci, L. (1989) 'The new immigration in Italy' in R. Leonardi and P. Corbetta eds *Italian Politics: A Review vol. 3,* London: Pinter, pp. 66–78

Cella, G.P. and Treu, T. (1986) 'Collective and Political Bargaining' in O. Jacobi et al. eds *Economic Crisis, Trade Unions and the State* London: Croom Helm, pp. 171–90

—— (1989) *Relazioni Industriali: Manuale per l'analisi dell'esperienza Italiana* Bologna: Mulino

CESOS (1988) *Le Relazioni Sindacali in Italia 1987–88* Roma: Edizioni Lavoro

D'Harmant, F.A. and Brunetta, R. (1987) 'The cassa integrazione guadagni' *Labour: Review of Labour Economics and Industrial Relations* 1, 1, pp. 15–56

Dal Co, M. and Perulli, P. (1986) 'The trilateral agreement of 1983: Social pact or political truce' in O. Jacobi et al. eds *Economic Crisis, Trade Unions and the State* London: Croom Helm, pp.157–70

Dell'Aringa, C. and Lodovici, M.S. (1990) 'Industrial relations and economic performance' *Review of Economic Conditions in Italy* (Jan.–Apr.) 1, pp. 55–83

Economist Intelligence Unit (1991) *Italy: Country Report No.1* London: Business International Limited

ETUI (1985) *The Trade Union Movement in Italy CGIL–CISL–UIL* Brussels: European Trade Union Institute Info. 11

Faustini, G. (1987) 'A new method of indexing wages in Italy' *Labour: Review of Labour Economics and Industrial Relations* 1, 2, pp. 71–91

Ferraresi, F. (1980) *Burocrazia e politica in Italia* Bologna: Mulino

Flanagan, R.J. et al. (1984) *Unionism, Economic Stabilization, and Income Policy: European Experience* Washington DC: Brookings Institution

Franzosi, R. (1989) 'Strike data in search of a theory: The Italian case in the postwar period' *Politics and Society* 17, 4, pp. 453–87

—— (forthcoming) *Strikes in Italy: An Exploratory Data Analysis* Madison, Wisconsin: University of Wisconsin Press

Garonna, P. and Pisani, E. (1986) 'Italian unions in transition: The crisis of political unionism' in R. Edwards, P. Garonna and F. Todling eds *Unions in Crisis and Beyond: Perspectives from Six Countries* Dover, Mass.: Auburn House, pp.114–72

Ginsborg, P. (1990) *A History of Contemporary Italy: Society and Politics* Harmondsworth: Penguin

Giugni, G. (1972) 'Recent trends in collective bargaining in Italy' in ILO *Collective Bargaining in Industrialised Market Economies* Geneva: International Labour Office

—— (1973) *Il Sindacato fra Contratti e Riforme 1969–1973* Bari: De Donato

—— (1984) 'Recent trends in collective bargaining in Italy' *International Labour Review* 123 (5), pp. 559–614. Reprinted in J.P. Windmuller *Collective Bargaining in Industrialised Market Economies: A Reappraisal* Geneva: International Labour Office, pp. 225–40

Golden, M. (1988) *Labor Divided: Austerity and Working-Class Politics in Contemporary Italy* Ithaca, N.Y.: Cornell University Press

Horowitz, D.L. (1963) *The Italian Labor Movement* Cambridge, Mass.: Harvard University Press

Jemolo, A.C. (1963) *Chiesa e Stato in Italia negli ultimi cento anni Roma*, quoted in Horowitz (1963), p. 96

Lange, P. (1977) *Studies on Italy 1943–1975: Selected Bibliography of American and British Materials in Political Science, Economics, Sociology and Anthropology* Torino: Fondazione Agnelli

Lange, P. and Vannicelli, M. (1982) 'Strategy under stress: The Italian union movement and the Italian crisis in developmental perspective' in Lange et al. (1982)

Lange, P. et al. (1982) *Unions, Change and Crisis: French and Italian Union Strategy and the Political Economy, 1945–1980* London: Allen & Unwin

Lanzalaco, L. (1990) 'Pininfarina, President of the Confederation of Industry, and the problems of business interest associations' in R. Nanetti and R. Catanzaro eds *Italian Politics Review vol. 4* London: Pinter, pp. 102–23

Locke, R.M. (1990) 'The resurgence of the local union: industrial restructuring and industrial relations in Italy' *Politics and Society* 18 (Summer), pp. 347–79

Martinelli, A. and Treu, T. (1984) 'Employers' associations in Italy' in J.P. Windmuller and A. Gladstone eds *Employers' Associations and Industrial Relations: A Comparative Study* Oxford: Clarendon Press

Negrelli, S. and Santi, E. (1990) 'Industrial relations in Italy' in S. Baglioni and C. Crouch eds *European Industrial Relations: The Challenge of Flexibility* London: Sage, pp. 154–98

OECD (1991) *Historical Statistics 1960–1989* Paris: Organisation for Economic Co-operation and Development

Pellegrini, C. (1983) 'Technological change and industrial relations in Italy' *Bulletin of Comparative Labour Relations* 12, pp. 93–209

——(1989) 'Italy' in M.J. Roomkin ed. *Managers as Employees: An International Comparison of the Changing Character of Managerial Employment* Oxford: Oxford University Press, pp. 228–52

Perulli, P. (1991) 'Industrial flexibility and small firm districts: The Italian case' *Economic and Industrial Democracy* 11, 3, pp. 337–53

Pyke, F., Beccattini, G. and Sengenberger W. eds (1990) *Industrial Districts and Inter-firm Cooperation in Italy* Geneva: International Institute for Labour Studies, International Labour Organisation

Piore, M. and Sabel, C. (1984) *The Second Industrial Divide: Possibilities for Prosperity* New York: Basic Books

Regalia, I. et al. (1978) 'Labour conflicts and industrial relations in Italy'

340 INTERNATIONAL AND COMPARATIVE INDUSTRIAL RELATIONS

340 INTERNATIONAL AND COMPARATIVE INDUSTRIAL RELATIONS

in C. Crouch and A. Pizzorno eds *The Resurgence of Class Conflict in Europe* London: Macmillan, pp. 101–58

Regini, M. (1987) 'Social pacts in Italy' in I. Scholten ed. *Political Stability and Neo-corporatism* London: Sage

Reyneri, E. (1989) 'The Italian labor market: between state control and social regulation' in P. Lange and M. Regini *State, Market, and Social Regulation* Cambridge: Cambridge University Press

Sabel, C.F. (1982) *Work and Politics: The Division of Labor in Industry* Cambridge, Mass.: Cambridge University Press

Salvati, M. (1985) 'The Italian inflation' in L.N. Lindberg and C.S. Mayer eds *The Politics of Inflation and Economic Stagnation* Washington D.C.: Brookings Institution

Santi, E. (1988) 'Ten years of unionization in Italy 77–86' *Labour: Review of Labour Economics and Industrial Relations* 2, 1, pp. 153–82

Sciarra, S. (1977) 'The rise of the Italian shop steward' in *Industrial Law Journal* 6, 1 (Mar.) pp. 35–44

Sforzi, F. (1990) 'The quantitative importance of Marshallian industrial districts in the Italian economy' in F. Pyke, G. Beccattini and W. Sengenberger eds *Industrial Districts and Inter-firm Cooperation in Italy* Geneva: International Institute for Labour Studies, International Labour Organisation, pp. 75–107

Sirianni, C.A. (1992) 'Human Resource Management in Italy' *Employee Relations* 14, 55, pp. 23–38

Solinas, G. (1987) 'Labour market segmentation and workers' careers: The case of the Italian knitwear industry' in R. Tarling ed. *Flexibility in Labour Markets* London: Academic Press, pp. 271–305

Treu, T. (1981–) 'Italy' in R. Blanpain ed. *International Encyclopedia for Labour Law and Industrial Relations Vol. 6* Deventer: Kluver

——(1983) 'Collective bargaining and union participation in economic policies: The case of Italy' in C. Crouch and F. Heller eds *Organizational Democracy and Political Processes* New York: Wiley

——(1987) 'Centralization and decentralization in collective bargaining' *Labour: Review of Labour Economics and Industrial Relations* 1, 1, pp. 147–75

Treu, T. and Roccella, M. (1979) *Sindacalisti nelle Istituzioni* Roma: Edizioni Lavoro

Veneziani, B. (1972) *La mediazione dei pubblici poteri nei conflitti colletivi di lavoro* Bologna: Il Mulino

Weitz, P. (1975) 'The CGIL and the PCI: From subordination to independent political force' in D. Blackmer and S. Tarrow eds *Communism in Italy and France* Princeton: Princeton University Press

Chapter 7   Industrial relations in France

Adam, G. (1983) *Le Pouvoir Syndical en France* Paris: Dunod

Ardagh, J. (1982) *France in the 1980s: The Definitive Book* London: Penguin

Auroux, J. (1981) *Report of the Right of Workers* Paris: Ministère du Travail

Bélier (1990) *Rapport* Paris: Ministère du Travail

Bellecombe, L.G. de (1978) *Workers' Participation in Management in France* Research Series 34, Geneva: International Institute for Labour Studies

Besse, D. (1992) 'Finding a new raison d'être' *Personnel Management* 24, 8, August, pp. 40–3

Bibes, G. and Mouriaux, R. (1990) *Les Syndicats Européens à l'Epreuve* Paris: Fondation Nationale des Sciences Politiques

Bridgford, J. (1990) 'French trade unions: crisis in the 1980s' *Industrial Relations* 21, 2, Summer, pp. 126–37

Brunstein, I. (1992) 'Human resource management in France' *Employee Relations* 14, 4, pp. 53–70

Bunel, J. and Saglio, J. (1984) 'Employers' associations in France' *Employers' Associations and Industrial Relations: A Comparative Study* J.P. Windmuller and A. Gladstone eds, Oxford: Clarendon Press

Delamotte, Y. (1985) 'Recent trends in the statutory regulation of industrial relations in France' *Labour and Society* 10, 1 (Jan.) pp. 7–26

——(1987) 'Industrial relations in France in the last ten years' *Bulletin of Comparative Labour Relations,* 16, pp. 59–76

——(1988) 'Workers' participation and personnel policies in France' *International Labour Review* 127, 2 pp. 221–41

Despax, M. and Rojot, J. (1987) *Labour Law and Industrial Relations in France* Deventer: Kluwer

Eyraud, F. (1983) 'The principles of union action in the engineering industries in Great Britain and France: Towards a neo-institutionist analysis of industrial relations' *British Journal of Industrial Relations* 21, 3 (Nov.), pp. 358–78

Gallie, D. (1978) *In Search of the New Working Class* Cambridge: Cambridge University Press

Goetschy, J. (1983) 'A new future for industrial democracy in France' *Economic and Industrial Democracy* 1, pp. 85–103

——(1987) 'The neo-corporatist issue in France' in I. Scholten ed. *Political Stability and Neo-Corporatism* London: Sage

——(1991) ' An appraisal of French research on direct participation' in R. Russel and Y. Rus eds *International Handbook of Participation in Organizations* Oxford: Oxford University Press

Goetschy, J. and Linhart, D. (1990) *La Crise des Syndicats en Europe Occidentale* Paris: Documentation Française

Goetschy, J. and Martin, D. (1981) 'The French system of industrial relations' *European Industrial Relations* IDE Group, Oxford: Clarendon Press

Hanley, D.L., Kerr, A.P. and Waites, H.H. (1984) *Contemporary France: Politics and Society Since 1945* London: Routledge & Kegan Paul

Hassenteufel, P. (1991) 'Pratiques représentatives et construction identitaire: une approche des coordinations' *Revue Française de Science Politique* 41, 1 (Feb.), pp. 5–26

Jobert, A. (1990) 'La négociation collective dans les entreprises multinationales en Europe' in G. Devin ed. *Syndicalisme: Dimensions Internationales* Paris: Editions Européennes Erasme

Jobert, A. and Rozenblatt, P. (1989) 'Les syndicats de salariés' and 'L'entreprise au coeur de la négociation collective' *L'Etat de la France* Paris: La Découverte

Jobert, A. and Tallard, M. (1992) 'Systèmes de classifications et structuration de la catégorie des techniciens' *Sociétés Contemporaines* 9, pp. 143–58

Kesselman, M. ed. (1984) *The French Workers' Movement: Economic Crisis and Political Change* London: Allen & Unwin

Lange, P., Ross, G. and Vanicelli, N. (1982) *Unions, Change and Crisis: French and Italian Union Strategy and the Political Economy, 1945–1980* London: Allen & Unwin

Lash, S. (1984) *The Militant Workers: Class and Radicalism in France and America* London: Heinemann

Liaisons Sociales (various issues)

Linhart, D. and Malan, A. (1988) 'Individualisme professionnel des jeunes et action collective' *Travail et Emploi* 36–7 (June–Sept.), pp. 9–18

Maurice, M., Sellier F. and Sylvestre, J.J. (1984) 'Rules, contexts and actors: Observations based on a comparison between France and Germany' *British Journal of Industrial Relations,* 22, 3 (Nov.), pp. 346–63

——*The Social Foundations of Industrial Power* Cambridge, MA: MIT Press

McAllister, R. (1983) 'Trade unions' in J. Flower ed. *France Today* London: Methuen

Morville, P. (1985) *Les Nouvelles Politiques Sociales du Patronat* Paris: La Découverte

Moss, B.H. (1980) *The Origins of the French Labour Movement 1830–1914: The Socialism of Skilled Workers* Berkeley: University of California Press

——(1988) 'Industrial law reform in an era of retreat: The Auroux laws in France' *Work, Employment and Society* 2, 3, September, pp. 317–34

Mouriaux, R. (1983) *Les Syndicats dans la Société Française* Paris: Fondation Nationale des Sciences Politiques

——(1986) *Le Syndicalisme Face à la Crise* Paris: La Découverte

Noblecourt, M. (1990) *Les Syndicats en Question* Paris: Les Editions Ouvrières

Reynaud, J.D. (1975) *Les Syndicats en France* Paris: Seuil

——(1978) *Les Syndicats, les Patrons et l'Etat* Paris: Les Editions Ouvrières

Rojot, J. (1983) 'Technological change and industrial relations' in G.J. Bamber and R.D. Lansbury eds *Technological Change and Industrial Relations: An International Symposium.* A special issue of the *Bulletin of Comparative Labour Relations 12*, pp. 175–93

——(1986) 'The development of French employers' policy towards trade unions' *Labour and Society* (Jan.), pp. 1–16

Rosanvallon, P. (1986) *La Question Syndicale* Paris: Calmann-Lévy

Rose, M. ed. (1987) *Work in the French Tradition* London: Sage

Rozenblatt, P. (1991) 'La forme coordination: une catégorie sociale révélatrice de sens' *Sociologie du Travail* 33, pp. 239–54

Ross, G. (1982) *Workers and Communists in France: From Popular Front to Eurocommunism* Berkeley: University of California Press

Segrestin D. (1990) 'Recent changes in France' in G. Baglioni and C. Crouch eds *European Industrial Relations: The Challenge of Flexibility* London: Sage, pp. 97–126

Sellier, F. (1984) *La Confrontation Sociale en France: 1936–1981* Paris: PUF

Shorter, E. and Tilly, C. (1974) *Strikes in France: 1830–1968* London: Cambridge University Press

Smith, R. (1984) 'Dynamics of plural unionism in France: the CGT, CFDT and industrial conflict' *British Journal of Industrial Relations* 22, 1 (Mar.), pp. 15–33

——(1987) *Crisis in the French Labour Movement* London: Macmillan

Sudreau, P. (1975) *La Réforme de l'Entreprise* Paris: Seuil

Touraine, A. et al. (1987) *Workers' Movement* Cambridge: Cambridge University Press

Visier, L. (1990) 'A l'épreuve des coordinations' *CFDT Aujourd'hui* 98, (July), pp. 21–32

Visser, J. (1990) *In Search of Inclusive Unionism* Deventer: Kluwer

Chapter 8 Industrial relations in Germany

Altmann, N. and Dull, K. (1990) 'Rationalization and participation: implementation of new technologies and problem of works councils in the FRG' *Economic and Industrial Democracy*, 11, 1

Baethge, M. and Wolf, H. (1992) 'The German system of industrial relations in transition?', paper presented to the MIT/OECD conference on *Recent Trends in Industrial Relations and Human Resource Policies and Practices*, Cambridge: Massachusetts Institute of Technology/Paris: Organisation for Economic Cooperation and Development

Berghahn, V.R. and Karsten, D. (1987) *Industrial Relations in West Germany* Oxford: Berg

Bergmann, J. and Tokunaga, S. (1984) *Industrial Relations in Transition: The Cases of Japan and the Federal Republic of Germany* Tokyo: Tokyo University Press

Boedler, H. and Kaiser, H. (1979) 'Dreissig jahre tarifregister' *Bundesarbeitsblatt*, p. 26

Budde, A. et al. (1982) 'Corporate goals, managerial objectives and organisational structures in British and West German companies' *Organisation Studies* 3, 1, pp. 1–32

Bunn, R.F. (1984) 'Employers' associations in the Federal Republic of Germany' in J.P. Windmuller and A. Gladstone eds *Employers' Associations and Industrial Relations: A Comparative Study* Oxford: Clarendon Press, pp. 169–201

Clark, J. (1979) 'Concerted action in the Federal Republic of Germany' *British Journal of Industrial Relations* 17, 2

Clark, J. et al. (1980) *Trade Unions, National Politics and Economic Management: A Comparative Study of the TUC and DGB* London: Anglo-German Foundation

Clasen, L. (1989) 'Tarifvertrage' *Bundesarbeitsblatt* p. 26
Daubler, W. (1989) 'The individual and the collective: No problem for German labor law?' *Comparative Labor Law Journal* 10, 4, Summer
Federal Republic of Germany (1978) *Co-determination in the Federal Republic of Germany* (translations of the Acts of 1952, 1972 and 1976) Bonn: The Federal Minister of Labour and Social Affairs
Florian, M. and Hartmann, H. (1987) 'German trade unions and company information' *Industrial Relations Journal*, 18, 4
Fox, A. (1985) *History and Heritage: The Social Origins of the British Industrial Relations System* London: Allen & Unwin
Fuerstenberg, F. (1978) *Workers' Participation in Management in the Federal Republic of Germany* Geneva: International Institute for Labour Studies
——(1983) 'Technological change and industrial relations in West Germany' *Bulletin of Comparative Labour Relations* 12, pp. 121–37
——(1984) 'Recent trends in collective bargaining in the Federal Republic of Germany' *International Labour Review* 123, 5, pp. 615–30
——(1985) 'The regulation of working time in the Federal Republic of Germany' *Labour and Society* 10, 2, pp. 133–50
——(1991) *Structure and Strategy in Industrial Relations* Special issue of *Bulletin of Comparative Labour Relations* Deventer: Kluwer
Fuerstenberg, F. and Steininger, S. (1984) *Qualification Aspects of Robotisation: Report of an Empirical Study for the OECD* Bochum: Ruhr Universität Bochum (mimeo)
Hartmann, G. et al. (1983) 'Computerised machine tools, manpower consequences and skill utilisation: a study of British and West German manufacturing firms' *British Journal of Industrial Relations* 21, 2, pp. 221–31
Hartmann, H. and Conrad, W. (1981) 'Industrial relations in West Germany' in P.B. Doeringer et al. eds *Industrial Relations in International Perspective: Essays on Research and Policy* London: Macmillan, pp. 218–45
Hassencamp, A. and Bieneck, H.J. (1983) 'Technical and organisational changes and design of working conditions in the Federal Republic of Germany' *Labour and Society* 8, pp. 39–56
Havlovic, S.J. (1990) 'German works councils: A highly evolved institution of industrial democracy' *Labor Studies Journal* 15, 2, Summer
Hutton, S.P. and Lawrence, P.A. (1981) *German Engineers: The Anatomy of a Profession* Oxford: Clarendon
Institut der Deutschen Wirtschaft (1988) *Zahlen zur Wirtschaftlichen Entwicklung der Bundesrepublik Deutschland* Köln: Deutscher Instituts-Verlag
Jacobi, O. and Müller-Jentsch, W. (1990) 'West Germany: Continuity and structural change' in G. Baglioni and C. Crouch eds *European Industrial Relations: The Challenge of Flexibility* London: Sage, pp. 127–53
Keller, B.K. (1981) 'Determinants of the wage rate in the public sector: The case of civil servants in the Federal Republic of Germany' *British Journal of Industrial Relations* 19, 3, pp. 345–60

Kissler, L. and Sattel, U. (1982) 'Humanization of work and social interests: Description and critical assessment of the state-sponsored program of humanization in the Federal Republic of Germany' *Economic and Industrial Democracy* 3, pp. 221–61

Lapping, A. (1983) *Working Time in Britain and West Germany* London: Anglo-German Foundation

Lawrence, P. (1980) *Managers and Management in West Germany* London: Croom Helm

McCathie, A. (1992) 'Germans go into training' *Australian Financial Review*, 24 July, p. 16

Maitland, I. (1983) *The Causes of Industrial Disorder: A Comparison of a British and a German Factory* London: Routledge & Kegan Paul

Markovits, A.S. (1986) *The Politics of the West German Trade Unions* Cambridge: Cambridge University Press

Marsh, A. et al. (1981) *Workplace Relations in the Engineering Industry in the UK and the Federal Republic of Germany* London: Anglo-German Foundation

Miller, D. (1978) 'Trade union workplace representation in the Federal Republic of Germany' *British Journal of Industrial Relations* 16, 3, pp. 335–54

——(1982) 'Social partnership and determinants of workplace independence in West Germany' *British Journal of Industrial Relations*, 20

Moses, J.A. (1982) *Trade Unionism in Germany from Bismarck to Hitler, vol. 1, 1869–1918; vol. 2, 1919–1933* Totowa, NJ: Barnes & Nobel

Mueller, F. (1992) 'Designing flexible teamwork: Comparing German and Japanese approaches' *Employee Relations* 14, 1, pp. 5–16

Mueller-Jentsch, W. (1981) 'Strikes and strike trends in West Germany, 1950–1978' *British Journal of Industrial Relations*, 20, 1982

Neal, A.C. (1987) 'Co-determination in the Federal Republic of Germany' *British Journal of Industrial Relations* 25, 2

Owen Smith, E. (1981) 'West Germany' in E. Owen Smith ed. *Trade Unions in the Developed Economies* London: Croom Helm

Pieper, R. ed. (1990) *Human Resource Management: An International Comparison* Berlin: de Gruyter

Projekttraeger Humanisierung des Arbeitslebens (1981) Das Programm zur Humanisierung des Arbeitslebens Frankfurt and New York: Campus

Reichel, H. (1971) 'Recent trends in collective bargaining in the Federal Republic of Germany' *International Labour Review* 104, 6, pp. 253–71

Seglow, P. et al. (1982) *Rail Unions in Britain and West Germany* London: Policy Studies Institute-Anglo-German Foundation

Sengenberger, W. (1984) 'West German employment policy restoring worker competition' *Industrial Relations* 23, 3, pp. 323–44

Schregle, J. (1987) 'Workers participation in the Federal Republic of Germany in an international perspective' *International Labour Review* May–June

Sorge, A. and Warner, H. (1981) 'Culture, management and manufacturing organisation: A study of British and German firms' *Management International Review* 21, pp. 35–48

Sorge, A. et al. (1983) *Microelectronics and Manpower in Manufacturing: Applications of Computer Numerical Control in Great Britain and West Germany* Berlin: International Institute of Management; Aldershot: Gower

Statistisches Jahrbuch (1991) Stuttgart: Metzler-Poeschel

Streeck, W. (1984) *Industrial Relations in West Germany: A Case Study of the Car Industry* London: Heinemann

——(1991) 'More uncertainties: German unions facing 1992' *Industrial Relations* 30, 3, pp. 317–49

Thelen, K. (1992) *Union of Parts: Labor Relations in Post-War Germany* Ithaca: Cornell University Press

Turner, L. (1991) *Democracy at Work* Ithaca: Cornell University Press

Wächter, H. and Stengelhofen, T. (1992) 'Human resource management in a unified Germany' *Employee Relations* 14, 4, pp. 21–37

Wiesner, H. ed. (1983) *Bismarck to Bullock* London: Anglo-German Foundation

Wiesner, H. (1979) *Rationalisierung* Köln: Bund-Verlag

Williams, K. (1988) *Industrial Relations and the German Model* Aldershot: Avebury/Gower

Wirtschaft und Statistik (1982 ff:) Statistische Monatszahlen, Stuttgart and Mainz: Kohlhammer

See also IIRA (1986) *Proceedings of the Seventh World Congress of the International Industrial Relations Association* Geneva: IIRA

Chapter 9   Industrial relations in Sweden

Abrahamsson, B. (1980) *The Rights of Labor* New York: Sage

Ahlén, K. (1989) 'Swedish collective bargaining under pressure' *British Journal of Industrial Relations* 27, 3, November, pp. 330–46

Albrecht, S. and Deutsch, S. (1982) 'The challenge of economic democracy: The case of Sweden' Conference paper, International Sociological Association

Asplund, C. (1981) *Redesigning Jobs: Western European Experiences* Brussels: European Trade Union Institute

Auer, P. (1985) *Industrial Relations, Work Organisation and New Technology: the Volvo Case* Berlin: Wissenschaftzentrum

Bosworth, B. and Rivlin, A. (1987) *The Swedish Economy* Washington D.C.: Brookings Institution

Bratt, C. (1990) *Labour Relations in 18 Countries* Stockholm: SAF

Delsen, L. and Van Veer, T. (1992) 'The Swedish model: Relevant for other European countries?' *British Journal of Industrial Relations* 30, 1, March, pp. 83–105

Edlund, S. and Nystrom, B. (1988) *Developments in Swedish Labour Law* Stockholm: The Swedish Institute

Elvander, N. (1990) 'Incomes policies in the Nordic countries' *International Labour Review* 129, 1, pp. 1–21

Evans, J. (1982) *Negotiating Technological Change* Brussels: European Trade Union Institute

Fry, J. ed. (1986) *Towards a Democratic Rationality; Making the Case for Swedish Labour* Aldershot: Gower

Fry, J.A. ed. (1979) *Industrial Democracy and Labour Market Policy in Sweden* Oxford: Pergamon

Fulcher, J. (1988) 'Trade unionism in Sweden' (Review Article) *Economic and Industrial Democracy* 9, pp. 129–40

——(1991) *Labour Movements, Employers and the State: Conflict and Cooperation in Britain and Sweden* Oxford: Clarendon Press

Gardell, B. and Svensson, L. (1980) *Co-determination and Autonomy: A Trade Union Strategy for Democracy at the Work Place* Ann Arbor: Institute for Social Research

Graversen, G. and Lansbury, R.D (1986) *New Technology and Industrial Relations in Scandinavia* Aldershot: Gower

Gunzburg, D. (1978) *Industrial Democracy Approaches in Sweden: An Australian View* Melbourne: Productivity Promotion Council in Australia

Hammarström, O. (1978a) *Negotiations for Co-determination* Stockholm: Swedish Working Life Centre

——(1978b) *On National Strategies for Industrial Democracy: Some Reflections on Ten Years of Industrial Democracy Development in Sweden* Stockholm: Swedish Working Life Centre

——(1982) 'Industrial Relations in Europe 1970–82' *International Issues in Industrial Relations* Sydney: Industrial Relations Society of Australia

Hammarström, O. and Piolet, F. (1980) *Evaluation of the Main Trends in Work Organisation within the Context of Economic, Social and Technological Changes* Brussels: European Communities

Hanami T. and Blanpain R. (1987) *Industrial Conflict Resolution in Market Economies: A Study of Canada, Great Britain and Sweden* Deventer: Kluwer

Himmelstrand, U. (1981) *Beyond Welfare Capitalism* London: Heinemann

Holzhausen, J. (1981) *Employee Representation on Company Boards* The Hague: ILO Industrial Relations Seminar

Industrial Relations Services (1983) 'Sweden: employee investment funds' *European Industrial Relations Review* 119, (Dec.), pp. 22–3

Jangenas B. (1985) *The Swedish Approach to Labour Market Policy* Stockholm: The Swedish Institute

Johnston, T.L. (1962) *Collective Bargaining in Sweden* London: George Allen & Unwin

Jones, H.G. (1987) 'Scenarios for industrial relations: Sweden evolves a new consensus' *Long Range Planning* 20, 3 pp. 65–76

Korpi, W. (1978) *The Working Class in Welfare Capitalism: Work, Unions and Politics in Sweden* London: Routledge & Kegan Paul

Lash, S. (1985) 'The end of new-corporatism?: The breakdown of centralised bargaining in Sweden' *British Journal of Industrial Relations* 23, 2, July pp. 215–39

Lawrence P. (1986) *Management and Society in Sweden* London: Routledge & Kegan Paul

Meidner, R. (1983) *Strategy for Full Employment* Stockholm: PSI Symposium

Neal, A.C. et al. (1981) *Law and the Weaker Party: An Anglo-Swedish Comparative Study, vol. 1, The Swedish Experience* Oxfordshire: Professional Books

Olson G.M. ed. (1988) *Industrial Change and Labour Adjustment in Sweden and Canada* Toronto: Garamond Press

Olsson, A.S. (1990) *Swedish Wage Negotiation System* Aldershot: Dartmouth

Peterson, R.B. (1987) 'Swedish collective bargaining: A changing scene' *British Journal of Industrial Relations* 25, 1, March pp. 31–48

Pontusson, J. and Kuruvilla, S. (1992) 'Swedish wage-earner funds: An experiment in economic democracy' *Industrial and Labor Relations Review* 45, 4, July, pp. 779–91

Rehn, G. and Viklund, B. (1990) 'Changes in the Swedish model' in G. Baglioni and C. Crouch eds *European Industrial Relations: The Challenge of Flexibility* London: Sage, pp. 300–25

Rosendahl, M. (1985) *Conflict and Compliance: Class Consciousness among Swedish Workers* London: Coronet Books

Sandberg, T., Molin, R. and Rudenstam, N.G. (1978) *The Swedish Industrial Relations System in an Economic, Social and Political Setting* Research Report 1978/1 Uppsala: Department of Business Administration

Schmidt, F. (1976) *The Democratisation of Working Life in Sweden: A Survey of Agreements, Legislation, Experimental Activities, Research and Development* Stockholm: TCO

——(1977) *Law and Industrial Relations in Sweden* Stockholm: Almqvist & Wiksell International

Swenson, P. (1985) *Unions, Pay and Politics in Sweden and West Germany* Ithaca: Cornell University Press

Tilton, T. (1990) *The Political Theory of Swedish Social Democracy* Oxford: Clarendon Press

Chapter 10 Industrial relations in Japan

Abeggen, J.C. (1958) *The Japanese Factory: Aspects of Its Social Organisation* Glencoe, Ill.: Free Press

——(1973) *Management and Worker: The Japanese Solution* Tokyo: Sophia University Press

Briggs, P. (1988) 'The Japanese at work: Illusions of the ideal' *Industrial Relations Journal* 19, 1, Spring

Chalmers, N.J. (1989) *Industrial Relations in Japan: The Peripheral Workforce* London: Routledge

Chusho Kigyo Cho (Small and medium-sized enterprise agency) (1983) *Chusho Kigyo Hakusho* (White Paper on SMEs) Tokyo

Clarke, R. (1979) *The Japanese Company* New Haven: Yale University Press

Cole, R.E. (1971) *Japanese Blue Collar: The Changing Tradition* Berkeley: University of California Press

Dore, R. (1979) *British Factory–Japanese Factory: The Origin of National Diversity in Industrial Relations* London: George Allen & Unwin, Berkeley: University of California Press

Ford, G.W. (1983) 'Japan as a learning society' *Work and People* 9, 1, pp. 3–5

Fuerstenberg, F. (1984) 'Japanese industrial relations from a western European perspective' *Work and People* 10, 2, pp. 11–14

Hanami, T. (1979) *Labour Relations in Japan Today* Tokyo: Kodansha-International

Hancock, K. et al. (1983) *Japanese and Australian Labour Markets* Canberra: Australian–Japan Research Centre

JIL *Japan Labor Bulletin* (monthly) Tokyo: Nihon Rodo Kenkyu Kiko (Japan Institute of Labour)

——(1979–89) *Japanese Industrial Relations Series* 1–12

JISEA (1984) *Japan 1990: An International Comparison* Tokyo: Keizai Koho Centre (Japan Institute for Social Economic Affairs)

Kamata, S. (1983) *Japan in the Passing Lane: An Insider's Account of Life in a Japanese Auto Factory* London: George Allen & Unwin

Karsh, B. (1984) 'Human resources management in Japanese large scale industry' *Journal of Industrial Relations* 26, 2, June pp. 226–45

Koike, K. (1988) *Understanding Industrial Relations in Modern Japan* New York: St Martin's Press

KoseiSho (Ministry of Health and Welfare) (1989) *Kani Seimei Hyo* (Simplified Life Expectancy Table)

Kuwahara, Y. (1983) 'Technological change and industrial relations in Japan' *Bulletin of Comparative Labour Relations* 12, pp. 32–52

——(1984) 'Employment and Japan's high-tech industries' *Euro-Asia* 3, 2, pp. 32–53

——(1985) 'Labour and management views of and their responses to microelectronics in Japan', paper presented to the International Symposium on Microelectronics and Labour, Tokyo

——(1989) *Industrial Relations Systems in Japan: A New Interpretation* Tokyo: JIL

Levine, S.B. (1984) 'Employers' associations in Japan' in J.P. Windmuller and A. Gladstone eds *Employers' Associations and Industrial Relations: A Comparative Study* Oxford: Clarendon, pp. 318–56

Levine, S.B. and Kawada, H. (1980) *Human Resources in Japanese Industrial Development* Princeton, N.J.: Princeton University Press

McMillan, C.J. (1985) *The Japanese Industrial System* 2e. New York: de Gruyter

Marsh, R.M. (1992) 'The difference between participation and power in Japanese factories' *Industrial and Labor Relations Review* 45, 2, January

Morishima, M. (1992) 'Use of joint consultation committees by large Japanese firms' *British Journal of Industrial Relations* 30, 3, September, pp. 405–23

Mueller, F. (1992) 'Designing flexible teamwork: Comparing German and Japanese approaches' *Employee Relations* 14, 1, pp. 5–16

Nakayama, I. (1975) *Industrialisation and Labor–Management Relations in Japan* Tokyo: Japan Institute of Labour

Ohta, T. (1988) 'Work rules in Japan' *International Labour Review* 127, 5, pp. 627–39

Olson, M. (1982) *The Rise and Decline of Nations: Economic Growth, Stagflation, and Social Rigidities* New Haven: Yale University Press

OECD (1977) *The Development of Industrial Relations Systems: Some Implications of Japanese Experience* Paris: Organisation for Economic Cooperation and Development

Orr, J.A., Shimada, H. and Seike, A. (1985) *United States–Japan Comparative Study of Employment Adjustment* Washington, D.C.: Dept of Labor

Rodosho (1991) *Rodo Kumiai Kihon Tokei Chosa* (The Basic Survey on Trade Unions) Tokyo: Rodosho (Ministry of Labour)

Shirai, T. ed. (1983) *Contemporary Industrial Relations in Japan* Madison, Wisconsin: University of Wisconsin Press

Somucho (1986) *Jigyosho Tokei* (Census of Establishments)

Tokunaga, S. and Bergmann, J. (1984) *Industrial Relations in Transition: The Cases of Japan and the FRG* Tokyo: University of Tokyo Press

Ward, B. (1958) 'The firm in Illyria: Market syndicalism' *American Economic Review* 68, pp. 566–89

Weitzman, M.L. (1984) *The Share Economy: Conquering Stagflation* Cambridge: Harvard University Press

Chapter 11 Conclusions

Adams, R. ed. (1991) *Comparative Industrial Relations Contemporary Research and Theory* London: HarperCollins

Baglioni, G. (1989) 'Industrial relations in Europe in the 1980s' *Labour and Society* 14, 3, July

Baglioni, G. and Crouch, C. eds (1990) *European Industrial Relations: The Challenge of Flexibility* London: Sage

Bamber, G.J. (1986) *Militant Managers? Managerial Unionism and Industrial Relations* Aldershot: Gower

Bamber, G. and Córdova, E. (1993) 'Collective bargaining in industrialised market economies: Is there scope for strategic choice?' in Blanpain (1993), forthcoming

Bamber, G.J. and Lansbury, R.D. (1989) *New Technology: International Perspectives on Human Resources and Industrial Relations* London: Unwin-Hyman

Blanpain, R. (1993) 'Comparativism in labour law and industrial relations' in Blanpain (1993), forthcoming

Blanpain, R. et al. eds (1993) *Comparative Labour Law and Industrial Relations* 5e. Deventer: Kluwer, forthcoming

Boyer, R. (1988) *The Search for Labour Market Flexibility. The European Economies in Transition* Oxford: Clarendon

Clarke, O. and Niland, J. eds (1991) *Agenda for Change: An International Analysis of Industrial Relations in Transition* Sydney: Allen & Unwin

Creighton, B. (1992) 'How the ILO works' *Workplace: The Australian Council of Trade Unions Magazine* Summer, pp. 36–9

Dowling, P.J. and Schuler, R.S. (1990) *International Dimensions of Human Resource Management* Boston: PWS-Kent

Ferner, A. and Hyman, R. eds (1992) *Industrial Relations in the New Europe* Oxford: Blackwell

Frenkel, S. and Clarke, O. eds 'Economic restructuring and industrial relations in industrialised countries' *Bulletin of Comparative Labour Relations* 20, Deventer: Kluwer

Galenson, W. (1981) *The International Labor Organization: An American View* Madison: University of Wisconsin Press

Gold, M. and Hall, M. (1992) *Report on European-level Information and Consultation in Multinational Companies: An Evaluation of Practice* Dublin: European Foundation for the Improvement of Living and Working Conditions

Johnston, G.A. (1970) *The International Labour Organisation: Its Work for Social and Economic Progress* London: Europa

Kahn-Freund (1976) 'The European social charter' in F.G. Jacobs ed. *European Law and the Individual* Amsterdam: North Holland, pp. 181–211

Lane, C. (1987) *Management and Labour in Europe: The Industrial Enterprise in Germany and France* Aldershot: Gower

Lipsig-Mumme, C. (1989) 'Canadian and American unions respond to economic crisis' *Journal of Industrial Relations* June, 31, 2, pp. 229–56

Moss, B.H. (1988) 'Industrial law reform in an era of retreat: The Auroux Laws in France' *Work, Employment and Society* 2, 3, pp. 317–34

Northrup, H.P. and Rowan, R.L. (1979) *Multinational Collective Bargaining Attempts: The Records, the Cases and the Prospects* Philadelphia: Industrial Research Unit, The Wharton School, University of Pennsylvannia

Northrup, H. R. et al. (1988) 'Multinational union-management consultation in Europe' *International Labour Review* 127, 5

OECD (1991) *Employment Outlook* Paris: Organisation for Economic Co-operation and Development

Oechslin, J. (1985) 'Employers' organisations' in R. Blanpain et al. eds *Comparative Labour Law and Industrial Relations* 2e Deventer: Kluwer, pp. 229–48

Smith, F. (1984) 'What is the International Labour Organisation?' *International Labour Reports* 6 (Nov.-Dec.), pp. 23–4

Stråth, B. (1987) *The Politics of De-Industrialisation: The Contraction of the West European Shipbuilding Industry* London: Croom Helm

Upham, M. ed. (1990) *Employers' Organizations of the World* London: Longman

Valticos, N. and Samson, K. (1993) 'International labour law' in R. Blanpain (1993) ed. *Comparative Labour Law and Industrial Relations* 5e. Deventer: Kluwer, forthcoming

Visser, J. (1989) *European Trade Unions in Figures* Deventer: Kluwer

Windmuller, J.P. (1982) 'International trade union movement' in

R. Blanpain (1993) ed. *Comparative Labour Law and Industrial Relations* 2e Deventer: Kluwer, pp. 98–116

Windmuller, J.P. and Gladstone, A. eds (1984) *Employers' Associations and Industrial Relations: A Comparative Study* Oxford: Clarendon Press/International Institute of Labour Studies

Appendix

Not all of these sources are cited explicitly in the Appendix. The following list includes others as an initial guide to sources of data relevant to the study of international and comparative industrial relations. The ILO and OECD also publish many useful works (including the bi-monthly *International Labor Review* and OECD *Observer*, the OECD annual *Employment Outlook* and its regular surveys of economic trends and prospects for each OECD country). Other useful sources include relevant publications from the World Bank, UN, EC, BLS, JIL, *European Industrial Relations Review, The Economist*, Economist Intelligence Unit and Incomes Data Services.

Adams, L.T. (1985) 'Changing employment patterns of organised workers' *Monthly Labor Review* Feb., pp. 25–31

Anderson, V. (1991) *Alternative Economic Indicators* London: Routledge

Australian Bulletin of Labour Adelaide: National Institute of Labour Studies, Flinders University (quarterly)

ABS (1990a) *Trade Union Statistics, Australia* Canberra: Australian Bureau of Statistics, Catalogue no. 6321.0

——(1990b) *Trade Union Members, Australia* Canberra: Australian Bureau of Statistics, Catalogue no. 6325.0

——1992 *Labor Statistics, Australia 1991* Canberra: Australian Bureau of Statistics, Catalogue no. 6101.0

Bain, G.S. and Elsheik, F. (1976) *Union Growth and the Business Cycle: An Econometric Analysis* Oxford: Blackwell

Bain, G.S. and Price, R.J. (1980) *Profiles of Union Growth: A Comparative Statistical Portrait of Eight Countries* Oxford: Blackwell

Bamber G.J. and Whitehouse G. (1992) 'International data on economic, employment and human resource issues' *International Journal of Human Resource Management* 3, 2, September, pp. 347–70

Batstone, E. (1985) 'International variations in strike activity' *European Sociological Review* 1, 1, May, pp. 47–64

Bean, R. ed. (1989) *International Labour Statistics: A Handbook Guide, and Recent Trends* London: Routledge

Bird, D. (1991) 'International comparisons of industrial disputes in 1989 and 1990' *Employment Gazette* 99, 12, Dec., pp. 653–8

——(1992) 'International comparisons of industrial disputes in 1991' *Employment Gazette* 100, 12, Dec., pp. 609–14

Blandy, R. and Brummitt, W. (1990) *Labour Productivity and Living Standards* Sydney: Allen & Unwin

Blyton, P. (1989) 'Hours of work' *International Labour Statistics: A Handbook Guide, and Recent Trends* R. Bean ed., London: Routledge, pp. 127–45

Bratt, C. (1990) 'International statistical comparisons' *Labour Relations in 18 Countries* Stockholm: Swedish Employers' Confederation (SAF) (intermittently)

Carter, M. and Gregory, R. (1981) 'Government pensions, benefits and the distribution of employment for males during a recession' Working Paper, Canberra: Research School of Social Sciences, Australian National University

Chamberlain, N.W., Cullen, D.E. and Lewin, D. (1980) *The Labor Sector* 3e. New York: McGraw Hill

Chang, C. and Sorrentino, C. (1991) 'Union membership statistics in 12 countries' *Monthly Labor Review* Dec., pp. 46–52

Clark, D. (1989) 'The problems in measuring GDP' *Australian Financial Review*, 12 July, pp. 36–7

Clarke, R.O. (1980) 'Labour–management disputes: a perspective' *British Journal of Industrial Relations* 18, 1, March, pp. 14–25

——(1987) 'The work of the OECD in the labour field' *The International Journal of Comparative Labour Law and Industrial Relations* 3, 4, Winter, 1987/88

Clegg, H.A. (1976) *Trade Unionism and Collective Bargaining: A Theory Based on Comparisons of Six Countries* Oxford: Blackwell

Creigh, S.W. et al. (1982) 'Differences in strike activity between countries' *International Journal of Manpower* 3, 4, pp. 15–23

Dore, R.P. and Sako, M. (1989) *How the Japanese Learn to Work* London: Routledge

Edwards, P.K. (1983) 'The end of American strike statistics' *British Journal of Industrial Relations* 21, 3, pp. 392–4

EC (1985) *Report on Social Developments Year* Brussels–Luxembourg: European Communities Commission (annually)

EC *EEC Labour Costs Survey* Brussels: Eurostat (triennially)

Economist 'Economic and financial indicators' London (weekly)

——(1991) *The Economist Pocket World in Figures* London: The Economist Books

Fisher, M. (1973) *Measurement of Labour Disputes and their Economic Effects* Paris: OECD

Flaim, P.O. (1982) 'The spendable earnings series: Has it outlived its usefulness' *Monthly Labor Review*, Jan.

——(1985) 'New data on union members and their earnings' *Employment and Earnings*, Jan.

Hart, R.A. (1984) *Shorter Working Time: A Dilemma for Collective Bargaining* Paris: OECD

Hussmanns, R., Mehran, F. and Verma V. *Surveys of Economically Active Population, Employment, Unemployment and Underemployment: An ILO Manual on Concepts and Methods* Geneva: International Labour Office

ILO (1976) *International Recommendations on Labour Statistics* Geneva: International Labour Organisation

——(1984) *World Labour Report Vol. 1: Employment, Incomes, Social Protection, New Information Technology* Geneva: International Labour Organisation

——(1985) *World Labour Report Vol. 2: Labour Relations, International Labour Standards, Training, Conditions of Work, Women at Work* Geneva: International Labour Organisation

——(1987) *World Labour Report Vol. 3: Incomes from Work: Between Equity and Efficiency* Geneva: International Labour Organisation

——a, *Yearbook of Labour Statistics* Geneva: International Labour Organisation (annually)

——b, *Bulletin of Labour Statistics* Geneva: International Labour Organisation (quarterly)

——c, *Social and Labour Bulletin* Geneva: International Labour Organisation (quarterly)

IMF (1991) *The Purchasing Power of Working Time: An International Comparison 1990* Geneva: International Metalworkers' Federation (annually)

Ingham, G.K. (1974) *Strikes and Industrial Conflict* London: Macmillan

Jackson, M.P. (1987) *Strikes: Industrial Conflict in Britain, USA and Australia* Brighton: Wheatsheaf/Sydney: Allen & Unwin

Japan Institute for Social and Economic Affairs (1992) *Japan 1992: An International Comparison* Tokyo: Keizai Koho Center (annually)

JIL (1991) *Japanese Working Life Profile: Labor Statistics* Tokyo: Japan Institute of Labour (annually)

Jones, B. (1982) *Sleepers, Wake! Technology and the Future of Work* Melbourne: Oxford University Press/Brighton: Wheatsheaf

Jonung, C. (1984) 'Patterns of occupational segregation by sex in the labour market' in G. Schmid and R. Weitzel eds *Sex Discrimination and Equal Opportunity: The Labour Market and Employment Policy* New York: St Martin's Press

Kaim-Caudle, P.R. (1973) *Comparative Social Policy and Social Security: A Ten Country Study* London: Martin Robertson

Korpi, W. (1981) 'Sweden: conflict, power and politics in industrial relations' in P. Doeringer et al. eds *Industrial Relations in International Perspective: Essays on Research and Policy* London: Macmillan

Leyland, J. (1990) *Business Comparisons: An Analytical and Statistical Survey of Europe and the USA* London: The Economist Intelligence Unit

Lynch, L. (1992) 'International comparisons of HR/IR practices and labor market outcomes: Evidence from national statistics' Mimeo., Cambridge: Massachusetts Institute of Technology, Sloan School of Management

Neef, A. and Kask, C. (1991) 'Manufacturing productivity and labor costs in 14 economies' *Monthly Labor Review* December, pp. 24–37

OECDa *OECD Employment Outlook* Paris: Organisation for Economic Co-operation and Development (annually)

——b *Labour Force Statistics* Paris: Organisation for Economic Co-operation and Development (annually, with a 20-year historical abstract)

——c *Quarterly Labour Force Statistics* Paris: Organisation for Economic Co-operation and Development (quarterly)

——d *OECD in Figures: Statistics on the Member Countries* Paris:

Organisation for Economic Co-operation and Development (an invaluable set of summary tables, with most data only two years old; it is usually published as a supplement to a mid-year issue of the *OECD Observer*)

——e *Historical Statistics* Paris: Organisation for Economic Co-operation and Development (annually; published as a companion volume to the mid-year *Economic Outlook*)

——f *Economic Outlook* Paris: Organisation for Economic Co-operation and Development (half-yearly; it includes OECD forecasts based on a review of each OECD member country)

Ross, A.M. and Hartman, P.T. (1960) *Changing Patterns of Industrial Conflict* New York: Wiley

Runciman, W.G. (1991) 'Explaining union density in twentieth-century Britain' *Sociology* 25, 4, pp. 697–712

Shalev, M. (1978) 'Lies, damned lies and strike statistics: The measurement of trends in industrial conflict' in C. Crouch and A. Pizzorno eds *The Resurgence of Class Conflict in Western Europe Since 1968, vol. 1,* 1978 London: Macmillan, pp. 1–20

——(1980) 'Industrial relations theory and the comparative study of industrial relations and industrial conflict' *British Journal of Industrial Relations* 18, 1, Mar., pp. 26–43

Smith, A.D. et al. (1982) *International Industrial Productivity: A Comparison of Britain, America and Germany* Cambridge: Cambridge University Press/National Institute of Economic and Social Research

Thurman, J.E. and Trah, G. (1989) 'Part-time work in international perspective' *Conditions of Work Digest* 8, 1, pp. 3–26

Turvey, R. ed. (1989) *Developments in International Labour Statistics* London: Pinter

UK Department of Employment *Employment Gazette* London: Her Majesty's Stationary Office (monthly)

UN (1971) *Indices to the International Standard Industrial Classification of all Economic Activities* New York: Department of Economic and Social Affairs, United Nations (intermittently)

US BLS (1985) *Handbook of Labor Statistics* Washington DC: US Bureau of Labor Statistics, Department of Labor (intermittently)

——*Monthly Labor Review* Washington DC: US Department of Labor (monthly)

——*News* Washington DC: Bureau of Labor Statistics Press Releases, US Department of Labor (intermittently)

——(1991a) *Hourly Compensation Costs for Production Workers in Manufacturing* Washington DC: US Bureau of Labor Statistics, Department of Labor (April) unpublished (mimeo., intermittently)

——(1991b) *International Comparisons of Hourly Compensation Costs for Production Workers in Manufacturing, 1975–90* Report 817 Washington DC: US Bureau of Labor Statistics, Department of Labor

——(1992) *International Comparisons of Hourly Compensation Costs for Production Workers in Manufacturing, 1991,* Report 825 Washington DC: US Bureau of Labor Statistics, Department of Labor

US GAO (1990) *Training Strategies: Preparing Noncollege Youth for*

Employment in the US and Foreign Countries Washington DC: US General Accounting Office

Visser, J. (1988) *In Search of Inclusive Unionism: A Comparative Analysis* Special Issue of *Bulletin of Comparative Labour Relations* Deventer: Kluwer

Walby, S. (1988) *Gender Segregation at Work* Milton Keynes: Open University Press

Walsh, K. (1983) *Strikes in Europe and the United States: Measurement and Incidence* London: Frances Pinter

——(1985) *The Measurement of Trade Union Membership in the European Community* Luxembourg–Brussels: Eurostat

——(1987) *Long-term Unemployment: An International Perspective* London: Macmillan

Walsh, K. and King, A. (1986) *International Manpower Market Comparisons* London: Macmillan

Waring, M. (1988) *Counting for Nothing: What Men Value and What Women are Worth* Wellington: Allen & Unwin/Port Nicholson Press

World Bank (1982) *World Development Report* Washington DC: International Bank for Reconstruction and Development

——(1991) *World Bank Atlas* Washington DC: International Bank for Reconstruction and Development (annually)

Index

Accord (Australia), 109, 112–13, 116, 117, 122, 125, 253–4, 256, 261
Act on Co-determination at Work (Sweden) (MBL), 210–11, 219, 258
Active Manpower Policy (Sweden), 272
Adams, R., 10
Adenauer, Konrad, 177
Advisory, Conciliation and Arbitration Service (UK) (ACAS), 42
Affirmative Action (Equal Opportunity for Women) Act (Australia, 1986), 119
AGA (company), 201
Agence Nationale Pour l'Emploi, 172
agricultural sector, 282; Australia, 100; France, 149; Germany, 175; Italy, 126, 141; Japan, 220, 278; Sweden, 197; United Kingdom, 28; United States, 58
AIDS, 71
Alfa-Laval (company), 201
All-Australian Trade Union Congress, 124
All-Canadian Congress of Labour, 99
All-Japan Federation of Labour Unions, 243
Allgemeiner Deutscher Gewerkschaftsbund (ADGB), 196
Amalgamated Engineering and Electrical Union (UK), 50
Amalgamated Clothing and Textile Workers (US), 66
Amalgamated Engineering Union (UK), 48, 49
Amalgamated Textile Workers Union (US), 77
America *see* United States
American Federation of Labor (AFL), 56, 81, 82
American Federation of Labor–Congress of Industrial Organizations (AFL–CIO), 65, 66, 79, 82, 263

American Federation of State, County and Municipal Employees, 66
American Federation of Teachers, 66
Americans with Disabilities Act (US, 1992), 71
Amiens Charter, 151, 173
Andreotti, Giulio, 130
arbitration, 5; *see also specific countries*
Arcata Graphics, 79
Assicredito, 135
Association for Services to the State through Industry (Japan), 242
Association of German Employers' Federations, 195
Association of Industrial Robot Producers, 235
Associazione Sindacale Aziende Petrolchimiche (ASAP), 135
Atlas Copco (company), 201
Auroux, Jean, 162
Auroux reforms (France), 162–3, 168, 172, 174, 259
Australia, 100–25; absenteeism, 110; Accord, 112–13, 116, 117, 122, 125, 256, 261; agricultural sector, 100; anti-discrimination legislation, 119; approaches to industrial relations, 120; arbitration, 101, 102, 104, 105, 108, 109, 256, 257; attempts to restrict strikes, 257; automotive industry, 4; bans, 110, 123; basic wage, 111, 124; centralisation, 120–1; collective bargaining, 108, 111, 114, 116, 261; conciliation, 101; consent awards, 108; Constitution, 101, 106; consumer price index, 100; decentralisation, 120–1, 122; decline in union density, 104; decline of AIRC, 273; deregistration of unions, 109; disparity between private and public sector, 107; dispute resolution,

357